AMIABLE SCOUNDREL

Amiable Scoundrel

Simon Cameron, Lincoln's Scandalous Secretary of War

PAUL KAHAN

Potomac Books

AN IMPRINT OF THE UNIVERSITY OF NEBRASKA PRESS

Library of Congress Cataloging-in-Publication Data
Names: Kahan, Paul, author.
Title: Amiable scoundrel: Simon Cameron,
Lincoln's scandalous Secretary of War / Paul Kahan.
Description: Lincoln: Potomac Books,
An imprint of the University of Nebraska Press, 2016. |
Includes bibliographical references and index.
Identifiers: LCCN 2016005061
ISBN 9781612348148 (cloth: alk. paper)
ISBN 9781612348476 (epub)
ISBN 9781612348483 (mobi)
ISBN 9781612348490 (pdf)
Subjects: LCSH: Cameron, Simon, 1799–1889. |
Cabinet officers—United States—Biography. |
Legislators—United States—Biography. |
United States—Politics and government—1849–1877. |
United States—Politics and government—1861–1865. |
Lincoln, Abraham, 1809–1865—Friends and associates. |
Maytown (Lancaster County, Pa.)—Biography.
Classification: LCC E415.9.C18 K34 2016 | DDC
973.7092—dc23
LC record available at http://lccn.loc.gov/2016005061

Set in ITC New Baskerville by M. Scheer.

To Jen, Alec, and Zoe—thanks for everything

CONTENTS

List of Illustrations   ix

Acknowledgments   xi

Introduction: "Warm Friends and Bitter Enemies"   1

1. "A Determined Will and a Right Purpose"   5

2. "The Great Winnebago Chief," 1838–45   29

3. "True-Hearted Pennsylvanian, Able, Fearless, and Unflinching," 1845–49   59

4. "Exclude Him from the Ranks of the Democratic Party," 1849–60   93

5. "What They Worship Is the God of Success," 1860–61   131

6. "Then Profit Shall Accrue," 1861–62   157

7. "Gentlemen, the Paragraph Stands," 1861–62   183

8. "A Man Out of Office in Washington," 1862–67   215

9. "Nothing Can Beat You," 1867–77   245

10. "I'll Behave Myself as Long as I'm Here," 1877–89   275

Conclusion: "I Did the Best I Could and Was Never Untrue to a Friend"   291

Notes   293

Bibliography   331

Index   359

ILLUSTRATIONS

Following page 134
1. Simon Cameron, c. 1860
2. Home of the Hon. Simon Cameron, Harrisburg
3. The Seventy-Ninth Regiment (Highlanders),
New York State Militia, c. 1861
4. Cabinet at Washington, July 13, 1861
5. The Committee on Foreign Relations
of the Senate, February 11, 1871

ACKNOWLEDGMENTS

Projects like *Amiable Scoundrel* reflect the assistance of dozens, if not hundreds, of people whose names do not appear on the cover, so I want to take a moment and thank them. Ashley Cataldo at the American Antiquarian Society, Beth Huffer at the Gilder Lehrman Institute of American History, Amanda Dean at the Historical Society of Pennsylvania, Debbie Hamm at the Abraham Lincoln Presidential Library Foundation, Mitch Fraas at the University of Pennsylvania Library, and Janet Mulligan Bowen at the Dauphin County Historical Society all took the time to track down various documents in their respective collections and send me digital copies. Stephanie Hoover provided invaluable assistance as a long-distance researcher, meticulously combing through various collections at the Pennsylvania State Archives and sending me digital copies of relevant documents. At the University of Nebraska Press, Kristen Elias Rowley (ably assisted by Emily Wendell) helped trim and shape the manuscript, while my friends Karen Momarella, Will Holbert, and Brian Dixon all read and commented on the book at various stages. My sister-in-law Tara Murphy proofread the manuscript, tirelessly crossing every *t* and dotting every *i*. Undoubtedly, *Amiable Scoundrel* is a much better book because of their help. Lastly, I want to thank my wife, Jennifer, and our children, Alec and Zoe, all of whom "picked up the slack" around the house so that I could have the time to write. *Amiable Scoundrel* is dedicated to them.

AMIABLE SCOUNDREL

Introduction

"Warm Friends and Bitter Enemies"

His contemporaries called him the "greatest of wire-pullers" and "corrupt as a dunghill."[1] Historians have been no kinder, branding him a "crafty manipulator with few scruples" and "a deadweight, an embarrassment."[2] The man they are describing, Simon Cameron, has become synonymous with corruption and graft during the Civil War, but as historian Brooks M. Kelly sagely noted more than a half century ago, "Cameron's reputation has stood in the way of an objective appraisal" of his life.[3] *Amiable Scoundrel* is an attempt to get past Cameron's reputation, but this book is far more than a simple biography. It is a portrait of an era that allowed—indeed, encouraged—a man like Cameron to seize political control by creating one of the most successful and long-lived political machines in American history. As historian A. Howard Meneely noted, "No politician of his generation understood the science of politics better than Simon Cameron; none enjoyed greater power, none had more success."[4] If Andrew Jackson was, as John William Ward has argued, a "symbol for an age," so was Cameron.[5]

Cameron's career highlights three key themes about American political life during the nineteenth century. First is the centrality of the "spoils system" to accruing and consolidating political power in nineteenth-century America. Second is the role that personality, rather than fidelity to party, played in building and exercising political power during the nineteenth century. Cameron was soft-spoken, informal, and genial, and his political success was rooted in his personal magnetism. A close friend described Cameron as "a man of warm temperament and ardent personal attachments."[6] According to a newspaper profile published in 1878, Cameron "seldom forgot a name or face . . . [and] he was a wonderfully good handshaker. . . . With his neighbors and immediate constituents he has always been a hail-fellow-well-met, walking along a country road he always has a pleasant word for those he meets. He knows all the babies for miles around, and is seldom without a red apple in his pocket for his favorites. It is because of these things that Simon Cameron, during a lifetime of political turmoil, could nearly always count on the popular support."[7]

The third theme is the fluidity of political identity until the Civil War. Historians have often cited Cameron's migration from the Democratic Party to the Know-Nothing and then finally the Republican Party as proof of opportunism and lack of principle. In truth, the key to understanding Cameron's long career is that he was, first and foremost, a protector of Pennsylvania's business interests. Seen through this lens, his migration from the Democratic Party to the Know-Nothing and then finally the Republican Party can best be understood as an attempt to forward and protect Pennsylvania's interests as he perceived them.

Moreover, despite his reputation as a craven and unprincipled scoundrel willing to do or say anything to win an election, Cameron's trademark virtues were loyalty and generosity. Gideon Welles, who served as Lincoln's secretary of the navy and disliked Cameron personally, nevertheless recalled "no man was more faithful to true and abiding friends than Simon Cameron. He never abandoned or neglected to serve if he had the opportunity those who had supported him."[8] Cameron himself once noted, "I never forget kindness."[9] His friendships transcended partisan and sectional lines, and though he vigorously prosecuted the war during its first year, at its conclusion he counted some former Confederates as his friends. Generous to his friends—and even to complete strangers—he was a devoted family man who passionately loved his wife and children.

At the same time, Cameron had an acerbic wit and was combative to people he perceived as enemies, seeing political conflict as a form of "take-no-prisoners" warfare. Thurlow Weed, the influential newspaper publisher, noted that, "Mr. Cameron during a long and stirring political life had made warm friends and bitter enemies."[10] As *Amiable Scoundrel* makes clear, Cameron ruthlessly exercised political power and sometimes resorted to questionable tactics to win elections. Furthermore, he never hesitated to reward political supporters and friends or to punish political opponents. As Cameron's biographer has noted, "Reward and punishment was the theme and soul of the Cameronian system. A pragmatist of the first order, Cameron knew his system was good because it worked."[11]

Amiable Scoundrel's most surprising revelation is that Cameron had rather progressive attitudes on race. Though historians have noted the fact that Lincoln forced Cameron out of the cabinet over the latter's recommendation that the government enlist slaves, many have argued that this was a smokescreen covering the real reason the president wanted to remove Cameron (corruption). Others have argued that Cameron's recommendation was a cynical attempt to ingratiate himself to congressional abolitionists, and thereby prevent Lincoln from firing him. Both explanations miss the mark; in reality, from the moment he became secretary of war, Cameron argued that attacking slavery was essential to winning the war. Though as a senator he had been a conservative on the issue of slavery, arguing that the federal government had no power to regulate it in states where it already existed, as a private citizen he paid to educate at least one escaped slave and, after the war, he used his political influence to improve conditions for former slaves. Put another way, there is substantial evidence to suggest that while Cameron may have used corrupt means to achieve political power and wealth, he frequently used both to further positive social change.

The point here, then, is not to defend Cameron's actions, many of which will strike modern readers as unprincipled, unscrupulous, and corrupt. Instead, *Amiable Scoundrel*'s goal is merely to put Cameron's actions into a larger historical context by demonstrating that many politicians of the time (including Abraham Lincoln) used very similar tactics to win elections and advance their careers and to remind us that he was a whole person: contradictory and complex, not the two-dimensional caricature of the grasping, unscrupulous politician so often depicted by historians.

1

"A Determined Will and a Right Purpose"

On his father's side, Simon Cameron was descended from the Lochiel family of the Clan Cameron. Two brothers—Duncan and Donald (the "foolish ones," according to family tradition)—fled Scotland after participating in the disastrous Battle of Culloden in 1746. Donald Cameron, along with his two sons, John and Simon, and their wives, settled in Lancaster County, Pennsylvania. Simon served as a private in the American army during the War of Independence, and his son Charles (born 1765), who had also migrated with the family, was apprenticed to a tailor in nearby Maytown. In 1794 Charles married Martha Pfoutz, who was descended from one of the earliest settlers of Lancaster County. One of eight children, her father had risen to local notoriety due to his service in the War of Independence. Shortly after they were married, Charles purchased a hotel. Future senator and secretary of war Simon Cameron was born in the hotel on March 8, 1799.

Cameron recalled being a "sickly little chap" who was "small for his age" and that his family was "not particularly overburdened with money."[1] Another person who knew Cameron as a child recounted that when he was eight or nine, the future war secretary needed a book for school that cost a dollar. Cameron scrimped for three months, managing to save only seventy-three cents. Lamenting this to the storekeeper one day, the boy broke into tears. Touched by the boy's obvious desire to learn, the storekeeper lent Cameron the twenty-seven cents, which he later paid back with interest. When he ran for president in 1860, Cameron's campaign biography described him as a child "possessing a mind that was craving for knowledge, and, to satisfy that appetite, he spent every leisure moment in reading."[2]

Charles Cameron's hotel failed in 1797, and his growing family was forced to move to a small frame house, where Charles tried to make a living as a tailor. This venture also failed and, in 1808 the family's furniture was seized and sold at auction by the local constable.[3] That same year, the Camerons moved to Sunbury, Pennsylvania, but bad luck followed them; in 1810 Charles died, leaving Martha a widow and unable to support her large family. As a result, the older children were adopted by some of the more prosperous local families in Sunbury. Simon, who had just turned eleven, had the good fortune to be taken in by Dr. Peter Grahl, a prominent local physician, and his wife. The Grahls were childless, and they treated Simon like a son. For the first time in his life, Simon Cameron had access to a multitude of books, which he read voraciously. Shortly after his seventeenth birthday, Cameron apprenticed himself to printer Andrew Kennedy, who was at that time the publisher of the *Sunbury and Northumberland Gazette, and Republican Advertiser.*[4] Reflecting on this decision decades later, Cameron noted, "Owing to my ill-health and physical delicacy of constitution, I was almost killed by this exacting labor. That part of the business which I could do without this extreme labor—the typesetting, &c.— was always pleasant to me, for it gave me all the opportunity a lean purse then permitted to secure the rudiments of education. Indeed this is why I chose the trade."[5]

Within a year, however, financial troubles forced Kennedy to release Cameron from his apprenticeship, and the young man migrated to Harrisburg. Here, he apprenticed himself to James Peacock, a local printer and publisher of the *Pennsylvania Republican.* Recalling these events during the Civil War,

Cameron claimed, "I came to Harrisburg—a poor, delicate, sickly boy—without any reliance but on the overruling control of Providence and the reward which I had been taught to believe would always follow proper actions." He stopped at the first printing office he found to ask for work, after which he "left with a feeling such as can be experienced only by those who are willing to work, are without money in their purse, and are destitute of friends upon whom to rely, when told 'we cannot employ you.' . . . The first place at which I stopped to rest my weary limbs after reaching the town was beneath the shade of an old willow tree in front of [Judge Hummel's] house. He came out and spoke kindly to me, inviting me into his home . . . a day or two after . . . I obtained employment."[6] Simon Cameron never forgot this kindness, and in adulthood, he returned the favor through generosity toward impecunious but talented young men.

Inevitably, apprenticing at the *Pennsylvania Republican* introduced Cameron to the chaotic world of Pennsylvania politics because, by the 1810s, newspapers were highly partisan businesses that relied on the patronage of influential politicians for their survival.[7] Looking back at his apprenticeship forty years later, Cameron noted, "In my position as a newspaper journalist, I necessarily came into contact with political theories and important questions of the day and never failed to advocate what I conceived to be a wise and beneficial state policy."[8] He made a point of regularly attending sessions of the Pennsylvania General Assembly, boasting in 1842 that he had been to "every session [of the assembly], more or less, since 1817. I have been upon the most intimate terms with the Legislature. Many years, I have known every member of the Legislature."[9]

Cameron's apprenticeship coincided with two important political developments: the emergence of a single dominant party in national and Pennsylvania politics and the growing enfranchisement of white males. Following John Adams's unsuccessful reelection bid in 1800, the Federalist Party went into sharp decline, becoming essentially a regional party thereafter. On the national level, U.S. politics became dominated by the Democratic-Republicans, who identified with Thomas Jefferson. Usually calling themselves simply "Republicans," they controlled the White House and Congress until the mid-1820s. At the same time, American politics became more democratic after 1800. Of the sixteen states in the Union in 1800, presidential electors of ten were selected by those states' legislatures, and only two selected electors through popular vote. A quarter of a century later, the legislatures of only six states still selected the states' electors. By the election of 1832, that number had dropped to one: South Carolina. Meanwhile, many states liberalized their suffrage qualifications. By 1824 most states allowed nearly all white males to vote.

Democratization required a substantial shift in the way politicians campaigned because "the management of the party type of politics required considerable manpower, demanded the expenditure of large amounts of time on routine or trivial matters, called for talents that were by no means restricted to the gentry, and offered tangible rewards in the form of patronage and prestige to attract men from many ranks and callings."[10] Surveying Pennsylvania's politics in this period, historian Richard McCormick concluded that "politics became the business of men who were interested in the tangible rewards of jobs and money"—in other words, professional political operatives.[11] In short, democratization, which was far along in Pennsylvania during the 1820s, created the ideal conditions for Cameron's rise to influence, and the rewards—patronage jobs and lucrative government contracts—were plentiful.

Because of the Republicans' dominance of national politics during this period, campaigns focused more on individuals than on political ideals. In the words of historian Richard P. McCormick, "Where virtually all leaders, candidates, and voters professed the same party allegiance, contests for offices . . . might be waged on the basis of personalities or between factions."[12] These "cults of personality"—there is no other phrase for it—were, in the words of Martin Van Buren biographer Ted Widmer, "little cabals dedicated to electing their leaders to higher office and willing to stop at nothing to do it."[13] However, "the abundance of state patronage did not, in Pennsylvania, serve as a cement for party organization."[14] If anything, the opposite was true: squabbles over patronage factionalized the party, so each side funded reliable newspapers (called "organs") to marshal support.

Given the important role newspapers played in American politics, it should come as no surprise that, while apprenticing with James Peacock, Cameron met the secretary of the commonwealth, Samuel D. Ingham. For a young man interested in social advancement, there was no better acquaintance than Ingham, who was a prosperous paper mill owner and a member of the U.S. House of Representatives. Ingham was politically well connected and a member of the Family Party. Created by George Mifflin Dallas, a prominent Philadelphia Democratic-Republican (known hereafter as "Republicans"), the Family Party took its name from the fact that its main leaders—Ingham, William Wilkins, Richard Bache, Thomas Sergeant, John J. Norvall, and Thomas J. Rogers—were all related to Dallas.[15]

Ingham clearly understood the important role that journalists and newspaper editors played in a rapidly democratizing political environment. At the moment Ingham met Cameron, the Family Party was locked in a bitter factional struggle for control over the Republican Party in Bucks County. In Doylestown, the county seat, two rival newspapers—Ingham's *Messenger* and the *Doylestown Democrat*—vied for control of the party. The *Messenger* survived primarily on state printing, which Ingham secured though his connections to state officials, though this appears not to have been enough to support its editor, Simon Seigfried.[16] When Seigfried left the paper, Ingham tapped Cameron to take it over, which the young man did on January 2, 1821.

From the beginning, Cameron sought to unify Bucks County's various Republican factions, which in practice meant avoiding any topic that might alienate potential voters. Under the headline "To the Public," he declared,

Having purchased the establishment of the *Bucks County Messenger* from Mr. Seigfried, I propose to continue its publication. In commencing my editorial career, I conceive it a duty on me to make known the principles on which I intend conducting the paper in the future. . . . I will briefly state that the character of the *Messenger* shall be purely democratic. At the same time, it will keep aloof from all local divisions or prejudices that may exist in the Republican ranks; nor shall it ever assail the character of private individuals. But it will keep a vigilant eye on the conduct of public men, and expose all errors as soon as detected.[17]

A few months later, he published "To Your Tents, O Israel," a plea for party unity in the October state elections. The column argued, "In the selection that has been made of candidates, dislikes may possibly be opposed to some one or other on the democratic ticket, but surely on such an occasion as the present, when union and activity are so necessary to support the general cause, candid men will not divide. It is not possible to please every individual; and perhaps it may appear in some instances that a better choice might have been made."[18]

Because Cameron wanted to extinguish, rather than stoke, partisan fires, the *Messenger* took few explicit editorial stands during his tenure as editor. Given his later flirtation with nativism, it is worth noting that, on January 16, 1821, the paper printed a message from Robert Wharton, the mayor of Philadelphia. Under the headline "Public Information," Wharton asserted "that there have been, for at least [twelve or fifteen years], a number of foreigners, of good address but of base and depraved principles, who have visited our country with forged credentials, counterfeit recommendations, and spurious statements of alleged losses. These sons of deception have traversed the country in every direction, exhibiting their false documents for the purpose of obtaining money for the ostensible object of redeeming some of their near relatives from Algerine Slavery, others to rebuild churches destroyed by fire or earthquakes, [or] to assist distressed villagers." Wharton sent this message

to the "printers of the United States," asking them to print it in their newspapers "when there is a dearth of news."[19] Cameron complied, printing the notice at least twice during the time he owned the paper, suggesting he agreed with the advertisement's sentiment, though it is also possible he was merely being a dutiful Republican.

Given Cameron's later prominence in banking, it is unsurprising that the *Messenger* strongly defended the Second Bank of the United States. In an article titled "United States Bank," which does not appear to have been reprinted from another newspaper, the authors claim, "The United States bank has been solemnly designed to be a constitutional . . . institution by congress, by the executive and the judiciary of the union. The conduct of Ohio, in thus attempting to outlaw that bank, in thus endeavoring to shield the citizens of that state, who owe the institution two or three millions of dollars, from the payment of their just debts, is not only hostile to the government and peace of the union, but is very little better than *an indirect method of sanctioning swindling*."[20]

These tantalizing clues about Cameron's political ideas can only be read backward, given what we know about his later beliefs, and should therefore be treated cautiously. Nonetheless, it appears that, by his early twenties, Cameron had embraced the pro-business nationalism that was a bedrock political belief for the rest of his life.

Cameron was in dire financial straits in Doylestown because the patronage Ingham had promised never materialized in sufficient quantity to support him. Out of desperation, Cameron merged the *Messenger* with the *Democrat*, partnering with the rival paper's editor, Benjamin Mifflin. In October 1821, Mifflin and Cameron published a "Valedictory," celebrating their achievements in "seeing the [party] of the county firmly united, notwithstanding the many attempts that have been made to prevent this desirable object." However, they announced that Cameron would be leaving, noting that "the increase of patronage, although considerable, has not been sufficient to warrant *two* editors, this we presume will be a sufficient answer to the many enquiries that may be made as to our reason for selling out."[21] After selling his share of the paper, Cameron left Doylestown at the end of 1821.

Following his departure from Doylestown, Cameron worked briefly as a compositor in Washington at the *Congressional Globe*, which published Congress's official proceedings. The work was ideal for a young man interested in politics, though the pay was so low Cameron found it impossible to save money.[22] At the end of the congressional session, Cameron briefly returned to James Peacock's printing office in Harrisburg. Soon, however, he managed to secure a loan from his uncle that allowed him to purchase the *Pennsylvania Republican*. Recalling the story years later, Cameron described how he accompanied his uncle to the older man's barn. There, his uncle produced a bundle of bills and slowly counted out $400. He recalled, "It looked to me the largest amount of money I ever saw up to that time. It was in one- and two-dollar notes, and as I took it in my hands I could hardly realize that I had control of so much money."[23]

Shortly after purchasing the *Pennsylvania Republican*, Cameron merged it with Charles Mowry's *Pennsylvania Intelligencer*. Mowry bought the *Intelligencer* in 1821 from Cameron's former master, James Peacock, and used it as a platform for vigorously supporting former governor William Findlay. Consequently, the *Intelligencer* was far more partisan than the *Messenger*. Mowry boasted to his readers in 1821, "This paper shall be a decidedly political one, devoted to the best interests of the *people*, on the republican principles which the editor is known to profess and practice. It shall not descend to littler, vulgar, personal squabbles, with its fellow-prints, nor ransack the Billingsgate catalogue, for epithets to apply to its opponents; yet the official conduct of public officers shall be scrutinized with a vigilant eye, and their errors fearlessly exposed, whenever the public good shall require it."[24]

Mowry and Cameron's avuncular partisanship paid off in 1823 when the Family Party managed to elect John A. Shulze governor of Pennsylvania. Cameron actively campaigned for Shulze, whose sister was married to Cameron's brother John.[25] Pennsylvania's constitution granted the governor sweeping appointive power, and Shulze directed a large share of the patronage at his disposal to Cameron's family.[26] Shortly after taking office, Governor Shulze appointed John Cameron to be Dauphin County's register of wills and recorder of deeds, and later made him justice of the peace. That was not all: Shulze made Cameron's brother William alderman of the City of Lancaster and, in 1829, named Cameron adjutant general of the state militia, a position Cameron held for the remainder of the governor's term in office. It was from his brief stint as adjutant general that Cameron earned the title "General," an honorific that he used for the rest of his life.

The new governor also directed state contracts toward the Camerons; during the legislative session of 1823–24, Pennsylvania's legislature abolished competitive bidding for printing contracts, instead awarding all of the state's printing to a single state printer. Almost immediately, Simon Cameron was appointed the commonwealth's official printer. In 1826 Shulze appointed Cameron's partner Charles Mowry a commissioner of the Pennsylvania Canal, which ensured that William and Simon Cameron received a contract to build a portion of this massive project. Meanwhile, Cameron and his brother James received a lucrative contract for state printing, and in December 1826 the Pennsylvania House of Representatives unanimously named Cameron and Mowry the body's official printers. This was a very desirable contract, yielding a payment of $200 in February 1827 and $300 two months later, though Cameron later recalled, "This was the period of my hardest labor. I do not think that I slept more than five hours of the twenty-four on average during that time; and then, utterly broken in health, I retired in ease with what I thought was then a comfortable fortune—about $20,000."[27]

Following Mowry's appointment to the canal commission in 1826, Cameron purchased his partner's stake in the *Pennsylvania*

Intelligencer and took on a new partner, Judge David Krause of Lebanon County, who had served as Governor Shulze's private secretary. By this time the *Intelligencer* had become the Republican Party's undisputed organ in Harrisburg. The following year, however, Cameron sold his interest in the paper to Krause and migrated to the *Pennsylvania Reporter and Democratic Herald*. Here too Cameron (along with his new partner, Samuel C. Stambaugh) received a substantial share of the state's printing, courtesy of Governor Shulze. When Shulze appointed Cameron adjutant general the following year, Cameron left the printing trade for good, but not before ensuring his lucrative printing contracts would be transferred to his younger brother James.[28]

As a young man, and despite his grueling work schedule, Cameron was extremely social. He developed a particular fondness for dry champagne, which he claimed had "medicinal value," and it was not unusual for him to drink a quart of the sparkling wine in a sitting.[29] Andrew Jackson's former gardener, who knew Cameron as a young man, recalled many years later that "young Simon was of a gay turn of mind and could tip his punch with any of them."[30] In between work and carousing, Cameron somehow managed to find time for romance, courting a local young lady named Mary Berryhill. Mary's father did not approve of the match because he feared Cameron had no future, so he sent his daughter away. Before she left, Cameron gave her a poem written on white satin that Mary had framed; and upon her death in 1892, it still hung in her house.[31] In 1822 Cameron married Margaretta "Margaret" Brua, the daughter of Peter Brua, a carpenter and local entrepreneur. It was a happy match that produced ten children, of whom six—Rachel (b. 1823), William "Brua" (b. 1826), Virginia (b. 1830), J. Donald (b. 1833), Margaretta "Maggie" (b. 1840), and Simon (b. 1844)—lived to adulthood.

These happy developments complemented Cameron's growing political influence. Erasmus D. Keyes, who first met Cameron around this time, described him years later, saying, "At that time his activity was astonishing, and all his movements indicated a determination to become rich and famous."[32] In 1824 Cameron attended the Harrisburg State Convention as a delegate from Dauphin County. The convention's purpose was to select the state party's presidential nominee. The election of 1824 was to be a four-way contest between Secretary of State John Adams, Speaker of the House Henry Clay, Secretary of the Treasury William Crawford, and former senator General Andrew Jackson, all of whom were nominally Republicans. The fact that four Republicans were jockeying for the presidential nomination was tangible proof that one-party rule, which had characterized American politics since Jefferson's election, was coming to an end. The Republican Party was splitting into two wings: the national Republicans, who advocated publicly financed internal improvements and a high protective tariff, and the democratic Republicans, who opposed these uses of federal power and eventually coalesced around Andrew Jackson. Like Cameron, Jackson had been born into poverty and had lost both of his parents at a very early age. Through a combination of battlefield victories and shrewd investments, Jackson managed to make himself one of the wealthiest and most politically influential men in Tennessee. His victory at New Orleans during the War of 1812, where he successfully repulsed a British attack, catapulted him to national prominence. Capitalizing on his renown, Jackson sought the presidency in 1824.

Although Jackson was extremely popular in Pennsylvania, Cameron did not yet support the former general; in a letter, he referred to Jacksonianism as a disease and predicted that enthusiasm for "Old Hickory" would soon wane. At a national tariff convention held at Harrisburg in the summer of 1827, future secretary of the navy Gideon Welles met a number of Pennsylvania's leading Democrats, including Cameron. Welles noted that Cameron was "not fully prepared to commit himself for Jackson," an accurate (if understated) assessment of the newspaperman's feelings that summer.[33] This put Cameron at odds with the Family Party, which nominated delegates to the convention committed to Jackson for president.[34] The Family Party's leaders did this because they saw it as the best chance for advancing South Carolina senator John C. Calhoun's presidential ambitions, in the belief that he would be ideally placed to run for president in 1828. Cameron's lack of enthusiasm for Jackson alienated him from his erstwhile patrons in the Family Party, though for the moment he remained on good terms with Samuel Ingham.

The election of 1824 was a turning point in American history that signaled the end of the "era of good feelings." Voting in the presidential election of 1824 had a heavily regional flavor, with Adams winning all of New England but very little of the South and the West. Crawford, who had been crippled by a stroke, took only two Southern states (Georgia and Virginia), while Clay won his home state of Kentucky as well as Ohio and Missouri. The exception to this pattern was Jackson, who (in addition to winning much of the South) swept Pennsylvania and New Jersey and won electoral votes from New York and Illinois. In fact, Jackson won the largest share of the popular vote (41.4 percent) but not a majority, so in accordance with the Twelfth Amendment to the United States Constitution, the contest went to the House of Representatives. Under the provisions of the Twelfth Amendment, the three candidates with the largest number of electoral votes (in this case, Jackson, Adams, and Crawford) became candidates in the House election. Importantly, the fourth candidate in the general election, Henry Clay, was then serving as the Speaker of the House, putting him in a position to play kingmaker. Clay hated Jackson and worked to prevent Old Hickory's election by throwing his support to Adams, who was elected on the first ballot. Jackson's supporters cried foul, particularly after Adams appointed Clay secretary of state. In those days, secretary of state was a stepping-stone to the presidency (four of the previous six presidents served as secretary of state prior to winning the presidency), which signaled to the Jacksonians that Adams was naming Clay his heir apparent. Claiming that Adams and Clay had struck a "corrupt bargain" (the presidency for Adams in exchange for the State

Department for Clay), Jackson's supporters began a four-year campaign designed to ensure Old Hickory's election in 1828.

In 1825, however, Adams was president and Henry Clay secretary of state for the next four years. Under federal law at the time, each state was allotted up to three newspapers that were paid out of the federal Treasury to print the laws and resolutions of Congress. Because the State Department was the custodian of congressional acts in their final form, the secretary of state was responsible for selecting the papers that would receive this government largess. Naturally, this quickly became a way of supporting papers friendly to the sitting administration. Cameron and Krause moved to secure a share of this lucrative printing, and, in exchange, they provided Clay with intelligence about the commonwealth's politics.[35] Following Pennsylvania's October 1826 congressional elections, Cameron reassured Clay about the result, asserting, "Our elections for members of Congress have not terminated just as we had reason to anticipate; but much more favorably to the administration than our enemies are willing to admit. In our district, in place of Mr. [Robert] Harris, we send Mr. [Innis] Greene, who is claimed as a *Jackson* man, but is known to me to have been an original *Adams* man, and when he shall get to Washington, he will, if nothing else shall govern him, be friendly [to the administration]."[36]

Cameron also offered Clay advice on how to improve Adams's electoral prospects in Pennsylvania, usually focusing on how to mobilize the federal government's considerable patronage to dampen popular enthusiasm for Jackson. In December 1826 he wrote to a friend of Clay's, who passed the letter along to the secretary of state. In it Cameron noted that he had nominated Joel Bailey (whom he described as "the most mad Jacksonian in the state") to represent Dauphin County at a convention meeting in Washington DC to promote the creation of the Chesapeake and Ohio Canal, a massive public works program that sought to connect the capital to Pittsburgh along a route parallel to the Potomac River. Cameron recommended that Clay pay Bailey some "little attention" (i.e., purchase his loyalty through patronage), in the hope of "curing" his Jacksonianism. Cameron also encouraged the secretary of state to shore up Adams's popularity in the state in preparation for the election of 1828. For instance, he noted in one letter that, while Adams had some support in Pennsylvania, he (Cameron) "is not sufficiently sanguine to believe that the vote will not go to [Jackson]."[37] The following summer, Cameron sought to placate any concerns Clay might have by bragging, "You will see that we have taken the field with vigor, and we have little doubt that a very large portion of the citizens of this state think with us, that the wise measures of Mr. Adams and his able cabinet deserve the support of every disinterested Pennsylvanian."[38]

Surely, there is an element of flattery in Cameron's letters, which is understandable: Clay controlled the government's printing contracts, so it behooved Cameron to ingratiate himself to the secretary of state. Moreover, as one of Cameron's political friends noted at the time, "he is fond of being noticed by those who are in power, at least by those whom his always valuable exertions have assisted placing there."[39] That being said, Cameron's efforts on behalf of the Adams administration were motivated by more than vanity. Throughout his career, Cameron constantly took positions that were consistent with the policies adopted by the Adams administration. For instance, in his first Annual Message to Congress, Adams had advocated a slew of internal improvements, including canals and roads, all financed by a high tariff, policies that Cameron applauded. Adams enthusiastically supported the Chesapeake and Ohio Canal and signed into law the Tariff of 1828 (called by Jackson's supporters the "Tariff of Abominations" because it raised prices for goods that the South imported). In short, while it made good business sense to aggressively support President Adams, Cameron was already inclined to do so.

Politics is a fickle business, however, and by late 1827, Cameron began moving into the Jacksonian orbit. The Adams administration lost control of the House of Representatives in the midterm elections of 1826, and Adams's Jacksonian foes widened their advantage in the Senate. Cameron and Krause started distancing themselves from the administration. A palpable chill is evident in the printers' relationship with Clay toward the end of 1827. On October 2 the *Pennsylvania Intelligencer* published an editorial that argued for supporting Adams's followers on the national level but supporting the Jacksonian candidates in Dauphin County. By the end of the month, Pennsylvania congressman John Sergeant described the changed tenor of the newspaper's editorials in a letter to Clay, noting, "At Harrisburg, you will have perceived the [somersault] the [*Pennsylvania Intelligencer*] is making, frightened by the threat of losing the Legislative printing."[40]

Despite Sergeant's snark, the matter was more complicated. Cameron's tilt toward Jacksonianism reflected the fact that he had hitched his wagon to James Buchanan, who was then trying to mold the anti–Family Party elements throughout the state into a coherent and dependable political organization. Cameron's budding political friendship with Buchanan brought him into the Jacksonian coalition, though he was more interested in serving Buchanan's interests than Old Hickory's. In 1834 Cameron described Buchanan to a friend as "a fine fellow . . . and . . . the only distinguished Pennsylvanian who we can expect to place in any of the high places at Washington."[41] It is unclear when Cameron first met Buchanan, though it seems likely that they met while Cameron's younger brother James apprenticed in Buchanan's law office in the 1820s. Nearly a decade older than Cameron, Buchanan had already distinguished himself politically by the time they met. Initially a Federalist, Buchanan had opposed the War of 1812 until the British invaded Maryland, at which point he volunteered to fight in the state militia. During the war, Buchanan was elected to the Pennsylvania House of Representatives, where he served from 1814 to 1816, and in 1821 he began a decade-long tenure in the U.S. House of Representatives, eventually serving as the chairman of the U.S. House Committee on the Judiciary. Seeing that the Federalist Party had no future, Buchanan briefly supported Henry

Clay before finally migrating into the Jacksonian camp.[42] As a reward for the Pennsylvanian's support, in 1832 President Andrew Jackson appointed Buchanan U.S. minister to Russia, a post he held for eighteen months before returning to Pennsylvanian in mid-1833 to run for the U.S. Senate.

By then a "Buccaneer" (a term Buchanan's enemies used to describe loyal supporters), Cameron worked hard (but ultimately unsuccessfully) to elect Buchanan to the U.S. Senate. The following year, however, another Senate seat opened up when William Wilkins decided not to stand for reelection. Cameron aided Wilkins in getting appointed U.S. minister to Russia, and then helped elect Buchanan to the Senate, all of which reflected Cameron's deep personal attachment to his friend. In May 1844, Cameron gushed to Buchanan, "So strong is my habit of being your friend, that I find myself advocating your cause whenever there is a chance of serving you. . . . Wherever your fortunes need a friend, I will be found."[43] In March of the following year, Cameron went so far as to describe Buchanan as someone "whom I have served only as a son serves a father . . . whom I have loved for his purity and honesty."[44] He was so close to Buchanan that he named one of his sons James Buchanan Cameron.

However, Cameron suffered a setback when George Wolf, the Family Party's candidate, won the Pennsylvania gubernatorial election of 1829. By now, Cameron was totally estranged from the Family Party, and because Wolf's administration was openly unfriendly to Buchanan, Cameron could expect no favors from the governor. As a result, Cameron quickly found himself on the outside looking in when it came to state patronage, so he focused on his growing business interests. Even in defeat, fortune favored Cameron, because Pennsylvania in the 1830s was abuzz with publicly funded works projects. New York's construction of the Erie Canal in the early 1820s had greatly concerned Pennsylvanians because it had the potential to undermine Philadelphia's status as America's leading port city. As a result, in 1824 the Pennsylvania General Assembly commissioned a study on the feasibility of connecting Philadelphia and Pittsburgh by canal. Two years later, the assembly authorized construction of the State Works, as the canal was called, despite the fact that it had not yet settled on a route. Thanks to his close relationship with Governor Shulze and canal commissioner Mowry, Cameron obtained contracts to build portions of the State Works. He quickly established himself as a much sought-after expert on canals and by 1829 he had started a business selling construction equipment.[45] At about that time, he and a business partner bid on a contract to build the Mississippi–Lake Pontchartrain Canal project then getting underway in Louisiana. Winning the contract, Cameron hired twelve hundred Philadelphians and sent them by sea to New Orleans while he made his way down the Mississippi. However, shortly after work began, Cameron's partner experienced some business reversals and closed shop. As a result, Cameron had to ask the board overseeing construction to release him from his contract; the board complied, but one of the companies selected to complete the canal hired Cameron as superintendent, allowing him to see out his original plans and make a tidy profit before returning to Pennsylvania.

While in New Orleans, Cameron wrote to former governor Shulze and detailed the variety of ways in which an entrepreneur could make a fortune in the Crescent City. One particular observation is worth noting: According to Cameron, raw materials in New Orleans were quite cheap, but paradoxically, finished goods were incredibly expensive. The reason, according to Cameron, was that local whites did not like to work, preferring to "depend on the Negroes."[46] Cameron's critique of slavery is an early example of what historians have called the "free labor ideology." According to free labor supporters, slavery threatened the economic independence of the white working class. It is worth noting that the free labor critique of slavery did not attack the "peculiar institution" as a *moral* wrong, only as an inefficient labor system that was holding New Orleans and other Southern cities from developing economically.

Cameron did not limit himself to canal building; he was an early and enthusiastic railroad man. By the late 1830s, railroads were quickly displacing canals as the preferred means of transporting goods and people. By 1833 Pennsylvania had constructed the largest number of railroads (fifteen) of any state in the Union and had ambitious plans for even more.[47] At about this time, the Pennsylvania General Assembly granted a charter to the Portsmouth & Lancaster Rail-road Company (later renamed the Harrisburg, Portsmouth, Mount Joy & Lancaster Railroad). Cameron and Buchanan were both listed as incorporators, and Buchanan even served as the railroad's president. Cameron even dabbled in the iron business, refining the very raw materials that made his expanding railroad businesses possible. Recalling his activities three decades later, he noted that he

> labored for years to secure the erection of a railroad from Harrisburg to Lancaster, though laughed at as a visionary boy who talked about carrying cars, wagons, and freight on rails by steam. I am reminded here of an expression made at one of the meetings which we held in favor of the railroad project. . . . During the course of my remarks, I had happened to say, "I have no doubt, gentlemen, there are many of you present who will live to see the day when a man can eat his breakfast in Harrisburg, go to Philadelphia (one hundred miles), take his dinner, transact big business there, and return home to Harrisburg to go to bed, as usual, in the evening."

When Cameron recounted this story, he said he did it "to show what may be accomplished by a determined will and a right purpose."[48]

Without a doubt, Cameron's most important business pursuit was banking. As early as 1829, Harrisburg's *Pennsylvania Reporter and Democratic Herald* had noted the need for a bank in the region. Three years later, Cameron and fifteen other commissioners began selling stock in the Bank of Middletown, which came into existence on May 12, 1832. Cameron moved his family from Harrisburg to Middletown, settling them in a small house attached to the bank. Working as the bank's cashier facilitated Cameron's growing political influence because it gave him the resources to loan influential Pennsylvanians large sums of money on extremely favorable terms. These "loans," which were often not repaid, ensured that Cameron had the recipients' ears when it came to requesting favors in the form of special legislation or assistance finding a job for a supporter.

Cameron's political ambitions did not stop at Pennsylvania's borders, and by the mid-1830s he had established a reputation for himself in the national Democratic Party, which is what the Jacksonians had taken to calling themselves. The Democratic Party was an unlikely coalition of what future president Martin Van Buren called "the planters of the South and the plain Republicans of the north," held together in the late 1820s and early to mid-1830s mostly by Andrew Jackson's popularity.[49] Jackson was particularly popular in Pennsylvania; one observer claimed at the time that "Jackson was more blindly worshipped in Pennsylvania than any other state in the union."[50] One reason for Old Hickory's popularity in Pennsylvania was his avuncular response to the Nullification Crisis. In 1830, while serving as vice president, John C. Calhoun nearly precipitated a civil war over nullification, or the doctrine that states could ignore federal laws they considered unconstitutional. The law in question was the Tariff of 1828, which raised the prices of goods that the South imported from Great Britain (making it harder for the British to pay for the cotton they bought from the South). South Carolinians rejected a compromise bill, the Tariff of 1832, and the state undertook military preparations to resist federal authority. It was only at the very last minute that a combination of carrot and stick—a lower tariff (called the Compromise Tariff of 1833) and a bill authorizing President Jackson to use military power to compel South Carolina's submission (called the Force Bill)—averted the crisis. Regardless, the damage was done: Vice President Calhoun was now thoroughly alienated from the administration and, because the tariff was extremely popular in Pennsylvania, from most of the Keystone State's voters.

A significant consequence of Calhoun's estrangement from Jackson was the marginalization of Pennsylvania's Family Party in Jackson's administration. Most of the prominent Family Party men initially close to Jackson (such as Samuel D. Ingham and George M. Dallas) were now alienated from Old Hickory. Ingham and Dallas always viewed Jackson's presidency as only a brief interregnum preceding Calhoun's ascension to the White House and they had supported Old Hickory merely as an expedient to achieving that goal. Calhoun's marginalization meant that his Family Party supporters could expect no favors from Jackson, particularly after Ingham left the cabinet in 1831, and Buchanan's supporters (including Cameron) quickly filled the vacuum.

Jackson found Cameron to be a useful lieutenant, employing the Pennsylvanian to create the impression that Jackson had been drafted for a second term. According to a story Cameron told numerous times throughout his life, in 1832 Andrew Jackson called the Pennsylvanian to the White House. During the presidential campaign of 1828, Jackson had promised to serve only one term, but as his time in the White House was getting short, he desperately wanted to run again. Cameron recalled a conversation he had with Jackson:

> When I arrived in Washington and met Gen. Jackson he told me he wanted me to do what I could toward helping him get a second term. He said, "Cameron, will you go home and get the legislature of Pennsylvania to pass a resolution asking me to stand for a second term?" I said: "No, I cannot do that; I am known as a one-term man. But I can have the resolution drawn up in Washington and get some one to take it to Harrisburg and have it passed." . . . This was done, and in due time the Legislature of Pennsylvania requested Gen. Jackson by resolution to reconsider his previous declaration not to be a candidate for re-election and stand for another term, which he [did].[51]

In Cameron, Jackson had found a political operative who could get things done.

Thus, when it came time for the 1832 Democratic National Convention, which Jackson had convened for the sole purpose of having former secretary of state Martin Van Buren named as his running mate, Jackson turned to Cameron. The president instructed his former secretary of war (and close personal friend), John Eaton, to contact Cameron and convince the Pennsylvanian to organize a delegation favorable to Van Buren to attend the National Democratic Nominating Convention. Held in Baltimore in late May, the convention was designed to be a coronation, whereby the overwhelming majority of the party would select Van Buren. Jackson's followers were explicitly warned to vote for no one other than Van Buren lest they "quarrel with the general."[52] As a result of such pressure, Van Buren received nearly three-quarters of the votes, besting his closest rival, Phillip P. Barbour, by a factor of more than 4 to 1. Reflecting on his role in the convention years later, Cameron noted that while his support of Van Buren caused difficulties for him in Pennsylvania, he "need not complain, for I had more enjoyment by pestering the fellows at Harrisburg until they actually swallowed the dose of Van Burenism than I have ever had in anything connected with politics."[53]

As a reward for Cameron's success in whipping the Pennsylvania delegation's votes for Van Buren at the nominating convention, Jackson appointed Cameron a visitor to the U.S. Military Academy at West Point (essentially a member of its board of directors). Though Cameron held this position only briefly, it apparently engendered a lifelong distaste for professional military officers. Cameron's appointment was a perfect example of a Jacksonian "spoils system," so-called because of New York senator William L. Marcy's infamous assertion "To the victor belong the spoils." In this case, the spoils of victory were the thousands of federal government jobs that the incoming administration could distribute among Jackson's supporters. In an era when the Republican Party was fracturing and party loyalty had frayed, the spoils system was designed to promote allegiance to Jackson's administration by giving recipients an incentive to promote Old Hickory's goals. The spoils system was nothing new; politicians had rewarded their supporters with government jobs and contracts well before Jackson became president, as Cameron's early relationship with Samuel Ingham demonstrates. However, because all of the presidents between 1801 and 1825 were from the same party, turnover of federal government jobs was quite small at the beginning of new administrations. Bucking this tradition, Jackson replaced nearly 10 percent of federal workers with his supporters, an unprecedented purge that involved removing some men who had held their positions since Washington's presidency![54] The new administration ruthlessly purged newspapers considered pro-Adams from the list of those receiving federal printing contracts, causing a turnover of approximately 70 percent during Jackson's first term.[55]

Jackson's election in 1828 opened new political opportunities for Cameron, but for all of the Pennsylvanian's political success in the 1830s, these years were not always joyful. Both he and his wife, Margaret, were frequently ill.[56] In 1830 Cameron's mother, Martha, died; though she had sent Simon and his brothers to live with local families when they were children, she remained close to the boys and they mourned her passing. Cameron and his wife lost multiple children during this time. His seven-month-old son, John Colin, died in June 1825, and in August 1831 he lost two daughters: three-year-old daughter Catherine Mary and one-year-old Ann Eliza. In late 1835 Cameron and Martha lost their son, James. Writing following the boy's death, Buchanan (for whom the boy was named) tried to comfort the grieving father by saying, "I feel sorry that he has been called away from us. And yet parents have many consolations for the loss of children in infancy. Their fate in future life is always uncertain, and we have the highest authority for believing that they are happy in death. 'Of such this the kingdom of heaven.'"[57]

Despite these tragedies, Cameron's wealth and political influence were unquestionable, and he remained active in state and national politics, ensuring his involvement in two important issues facing Pennsylvania in the 1830s: public education and slavery. In the early 1830s, Cameron supported the Free School Act of 1834, which encouraged the creation of taxpayer-funded public schools. Cameron's support of the public education law seems rooted in two impulses that reflected his impoverished childhood: generosity and a belief that formal education was important. Certainly, his belief in the importance of education was reflected in the fact that he used a considerable portion of his growing wealth to provide for his children the exclusive education he never had. At least four of his children—Brua, Donald, Margaret, and Virginia—attended the local private school with the scions of the region's leading families, and the boys attended college at Princeton. In addition, his daughter Rachel and his son Brua attended the local Sunday school, where Cameron apparently paid the tuition of an indigent child named George A. Minshall, a perfect example of the generosity for which Cameron was widely known.[58]

The other important issue facing Pennsylvania and the nation in the 1830s was slavery. In many ways, Pennsylvania was a natural battleground for those opposed to and supportive of slavery because the Keystone State's southern border coincided with the Mason–Dixon Line, which demarcated the free North and the slave South. Slaves escaping from Maryland or Virginia almost always passed through Pennsylvania, and the state housed a large free black population. As a result, Pennsylvania's relationship with its Southern neighbors grew strained following Nat Turner's Rebellion in 1831, the nullification crisis of 1832, and the imposition of the gag rule in the House of Representatives in 1836. In an attempt to address the simmering tension, a number of prominent Pennsylvanians met in Harrisburg in May 1837 for a "Convention of the Integrity of the Union." All of Pennsylvania's counties sent delegates; Cameron attended as one of the representatives of Dauphin County, while his brother James represented Indiana County. The convention affirmed that states had the right to choose for themselves whether to permit slavery, and the federal government or other states had no right to interfere with or influence that choice.

Because Cameron was only a candidate to this convention and no official minutes exist, it is difficult to know whether he personally agreed with these sentiments. However, in a letter to James Buchanan, Cameron expressed opinions similar to the convention's resolutions. According to Cameron, "The question [of slavery], however, I am afraid will occupy more of public attention during the coming year than will comport with the peace and good order of our state. Every village is now cursed with some hired lecturer who is daily engaged in adding fuel to the growing flame. Those of the leaders, however, who calculate upon gaining votes to the opposition by abolitionism will be much disappointed: Our people do not like the Negroes."[59]

Cameron's presence at the "Convention of the Integrity of the Union" certainly demonstrates that, by the late 1830s, he had emerged as one of Pennsylvania's leading Jacksonian Democrats. Writing to Buchanan in March 1842, Cameron noted the birth of a son, whom he named Simon: "By the way, I have another son, born on my birthday, 8th March. He is to be called Simon. If he is to have as many fights in the course of the next forty years as his worthy namesake has had for the cost to keep his head above water, then God help him. And still, after all the turmoil, I have had much fun in my time, and as many triumphs on a small scale as most men."[60] Despite his earlier antipathy toward Andrew Jackson, by 1832 Cameron had established himself as one of the most influential Democrats in Pennsylvania, submerging whatever doubts he harbored about the Jacksonians in the mid-1820s under a sea of patronage and political influence. Cameron campaigned hard for Old Hickory's hand-picked successor, Martin Van Buren, in 1836. However, Cameron's bond with the Jacksonians faced serious strains in the late 1830s and early 1840s over two issues: a scandal resulting from his appointment as commissioner to adjudicate the repayment of claims against the Winnebago Indians, and the Jacksonians' "hard money" and anti-banking policies.

2

"The Great Winnebago Chief," 1838–45

Beginning in the mid-1830s, Cameron sought to leverage his political influence to secure a patronage job. In a July 1834 letter to Andrew Jackson, James Buchanan told the president that Cameron's "influence is extensive and powerful throughout [the] State, and to my knowledge many of the Democratic members of our last Legislature were among his warmest friends."[1] A few days later, Auditor of the Treasury William B. Lewis noted that he had received numerous letters from Pennsylvania Democrats recommending Cameron be appointed governor of the Michigan Territory.[2] This was not a spontaneous outpouring; in fact, Cameron had engineered the letter campaign, and it seemed to succeed.[3] A few weeks after receiving Lewis's letter, Jackson included Cameron among a number of potential candidates for the governorship of Michigan, but the president ultimately appointed someone else.[4] No other patronage appointments were forthcoming, a fact that clearly annoyed Cameron, especially following Van Buren's election to the presidency in 1836. At one point, Cameron reminded Buchanan, "There was a time when Mr. Van Buren had few friends in this state, and he never could have secured its vote if a few men had not so early as 1832 taken ground in his favor in opposition to the views and exertions of the then state administration."[5] In other words, under the rules of the spoils system, Cameron felt he was owed his share of patronage, and he was now coming to collect.

A prime opportunity for Van Buren to reward Cameron's loyalty came when the United States signed a treaty with the Winnebago Indians in November 1837. Under the treaty's terms, the Winnebagos ceded land west of the Mississippi River. The Winnebagos also agreed to use the lands just west of the Mississippi River for hunting only and not for settlement. In exchange, the treaty obligated the U.S. government to pay $200,000 in a mix of direct cash payments to individuals specifically named in the treaty and payments to traders for the Winnebago nation's debt. In addition, the treaty bound the U.S. government to pay out $100,000 to individuals of mixed race (i.e., "half-breeds") who were at least one-quarter Winnebago. The treaty also empowered the president to appoint commissioners to investigate and adjudicate traders' claims under the treaty, which was standard practice when it came to dealing with Native Americans.[6]

Once the Senate ratified the treaty, Cameron requested Buchanan's help in obtaining an appointment as one of the commissioners. In late December, Cameron thanked Buchanan for the "prompt manner" in which the senator responded to his request for help in getting the appointment, but when it was not immediately forthcoming, Cameron sent multiple letters asking about it.[7] Eventually, Van Buren's secretary of war, Joel R. Poinsett, named Cameron one of two commissioners charged with examining "claims of half-breed relatives of the Winnebago Indians, and debts due by the same Indians."[8] In a letter to his friend Lewis S. Coryell, Cameron ruefully noted, "My instructions came the day before yesterday and I am instructed to be in Prairie du Chien [Wisconsin] by the 20th inst."[9]

Commissioner of Indian Affairs Carey A. Harris dispatched instructions to Cameron and his co-commissioner, James Murray of Maryland, directing them to arrive at Fort Snelling by August 25 and to immediately announce a time and place for the commission to conduct its work, which was twofold. First,

Cameron and Murray needed to compile a list of the individuals claiming at least one-quarter Winnebago blood and submit it to the leaders of the Winnebago nation for verification. Next, the commissioners were to investigate and adjudicate the claims of traders in the region to whom individual Winnebagos and the nation as a whole owed money. The actual specie for paying the "half-breeds'" claims was to be forwarded to Major Ethan Allen Hitchcock, the local U.S. Army official in the area, who would actually pay the claims. Crucially, Harris's instructions made clear "there will no doubt be a number of minors, or orphans, and of persons incompetent to make the right disposition of the sums allowed them. . . . [In such cases], you are authorized to place their respective shares in the hands of some trustworthy person, who will apply it faithfully for their benefit. . . . The same course may be taken in the cases of Indians you deem incompetent to manage their affairs."[10] The commissioners' broad interpretation of this mandate laid the groundwork for a scandal that haunted Cameron for the rest of his life.

Cameron took his family with him to Wisconsin. He also took $5,000 in Middletown Bank notes (currency printed by the bank and redeemable for specie); he apparently decided to look for opportunities for land speculation while in Wisconsin.[11] His critics later seized on this fact as proof that Cameron had corruptly used his office for personal gain. More important, it also appears that he (and later Murray, when the second commissioner joined the Camerons) traveled with Daniel M. Brodhead, a Philadelphia lawyer and banker, on a steamship from Detroit to Chicago. Brodhead intended to peddle his services to "half-breeds"; his presence on the trip caused much of the ensuing controversy. Murray later claimed in a letter to the committee that he had not known Brodhead before encountering him on the steamboat.[12] Cameron also signed the letter, implying that he too did not know Brodhead, but this was not the case: Cameron was certainly acquainted with Brodhead, at least superficially, because the two were often in Harrisburg advocating for their respective banks, though the depth and character of their relationship is unknown, which only added to the later speculation that Cameron was actively working to cheat the Winnebagos of their money. At this point, however, all of that was in the future, and Cameron saw the enterprise as an opportunity to craft a national reputation for himself and make some money in land speculation.

Due to delays, Cameron and Murray did not arrive in Prairie du Chien until August 29. On the advice of some locals, the commissioners elected to remain in Prairie du Chien and conduct their commission there rather than go out into Winnebago territory. From the start, the commissioners were at a disadvantage. As they later noted, they were "entire strangers in the country, having no knowledge of the mixed breeds, of their present or previous standing, [were] ignorant of their history . . . and limited in time" and were therefore "thrown for information upon the community of Prairie du Chien."[13] Though obligated to "require the respective creditors to deposite [*sic*] with us transcripts of their claims, exhibiting names, dates, articles, prices, and the original consideration of each claim,"[14] the commissioners quickly found this to be an impossible task; most traders had no such documentation and therefore would be unable to present their claims if the commissioners followed these instructions. In a letter, Cameron described the challenges he and Murray faced:

> The claimants are a <u>queer</u> sort of people and they present their claims in a <u>queer manner</u>. I cannot consent to make any decision which I may not feel fully satisfied is right, and which will be sustained by evidence. . . . The principle upon which they wish our decision is that every trader shall make a statement of what he believes he lost and get some writings to make a deposition. . . . We want some evidence that <u>some goods at least</u> went into the hands of the Indians above the amount they paid for. . . . We will not be [illegible] nor frightened. . . . My colleague goes for doing all things according to instructions, and I agree with him.[15]

Cameron and Murray decided that, under the treaty, the Winnebagos had essentially conceded that they owed the traders money; therefore, the issue was no longer providing *that* the traders were due payment, it was only a matter of *how much* money was due. Again, the commissioners liberally construed their instructions: Based on the traders' testimonies, Cameron and Murray devised an average for the claims that allowed them to pay a little more than ninety-three cents on the dollar for each claim they considered legitimate.[16]

Had this been the only issue with the commissioners' work, it is unlikely that anyone would have complained; after all, the amount paid was nearly the total amount due on the Winnebagos' debt, and the traders agreed to the discounted amount they received. Settling the traders' claims was only half of Cameron and Murray's charge; they also had to disburse money due to "half-breeds." The controversy arose over the fact that, most of the individuals claiming eligibility to receive payment as "half-breeds" signed over their power to plead their cases to other people (in this case, white men) who acted as the claimants' advocates. This was not unusual; as the commissioners later noted, "If the claims had belonged to white citizens . . . it would not have been at all a matter of surprise that they should appear by attorney, it certainly being the most convenient and best course. . . . Their right so to appear was not in any case questioned, and the instructions did not forbid it."[17] It is important to remember that people claiming Winnebago ancestry had to persuade the commissioners of the veracity of their claims; doing so required definitive evidence or, in the absence of evidence, a really strong circumstantial case. Thus, from Cameron and Murray's perspective, they did nothing wrong in allowing representatives, or attorneys-in-fact, to plead the claimants' cases.

Major Hitchcock did not share the commissioners' broad interpretation of their mandate. On November 6 he wrote to Commissioner of Indian Affairs T. Harley Crawford (who had recently replaced Harris in that position) to advise that, from a sense of duty, "I have been compelled . . . to suspend payment of the Winnebago half-breed money until I receive your instructions." According to Hitchcock, the problem was that the Winnebagos' attorneys-in-fact were attempting to collect the claimants' money. This was a problem to Hitchcock because "it is against all knowledge (although there may be exceptions) to suppose the half-breeds are acquainted with the nature of powers of attorney and bills of exchange and to discuss a question concerning them, upon a presumption of their moral responsibility to our laws and usages, is, to my mind, an absurdity." He believed that the "half-breeds'" alleged intellectual inferiority prevented them from understanding what it meant to grant power of attorney to a third party and they were therefore being taken advantage of by their representatives. Putting aside the obvious and distasteful racism inherent in Hitchcock's assumptions, there is some reason to believe he may have been correct that the Winnebagos were being fleeced. He noted that "a moneyed man [Daniel M. Brodhead], who travelled from Philadelphia with a large amount of Philadelphia bank notes" represented many Winnebago claimants and was therefore collecting their money.[18]

Cameron and Murray argued with Hitchcock over the payment suspension but to no avail. In a letter to the War Department, Hitchcock asserted, "Their instructions were given under the presumption that the money would be on the spot, to be *distributed* by them to the *proper claimants*; that the money not being there presented a contingency not anticipated [the money had been delayed]; and that, in point of fact, their duties would not be executed."[19] Later, he sent the commissioner of Indian Affairs another letter, this one expanding on his assertions regarding Cameron and Murray's malfeasance. The major grandiloquently proclaimed, "I have crossed the purposes of a band of greedy speculators and brought upon myself the maledictions of many who pretend an infinite degree of sympathy for the very half-breeds whom they cheated and almost robbed. . . . Be the consequences what they may, I rejoice that I have, for a few weeks at least, suspended the execution of this business."[20] By way of evidence, he repeated as fact speculation and innuendo regarding the claimants' representatives and the commissioners.

For instance, Hitchcock claimed that he knew of one attorney-in-fact who had a note entitling him to collect $1,500 for his "half-breed" client but had instead used the note to pay off his own debt. He also reported that he was "informed, and have not the slightest doubt of the fact," that "half-breed" claimants were regularly pressured to sell the notes entitling them to payment for pennies on the dollar.[21] In another letter, dated December 3, Hitchcock cited as evidence "the statements of correct persons here, [attesting to] the most shameful bribing and favoritism [having] been practiced."[22] Two days later, the major sent another letter to the War Department, in which he cited "public rumor" as proving that the "half-breeds were shamefully cheated out of their rights." He further noted that he believed "this is the general impression of the disinterested party of the community at Prairie du Chien." However, he acknowledged that he had not "inquired into the true origin of the reports which came to my knowledge in this affair" and he therefore declined "giving any facts at present," though he promised to at a later date.[23] The lack of evidence, coupled with the vague assertions of corruption, became a hallmark of this scandal, and it is one of the reasons why it is so hard for historians to assess who was actually telling the truth.

Hitchcock also asserted that Brodhead was colluding with the commissioners to defraud the "half-breeds," yet he again failed to produce any evidence. On November 10 Hitchcock sent Crawford a letter in which he charged that

Lockwood and Dousman [two other men acting as attorneys-in-fact], in conjunction with a Mr. Brodhead (the latter with the commissioners, and bragged that he had made $60,000 out of the claims and half-breeds), decided the cases, and the commissioners only confirmed their acts officially. Let any man of common sense and honesty look at the treaty, and then place the half-breeds in classes, if they can; and that, too, has no relation to half or quarter blood, but they are classed by *favor*. A quarter blood is in the *first* class, and a half in the *third class*. If the case was presented by Mr. Brodhead, or Mr. Dousman, or Lockwood, strongly, it was in the first or second class; if not advocated by either of these potent characters, the case went into the third class.[24]

While Hitchcock deluged the War Department with letters detailing his concerns, the commissioners submitted a lengthy defense of their actions. Citing time limitations and their inability to gather reliable records, and the fact that the specie to pay the claims was late, Cameron and Murray rationalized their behavior as within the spirit, if not the exact letter, of their mandate. Three days after Christmas, Murray sent the commissioner of Indian Affairs a second letter that contained the commission's records, purporting to demonstrate that the commissioners' actions were beyond reproach. The letter notes only a single questionable instance regarding attorneys-in-fact, namely, that Brodhead had received a note for Julia Grignon, payable to himself, that should have gone to the girl's actual attorney-in-fact, Aimable Grignon. Murray explained this error by noting, "The power of attorney is endorsed on the back, as if given to Mr. D.M. Brodhead, and the commissioners may have thus been led into error. Mr. Brodhead has been written for an explanation."[25]

By now Hitchcock was not the only person criticizing Cameron and Murray's conduct. In a January 1839 letter to the commissioner of Indian Affairs, a Philadelphian named C. A. Rogers reported that Cameron boasted of having made $100,000 by defrauding the Winnebagos through the use of Brodhead as attorney-in-fact, though he produced no proof to support this allegation.[26] As a result of the rumors of fraud, Commissioner of Indian Affairs Crawford recommended to Secretary of War Poinsett that payments of Winnebago certificates should immediately be halted pending a new commission being sent to investigate Cameron and Murray's actions. According to one investigator, "The [commissioners'] instructions point plainly to the payment of money to the Indians; and if they did not, it seems to me the appearance by attorney-in-fact, and the granting of certificates to those representatives, opened so wide an entrance to fraud that I cannot repress the expression of my surprise that such a course should have been deemed proper. The money was to be paid to the *respective persons entitled to it*, except in instances of minors, orphans, and incompetents. The execution of the treaty, in either its spirit or letter, forbade any other procedure."[27] Poinsett endorsed Hartley's letter, writing on it, "The Department will in no manner recognize these transactions. A new commission will be forthwith appointed."[28]

A week later, Hitchcock obtained a statement from one "half-breed" who claimed that Brodhead and another individual, Nicholas Boilvin, had pressured him into selling his and his children's claims, which totaled $1,600, for $800 (which was eventually raised to $1,100).[29] Indian agent Joseph M. Street, who lived among the Winnebagos, detailed other cases of Brodhead purchasing the "half-breed's" certificates at steep discounts, though there is no evidence of outright fraud.[30] Street's most important claim, as it relates to Cameron, was that "Mr. Brodhead said that General Cameron and himself had brought on $40,000 or $60,000 with them. Mr. F[eatherstonhaugh], the secretary, also said the commissioners did not care whether the disbursing agent paid their private draft, for that the commissioners had brought on a large amount of money; and the money paid out here, was on a bank of which General C. is president. What could all this money be brought here for by the commissioners and Mr. Brodhead?"[31]

Called to account for their actions, in mid-February, Cameron and Murray submitted a lengthy statement defending their conduct, asserting that the only issue with their report, which they charged had been "harshly" set aside, was the fact that they had granted the "half-breeds" certificates in lieu of specie. The commissioners defended themselves by reminding Hartley that "we did not *pay the money*; that part of the duty was to have been performed by another officer of the Government, who did not reach the county during our protracted stay there, and whose presence at the proper time might have saved the necessity of giving certificates."[32] Furthermore, they noted, the War Department had instructed them to *"pay the parties interested,"* which, Cameron and Murray claimed, "might mean even assignees, but, without doubt, as we conceive, attorneys-in-fact." The two commissioners claimed that they "thought our guardianship ended when the final award was made; and that the persons in whose favor awards were made, had as good a right to direct us to pay A, B, or C (we mean when there was no allegation of fraud) as themselves." Finally, and rather boldly, the two men declared, "[If] the department is in possession of any information impugning our motives, or charging against us corruption of any kind, we are sure that we shall be excused if we demand that it be produced in order that we may defend ourselves."[33] This was a smart strategy on Cameron and Murray's part because the case against them relied entirely on hearsay, innuendo, and rumor. In a letter to Poinsett, Murray accurately characterized the majority of Hitchcock's letters as "artful inferences, drawn entirely from an assumed connexion between Mr. Brodhead and the commissioners." He then asked, rhetorically, "Is this connexion proved? Is any fact stated, from which this presumption is fairly deductible?"[34]

Murray's question is worth considering. Though Hitchcock was sure of his own rectitude, Murray was absolutely right that the major lacked any solid evidence of collusion between Brodhead and the commissioners. Moreover, the tone of Hitchcock's letters to the War Department indicates that he bore some animus toward the commissioners, seeing them as guilty without investigating their version of events. Cameron himself pointed this out when, after reviewing Hitchcock's letters, he complained of "the means used by your disbursing agent to blacken the reputation of the commissioners."[35] The commissioners' secretary, George W. Featherstonhaugh, lauded Cameron and Murray's work and asserted that it was "highly improbable any allegation of improper or interested collusion between the commissioners and any other parties" was true. He based this conclusion on the antagonism that almost all of the claimants had for the commissioners upon their arrival and how, at the commission's conclusion, "almost each and every claimant . . . expressed the highest satisfaction for having what was termed substantial justice."[36]

Given the fact that no evidence of corruption had been presented, Congress exonerated Cameron and Murray in March 1839 but, by the same token, reinforced the suspicion that *something* was amiss by dispatching a new commissioner, John Fleming Jr., to readjudicate the Winnebagos' claims. The confusion annoyed the "half-breeds" and the traders. In letters to Cameron, Boilvin recounted the confusion caused by the new commission. In the first place, a new set of claimants appeared, as well as some of the ones Cameron and Murray had adjudicated the previous year. In late August, Boilvin claimed there was "trouble" between the two groups, and the following month he reported to Cameron "the Indians had a council and told the Com[missioner] that they would not do over what was done last year. It was well done." The letter doubtlessly pleased Cameron because it vindicated his and Murray's actions, a fact reinforced in March 1840 when John Fleming Jr. sent Cameron a letter celebrating the fact that the Pennsylvanian had "come out triumphant."[37]

Yet the *perception* of corruption became impossible for Cameron to shake. In autumn 1839, Cameron wrote to Buchanan asking to see any correspondence that Buchanan had received about the commission; Buchanan refused, saying, "I have never in a single instance, and I cannot think that I ever shall show . . . to my nearest friend a letter written against him to me because I consider it a breach of confidence."[38] Buchanan's response irritated Cameron and, in retrospect, was an early indication of the coming break in their friendship. Despite there being no hard evidence that Cameron and Murray had done anything wrong, in April 1840 the chairman of the House Committee on Indian Affairs, Ambrose H. Sevier, sent Cameron a letter notifying him that the committee was *again* investigating the Winnebago commission. Cameron was apparently ill at the time and did not go to Washington. This prompted Brodhead to write a panicked letter imploring Cameron to meet with the committee. Brodhead told him, "I think you had better come down [to Philadelphia] immediately and go on to Washington. . . . I feel as though the report of the Com[mittee] was of vital importance to you officially and collaterally to me as an individual."[39] This apparently did not stir Cameron to action, because two months later he received another letter begging him to come speak to the committee, though it appears he never did.[40]

The committee found no proof of wrongdoing, and its desire to investigate the Winnebago commissioners eventually waned, so Cameron faced no legal consequences for his actions.[41] Whether Cameron and Murray actually cheated the Winnebagos, however, mattered little; henceforth, Cameron's political enemies routinely derided him as the "Great Winnebago Chief," an epithet that always aroused his anger. The fallout from the Winnebago Treaty scandal was a major blow to Cameron's political ambitions, with many people believing that he was politically toxic and should therefore be held at arm's length. Writing to Buchanan, Cameron complained that one of their mutual acquaintances

> wanted to use my money and influence and at the same time avoid what he considered my unpopularity and that of my friends. I am tired of such slang. I do not choose to be used by any man who will not openly own his connection with me. I know well my own capacity for good or evil, & I feel deeply the indignities that have been heaped upon my reputation by such men as I could name who have feared my rivalry, while they have at the same time been pretending friendship, using my services and in secret slandering me by innuendo.[42]

His bitterness at his fellow Democrats' treatment of him was the first of many signs that his attachment to the Jacksonians was waning.

Heightening his alienation was the fact that Cameron had drifted into the orbit of a coalition of Pennsylvania Democrats known as the "Improvement Men," for their unswerving devotion to publicly funded internal improvements, a protective tariff, and a strong banking sector. These policies were at odds with the Jackson and Van Buren administrations, which opposed protective tariffs, central banking, and the use of federal funds for internal improvements. Worse, as the election of 1840 approached, the Van Buren administration was becoming more, not less, dogmatic on these issues. Van Buren's prospects for reelection in 1840 were not good; with Jackson retired, the general's magnetism no longer held together the disparate (and in many cases antagonistic) elements of the Jacksonian coalition. One consequence was that, for the first time, the party laid down a platform embracing the very hard-money, anti-improvement, anti-banking positions that were anathema to men such as Cameron. As Kelley has noted, "The Democrats had been successful in Pennsylvania because they had effective party leadership," but now the party was attempting to substitute allegiance to doctrine for attachment to individuals.[43]

Unfortunately for the Democrats, a party platform failed to overcome voter anger over the depression caused by the Panic of 1837, and Van Buren lost his bid for reelection that fall to the Whig candidate, William Henry Harrison. Harrison's victory in 1840 freed Pennsylvania's Democrats from adherence to Jacksonian dogma because, without a national Democratic administration, local and state party leaders had greater autonomy when it came to choosing candidates and taking stands on issues.[44] The price to be paid for decentralization was that the commonwealth's Democrats quickly "turned to their own devices," often exacerbating divisions between the party's various factions.[45] In Pennsylvania, Democrats divided into two main camps: those who wanted Van Buren to run for president in 1844 and those who supported Governor David Porter's administration.

Porter was a former state senator and longtime friend of

James Buchanan who advocated many of the "Improvement Men's" goals. Cameron supported Porter in part because he had appointed Cameron's brother James superintendent of motive power in February 1839. Cameron attended the Democratic State Convention in March 1841, where his ally Hendrick B. Wright nominated Porter for reelection as governor. Cameron worked hard on behalf of Governor Porter's reelection that year, and some Whig newspapers even went so far as to call Porter the "Cameron candidate," an attempt to tar the candidate with the residual stench of the Winnebago Scandal.[46] Cameron's conspicuous and avuncular support for Porter aroused the ire of Van Buren's supporters, which suited Cameron just fine. In January 1844 he complained to Buchanan of a great Democratic meeting taking place nearby, claiming he was "very much inclined to go into it and make a speech against Van Buren. The [illegible] are in an uproar, and only need a leader to make them blow up every chance of Van Buren's success in this state."[47]

Despite Cameron's efforts to prevent it, in 1844 the Pennsylvania State Convention chose Van Buren for president. In response, Cameron and the U.S. attorney for the Eastern District of Pennsylvania, John M. Read, called a meeting of the Democratic State Central Committee with an eye toward freeing the commonwealth's delegates from their pledges to support the former president and reinstructing them to support Buchanan. The lack of a quorum prevented this tactic from succeeding. At the end of May, Cameron journeyed to Baltimore for the Democratic National Convention. Cameron's fellow "improvement man" Hendrick B. Wright chaired the convention, and he got the delegates to adopt the two-thirds rule in an attempt to thwart Van Buren's nomination. The two-thirds rule required that a nominee had to win the votes not just of a majority of convention delegates but of two-thirds. Ironically, this rule dated to the first Democratic national nominating convention in 1832, when Jackson was nominated for reelection. The rule applied to Jackson's running mate, Martin Van

Buren, who secured the necessary two-thirds vote and won a place on the ticket.

Though successive Democratic nominating conventions retained the two-thirds rule, it had little impact on the conventions of 1836 or 1840, but 1844 was a different matter. The two-thirds rule magnified the South's power because the number of convention delegates a state had was dictated by the state's electoral votes; due to the three-fifths clause (which allowed the South to count five slaves as if they were three white men) in the Constitution, the South's share of electoral votes was far higher than its white population warranted. Thus, by 1844 the Democrats had become a Southern-dominated, pro-slavery party that contained a compliant Northern wing.[48] Van Buren had alienated many Southerners by publicly opposing the annexation of Texas, which he knew would upset the delicate balance between the Southern and Northern wings of the Democratic Party. Writing in April 1844 to Mississippi congressman William Hammett, Van Buren asserted, "The acquisition of so valuable a territory by means which are of questionable propriety, would be a departure from those just principles upon which this government has ever acted, and which have excited the admiration and secured the respect of the dispassionate and enlightened friends of freedom throughout the world."[49] This was hardly a response designed to endear the former president to the Southern Democrats he would need to win the party's nomination and the general election. After reading Van Buren's letter, James Buchanan compared the former president's chances of being elected to those of a "dead cock in the pit."[50]

In truth, the party's Southern wing never fully trusted Van Buren; since he was a New Yorker, many Southerners believed that he was insufficiently committed to the protection of slavery. Because Southerners had an outsized number of delegates, losing the South was a body blow to any candidate. Practically speaking, the two-thirds rule sank Van Buren's chances of winning the nomination because, while the former president could be assured of receiving a simple majority of the delegates' votes, two-thirds was simply too high a hurdle for either the New Yorker or his main rival, former Michigan governor Lewis Cass. The two-thirds rule essentially enshrined the principle that "a well-organized minority could derail the candidate of the majority and dictate terms."[51]

In 1844 that is exactly what happened: the convention nominated former Speaker of the U.S. House of Representatives James K. Polk. Polk was close to Jackson—he was known as "Young Hickory"— but he was not married to Jacksonian orthodoxy, which appealed to northern Democrats who had grown accustomed to their freedom of action on issues like the tariff and banks. In addition, Northern Democrats comforted themselves with the fact that the convention called for not just the annexation of Texas but the "reoccupation" of Oregon, meaning that the country would add both slave and free territory.[52] Yet the bitter split in the party became evident when the convention chose Silas Wright Jr. as its vice presidential nominee. Wright, a prominent New York State politician, was closely aligned with Martin Van Buren and declined the nomination out of fealty to the former president. The method of Polk's selection, and the underlying sectional tension it exposed, had far-reaching consequences for the Democratic Party and for the country.

Cameron's exact role in the struggle over the two-thirds rule is murky at best. Biographer Lee F. Crippen found no direct evidence connecting him to the movement for the two-thirds rule, though he does note that Pennsylvania's delegation (which was formally pledged to Van Buren) voted for the rule, which was effectually a vote *against* the former president.[53] In a similar vein, one of Jefferson Davis's early biographers claimed that the two-thirds rule and Polk's selection as the Democratic nominee resulted from the machinations of a cabal of anti–Van Buren politicos that included Cameron, Mississippi senator Robert J. Walker (one of Cameron's personal friends and soon to be Polk's secretary of the Treasury), and Thomas Ritchie (an acquaintance of Cameron's and soon to be the editor of the Polk administration's official newspaper); he, like Crippen, provides no evidence for this assertion, though it is worth noting that Polk rewarded two of the three individuals named (Walker and Ritchie) with plum patronage jobs.[54]

Regardless, Polk was the Democratic presidential nominee. However, he had a problem: his stand on the tariff. The tariff served two functions: it provided revenue (in this period, the federal government's operating expenses came mostly from tariff revenue) and it increased the price of imported goods, thereby protecting American industries. While some level of taxation on imports was necessary for the federal government to operate, whether the government should encourage domestic manufacturers by using the tariff to protect them had become one of the most contentious issues in American politics during the 1830s and 1840s. In general, Pennsylvanians (Democrats included) demanded protection for the commonwealth's burgeoning industries, but Polk had consistently advocated a tariff low enough to fund the federal government and had opposed all legislation designed to use the tariff to protect American industries.[55] This was not going to win him many votes in Pennsylvania, the state with the second-highest number of electoral votes. Clearly, he needed to "massage" the issue to make himself palatable to the Keystone State's voters without alienating the anti-tariff South.

He achieved this by writing a letter, designed for publication, to Philadelphia politician John K. Kane, a Jacksonian Democrat who had broken with Van Buren and now considered Polk a personal friend. In the letter, Polk asserted that it was "the duty of the Government to extend as far as it may be practicable to do so by the revenue laws & all other means within its power, fair and just protection unto all the great interests of the whole Union, embracing agriculture, manufactures, the mechanic arts, commerce, and navigation."[56] Polk's statement was vague enough that both advocates of protection and supporters of free trade were convinced that the president agreed with them. At another point, Polk claimed, "In adjusting the details of a revenue tariff, I have heretofore sanctioned such moderate discriminating duties as would produce the amount of revenue needed, and at the same time afford reasonable incidental protection to our home industry."[57] Based on these statements, Pennsylvania's voters could be forgiven for concluding that Polk supported using the tariff to protect American industry from foreign competition. Though Polk did not lie outright, his letter was nonetheless calculated to create a false impression about the policies his administration would pursue if he were elected president. In October 1844, Cameron confirmed that Polk's letter to Kane had falsely "fixed the belief that [Polk was] as good a tariff man as Clay." He also emphasized to Polk that no one who was suspected of being anti-tariff could possibly win Pennsylvania, whose electoral votes were absolutely essential to winning the election.[58] Kane's letter worked; on election day, Polk squeaked to victory, winning 49.5 percent of the popular vote (to Clay's 48.1 percent), and carrying not only all of the deep South but Pennsylvania and New York as well.

Polk's defeat of Van Buren for the Democratic nomination and victory in the general election signaled the end of Jacksonian control over the party, which boded well for Cameron. Nowhere was the Jacksonians' waning power more evident than in Polk's first priority: establishing a loyal newspaper in Washington. This was hardly unusual, as many politicians at the regional, state, and national levels subsidized newspapers favorable to their policies and careers as a means of connecting with voters; recall that this was how Cameron had entered state politics a generation before.

The problem was that the capital already had a Democratic organ, the *Globe*, a Jacksonian paper edited by Francis P. Blair. The paper had served as the Jackson and Van Buren administrations' main mouthpiece. In the lead-up to the 1844 Democratic nominating convention, the *Globe* had enthusiastically supported Van Buren, to whom Blair was "fanatically loyal," angering the vindictive Polk.[59] The president-elect was not the only Democrat with an ax to grind when it came to the *Globe*. Other prominent Democrats alienated from the dominant Jacksonian wing of the party, such as John C. Calhoun, pushed Polk to oust Blair if the Tennessean won the presidency, while incoming secretary of state Buchanan hated Blair and the *Globe* because he believed the newspaper had been hostile toward him.[60] In other words, Blair had to go.

Polk tried to convince Jackson of the need for new leadership at the *Globe*, writing shortly after his inauguration, "The *Globe* it is manifest does not look to the success of the glory of my administration so much as it does to the interests, and wishes of certain prominent men who are looking to succeed me in 1848. The arrangement which above all others I would prefer would be that, the owners of the *Globe*, would agree to place it in the hands of a new editor, still retaining the proprietorship of the paper if they choose."[61] The ailing former president (Jackson would be dead within three months) wrote to a mutual acquaintance in April 1845, noting, "I find that Mr. Blair and the President have got into some difficulty about the *Globe* (with Mr. Blair as its Editor) being the executive organ. This is a difficulty where I can see no result but injury to him, and no justifiable cause of the President's part for [*sic*] it. He believes Mr. Blair has become unpopular with part of the democracy—[Polk] has opened his ears to bad advisors. Mr. Blair has more popularity with the democratic members of Congress and the democracy of the United States than any editor in them."[62] Despite Jackson's pleas that Polk should leave Blair in place, "Young Hickory" was determined to have a reliable propagandist editing the administration's paper. Less than a month after the election, Polk was plotting how to loosen Blair's grip over the *Globe*.

The man Polk asked to push Blair out of the *Globe* was John P. Heiss, then coeditor of the Nashville *Union*. Heiss was born in Pennsylvania and worked as a ship's carpenter and as a clerk. At one point he lived in Bucks County, and it is possible that he briefly worked for Cameron at the *Messenger*.[63] By 1840 Heiss had moved to Tennessee and was working at the *Union*, where he had made Governor Polk's acquaintance. In 1842 Heiss became coeditor of the *Union* along with Thomas Hogan (another Pennsylvanian who had migrated to Tennessee). Hogan's death in 1844 left Heiss in sole control of the paper. Under Polk's encouragement, Heiss transformed the *Union* into an aggressive supporter of the former governor's bid for the vice presidency. Thus, when Polk sought to transform the *Globe* into an effective and unswerving supporter of his policies, it was natural that he turned to Heiss.

Given the potential backlash from ousting Blair, Polk considered allowing him to maintain ownership of the *Globe* while installing a more pliable editor. Voices inside and outside of Polk's cabinet suggested Andrew Jackson's nephew, Andrew Jackson Donelson, who quickly became the front-runner. Approaching Donelson about such a ticklish matter required someone who was both reliable and discreet, so Polk turned to Simon Cameron. In March 1845, Cameron, claiming to represent Polk's brother-in-law, wrote to Donelson about the possibility of taking over the *Globe*. Cameron was the ideal person for such a sensitive mission; a former newspaperman himself, he had successfully created or funded organs for friendly administrations or candidates in the past, giving his offer to Donelson credibility.[64] Donelson almost immediately wrote to Polk, expressing skepticism about the offer and concluding that, in all likelihood, "the proposition was unknown to you." He then mildly rebuked Polk, saying, "If [the offer was] with the sanction of Mr. Buchanan and the other members of your cabinet it ought to have been communicated by someone better authorized to approach me on the question of so much delicacy and importance."[65]

Ten days later, Polk responded to Donelson's letter. On the one hand, he claimed "the letter to you by Mr. Cameron was written without my authority." On the other, the president wrote, "But though this be the case, the subject to which it related had been one of anxious thought by my friends, who with few exceptions concur in the opinion that a new organ will be indispensible to unite the whole democracy, and consequently, for the success of my administration. In speaking of an organ to one or two confidential friends, I had expressed the opinion that I would desire to have you connected with it, if it was consistent with your views, and I suppose Mr. Cameron had in some way heard this when he wrote to you."[66]

Polk was being disingenuous; as early as January, a correspondent of his referred to the scheme, mentioning Cameron by name.[67] Late the following month, Heiss wrote to Polk to request a short interview with him to discuss the *Globe*'s future, noting, "I am backed by *Pennsylvania* and many more of your strong friends in proposing to establish a 'new press,' to be under the *control of any true friends of yours* whom you may select, myself to be the businessman of the concern, and organized *entirely* with the view of sustaining your administration."[68] Heiss almost surely meant Cameron when he referred to "Pennsylvania," so there is no reason to believe Polk's assertion to Donelson that he was unaware of the Pennsylvanian's machinations.

When Polk asked Blair to accept Donelson as a partner and nominal editor at the *Globe*, Blair refused. Believing he had no other choice, Polk forcibly ousted Blair, replacing him with long-time newspaperman Thomas Ritchie, who had published the *Richmond Enquirer* for more than forty years. Ritchie's political credentials were beyond reproach: writing in 1823, Thomas Jefferson called the *Enquirer* "the best [newspaper] published or [that] ever has been published in America."[69] Ritchie ingratiated himself with Andrew Jackson by supporting the general's bid for the presidency in 1828 and then further cemented his position as a Jackson favorite by opposing both John C. Calhoun and Henry Clay, two of Old Hickory's main antagonists. During the 1844 presidential campaign, Ritchie vigorously supported Polk, making him everything the president-elect wanted: a reliably Democratic newspaper editor who would provide unqualified backing for the incoming administration.

The problem was that Ritchie was $30,000 in debt and had no cash with which to buy the *Globe*. Consequently, when describing the deal in March 1845, Polk promised Donelson, "Neither of you [Donelson or Ritchie] would be required to pay a cent."[70] Though in the same letter Polk had asserted that Cameron would not be involved in funding the transaction, in reality the Pennsylvanian was in an ideal situation to do just that. In 1844 then senator Buchanan recommended to the Tyler administration that it place $50,000 of federal government money in Cameron's Middletown Bank, most likely as a reward for Cameron's political support. Shortly thereafter, Tyler's secretary of the Treasury, George M. Bibb, apparently transferred the money from a bank in Philadelphia to Cameron's bank, a move that led the acerbic Thomas Hart Benton (a noted Cameron antagonist) to comment that the money had been moved to a place "where there was not public use for it, and where [its] safety was questionable."[71] The money remained in Middletown until a cabal of Democratic notables (Cameron, Pennsylvania businessman and politician Lewis S. Coryell, longtime treasurer of the United States William Selden, Representative Aaron V. Brown, Secretary of the Treasury Robert J. Walker, and Thomas Ritchie's son-in-law Thomas Green), attracted by the scent of lucrative government printing contracts, arranged for some of it to be loaned to Ritchie. Writing to Coryell at the end of March, Cameron assured his friend, "I have my eyes on the 'Organ,' and am to be informed when the funds are needed."[72]

Heiss, Cameron, and company expected Ritchie to repay the loan from the highly profitable government printing contracts that they imagined the administration and Congress would steer the *Globe*'s way. Polk had promised as much to Donelson in March when the president wrote, "There can be no doubt that with the printing of Congress which you could certainly obtain you would make a fine fortune in a very short time and that without any risk except your time."[73] The new paper was called the *Washington Union*, and Heiss became its business manager while Ritchie essentially functioned as Polk's press secretary.[74] Following the *Union*'s establishment, Cameron played no role in its operation, and by 1847 Heiss had bought out the Pennsylvanian's stake.[75]

Polk's ouster of Blair from the *Globe* enraged Andrew Jackson, but Old Hickory focused his anger on his former lieutenant, Cameron, whom he saw as dividing the party. On April 7, 1845, Jackson wrote to Polk and predicted, "If such men as Cameron is to have any interest in, or control over, [the *Globe*'s] columns, the democracy will be split to pieces, and instead of that smooth and pleasant road that opened to you, at the commencement of your administration [the path] will become thorns and briars."[76] To others, Jackson was even blunter. In a letter to Blair, Old Hickory complained, "And you know Cameron who boasts he had $50,000 to invest in a new paper. I view him as a bankrupt in politics and property, and not to be trusted by any one in any way or by any body."[77] Ironically, Polk had come to the conclusion Jackson had during the latter's presidency: namely, that Cameron was a useful ally who could be counted on to carry out delicate tasks.

That being said, Cameron was still tainted by the Winnebago scandal, so the president tried to keep him at arm's length. At the same time Polk offered Donelson the position as editor of the *Globe*, he specifically said that Cameron would *not* serve as Donelson's business partner, exposing the fact that while Cameron was useful, many Democrats still preferred to keep distanced from him.[78] For instance, Jesse Miller, a Democrat from Harrisburg, cautioned Polk about Cameron, predicting, "This man Cameron will come to you in the most plausible manner and profess friendship and willingness to aid you and your administration, for the purpose of getting some of the Scoundrels Who aided him in his election office to repay them for their services. It was openly avowed during the Canvass that Cameron could serve his friends better than any other man & must therefore be elected. You cannot distrust this man too much."[79]

Meanwhile, Pennsylvania's 1844 gubernatorial contest split the Keystone State's Democratic Party into two factions. Early on, Cameron had supported Henry A. Muhlenberg, scion of the famed Pennsylvania Muhlenbergs. Muhlenberg's death in August 1844, shortly after his nomination for governor, ended his chances of being elected, and Pennsylvania's Democrats then nominated Muhlenberg's main opponent, Francis R. Shunk. The Improvement Men were concerned about this twist of fate, fearing that Shunk (whom historian Charles McCool Snyder described as "vindictive") would exclude them from patronage if elected.[80] Under these circumstances, it fell to Buchanan to try to forestall a rift in the party on the eve of an extremely close election. Conciliator was a role for which Buchanan was particularly well suited because both factions trusted him. He prompted Shunk to reach out to Muhlenberg's supporters in general, and Cameron in particular, whom the senator described as "a man of warm temperament and of strong personal attachments."[81] Meanwhile, Buchanan pushed Cameron to support Shunk, which he did, though out of a sense of expediency and party loyalty. In 1844 Shunk secured the governorship by a razor-thin margin of less than five thousand votes, but recognizing the shallowness of Cameron's support and despite Buchanan's best efforts, the governor-elect's closest supporters opposed any rapprochement between the two factions.

The ongoing conflict became evident when the Pennsylvania legislature met in January 1845 to elect a senator. Neither the Muhlenberg nor the Shunk factions could nominate their preferred candidates, Nathaniel B. Eldred and George W. Woodward, respectively. As a compromise, the Shunk and Muhlenberg men reelected the incumbent, the so-called "silent senator" Daniel Sturgeon, who was reputed to have made only a single speech in his entire time in the Senate. According to historian Charles McCool Snyder, Sturgeon's election was "a turning point in the Shunk administration. It convinced the Muhlenberg men that they could expect no favors by acting in concert with the Shunk group." Consequently, shortly after Sturgeon's reelection to the Senate, Cameron notified Buchanan of his clique's intention to "resist further attempts of the Administration to reward favorites with office."[82]

Cameron's chance to frustrate the Shunk administration was not long in coming. Within a few weeks, the Pennsylvania State Senate needed to elect a replacement for Buchanan, who was going into Polk's cabinet (a reward for his help in delivering the state and an attempt to balance the demands of his supporters with those of Vice President Dallas). Given all of Cameron's service to Polk's administration, it was perhaps natural that the Pennsylvanian believed he was owed a reward. The election had been on Cameron's mind since at least early December, when he wrote to Buchanan to report that several supporters had suggested that he ought to run, though he faced an uphill battle.[83] Shunk's faction again promoted George W. Woodward, a Polk favorite. Though only thirty-five, Woodward had already distinguished himself in the commonwealth's politics. At the time of his nomination for senator, he was the presiding judge of the fourth judicial district. He was a devoted acolyte of Thomas Hart Benton, the longtime senator from Missouri who advocated "hard money," and he advocated lowering the tariff, which certainly did nothing to endear him to Cameron's Improvement Men.[84] Cameron's approximately two dozen protectionist supporters in the Democratic caucus boycotted the nomination convention, so only a bare majority of Democrats supported Woodward.[85]

On the same day that the Democratic caucus nominated Woodward, some prominent Pennsylvania Whigs and nativists (men committed to decreasing immigration to the United States) sent Cameron a letter requesting his views on the tariff and immigration. They wanted assurances of Cameron's support among Democrats dissatisfied with Woodward's nomination. Cameron promised the Whigs that he would oppose any changes to the Tariff of 1842, writing, "I have no hesitation in declaring that I am in favor of the tariff of 1842, and if elected to the Senate of the U. States, I will sustain it without change."[86] Cameron's appeal to the nativists was less forthright; while he did not explicitly endorse nativism, he implied that the government should increase the length of time necessary for immigrants to become citizens. The overall effect was to cement nativist and Whig support for Cameron, which, added to his support among protectionist Democrats, would be enough to win the Senate seat.

That being said, Cameron left nothing to chance. Alexander McClure, who became one of Cameron's most persistent and vociferous critics, claimed that Cameron even went so far as to appeal to a number of local Presbyterian ministers, who in turn pressured some Whig holdouts to vote for Cameron. As a result, Cameron succeeded in building a majority coalition of Whigs, a few nativists, and sixteen dissident Democrats. During balloting on March 13, 1845, Cameron's vote total was sixty-six (to Woodward's fifty-five), and he was declared the new senator from Pennsylvania.

However, that was not the end of the matter. Caucus Democrats were horrified that Woodward had been beaten through what they saw as an unethical coalition of Whigs, nativists, and "bolting" Democrats. Cameron's political enemies claimed that he secured the sixteen protectionist Democrats' votes through corrupt means.[87] The day after Cameron's election, the caucus Democrats met in Harrisburg and unanimously approved a motion to create a committee of seven to draft an address to the state Democratic Party about the methods the new senator had used to win. They sent letters to Vice President Dallas and Secretary of State Buchanan complaining about Cameron's election. Buchanan asked Cameron to respond to the committee's charges, which he did on March 27. In a letter that accompanied his response, Cameron complained, "I am told that they say you have agreed to reply to their letter denouncing me. This of course I do not believe. It is bad enough to be slandered by your confidential friends, but I should weep for human nature if I could believe that you . . . who I have loved for his purity and honesty—could suffer fears engendered by the clamor of disappointed opponents to induce you to use your position, which I have so materially aided in making, to do me wrong."[88] Buchanan seems not to have made any move toward silencing his "confidential friends," an indication that his political aspirations were now in conflict with his friendship with Cameron. As early as 1843, evidence of a rift between the two men was visible. By the following year, Cameron still felt alienated from Buchanan, writing, "I don't feel as if I get your wishes and opinions with the same unreserved confidence as I used to, and thereupon I have a delicacy in acting for you as I would, if I knew that my acts would be properly construed. It may be that the feeling is all on my side, and that the bad, very bad treatment I have received from your intimate friends at Lancaster, makes me cool towards you without knowing it myself."[89]

At least some of the attacks on Cameron originated from Shunk's allies, a fact that the senator-elect would not soon forget. In a letter to Polk, former representative David Petrikin asserted that Cameron's loudest critics were Shunk men venting their spleens against one of Muhlenberg's most prominent supporters.[90] Another letter Polk received a short time later, this one from former secretary of the Commonwealth Jesse Miller, supports Petrikin's conclusions. Miller was a Shunk partisan, and he attacked Cameron's supporters as a "rule-or-ruin clique," claiming, "I feel as confident as I do of my own existence that [Cameron] & those who act with him are determined to break down our State administration if they can. They are essentially dishonest and as they know they cannot have the confidence of the State administration they will produce a division or join the opposition to break it down if they think they can succeed, and all they gain in appointments or influence at Washington is so much gained for our destruction."[91] While Cameron probably did not know specifics, he was undoubtedly aware that Shunk's supporters were trying to alienate him from the president. Polk himself took no steps to end the fighting, perhaps because he had openly supported Woodward for the Senate seat; this was a portent of the conflict to come.

In April, Pennsylvania's caucus Democrats published its "Address to the Democracy of Pennsylvania," copies of which were forwarded to both Dallas and Buchanan. The "Address" was extremely aggressive, demanding that the secretary of state and the vice president condemn "the disorganizing conduct of an individual whose pledges to the Natives and the Whigs should, and we believe will, sever him from the association and confidence of the Democratic party."[92] Both Buchanan and Dallas tried to avoid antagonizing either faction by temporizing. The vice president noted that he was "unwilling to overstep, in the slightest degree, the proprieties incident to the official position in which yourselves, with the rest of the American democracy, have placed me, and cannot, therefore, venture to review, for the purpose of censure, the personal conduct of a member of the body over which it is my duty to preside with an unbiased and impartial spirit."[93] Buchanan's response was even more tepid than the vice president's. The secretary of state replied to the committee's demand that he censure Cameron by first remarking upon the "most profound and grateful respect" he had for the committee members. However, he noted, "after much reflection," that he had decided "that it would be improper for me, especially since I have become a member of President Polk's cabinet, to criticize or condemn the legislature of a sovereign state, for electing whom they pleased to the senate of the United States."[94]

Neither Dallas's nor Buchanan's statements satisfied Pennsylvania's disgruntled caucus Democrats, and the controversy refused to die. In August, the Bedford County chapter of the Democratic Party adopted a resolution denouncing "the election of Simon Cameron (Cashier of the Middletown Bank) to [the Senate of the United States]" as "a gross political fraud upon the Democratic Party—as an outrage upon the People's rights—and as a violation of all Republican principles." The group went even further, calling Cameron a "Federal Whig" and a "Bank Whig."[95] Clearly, at least some elements within Pennsylvania's Democratic Party were not content to "live and let live," and in this, Cameron's attackers were not alone: in his letter to Buchanan after the election, Cameron had noted, "I have told all leading men here who are about the Governor that I prefer peace, but if war is to wage it shall not be a one-sided war."[96]

Though Cameron did not know it at the time, "war" would be an accurate description of his tenure in the Senate. Alienated from many of Pennsylvania's Democrats, he surely knew that the commonwealth's Whigs viewed him as something akin to the lesser of two evils, a stop-gap measure to be replaced as soon as circumstances permitted. Worse, though he had actively supported Polk's presidential candidacy, the return of a Democrat to the White House signaled the end of the autonomy state Democratic parties had enjoyed following Van Buren's defeat in 1840. Polk expected Pennsylvania's Democrats to fall to unquestioningly support his low-tariff, anti-bank policies. Over the next four years, Cameron found himself at odds with the Polk administration, which pursued an ambitious, pro-Southern agenda at odds with the Pennsylvanian's pro-business nationalism.

3

"True-Hearted Pennsylvanian, Able, Fearless, and Unflinching," 1845–49

Two days after winning his seat, Cameron appeared in the U.S. Senate. Vice President Dallas laid the new senator's credentials before the upper chamber, and on March 17, 1845, Pennsylvania's senior senator, Daniel Sturgeon, presented Cameron to his colleagues. A few minutes later, Cameron took the oath of office and began his duties as Pennsylvania's junior senator. He was overjoyed to find that his desk was directly behind that of John C. Calhoun; though the two frequently disagreed during Cameron's time in the Senate, the Pennsylvanian nonetheless respected the South Carolinian and came to see the former vice president as a friend.[1]

Cameron arrived in Washington during a particularly tumultuous moment in the nation's history. Though the Twenty-Ninth Congress occurred toward the end of what has been called the Senate's "Golden Age (c. 1820 to c. 1850)," the chamber was nevertheless the setting for political intrigue, backroom deals, and even violence. Senators and observers at the time noted the prevalence of alcohol consumption during Senate business. Whatever wonder Cameron might have experienced when he arrived in Washington as senator-elect quickly dissipated; he later confided to Buchanan, "I regret Congress is so near its 2nd session, for I much prefer home."[2]

Cameron's election to the Senate placed him in a uniquely powerful position. Though Polk's Democrats nominally controlled the Senate, the president could not count on party discipline to ensure that the body enacted his legislative agenda; he would have to negotiate with senators, which theoretically gave them leverage over him. In fact, up until the 1840s, "senators performed their tasks as individuals rather than as Democrats or Whigs, [and] if at times they gave weight to the recommendations of a platform or the suggestions of a President, that was testimony to a coincidence of aims, not the power of a party."[3] Vice President Dallas noted, "It can hardly be said that the Administration has a majority in the representative chamber: in the Senate, on all measures beyond mere form, it is in a decided minority."[4] Given that President Polk entered office with four ambitious (and controversial) goals—acquire Texas, settle the dispute with Great Britain over the Oregon Territory, lower the tariff, and reestablish an independent Treasury—he would need to work hard to maintain his party's fragile majority in Congress.

Measured against these goals, the Polk administration can be called an unqualified success, given that the president accomplished all four. Yet, Polk paid a price for his success. Daniel Webster, a Whig then serving as U.S. senator from Massachusetts, complained in a letter about Polk's stranglehold on Congress. Polk tried to dictate to Congress, and he was not above strong-arming resistant congressmen. In his first seventeen months in office, he handled Congress with a firm hand, successfully pushing through major pieces of legislation. According to Webster, "[There] are a dozen members of the Senate who are alarmed, & would gladly change the present state of things. But each one is afraid."[5] Representatives and senators who failed to toe the administration's line could expect a personal visit from a cabinet officer who would pressure the errant legislator. If that failed, the *Washington Union* provided a useful outlet for attacking wayward congressmen. Finally, Polk was not above denying requests for federal patronage and jobs to legislators who went afoul of the president. Naturally, this did not make him popular on Capitol Hill.

By the start of his third year in office, Polk bragged that he had alienated almost two dozen congressmen by refusing their requests for federal appointments. This was partially due to principle—he genuinely did not like the scramble for patronage, which he found to be corrupt—and was partially due to his belief that patronage weakened both the Democratic Party and the office of the president.[6] This belief was totally wrong; if anything, patronage kept the fractious party together. As historian Allan Nevins noted, "Public appointments [were] not merely [rewards] to members of the victorious party, but [a means] of preserving equilibrium or discipline among the various factions."[7] Thus, while concerns about the corruption inherent in the spoils system may have been legitimate, it was nonetheless naïve to believe that Polk could simply "junk" a system that essentially held the disparate factions of the Democratic Party together.

Ironically, though patronage was the one thing that kept the Democratic Party united, it also caused a substantial amount of the discord within the administration. Early in Polk's administration, Jackson noted in a letter to *Globe* editor Francis P. Blair that if the president "does not look well to his course, the divisions in Newyork [*sic*] and Pennsylvania will destroy him."[8] Pennsylvania accounted for most of the president's patronage headaches because both Dallas and Buchanan wanted desperately to succeed Polk, an ambition that necessitated consolidating their control over Pennsylvania's democracy and neutralizing the other.[9] Dallas's election to the vice presidency was seen as a defeat for Buchanan's supporters, who naturally assumed that they would be shut out of federal patronage in favor of the vice president's supporters. As a result, shortly after the election, Buchanan's supporters pressured Polk to take the senator into the cabinet. It would have taken a deft politician to balance the claims of these important Pennsylvania politicians without alienating any of them, and Polk failed miserably in this regard. The president was simply unwilling to dole out patronage in a way that would meet his supporters' expectations. He therefore constantly disappointed both Buchanan and Dallas, aggravating the factionalism in Pennsylvania.

Complicating this scramble for power was Cameron's election to the Senate, which came during a bitter fight between Dallas and Buchanan over a plum patronage position: the collectorship of the Port of Philadelphia. President Polk wanted Philadelphia Democrat Henry Horn, who had served one term in the House of Representatives during the early 1830s. Horn's claim to the office was rooted in the fact that he was nominally a Van Buren supporter as well as Polk's personal friend and therefore represented a crucial fig leaf from the president to the former president's supporters. Buchanan opposed the nomination, so Polk (using Vice President Dallas as his intermediary) convinced Horn to remove himself from consideration in exchange for a promise of another patronage position. It was during these negotiations that Cameron was elected to the Senate. Polk, angered by Cameron's election and Buchanan's failure to publicly condemn it, refused to consider the secretary of state's preferred candidate for the collectorship, George F. Lehman. Unfortunately for Polk, the Pennsylvanians' struggle for control of patronage was becoming an embarrassment for the administration. In Philadelphia, Roberts Vaux's *Keystone*, a newspaper supporting Dallas, was involved in a bitter war of words with Buchanan's paper in the city, John W. Forney's *Pennsylvanian*. This battle put the administration's internal divisions on display for all to see, sending the message that Polk had lost control of his administration.

Polk tried to end the struggle by appeasing both sides. He appointed Horn to the collectorship as he had originally intended (a nod to Dallas), gave Lehman the postmastership of Philadelphia, and gave Henry Welsh (a friend of Buchanan's) control of Philadelphia's customhouse. However, Polk's attempt to end the patronage feud enraged Dallas, who briefly cut off all contact with the president. The deal favored Buchanan's

forces, so Polk tried to seal the rift by writing Dallas a conciliatory letter in which he offered to make Dallas's friend Richard Rush the treasurer of the Philadelphia Mint, but the vice
president refused to be mollified. The *Pennsylvanian*, reflecting
Dallas's alienation, published an article in June 1845 disassoci-
ating the vice president from Polk's administration.[10]

Worse, Polk's compromise angered Cameron, who nursed
a grudge against Horn. Horn had denounced Cameron's election to Polk in a letter the previous March, saying, "You will
perceive that our party has been betrayed, defeated, and disgraced at Harrisburg and some of those who have recently been
making great professions of friendship to you at Washington I
believe have been instrumental in producing this deplorable
result. I blush for Penn[sylvani]a."[11] Cameron was surely aware
of Horn's hostility and complained to Buchanan that he was
"mortified and disappointed" by the compromise; the secretary
of state could only respond meekly that Polk made "his own
appointments."[12] Horn's nomination signaled that Polk had
taken sides, however subtly, in Pennsylvania's internal politics,
which soured his relationship with Cameron. Polk was personally and politically close to members of Governor Shunk's faction, including John K. Kane, who the governor had recently
appointed state attorney general. Cameron's defeat of Woodward, Polk's preferred choice, had provoked howls of rage from
Woodward's supporters and certainly did nothing to endear
Cameron to Polk.

Despite his frustration over Woodward's loss (and the manner of Cameron's election), Polk would have been well advised
to work with Cameron. Hailed in early 1844 by the *Democratic-
Union* in Harrisburg as "one of the most consistent and influential Democrats in the State," Cameron had initially advertised
himself as a strong supporter of Polk's administration and would
have proven a valuable ally in the Senate, where Polk needed
all the friends he could get.[13] Recognizing this reality, Polk's
brother-in-law James Walker counseled him to work with Cameron, predicting, "If Cameron is let alone, he will be a firm sup-

porter of your administration. The manner of his election is to be regretted but why throw him into the opposition when a majority in the Senate is so important?"[14] Walker's advice fell on deaf ears, however, as Polk's actions over the next few months made an enemy out of a potential ally.

As a result of Polk's enmity, Cameron decided to derail Horn's nomination. On January 3, 1846, he introduced to the Senate a resolution calling for the president to disclose the recommendations that had led him to appoint Horn. This move was a portent of the rocky road ahead for Horn. That evening, the Senate secretary met with Polk to apprise him of Cameron's actions and to inform the president that his research had yielded no precedent for such a request. Shortly thereafter, North Carolina senator William H. Haywood Jr., then chair of the Committee on Commerce, called on Polk to discuss Cameron's motion. Haywood was offended by Cameron's actions because the Pennsylvanian had not approached the committee, to whom Horn's nomination had been referred, to see what information its members had. Cameron's actions infuriated Polk, who was incredibly sensitive to any encroachment on presidential authority. Privately, the president suspected (correctly as it turned out) that Buchanan had egged Cameron on. In fact, the secretary of state admitted as much to an acquaintance, saying that Cameron was with him "heart and hand."[15] Shared antagonism toward the president had aligned Cameron and Buchanan's interests, briefly sealing the rift that had developed between the two men.

At about the same time, Cameron blocked Polk's nominee for the Supreme Court, George W. Woodward, the former's opponent in the senatorial election. Polk nominated Woodward over Buchanan's strenuous objections that doing so would only cause the president political trouble, seeing the nomination as a way to rectify what Polk saw as the colossal injustice of the Pennsylvania senatorial contest.[16] On Christmas Day 1845, Cameron sent Buchanan a letter complaining about the nomination, noting that he thought he understood from Polk that "the president did not intend to do it." As a result, Cameron was hurrying back to Washington and asked to see Buchanan on the following Sunday afternoon.[17] Clearly, the two Pennsylvanians were plotting to prevent the nomination.

On January 22, Cameron called up Woodward's nomination, and it was soundly defeated with the help of five other Democrats, infuriating the president.[18] Polk fulminated that one of the five Democrats, Florida senator James D. Westcott Jr., was "a Whig in disguise."[19] According to Polk's diary, Cameron called on the president to gloat. During their meeting, Cameron apparently "put on a smiling and hypocritical air and acted as though he had been one of my friends."[20] Recognizing that he had lost (at least for the moment), Polk eventually nominated Robert C. Grier, a solid Jacksonian then serving a patronage appointment to the District Court of Allegheny County, Pennsylvania. The Senate confirmed Grier's nomination on August 4, the day after Polk submitted it, but the vindictive president never forgave Cameron. Polk complained in his diary that "Mr. Buchanan had been willing to see my nomination of Mr. Woodward rejected by the Senate, in order to obtain the office himself. . . . Of one thing, however, I am satisfied and that is that Mr. Buchanan did not interfere with Mr. Cameron, Mr. Sevier & others of the Senate to have Mr. Woodward rejected, at least he took no interest in [Woodward's] confirmation and was willing to see him rejected."[21]

Political defeat brought out the worst in Polk, and though the president grudgingly changed course on Woodward's nomination, he decided to push forward with Horn's. His anger and pride (not to mention his fanatical devotion to maintaining presidential prerogatives) impelled him to do so. Cameron met with him to discuss the situation and, to his diary, Polk claimed the Pennsylvanian conceded that Horn was both qualified for the office and an honest public servant. Furthermore, Polk asserted that Cameron offered to stop opposing Horn if only the president would instruct the nominee to "reach an understanding" with the Pennsylvanian. Polk indignantly refused and girded for a showdown with Cameron, which was not long in coming.[22]

Another reason for Polk's intransigence related to a joke that Cameron had made about the president in the Senate. At about this time, David Wilmot, a congressman from northern Pennsylvania, sent the president a note alleging that Cameron had said of the president, "The only way to treat an ugly negro who was unruly was to give him a damned drubbing at the start and he would learn to behave himself."[23] The exact nature of the remark was not clear; apparently, Cameron had been speaking to Pennsylvania representative William S. Garvin and, during the course of the conversation, quoted a remark made by Senator James D. Westcott Jr. (one of the men who had helped Cameron torpedo Woodward's nomination), who was standing nearby. Regardless of who actually made the comment, Polk complained, "I consider both [Cameron and Westcott] therefore as guilty of gross rudeness and vulgarity."[24]

In mid-February, Cameron again met privately with the president and related to Polk his reasons for opposing Woodward's nomination. Polk noted in his diary that he found Cameron's reasons "unsatisfactory, though I did not deem it to be necessary to tell him so; indeed I did not think they were the real reasons."[25] Polk finally cut to the chase by saying to Cameron, "The public understood that there was a Democratic majority of six in the Senate, and the effect of rejecting my principle nominations at the commencement of my administration, and especially as the Senate sat with closed doors & the public could not know the reason of the rejection, was calculated to weaken my administration, and destroy or impair my power and influence."[26]

Here was the real issue: Polk, who jealously guarded presidential prerogatives, was aggravated by the Senate's unwillingness or incapability to simply rubber-stamp his nominations. Complaining to his diary, Polk claimed, "The truth is Mr. Woodward's rejection was facetious, Mr. Cameron and five other professed democrats having united with the whole Whig party to effect [it]."[27] Clearly, it had never occurred to Polk nominating Woodward, whom Cameron had beaten only narrowly, might aggravate the sort of party division that the president now faced. Projecting all the blame onto Cameron, Polk then moved to the senator's alleged remark. Cameron denied having made the remark, but Polk refused to let it go, saying that "I had done nothing to merit such epithets or reproach; that I had exercised my constitutional power in making the nomination of Judge Woodward, and the Senate had a right to reject him, but that no man had a right to use such terms."[28] During this meeting, the two men discussed Horn's nomination as well. Polk noted that, early in his term, Buchanan had asked Polk not to nominate Horn to a position. Polk had agreed to Buchanan's request but (according to the president) informed the secretary of state that he reserved the right to nominate whomever he wanted whenever he wanted, and the president made clear his intention to proceed with the nomination.

In late May, Cameron called up Horn's nomination for approval, taking advantage of the absence of seven Democratic senators. Working with the Senate's Whigs (who were eager to do anything that might split and thereby weaken the Democratic Party), Cameron encouraged a number of Democrats who were alienated from the administration to oppose the nomination, and it was rejected. Believing that Horn's nomination was dead, a number of prominent Pennsylvanians pressed their preferred candidates on the president, but Polk insisted that he would have Horn or nobody. Polk reached out to the seven Democrats who had been absent from the Senate and, confident of their votes, resubmitted the nomination. What he did not count on was Cameron's ability to find three other disgruntled Democrats whose votes, in combination with those of Cameron's supporters and the Senate's Whigs, again sent Horn's nomination down in flames, a reflection of just how badly Polk had managed relations with members of his own party. At this point, Polk tried to play Cameron's game: instead of nominating Horn a third time, the president submitted another nominee, and Cameron did not contest the nomination. Yet the point had been made: the president was weak, and resistance from even a small number of Senate Democrats could frustrate his agenda.

The most important dispute between Cameron and Polk was the tariff.[29] Within months of being confirmed as secretary of the Treasury, Robert J. Walker began working on proposals to revise the Tariff of 1842, known to its opponents as the "Black Tariff." On average, the "Black Tariff" doubled the rates established under the Tariff of 1833. The tariff on iron goods was increased to more than 66 percent, while some specific iron items, such as nails, were subject to a tariff exceeding 100 percent. Finally, it increased the number of imported goods subject to tariff rates by more than 70 percent. As a result, prices around the nation increased, and the total amount of imports declined by nearly one-fifth. The Tariff of 1842 was widely supported by protectionists across the North who saw it as the cause of American prosperity, but it was just as vociferously attacked by Southerners, who saw it as a tax they paid to support northern industries.

During the autumn of 1845, it was nearly impossible to meet with Walker, who was consumed day and night with revising the tariff. Published in December, his report on the tariff, which recommended a number of revisions, created a sensation. According to Walker, the first principle of revising the Tariff of 1842 was "that no more money should be collected than is necessary for the wants of the Government, economically administered." If anyone missed his meaning, he went on to declare, "A direct tax or excise, not for revenue, but for protection, clearly would not be within the legitimate object of taxation."[30] In addition, the tariff differed from most previous tariff schemes, which had set fixed rates on specific items on a case-by-case basis. By contrast, the report created general schedules of types of goods into which specific items could be categorized and applied *ad valorem* rates of taxation, based on the goods' value. For most goods (luxury items were an exception, as was alcohol), the net effect was a lower rate of taxation, which appealed to southerners, but provided no protection for northern industries.

The president endorsed Walker's scheme in his Annual Message to Congress, dated December 2. According to Polk:

> The object of imposing duties on imports should be to raise revenue to pay the necessary expenses of Government. Congress may undoubtedly, in the exercise of a sound discretion, discriminate in arranging the rates of duty on different articles, but the discriminations should be within the revenue standard and be made with the view to raise money for the support of Government. . . . In recommending to Congress a reduction of the present rates of duty and a revision and modification of the act of 1842, I am far from entertaining opinions unfriendly to the manufacturers. On the contrary, I desire to see them prosperous as far as they can be so without imposing unequal burdens on other interests. The advantage under any system of indirect taxation, even within the revenue standard, must be in favor of the manufacturing interest, and of this no other interest will complain. I recommend to Congress the abolition of the minimum principle, or assumed, arbitrary, and false values, and of specific duties, and the substitution in their place of *ad valorem* duties as the fairest and most equitable indirect tax which can be imposed.[31]

Though Polk opposed compromises, as the bill enacting the new tariff rates wound its way through the House Committee on Ways and Means, committee members amended it to make it more palatable to Northern Democrats. One important change maintained the existing duties on coal and iron, which was a sop to Pennsylvania's congressional delegation. Polk insisted to Committee on Ways and Means chairman James Iver McKay that the tariff bill be preserved as written, and Pennsylvania's representatives were equally adamant that no change be made to rates on iron and coal specified in the Tariff of 1842, setting in motion a confrontation. By March, the committee was flooded with examples of British goods that would be cheaper as a result of lowering the tariff (helpfully submitted by individuals opposed to the tariff) and counterexamples of American goods that would be hurt by lowering the tariff (helpfully submitted by American manufacturers who would be affected by the tariff reduction). As a result, when the Committee on Ways and Means reported the bill to the full House in the middle of April, several adjustments had been made, including retaining the 30 percent tariff on coal and iron.[32]

Initially, it looked as though (with a few minor tweaks) the bill would pass the House of Representatives by approximately ten votes. However, when McKay scheduled a caucus of Democrats, the representatives of both Pennsylvania and New York failed to show up, while representatives from western states intimated that they wanted to move some of their own legislation before considering the tariff bill. It was therefore not until June that enough votes could be found in the House to even begin debating the bill. As the debate progressed, the administration was forced to make compromises, including abandoning the tariff on tea and coffee and increasing the rate on luxury goods to 40 percent. McKay even offered to raise the tariff on iron and coal to 40 percent in an attempt to appease Pennsylvania's delegation, but to no end. When the bill finally made it to the House floor, eleven of Pennsylvania's twelve Democratic representatives voted against it. Fearing a debate that might lead to further modifications and necessitate reconciling competing House and Senate versions of the tariff bill, the Senate's Democratic leadership decided to force the bill through the upper chamber without a debate; senators could only vote for the House's bill as it was with no amendments.

Polk was concerned about the bill's fate in the Senate, and rightly so: the defection of only a few Democrats could sink the bill if all the Whigs voted against it. As the Senate debated the bill in July, a considerable number of manufacturers descended on Washington to lobby against it, and (because Polk was afraid that some Democratic senators might go "wobbly" at the last moment) the president was (reluctantly) willing to make a deal.

The manufacturers proposed making the tariff reductions gradual over a period of years and possibly limiting the number of items affected. Polk agreed to these suggestions provided the amendments came from Pennsylvania's senators, Simon Cameron and Daniel Sturgeon. According to Polk's diary, he told the manufacturers that he needed the Pennsylvanians to walk point on any amendments because "if made by them . . . it would probably be entertained by the other Democratic members of Congress. . . . They must pledge themselves that if the amendment of Compromise was adopted they would vote for the bill as amended & that the Pennsylvania Democratic members in the [House] would vote for it also."[33]

Polk's decision to shift responsibility for these amendments, which might have attracted some Northern Democratic support, to Pennsylvania's senators was foolhardy, to say the least. In the words of historian Charles McCool Snyder, Cameron "neither owed anything nor expected anything from the Polk administration," and he could therefore set his own course.[34] According to Polk's diary, Cameron had told the president that Pennsylvanians might "scratch a little bit" about the tariff bill but in any event would eventually fall in line behind the president. Most historians have accepted Polk's recollection as fact, but there are at least two reasons to be skeptical of his claims. The first is that the tariff was *the* central issue in Pennsylvania politics. Even James Buchanan and Daniel Sturgeon, otherwise stalwart Democrats, had voted for the Tariff of 1842 (though both later disingenuously claimed they did so only to ensure that the U.S. Treasury had enough revenue to fund the government).[35] Cameron told the president in October 1844 that no anti-tariff candidate could possibly expect to win in Pennsylvania, and Polk's 1844 letter to John K. Kane demonstrates that "Young Hickory" agreed with this assessment.[36] The following year, Cameron won his Senate seat by promising to sustain the Tariff of 1842 "without change."[37]

Furthermore, both houses of the Pennsylvania General Assembly had passed resolutions asking the commonwealth's House delegation and its two senators to oppose any revision of the Tariff of 1842. During the Senate debate over the tariff, the miners of Schuylkill County resolved "that we have full confidence in the integrity and ability of our senators in Congress, the honorable Simon Cameron and the honorable Daniel Sturgeon, who are requested to use all honorable means to defeat the iniquitous bill now before the senate." The miners also noted with some unhappiness that the Walker Tariff was "contrary to the principles avowed by Mr. Polk through his friends and in his letter to John K. Kane."[38]

This was not the only memorial from Cameron's constituents opposing tariff revision. That July, Cameron noted in the Senate that he had "attended, perhaps, every Democratic meeting within my reach in [Pennsylvania] . . . , and at all these meetings the watchwords and the mottoes were, 'Polk,' 'Dallas,' and (before his lamented death) 'Muhlenberg,' and 'The Tariff of 1842.' And after the death of our candidate for the gubernatorial chair, they were, 'Polk,' 'Dallas,' 'Shunk,' and 'The tariff of 1842.' Neither of the three would have got the vote of Pennsylvania without the last—the tariff of 1842."[39] A week later, he reiterated this claim and warned of "the danger of arousing the indignation of the Democracy of [Pennsylvania]."[40] It is therefore extremely unlikely that Cameron would have so blithely dismissed his constituents' desires regarding a reduction in the tariff, if for no other reason than it would have been political suicide.

Another reason to doubt Polk's recollection is that Cameron had a personal stake in maintaining the Tariff of 1842. He was an industrialist himself who owned significant iron interests, and the Walker Tariff cut the tariff on imported pig iron from a fixed rate of approximately $10 per ton to a fixed *percentage* that varied with the price of pig iron. Thus, the tariff rate on imported pig iron fell to $5.75 in 1847 and to $3.05 in 1852. Even though it increased slightly by 1855 to $6.00 per ton, it never reached the high of $10.00 mandated under the Tariff of 1842. A dramatic reduction in protection undoubtedly affected

Cameron's business interests, so it again strains credulity that he would have assented to the Walker Tariff.

In any event, Cameron soon demonstrated that he planned not only to scratch about the Walker Tariff, he would fight it tooth and nail. On July 22, 1846, Cameron made an impassioned speech on the Senate floor in favor of retaining the Tariff of 1842. The speech embarrassed the administration by quoting at length from a speech Vice President Dallas had given years earlier in support of the Tariff of 1842. Worse, Cameron implied that Polk had intentionally misled Pennsylvania's voters who would never have supported candidates committed to lowering the tariff. Cameron's efforts did not go unnoticed; Daniel Webster, who also opposed reducing the tariff, commented in an editorial published in the *National Intelligencer*:

> The Petitions [in opposition to the Walker Tariff] which are pouring in upon the Senate on Saturday, by Mr. Cameron, effectually put to flight these false and miserable subterfuges [that opposition to the Walker Tariff was confined to a few wealthy industrialists]. We hope to see this Petition presented by Genl Cameron spread out, & displayed, in the columns of the *Union*; although we doubt whether it will make its appearances there, unless the Honorable Senator who presented it shall satisfy the venerable Editor, that the voice of so large a part of the "Democracy" of Pennsylvania is not to be stifled.[41]

Cameron tried to get Polk to compromise on the tariff by agreeing to an amendment that would reduce the duties gradually over a decade (the very deal Polk had offered to the industrialists a few months before); Polk refused, and Dallas fumed that Cameron and the senior senator from Pennsylvania, Daniel Sturgeon, might have accomplished a compromise on their own, but they "shrank from the responsibility."[42] Dallas's pique resulted from being placed in an awkward position: When the bill to modify the tariff came up for a final vote on July 28, the Senate tied 27 to 27, leaving the deciding vote to Vice President Dallas. He voted for the revision, and Cameron responded by promising his colleagues that the Democrats of the North "would not cease until [they] had triumphed" in returning the country to the Tariff of 1842.[43] Cameron lashed out at Democrats who criticized his actions, complaining about rumors that he was a Whig. Writing to Buchanan in September 1846, he complained, "A man of forty-seven years of age, who has voted the democratic ticket for twenty-six successive years, should not have his democracy doubted by his friends whatever his enemies may do in regard to him."[44] Yet, for all his fury, he was unable to prevent the Walker Tariff from becoming law.

Even after the Walker Tariff was enacted, Cameron attacked it in the hope of getting it modified. In January 1847, the Pennsylvanian submitted a resolution to the Senate that directed Walker "to report to the Senate on what articles embraced in the tariff act of 1846, the duties can be increased beyond existing rates, and to what extent the said duties can be increased, and where additional revenues would accrue there from."[45] Two days later, he defended his resolution as an economic necessity, noting that "by the bill of 1846, there will be a loss in the revenue upon the importation of 1845 of over one million dollars. This, too, in a time of war, when our expenses are greatly increased, and at a time, too, when our credit has sunk, so that our loans have already fallen about 16 percent, only because capitalists fear that revenue will not be sufficient to insure prompt payment of interest."[46] The senator complained about the tariff to any who would listen. Writing to Buchanan in late October 1846, he counseled, "It will be hard to [elect Democrats because of the tariff], but it can be done, if the would-be leaders will follow instead of attempting to drive the people."[47] All of this was to no avail, of course, and the Walker Tariff remained the law of the land.

In the long term, the Walker Tariff worked to Cameron's political advantage because, according to historian John F. Coleman, the senator "by the bitterness and persistence of his opposition [to the Walker Tariff], earned the special affection of many influential Pennsylvanians who began to regard him as the genuine voice of Pennsylvania interests."[48] The Democratic Convention of Northumberland County passed a resolution nominating Cameron for governor in 1847, commending him for being a "true-hearted Pennsylvanian, able, fearless, and unflinching in defense of [Pennsylvania's] rights and her interests." In his response, the senator thanked the convention for the honor it had bestowed upon him but demurred, saying, "I feel that I have no claim to it; and having recently been elevated to a high place, mainly to aid in the protection of the interests of my native state, I could not, in accordance with my sense of propriety, desert the post while those interests are in danger, for any personal distinction high and honorable as it might be."[49]

If Cameron's political future seemed brighter due to the Walker Tariff, the same could not be said for many of Pennsylvania's other federal office holders: within a few days of the vote, Vice President Dallas was hanged in effigy in Philadelphia, and he actually sent the Senate's sergeant-at-arms to the city to escort his family to Washington out of fear that they might be targeted by rioters.[50] In the October statewide elections (generally a bellwether of the federal elections in November), the Whigs displaced the incumbent canal commissioner (a Democrat). Moreover, the Whigs won control over both houses of the Pennsylvania General Assembly. However, the worse defeat came the following month, when Pennsylvania's Democratic House contingent lost six of its twelve members, a stunning defeat by any measure. Polk had gotten his tariff but at a fearful cost to Pennsylvania's Democratic Party, vindicating Cameron's prediction: "Pass this bill, and the democratic party must again be defeated."[51]

There was also an important subtext to Cameron's fight against the Walker Tariff: the growing rift between the Northern and Southern wings of the Democratic Party. Fights over issues such as the tariff always had a sectional flavor, but that dynamic became more pronounced during Polk's administration. In his fight against the tariff, Cameron referred to free trade as a principle of "Southern Democracy," and he argued that Southerners "would rob the poor man of his labor, and make him dependent on the capitalists of England for his scanty subsistence."[52] In other words, Southern Democrats' free-trade policies would reduce Northern free laborers to slaves. If anyone missed the sectional nature of these remarks, the point was further driven home in Cameron's response to Florida senator Ambrose H. Sevier's disparaging comments about Pennsylvania's workers. Sevier, Cameron's erstwhile ally in the fight against Polk's nomination of George W. Woodward to the Supreme Court earlier in the year, called Pennsylvania's laborers dependents on the government because they demanded protection for their industries. Cameron responded by acidly remarking that "the laborers of Pennsylvania were white men; they were free men; and they asked no favors from the Government but to be let alone in the enjoyment of their labor . . . and he desired to learn no new democracy from gentlemen who compared his laboring fellow citizens with the Negro laborers of the South."[53]

The issue that most aggravated the country's growing sectionalism was another key Polk policy: the annexation of Texas. Absorption of Texas into the United States had appealed to Americans at least since the mid-1830s, when President Andrew Jackson had unsuccessfully (and ineptly) tried to purchase the territory from Mexico. When the newly independent republic requested admission to the United States in August 1837, President Martin Van Buren rejected the request for fear that it would upset the balance between free and slave states, which could aggravate sectional tensions. John Tyler (who had assumed the presidency following William Henry Harrison's death in 1841) tried to use the Texas issue to buoy his sagging political fortunes. Beginning in 1843, he purged the executive branch of appointees hostile to annexing Texas, replacing them with individuals committed to bringing the territory into the United States.

Almost immediately, the Texas issue reignited the debate over slavery, in large part due to John C. Calhoun, who became Tyler's secretary of state in March 1844. Though a fervent nationalist earlier in his career, Calhoun became increasingly obsessed with perceived threats to slavery (real and imagined) during the 1820s, morphing into a vocal advocate of states' rights. As historian Ted Widmer sagely noted, by 1830 Calhoun had entered "a lifelong mania against Northern political power."[54] In 1840 he and his congressional supporters had demanded an outright ban on anti-slavery petitions; the previous practice, instituted in 1836, had been to hold a *pro forma* vote in the Senate on the question of whether to receive the petition, with the rejection of the question a given. Though Calhoun's more militant position achieved the same end—anti-slavery petitions were ultimately not presented to the Senate—it incensed many Northern senators, who saw in it an abridgement of citizens' fundamental right to petition the government. As such, Calhoun's actions were another in a long series of irritants fraying the ties of party uniting Northern and Southern Democrats.

Calhoun's brief tenure as secretary of state played an enormous role in fusing the issue of Texas to slavery. In December 1843, the British government sent a letter addressed to the secretary of state. The letter's author, George Hamilton-Gordon, Lord Aberdeen, wrote, "We should rejoice if the recognition of [Texas] by the Mexican government should be accompanied by an engagement on the part of Texas to abolish slavery eventually and under proper conditions . . . but we shall not seek to compel, or unduly control, either [the governments of Texas or Mexico]."[55] Calhoun's response, a passionate defense of slavery, was as aggressive as Aberdeen's statement was conciliatory. Calhoun's letter transformed the Texas issue into a fight over slavery, which in turn mobilized abolitionists to oppose annexation. Predictably, the growing numbers of abolitionists began a sustained campaign against the annexation treaty, and in June 1844 the Whig-dominated Senate rejected the treaty. Tyler decided to annex the territory through a joint resolution, which passed both houses of Congress in February 1845. Tyler signed the joint resolution into law on March 1, a scant three days before his term expired.

The joint resolution granting Texas admittance to the United States failed to settle a long-running dispute between Texas and Mexico: the location of Texas's southern border. Since declaring its independence, Texas's government had argued that its territory stopped at the Rio Grande, while Mexico's government argued that it ended at the Nueces River. A few months after his inauguration, Polk decided to push the issue by dispatching a small force under General Zachary Taylor to occupy the disputed land. Following a confrontation between Mexican and U.S. soldiers in the disputed territory, the Polk administration sought and received a declaration of war from Congress in May 1846. Following a series of U.S. victories, the Mexican government capitulated and, on February 2, 1848, signed the Treaty of Guadalupe Hidalgo. Under the terms of this treaty, the U.S. received undisputed control of Texas (whose southern border was fixed at the Rio Grande) as well as most of the territory comprising the contemporary states of California, Nevada, Utah, Arizona, New Mexico, Oklahoma, Kansas, Wyoming, and Colorado. In exchange, the U.S. government compensated Mexico with a direct payment of $15 million and an agreement to assume the debt of $3.25 million that Mexico owed to American citizens.

At first, the war was extremely popular in Pennsylvania, and Cameron vigorously supported what came to be known as "Mr. Polk's War," noting that he "agreed with the president in every particular" regarding Mexico.[56] Cameron had long supported the annexation of Texas, gushing in 1836 that he was "delighted with the news in relation to the [independence of] Texas."[57] Initially, Pennsylvania was allotted six regiments, but by the July cutoff date for enlistment, substantially more men had volunteered. At about the same time, Cameron recommended to Polk to send the regular forces stationed at Fort Mifflin, a fortress located just south of Philadelphia. Cameron reasoned that the regulars could be replaced by volunteers, which would give the president a further supply of more seasoned troops to send to Mexico.[58] In December 1846, the War Department asked Pennsylvania for more men, and a second Pennsylvanian regiment—Company G of this regiment was Dauphin County's Cameron Guards—was organized and equipped for service. In January, Cameron gave, through proxy, each of the commissioned officers of the Cameron Guards swords ("said to be of splendid finish") as gifts.[59] In December 1846, Cameron introduced and the Senate adopted a resolution instructing the Committee of Military Affairs to investigate the feasibility of granting 160 acres of annexed land to noncommissioned volunteers and increasing their compensation, a reflection of his genuine concern for America's volunteer soldiers.

Cameron's connection to the war was personal: his brother James and one of his brothers-in-law volunteered to fight. Interestingly, his son Brua appealed to Buchanan for help in securing a lieutenant's commission in the regular army. It is unusual that Brua reached out to Buchanan, given that Cameron could have arranged a commission for his son. The reason for Brua's actions is revealed in a letter Cameron wrote to Buchanan a few days after the secretary of state received the younger Cameron's request. Cameron wrote,

> I would have had no objection to his having gone with a volunteer co. for a year and six months at the beginning of the war, or even now if the country needed him—but I have a horror of men living off the public + nothing would pain me more than to see my son entering the army for a living or expecting to be supported by the Govt. in any way. The commission now would occupy the time necessary to fit him for his profession and perhaps forever preclude him from taking my place + my business as I desire him to do.[60]

This letter is an important window into Cameron's thinking about the military. While he was extremely supportive of the volunteers, he was suspicious of professional soldiers, who he believed were essentially living on government handouts, a byproduct of his time as visitor to the United States Military Academy at West Point. This suspicion would resurface during his time as secretary of war, causing tension between him and the officers who served under him.

For all its initial popularity, the war did exacerbate sectional tension, just as Martin Van Buren had predicted. The *Boston Whig* noted this in August 1846, when it said, "As if by magic, [the war] brought to a head the great question which is about to divide the American people," particularly in Pennsylvania, was an important battlefield for this debate because most escaped slaves had to go through the state.[61] Pennsylvanians had been growing more resistant to what they saw as Southern encroachments on the Keystone State's rights, particularly regarding the commonwealth's right to be a free state. Furthermore, many Northerners correctly saw the war in Mexico as an attempt to create more slave states and thereby upset the delicate balance between free and slave states in Congress. Northern Democrats' growing opposition to the expansion of slavery was a natural outgrowth of Jacksonianism, which had always harbored a paranoid fear that some large conspiracy existed to deprive citizens of their rights. Northern Democrats identified the horrific demon in their midst: "the slave power." According to historian David G. Smith, "The [Pennsylvania] anti-slavery movement's emergence looks suspiciously like a political tool being developed as the basis to rally Northerners against a new, politically dominant conspiracy."[62] Increasingly, Northern Democrats believed that the "slave power" extremists bent on the unlimited expansion of slavery had hijacked the party.[63] This perception was confirmed by the aggressiveness and irritability about abolitionism shown by Southerners such as John C. Calhoun and the increasing numbers of Northern politicians who, for one reason or another, indulged slave owners' demands.[64]

The most concrete expression of the Northern Democrats' growing anti-Southernism was the Wilmot Proviso, an amendment attached to an appropriation bill that excluded slavery from any territory purchased from Mexico. Named for Pennsylvania congressman David Wilmot, the proviso grew out of Polk's request in August 1846 for $2 million from Congress to buy the disputed land from the Mexican government. In response, New York Whig Hugh White (who most likely was aware of Wilmot's plan) requested that the Democrats offer an amendment to prevent slavery in the newly acquired land. After New York's Bradford Ripley Wood, an anti-slavery Democrat, yielded his floor time to Wilmot, the Pennsylvanian offered a proviso to the appropriation bill stipulating that "neither slavery nor involuntary servitude shall ever exist" in any land acquired from Mexico. The House, which was about to break for recess, passed the amendment as well as the amended appropriation bill.

Despite Cameron's antipathy toward Wilmot, he supported the proviso, noting that while Pennsylvanians did not wish to interfere with slavery where it existed, they would be willing "to pour out their blood and treasure to sustain the union or to protect from wrong the people of the southern States," and nonetheless, the Keystone State's citizens remained "united in the wish that no more slave territory should be acquired."[65] Cameron's personal attitude toward slavery is difficult to discern. On the one hand, many of his contemporaries (including critic Alexander McClure) asserted that he was an abolitionist by the mid-1840s. His vocal support of the Wilmot Proviso seems to support McClure's conclusion. On the other hand, William Lloyd Garrison, writing in the *Liberator*, called Cameron a "doughface," a derogatory term meaning Northerners who kowtowed to Southern demands.[66] It is undeniable that Cameron socialized with many Southerners while in the Senate and counted slave owners, including Jefferson Davis, Willie P. Mangum, and David Outlaw, as friends. However, as historian Rachel Shelden has ably demonstrated, cross-sectional friendships were the norm in Washington during this period, and congressmen's personal closeness did not preclude them from taking opposite positions in the Senate or the House.[67] Despite his close friendships with many Southern congressmen, Cameron was no doughface: he saw slavery as inefficient and backward, and he was committed to protecting Pennsylvania's interests by preventing the spread of slavery into the territories. These positions were consistent with his statements on slavery from the 1830s and matched those expressed in a speech he delivered to the Senate in May 1848. According to Cameron, "Pennsylvania has no sympathy with the ultra abolitionists. . . . The masses of the people [of Pennsylvania] were entirely willing to leave the domestic institutions of other States with them. What they claim for themselves, they cheerfully accord to others—the right to regulate their own affairs. They are opposed to slavery in the abstract, and have long since abolished it within their own borders. They are willing, as they should be, to let other States act for themselves in this and other domestic matters."[68] Until the Civil War, Cameron consistently advocated this principle—that states (but not the territories) should decide for themselves whether to be slave or free—and it became one of the basic policy statements of the Republican Party during the 1860 campaign.

However, Cameron hedged about the proviso, as his comments (later printed in the *Congressional Globe*) demonstrate.

> He was free to say that he would not obey instructions in accordance with the opinions and wishes of the people who had elected the legislature giving them; or, if they should instruct him to do an act which subsequent information should convince him they had adopted upon wrong information, he would not hesitate to take the responsibility of disobeying them, and would rely with confidence on the purity of his intentions and the result of his vote as justification with the people, who were common masters of all representatives. But upon a question on which public opinion was clear, he should never hesitate, and would cheerfully obey—for, in his opinion, no principle was more clear that the agent was bound to carry out in good faith the wishes of his principle.[69]

In December 1847, Polk extracted a promise from Wilmot not to reintroduce the proviso, though the Pennsylvanian disingenuously claimed that he would be compelled to vote for it if someone *else* introduced it. On January 4 New York representative Preston King sought to attach it to the administration's request for funds (which had now increased to $3 million). Preston was a Martin Van Buren supporter, and his actions were a message to Polk that the former president's supporters had neither forgiven nor forgotten the real and perceived slights the New Yorker had received from the Tennessean. In February the House again voted to attach the Wilmot Proviso to the administration's appropriation request, and the Senate responded by passing the appropriation bill but stripping it of the proviso. This bill was eventually returned to the House, where it passed when twenty-two Democrats who had previously voted for the proviso now voted for the bill without it. The president had gotten his appropriation but at the cost of splitting the party over slavery.

The Mexican-American War, however, was not the only thing aggravating sectional tension during this period: many Northern Democrats were unhappy with Polk's policies regarding Oregon. During the campaign, Polk argued that the United States had a legitimate claim to the Oregon Territory as far north as 54°40' north, while the British government maintained that the northern boundary of the United States was at 54°42' north, and the conflict led to tension between the two governments. Northern Democrats had expected Polk to show the same zeal in prosecuting America's claim to this territory that he had in pursuing Texas.[70] In April 1845 both houses of Congress voted for a joint resolution giving notice to Great Britain terminating its right to joint occupation of the Oregon Territory. Cameron strongly supported this resolution and implored his colleagues to make it unanimous in order to give the president the strongest hand in bargaining with Great Britain. According to Cameron, the United States' northern boundary "terminates only where the Russian line begins, at 54 degrees 40."[71]

That same month, both Cameron and Buchanan traveled to Lancaster, Pennsylvania, where the secretary of state argued that the United States had a right to the Oregon Territory. According to the *Somerset Herald and Farmers' and Mechanics' Reg-*

ister, Buchanan was "chock up for 54–40, or war. But he says that there is no danger of that."[72] Their efforts paid off: Pennsylvanians supported "reoccupying" Oregon. In January 1846 Cameron presented three memorials from his constituents in the Wyoming Valley demanding that Polk make clear that U.S. territory extended to 54° and "remonstrating against the relinquishment of any of our claims to the said territory."[73] Expansionists in Congress pressured the new president to push the United States' claims to 54°, but Polk (concerned by the prospect of fighting two wars simultaneously) offered to compromise with the British at 49°. The Senate ratified the treaty establishing the new boundaries in June 1846 by a vote of 41 to 14, but Polk's willingness to go to war with Mexico but to capitulate to Great Britain without a shot being fired convinced many Northerners that the president and the party were controlled by the "slave power" and were therefore working for the good of the South at the North's expense. Campaign literature for Cameron's run for the presidency a dozen years later pointed to what the authors viewed as Polk's subservience to the South: "The entire cotton growing portion of the [Polk] Administration began to manifest weakness in the knees on [the Oregon question]. War with England, and an abrupt close of the English market for their cotton, was seriously apprehended by [Southerners], and they were, therefore, disposed to shirk one of the issues made by themselves, on which Mr. Polk was elected."[74]

Oregon became a battlefront in the fight over slavery when, in January 1847, the House Committee on Territories reported a bill that specifically excluded slaves from any of the Oregon Territory. Given the fact that Oregon's climate was totally unsuited to plantation agriculture and that the entire territory lay above the line established by the Missouri Compromise, this should not have been an issue, but in the tense atmosphere created by the Wilmot Proviso, the issue took on added significance. Martin Van Buren had said as much when he warned Polk that expansionism would exacerbate sectional tensions within the party by forcing Northern Democrats to choose between supporting the administration and fighting the spread of slavery.[75] Polk got the same advice from Buchanan, who warned the president early in the administration that westward expansion would provoke a congressional debate over slavery; the president, as was his wont, had ignored his secretary of state's advice.[76] Thus, the irony of Polk's success in achieving his main policy goals is that the Democrats paid a heavy price in the 1846 midterm elections, losing control of the House of Representatives. The Whig victories in the midterm elections of 1846 hit close to home for Cameron; his home county of Dauphin and his representative district both elected Whigs that year, a fact that he noted bitterly in a letter to Buchanan.[77]

Meanwhile, Pennsylvania's gubernatorial election was fast approaching, and the commonwealth's Improvement Men remained opposed to Governor Shunk's administration. Buchanan's efforts to forge a rapprochement between Cameron's adherents and Shunk's supporters in 1844 had failed; in a letter to Buchanan following the election, Cameron confessed, "I pretend no personal attachment to Mr. Shunk. . . . I merely did my duty to the democratic party [in voting for him]."[78] After his election to the governorship in 1844, Shunk had followed Buchanan's advice and tepidly reached out to Muhlenberg's followers: following Polk's appointment of Kane to the federal bench in 1846, Shunk had replaced him as attorney general by offering the job to John M. Read, a committed Muhlenberg man. This fig leaf quickly rotted, however, when opposition to his appointment among Shunk's followers caused Read to resign after only five months. This was the last concession Shunk offered to the Muhlenberg faction, ensuring their opposition to his reelection.

Buchanan, eyeing the 1848 Democratic presidential nomination, sought to unify Pennsylvania's Democratic Party. Buchanan's strategy involved enthusiastically supporting Shunk's renomination and reelection, a move that further alienated him from Cameron's Improvement Men. Despite the Democrats' factionalism (and Cameron's antipathy toward the governor), Shunk won reelection, more than quadrupling his 1844 electoral margin, and the Democrats retook control of the Pennsylvania House of Representatives (though the Pennsylvania State Senate remained under Whig control). Cameron played almost no role in the gubernatorial campaign of 1847, consumed as he was with senatorial business, though rumors circulated that he had not voted for Shunk or, worse yet, had conspired with the Muhlenberg faction to elect the Whig candidate, James Irvin. Cameron was upset by these rumors because, while he did not like or support Shunk, he had not tried to tilt the election toward Irvin.

Buchanan was not the only Democratic candidate; potential nominees included Vice President Dallas, former secretary of war Lewis Cass, and former president Martin Van Buren, who was trying to regain control of the party he had created. Some Democrats, however, were unhappy with these choices, and they went looking for a more attractive candidate. Many settled on Major General Zachary Taylor, former commander of the Second Department of the U.S. Army's Western Division. Taylor rose to national prominence by winning a number of decisive victories in the Mexican-American War, and his growing popularity caused friction with Polk, which only increased the general's appeal to Democrats disaffected with the current administration. These "Democrats for Taylor" were strongly rebuked by the *Union* as "unsound" and "mongrels." The *Somerset Herald and Farmers' and Mechanics' Register,* a Pennsylvania newspaper that supported Taylor, fired back at the *Union,* noting the prominence of the Democrats who participated in the convention and wondering, "how these gentlemen will relish this kind of 'flattery'" and commenting that "[it] will, we opine, scarcely 'bring them back into the fold.'"[79] In other words, rather than unifying the party, the presidential election of 1848 only exacerbated Democratic factionalism.

In July 1847 a group of Pennsylvania Democrats held a meeting in Harrisburg to promote Taylor's candidacy for the presidency, and Cameron was appointed to the committee of correspondence. According to *Niles' National Register*, he "took an active part [at the convention] on behalf of General Taylor as the next candidate for the presidency."[80] Colonel Samuel Patterson, editor of the Democratic *Norristown Register*, asked Cameron to investigate Taylor's politics. Cameron's response, which was later published in the *Bradford Reporter*, claimed that Taylor "has been a Democrat all his life and this agrees with all the information on the subject. He was the personal and political friend of General Jackson, and the firm supporter of his administration and measures. . . . If I have not, my dear sir, said enough to convince you that General Taylor is a good Democrat, of the Jeffersonian, Jacksonian school, I shall be glad to hear what will make a Democrat."[81] The senator even went so far as establishing a pro-Taylor newspaper in Lancaster, Pennsylvania, with his brother James as editor.[82] All of this effort was at least partially motivated by the possibility that Cameron would be Taylor's running mate in 1848, an idea that floated around Democratic circles. James wrote to Cameron in early 1847, predicting that Taylor would win and suggesting that Cameron might find a place on the general's ticket as the Whig vice presidential nominee.[83] That summer, Cameron played a prominent role in a convention held in Harrisburg that endorsed Taylor for the presidency and, incidentally, suggested Cameron as a potential running mate.

In a June 23 letter to a friend, Taylor wrote, "I regret to see Genl Cameron's letter published, notwithstanding I am and always have been a democrat of the Jeffersonian school, which embodies very many of the principles of the whigs of present day."[84] Taylor's statement, plus a letter dated May 18 that was subsequently published, provided evidence for concluding that he was both a Democrat *and* a Whig, which was surely the intention: Taylor's supporters wanted to make the candidate appealing to the widest group of potential voters. That there was some intentional obfuscation of Taylor's actual politics is indicated in an exchange of letters between Cameron and Jefferson Davis. In July, Cameron wrote to Davis suggesting that it was best for Taylor to avoid making any public statements or answering any questions about his political beliefs. Writing to Cameron on July 26, Davis said, "I agree with you as to the propriety of [Taylor's] declining to answer letters written either to draw out his opinions or to connect him with little cliques or political hacks in newspaper publication."[85] In the same letter, Davis noted that he expected Taylor to get the Democratic nomination.[86]

However, Taylor's newfound attachment to the Democratic Party was widely questioned, and the general undercut assertions of his Democratic leanings by offering to run for president but not as the candidate of any party, which cooled Democratic enthusiasm for him. Then, in early August, Taylor sent a letter to Philadelphia congressman Joseph R. Ingersoll in which he declared himself, "a Whig—not indeed an ultra Whig—but a Whig in principle."[87] Taylor's statement killed the nascent "Democrats for Taylor" movement, leaving Cameron without a candidate to support. Thus, when Pennsylvania's Democratic Party selected Buchanan as the commonwealth's nominee for president in March 1848, Cameron fell into line and supported his friend's candidacy.[88] In the words of Cameron biographer Lee F. Crippen, "Despite whatever aid and encouragement Cameron and his men may have given to the Whig supporters of General Taylor during the winter of 1847–48, Cameron was himself in the Democratic ranks." Once the state caucus nominated the secretary of state, "Cameron boarded the Buchanan bandwagon and went to the convention as a member of the Pennsylvania delegation."[89] Ominously for Buchanan, Pennsylvania's convention selected Cass as its second choice. More unfortunate for the secretary of state was that, due to opposition from Vice President Dallas and Congressman Wilmot, the actual committee of delegates selected to go to the national Democratic Party nominating convention in Baltimore was only loosely committed to Buchanan. Cameron attended the national convention and wrote to Buchanan daily, updating the secretary of state about the proceedings. The Pennsylvania delegation voted solidly for Buchanan, through four straight ballots, but it could not stem the rising tide for Lewis Cass, who was selected as the Democratic nominee.

Shortly after the convention, rumors began circulating that Cameron had betrayed Buchanan by surreptitiously packing the Pennsylvania delegation with delegates he knew would abandon the secretary of state. In the 1850s, John Weidman, a small-time Democratic politician and one of Cameron's enemies, published a pamphlet claiming that the senator had bullied some of the voters selecting delegates to the national convention, going so far as to threaten bankrupting one's business unless he voted for Cameron (whose opponent in this race was, naturally, Weidman). When the delegates instead voted for another candidate named David Pool, Cameron allegedly convinced Buchanan to find Pool a federal job in exchange for Pool giving up his place on Pennsylvania's delegation, which Cameron would now fill. According to Weidman, at least some of the other delegates were resistant to this because they did not "recognize" Cameron as a Democrat, which required further intercession from Buchanan. Apparently, Cameron repaid this courtesy by working against Buchanan's nomination. Weidman claimed he witnessed Secretary of the Navy John Y. Mason telling Buchanan that Cameron was spreading rumors among the other states' delegates that "Pennsylvania's resolutions in your favor are a sham, the convention itself was opposed to you, was induced to give you a formal endorsement, not intended to actually secure your nomination; that you are not popular in your own state and cannot carry it, and by these and the like arguments, professing at the same time a warm and personal friendship for you."[90]

The truth of Weidman's charges is impossible to ascertain. The sequence of events is taken from a pamphlet he published in 1855 while trying to derail Cameron's election to the Senate; as such, there is reason to be skeptical about his claims. There do not appear to be any surviving letters among Cameron's papers indicating that he was working against Buchanan, though his relationship with the secretary of state had definitely cooled over the previous few years. Yet, Cameron had always been extremely loyal to Buchanan, and there was nothing to be gained politically by supporting Cass over Buchanan. Still, Buchanan believed Weidman, especially when, out of party loyalty, Cameron supported Cass in the general election.

Cameron and Buchanan's falling-out was not the only schism weakening the Democratic Party that fall. Cass's nomination alienated Van Buren's supporters, who saw his selection as a sop to the Southern wing of the party. In August, a group of Van Buren supporters held a convention in Buffalo, New York, and organized a new party, which they called the Free Soil Party. At the same convention, the Free Soilers (as they came to be known) nominated Van Buren for president and Charles Francis Adams (son of former president John Quincy Adams, who had become a leading anti-slavery voice in Congress after leaving the White House) for vice president. All across the North, the Free Soilers' cry of "Free Soil, Free Speech, Free Labor, and Free Men" could be heard. Polk's actions had split the Democratic Party, and Whig leaders channeled much of their support to the Keystone State in order to remind voters about Polk's (and by extension the Democrats') perfidy on the tariff issue, which certainly improved Taylor's prospects.[91] Taylor won the state by a wide margin and received Pennsylvania's twenty-six electoral votes, which won him the presidency. Worse from Cameron's perspective, Taylor swept a Whig majority into the Pennsylvania General Assembly. Under such circumstances, Whigs in the Pennsylvania State Senate would be able to elect a Whig to replace Cameron, whose term was ending in March 1849.

Though the Whigs were now in the majority, they had a hard time uniting on a candidate. Former Speaker of the Pennsylvania House of Representatives James Cooper had the support of most of the incoming Whigs, but the legislature's nativists opposed him. This created an opportunity for Cameron: he might be able to secure reelection if he could create a coalition of Democrats, nativists, and enough anti-Cooper Whigs. To do so, he would need help corralling the legislature's Democrats, most of whom were still unhappy with the circumstances of his election in 1845. To do this, Cameron turned to Buchanan. According to Cameron biographer Erwin Stanley Bradley, "No one was in a better position in 1849 to influence the outcome of a Democratic state caucus nomination than was James Buchanan, recognized leader of the state's democracy."[92] Buchanan, however, refused to exercise his influence on Cameron's behalf, believing that his former friend had betrayed him at the Democratic nominating convention the previous summer. As a result, on the third ballot, the legislature elected James Cooper to succeed Cameron. Four days later, on January 12, Vice President Dallas laid Cooper's credentials before the Senate, and on March 4 Cooper was sworn in as Pennsylvania's new junior senator. Cameron, who prized loyalty over all else, was aghast at what he considered Buchanan's betrayal, and he was unhappy leaving the Senate. Despite his political enemies taunts, this was not the end for Cameron, who, after all, used a letterpress that depicted a printing press and stated his personal motto: "Persevere."[93] As he had noted in an 1839 letter to Buchanan, "[My] usual course has been to fight through my difficulties, and in so doing, I have generally succeeded."[94]

4

"Exclude Him from the Ranks of the Democratic Party," 1849–60

ameron's departure from the Senate coincided with an industrial boom in Pennsylvania. Between 1850 and 1860, the amount of capital invested in the commonwealth more than doubled, while the value of Pennsylvania's industrial output surged by almost 100 percent.[1] Just as before his time in the Senate, Cameron was involved in a diverse, but interlocking, series of business ventures that not only enriched him, they kept him in close contact with important politicians. In March 1856, for instance, he was listed as president of the Commonwealth Insurance Company of Harrisburg, and in April of that year the *Democrat and Sentinel* (which had viciously attacked Cameron and his supporters just a few before) ran an advertisement for the West Branch Insurance Company of Lock Haven, Pennsylvania, that listed Cameron as a reference.[2] In addition, Cameron was still cashier of the Middletown Bank, though by far, his most important business venture during this period was railroads.[3]

In 1851 Cameron chaired a convention held at Sunbury, Pennsylvania, designed to standardize and consolidate the various railroads bisecting Pennsylvania into a single uniform line. Two years later, he was elected president of the newly formed Lebanon Valley Railroad, which connected Reading and Harrisburg, bringing to three the total number of railroad presidencies he held at this time.[4] He also owned a number of construction companies that built the lion's share of the Baltimore & Susquehanna's rail lines.[5] In 1854 the Pennsylvania and Maryland legislatures created the Northern Central Railroad. The goal was to create a single railroad that ran from western New York through Harrisburg to Baltimore. Up until the late 1850s, all railroad traffic between New England and Baltimore passed through Philadelphia over two lines: the Camden & Amboy and the Philadelphia, Wilmington & Baltimore Railroads. There was only a single railroad line from Baltimore to Washington DC, the Baltimore & Ohio (B&O). The Northern Central might be able to break this monopoly (and enrich its shareholders) if it could provide a credible alternative route through central Pennsylvania.

Cameron saw the railroad's potential and was one of the line's original incorporators, eventually sitting on the board of directors. In late 1858 and early 1859, Cameron and his brother-in-law bought enough Northern Central stock to get Cameron, his brother William, and some like-minded supporters elected to the railroad's board of directors. Cameron and his supporters were in the minority, so he next turned to J. Edgar Thomson and Thomas A. Scott of the Pennsylvania Railroad (PRR) for help. Thomson ascended to the PRR's presidency in 1852 and began a campaign of expansion that made the PRR the largest business enterprise in the world by the mid-1870s. Scott, like Cameron, recognized the importance of maintaining close ties with the General Assembly, so he frequently worked from an office in the state capitol building adjacent to the legislative chamber. Furthermore, the PRR flexed its economic might by placing advertisements in newspapers across the state, which strongly encouraged those papers' editors (who were always hungry for revenue) to support the company with favorable editorial coverage.[6]

Cameron and the PRR had a (generally) friendly relationship, at least as long as their interests converged. In the summer of 1860, Cameron convinced Thomson to buy Northern Central stock in order to gain control of the railroad's board of directors in return for the Pennsylvanian's support in the Senate for repeal of the tonnage tax, which the PRR's management desperately wanted. Cameron's allies in the Pennsylvania legislature were crucial to getting the tax law amended, so Thomson had every incentive to provide the cash necessary to buy Northern Central stock.

The B&O's president, John W. Garrett, recognized the challenge that the Northern Central represented to his railroad and moved decisively to neutralize it. Joining forces with the Philadelphia & Reading Railroad (who also feared a loss of business to the Northern Central), Garrett purchased enough stock to control the Northern Central and thereby prevent it from cutting into the B&O's business. When this proved insufficient, Garrett successfully pressured the Commonwealth of Maryland to instigate foreclosure proceedings against the Northern Central to force the railroad to repay state loans. The plan backfired when the foreclosure proceedings sent the Northern Central's stock price tumbling, encouraging Garrett's allies to sell their stock, which Cameron's associates were only too happy to purchase, solidifying his control over the railroad.[7] At the March 1861 stockholders' meeting, Cameron was able to transfer the presidency of the Northern Central to his brother-in-law, while John Cameron became the company's vice president and Cameron's son J. Donald was elected to the board of directors.[8] The Civil War so badly damaged the B&O (a circumstance that Cameron's War Department helped facilitate) that Garrett was forced to sell his railroad's remaining stake in the Northern Central to the PRR, which eventually owned about 55 percent of the line.[9]

Though Cameron was well known for his soft-spoken good-humor, the former senator was a dangerous man to cross. David Taggart was a young Whig then representing portions of Dauphin and Northumberland counties in the Pennsylvania Senate who had viciously attacked Cameron during the latter's failed senate run in 1855. In response, Cameron used proxies to buy stock in the Northumberland Bank, which provided the Taggart family with the majority of its income. Once Cameron controlled a majority of the bank's stock, he engineered the Taggarts' removal from the bank's board of directors. The lesson was not lost on Taggart, and he quickly fell in line as a Cameron supporter. The coda to this story is also revealing about Cameron's character: while he was never afraid to use bare-knuckle tactics against an opponent, he was willing to let bygones be bygones, if doing so was politically expedient. As secretary of war, Cameron appointed Taggart as a paymaster in the army, which at the time was a much sought-after lifetime appointment.

At the same time, Cameron had a well-deserved reputation for generosity and civic engagement. His papers at both the Dauphin County Historical Society and the Library of Congress contain letters to him from strangers asking for charity, requests that he often obliged. For instance, in 1859 a man named Frank T. Reamen wrote to Cameron and solicited a $150 loan to pay the balance of his tuition at a local seminary.[10] In 1854 Cameron contributed $20 for cholera relief in Lancaster County, and later donated a bell to the Union County Court House at a cost of $267.[11] In 1860, following a solicitation from a member of the congregation, Cameron donated $50 to the German Reformed Church to replace the building's roof, and during this period he served on the Pennsylvania Female College's board of trustees.[12] Prominent Lancaster County Democrat Reah Frazer (known as the "Lancaster War-Horse," and a former Cameron opponent) gushed in a letter that Cameron had "a great-big heart" and "never deserts his friends, who stands in the house of adversity and peril, closer, truer, and nearer, and, as the blow approaches, wards it off with the strength of his own right arms."[13] One visitor, who knew Cameron only by reputation up to this point, described the Pennsylvanian as "certainly a genial, pleasant, and kind hearted man, & many prejudices that I have heretofore entertained have been removed."[14]

Despite being out of office, Cameron still enjoyed wide political influence. For instance, in October 1853, W. A. Hollinger asked Cameron to support his reappointment as a Pennsylvania Canal collector. Hollinger wrote, "As the time is fast approaching for the appointments to be made by the Canal Commissioners, and I have no doubt but that you will be in Harrisburg at that time, I again most respectfully ask your influence for my reappointment."[15] From at least 1850, savvy political spectators assumed that Cameron would make another run for the U.S. Senate, an impression reinforced by the fact that his sons Brua and Donald played increasingly active roles in Cameron's various business ventures. Once the Democrats recaptured the Pennsylvania General Assembly in 1850, it was a given that a Democrat would be elected to fill Daniel Sturgeon's seat when the senator's term of office ended early the next year. Cameron actively, though subtly, campaigned for the nomination, and two days before the election was one of five candidates; the other four were Woodward (the perennial candidate), Jeremiah S. Black, Henry D. Foster, and former congressman Richard Brodhead. On the twelfth ballot, Brodhead was elected senator. While the defeat was a stinging one for Cameron, the silver lining was that Brodhead was the candidate that the former senator most wanted in the position (after himself). Cameron smartly cultivated a relationship with the senator-elect, and the two became political allies.

Over the course of the early 1850s, Cameron's estrangement from Buchanan grew wider and more personal. At this point, Buchanan's faction was stronger than Cameron's, though Cameron's men (who had taken to calling themselves "Cameron Democrats") generally dominated the canal board, which was a rich source of patronage. In the words of Roy F. Nichols, "Using this, they carried on a constant guerilla warfare within the party for delegates and legislators," using the state's partisan newspapers to try and undermine Buchanan.[16] Cameron spread rumors that Buchanan enjoyed limited support in Pennsylvania, implying that "Old Buck" might not even be able to win his home state if he received the party's 1852 presidential nomination. To stir up trouble with the Southern wing of the party, Cameron passed to his former Senate colleague Jefferson Davis a newspaper article from 1820 reporting that Buchanan had signed an anti-slave resolution. Cameron certainly understood how explosive this revelation could be—he knew the Southern senators well and had witnessed the controversy caused by the Wilmot Proviso—and he surely thought the article would derail Buchanan's chances of securing the Democratic presidential nomination in 1852. This was a bold move, even in the "take-no-prisoners" world of Pennsylvania's politics. Writing to Buchanan in March 1850, Buchanan's intimate friend and former roommate, William R. King, noted,

> Col. Davis has shewn me your letters to him. I was fully aware of the hostile movements of that unprincipled intriguing fellow Simon Cameron. He has long been your enemy; but I trust his entire destitution of all political principle, and I would add in my opinion moral honesty, is too well understood in Pennsylvania to enable him to injure you. I know no man more unfortunate than yourself in having his opinions on this Slavery question tortured and misrepresented, to subserve their selfish purposes. I doubt not you will live them down, and that your patriotic course will in the end be appreciated by the American people.[17]

Buchanan lamely asserted that he had signed the seemingly antislavery resolutions out of "a great veneration for the chairman of the Committee as my legal preceptor," but the few Southerners believed this rationalization.[18]

The internecine warfare between the two men's supporters worried prominent Democrats, who believed that endangered the party's chances of carrying the state in 1852. One Democrat wrote to Buchanan in May 1851, trying to convince him to call off the attacks on Cameron in the press and repair their relationship, noting, "You & Gen. Cameron ought to be friends. Living in the same section of the State, and having so many interests in common, it is worse than idle for you men to be enemies. If the *Pennsylvanian* [Forney's paper, widely recognized to be Buchanan's organ in the state] would cease to attack him, (which he charges to you) I have little doubt but a better understanding could be brought about between you."[19] Buchanan responded testily, blaming Cameron for having "made war upon me without any cause." He further denied inciting the personal attacks against Cameron in the *Pennsylvanian*, admitting only that "so far as that paper exerted itself to defeat the attempt to disorganize the party in the Legislature & elect him to the Senate by Whig votes, it received my approbation."[20] A few months later, in a letter to Cave Johnson, Buchanan lumped Cameron in with "all that corrupt clique who are, par excellence, the special friends of General Cass."[21]

Cameron struck back at Buchanan in June 1851 at the Democratic gubernatorial nominating convention. Buchanan arrived at the convention expecting to control it and was rudely surprised to find that Cameron had covertly challenged his authority by attempting to seat delegates who were the former secretary of state's political opponents. Cameron's goal seems to have been to put the Democratic nominee, William Bigler, into his debt.[22] Though Bigler had strongly supported Woodward in the 1845 senatorial election, Cameron recognized that his own success was tied to Bigler's ability to unify Pennsylvania's Democratic Party. Consequently, throughout 1850, Cameron assiduously courted Bigler by subtly corralling influential supporters to vote for Bigler's nomination. Bigler's uncle, William Dock, acted as an intermediary between the two men by passing along Bigler's plea for aid to the former senator. Cameron delivered: at the convention, a number of counties Cameron was thought to control supported Bigler.[23] Cameron thus made it appear that Bigler owed his nomination to the former senator, an outcome that enraged Buchanan. In a letter to Bigler congratulating the governor-elect on his win, Buchanan could not pass up the opportunity to blame Cameron for the fact that the state had also elected a Whig majority to the state senate. The former secretary of state went so far as to claim that Cameron had "done a deed which forever must exclude him from the ranks of the Democratic party," which did nothing to unify the fragmented party.[24]

As a result, when the Pennsylvania Democratic nominating convention convened in early 1852, the acrimony between Buchanan and Lewis Cass's supporters (of which Cameron now counted himself) was palpable. In a letter to Cave Johnson that month, Buchanan claimed that Cass's chances of winning in Pennsylvania were low due to his "close identification with Cameron and his clique."[25] Buchanan's forces triumphed, getting their man the state convention's nomination and succeeding in passing a resolution binding the delegates to vote for Buchanan "to the last" at the national Democratic nominating convention in Baltimore.

Cameron attended the national convention as a Cass lieutenant entrusted with engineering the Michigander's nomination. Cass (who appeared the strongest) and Buchanan were joined by Illinois senator Stephen A. Douglas and former New York governor (and Polk's secretary of war) William L. Marcy as potential nominees. Cameron continued his efforts to disrupt Buchanan's nomination. At one point, Cameron's lieutenants circulated a rumor that they had offered to bet Buchanan's men $10,000 that Buchanan could not carry Pennsylvania; though it appears Buchanan's men took the bet, the story circulated that they had refused out of concern over Buchanan's prospects, a rumor that hurt the Pennsylvanian's chances of getting the nomination.[26] Tactics like these succeeded, at least insofar as they prevented Buchanan from winning enough votes to capture the nomination.

In fact, over three days no candidate garnered the necessary three-fifths majority to claim the nomination, and their supporters began casting about for potential compromise candidates who could command enough votes. Ultimately, the convention turned to Franklin Pierce, a former U.S. representative and senator from Maine who served as a general in the Mexican-American War. Though a Northerner who claimed to "detest" slavery, Pierce thought the preservation of the Union was more important and was therefore willing to make concessions to the South in order to achieve this goal, which made him acceptable to both Northern and Southern Democrats. On the thirty-fifth ballot, Pierce was nominated by Virginia. Over the next dozen or so ballots he consolidated his strength, eventually receiving the convention's unanimous nomination on the forty-ninth ballot. As an olive branch to Buchanan's supporters (Pennsylvania was, after all, a crucial state), the convention nominated Buchanan's close friend Alabama senator William R. King for vice president. In November, Pierce won 50.8 percent of the popular vote, besting the Whig candidate, General Winfield Scott.

Pierce's election temporarily closed some of the fissures caused by Polk's actions in the 1840s. Two years earlier, Congress had passed a series of five bills collectively known as the Compromise of 1850. The most important elements of the compromise included banning the slave trade (but not slavery) in Washington DC; the rejection of the Wilmot Proviso; the substitution of "popular sovereignty" (essentially that the question of whether to become a free or slave state would be decided by the voters of each territory) for the line established by the Missouri Compromise as a mechanism for determining whether newly admitted states would be slave or free states; and a much stronger fugitive slave law. By making the finality of the Compromise of 1850 the campaign's main issue, the Democrats effectively soothed the sectional tensions caused by the annexation of Texas and the Wilmot Proviso. Moreover, "northern and southern Democrats alike had smelled victory and, with a lively anticipation of the patronage to come, had worked together with such effect that they carried all but four states and won top-heavy Congressional majorities."[27]

While sectional tension seemed to have eased for the moment, the acrimony between Cameron and Buchanan got worse. Pierce turned to the former secretary of state for advice on patronage appointments, and Buchanan promoted two of Cameron's political enemies, former Pennsylvania governor David R. Porter and James Campbell. Campbell was a Philadelphia Democrat whom Porter had appointed to various state judicial posts in the 1840s. In 1852, he worked tirelessly to secure the Democratic presidential nomination for Buchanan, leading the perennial candidate to call the younger man "by far the best and most influential politician in Philadelphia and . . . a friend who sticks closer than a brother."[28] Due in large part to his Catholicism, which aroused the animus of nativists, Campbell was the only Democrat defeated for the Pennsylvania Supreme Court in 1850. As a result Governor Bigler appointed Campbell Pennsylvania's attorney general, a position he held until Pierce, in a nod to Buchanan, appointed him postmaster general. Cameron Democrats furiously protested the move, correctly seeing it as a major triumph for Buchanan. Pierce ignored their complaints and, in a letter to Buchanan, argued that Cameron and his followers had always been "disorganizers whenever their personal interests came into conflict with the success of the party."[29] Shortly after the election, Cameron called on the president-elect but did not appear to get anywhere, and feared he would spend another four years without any influence.

Yet the situation soon reversed itself, and, within a short time, Cameron was more successful than Buchanan in obtaining patronage for his supporters.[30] Pierce excluded Buchanan from the cabinet because he had decided not to appoint anyone who had previously served in that role, leaving Buchanan to fume that it made little sense to "ignore the great talents Polk had given employment."[31] Within a few months of Pierce's inauguration Buchanan was reduced to grousing, "The faction which was defunct [Cameron and his followers] has been galvanized by the present Administration. . . . The President seems determined to infuse new life and vigor into that corrupt faction, and thus may possibly succeed (I hope not) in alienating his true friends . . . It is a remarkable fact I have not succeeded in obtaining the appointment of a single individual whom I recommended, beyond the limits of my own County."[32]

Patronage was far from the most pressing item on Pierce's agenda, however. Despite the hope that the Compromise of 1850 had finally settled the issue of slavery, if anything the conflict over the South's "peculiar institution" got worse. In December 1853, Iowa senator Augustus C. Dodge introduced a bill organizing Nebraska as a territory, which was referred to the Senate Committee on Territories. The committee, chaired by Illinois senator Stephen A. Douglas (who was then eyeing a presidential run in 1856), reported a bill that allowed the people of Nebraska the right to enter the union "with or without slavery." This spurred a great deal of debate, and the final bill ended up creating two new states, Kansas and Nebraska. Eventually, the bill passed both the House and the Senate and was signed into law on May 30, 1854. The reaction across the North was electric, and largely negative. The Kansas-Nebraska Act, as the bill became known, was a turning point for both the Pierce administration and the country as a whole. Pennsylvania's voters generally saw the bill as a power grab by the slave power, and the commonwealth's Democratic press vigorously opposed it. Nearly a third of Pennsylvania's Democratic congressmen voted against the bill, and one of Cameron's correspondents advised him not to go "too strongly for the Nebraska Bill; though it will pass the Senate by a thundering majority, it will not the pass the House in a hurry."[33] Another correspondent observed, "Those opposed to the Nebraska bill have the moral and religious feeling and sense of the community to fall back upon." As a result, he concluded that "those who have supported it must sooner or later fall."[34] Though the Keystone State's Democratic newspapers supported the bill, the bill's naked appeasement of the South cost Northern Democrats dearly, with nearly three-quarters losing their seats in the 1854 midterm elections.[35]

The Kansas-Nebraska Act split the Democratic Party into pro- and anti-administration factions, and factionalized the Whigs, essentially destroying that party as a viable national organization. Consequently, Pennsylvania's Whigs began casting about for a new political party committed to opposing the expansion of slavery and the protection of the North's interests. Out of this disorder, Cameron saw an ideal opportunity for returning to the Senate. Naturally, Cameron worked extremely hard at cultivating the state press with an eye toward furthering his own career. Evidently, in late 1853 or early 1854, Cameron thanked George Lochman, editor of the *Bedford Gazette*, for a column suggesting that Cameron had the right to be a candidate for the Senate. Lochman responded to the flattering letter, writing, "My highest ambition is to do <u>justice</u> to <u>all men</u>—and it was this disposition that induced me to pen the paragraph to which you so kindly allude."[36] Other times, Cameron's support was more direct. Writing on behalf of one editor, Edward Fox solicited a "donation" of $40 or $50 to help him meet expenses. Fox noted, "I think matters are working well here for your interests and I am well satisfied that Stillwell is making friends for you wherever he can."[37] The *Youth's Companion*, a magazine that its editors designed to promote "virtue and piety," celebrated Cameron as "The Barefoot Printer Boy," marveling that he "entered a printing office at Harrisburg, hungry and weary laid down his bundle on a pile of wet paper and asked to become a printer's apprentice, [and was later] elected Senator."[38]

Press support alone was not enough to win the election. To win the Senate seat, Cameron had to line up state legislators' votes. The 1854 legislative elections had weakened Pennsylvania's Democrats, and the new legislature was majority Whig, with a strong Democratic contingent and a powerful minority of Know-Nothings. Throughout the fall of 1854 and into early 1855, Cameron relentlessly pursued the Senate seat, writing to his friends and allies across the commonwealth in order to marshal their support. Naturally, this involved a fair amount of horse trading and promises of patronage. In December 1853, William Breten wrote to Cameron, informing him that some of his supporters met with their local state senator, who would not pledge his support to any candidate. At the same time, the legislator noted that he wished to secure an appointment for one of his political friends, and he authorized Cameron's supporters to tell the general "that he knew [the appointment] lay in [Cameron's] hands . . . [and it would be] exceedingly gratifying to [him], and would strongly induce him to feelings of kindness and a desire to gratify the person who should secure [the] appointment."[39]

Breten's letter was hardly unique; Cameron was inundated with requests for money to aid in the requestor's campaign to elect friendly candidates to the legislature. One Cameron biographer has asserted that Cameron considered these requests as blackmail, but, more often than not, sent the requested funds. In addition, he "loaned" legislators and prominent party operatives money, apparently with no expectation of repayment. When his son Donald tried to collect these loans in mid-1857, at least two of the recipients sent Cameron letters expressing their shock, noting that they had understood that these "loans" would never be called. Whether they were given this impression by Cameron is a mystery; in both cases, he wrote them back and explained to them that they needed to repay the loans, which both (grudgingly) did.[40] One Cameron lieutenant alluded to some form of skullduggery when he informed the candidate in 1854, "I have directed my brother-in-law to see that every vote from Lancaster County goes in and goes right."[41]

It quickly became apparent that in order to win, Cameron needed the legislature's Know-Nothings. The Know-Nothings were nativists who wanted to limit Catholic immigration to the United States and make it more difficult for immigrants to become citizens. Believing that Catholics' attachment to the Pope made them unsuitable citizens for a republic, Know-Nothings became concerned by the growing influx of Irish and German immigrants to the United States in the middle third of the nineteenth century. Being a Know-Nothing did not exclude people from other party affiliations; there were Know-Nothing Democrats and Know-Nothing Whigs. Though the Know-Nothings signature issue was anti-Catholicism, in reality what united these disparate groups in the North was opposition to the spread of slavery. According to historian Tyler Anbinder, the Know-Nothings had earned an anti-slavery reputation, so when the Whig and Democratic parties disintegrated after the Kansas-Nebraska Act, many Northerners opposed to the "slave power" migrated to the Know-Nothings.[42]

Cameron's migration into the Know-Nothing ranks seems to have been more about political opportunism and concern about the slave states' infringements on northern states' rights than any real commitment to the party's anti-Catholic nativism (though it is worth noting that, in 1875, some newspapers affiliated with Cameron engaged in nativist attacks on Catholic schools).[43] Described by Michael Holt as "new and leaderless," the Know-Nothings provided a quick road to political power for those Democrats frustrated by fact that men Buchanan controlled the Democratic party in Pennsylvania.[44] In fact, many prominent anti-Buchanan Democrats in Pennsylvania jumped aboard the Know-Nothing bandwagon following the Kansas-Nebraska debacle, and the new legislature's composition gave the Know-Nothings power beyond their numbers because either of the two other parties would have to attract some Know-Nothing votes in order to elect a senator.[45] Moreover, it gave bolting Democrats a plausible reason to jettison unpopular positions in favor of those espoused by the Know-Nothings.[46] More than anything else, Cameron's migration into the Know-Nothing camp reflected the simple fact that party attachment was incredibly fluid during the 1850s; as one historian has noted, "Political mutation was simple and few questions were asked."[47]

In February 1854 John M. Kirkpatrick, then serving as a member of the Pennsylvania House of Representatives and a recent convert to the Know-Nothing cause himself, addressed to Cameron a series of ten interrogatories dealing with contemporary political issues. Of the ten questions Kirkpatrick posed, six dealt with slavery, three with protection and internal improvements, and only one (the last) dealt with immigration reform.

Cameron's responses provide the best insight into his attitudes toward slavery. To Kirkpatrick's question about his feelings on the Kansas-Nebraska Bill, Cameron replied, "From the day it was introduced in the Senate, to this time, I have been opposed to the bill." Cameron agreed that, if elected to the Senate, he would look for "an honorable and just means to affect the restoration of the . . . Missouri Compromise." With regard to the Fugitive Slave Law of 1850, Cameron asserted that the South had been the first to violate it and pledged to work for its revision, in all cases voting with the North. He furthermore recognized the right of Congress to legislate with regard to slavery in the territories and, citing his consistent support of the Wilmot Proviso while a senator in the late 1840s, "emphatically answer[ed] in the affirmative" to Kirkpatrick's question "Would you oppose by all honorable and fair means in your power the extension of Slavery?" Naturally, Cameron also committed himself to a strong protectionist stand and voiced his support of internal improvements. As far as restrictions on immigration, Cameron claimed that he was in favor of "such a change in our nation's laws pertaining to the naturalization of foreigners."[48]

Based on Cameron's responses, he is best described as a conservative or moderate on the issue of slavery. Though he later claimed to "abhor" slavery, Cameron's objections to slavery mostly concern the South's encroachment of Northern states' rights. At no point did he argue that slavery was unjust or should be abolished, only that it should not be extended beyond where it already existed and that Congress had the power to prevent its expansion, assertions that were consistent with his stances as a senator in the 1840s. In a response to another set of inquiries the following year, Cameron claimed, "I am opposed, and have long been, to the admission of any new states into the Union, whose constitutions contains slavery, and if elected to the United States Senate I will vote against any proposition to legalize slavery in any of the territories or otherwise encourage its extension."[49]

In the end, Cameron's efforts to court the Know-Nothings

seemingly paid off: at a mass meeting held in February 1855, they resolved "that with a view to promote the harmony and success of the great . . . party, our Senator and members of the House of Representatives at Harrisburg, be and they are hereby requested and instructed to vote for Simon Cameron."[50] At the same time, prominent furnace operator Charles Forney sent Cameron a letter promising, "Your Democratic friends have every thing in shape [here]. . . . Your friends here have . . . pledged their efforts in your behalf, with something of the ardor, that inspired Constantine and his followers of old."[51] Statements like these reinforced Cameron's confidence that the legislature would return him to the Senate.[52]

In an effort to derail Cameron's candidacy, his political enemies raised the long-dormant Winnebago issue. Leading the charge was John Weidman, with whom Cameron had tangled in 1848 over the delegation to be sent to that year's Democratic nominating convention. In January 1855 Weidman anonymously published a pamphlet addressed to Pennsylvania's state legislators, accusing Cameron of corruption and fraud. Weidman selectively included documents from the 1839 and 1840 House investigations into the Winnebago debacle. On February 6 Cameron published his own pamphlet, refuting Weidman's charges. Presenting some of the documents Weidman had not included, Cameron argued they would be "sufficient to convince every candid mind of the utter falsity of the charges."[53] Cameron's response failed to convince critics like Weidman, who dismissed it as "lame," and it was a stark reminder that, even after twenty years, Cameron had not shaken the "Winnebago Chief" smear.[54]

Ultimately, Weidman and Cameron's pamphlet war had little impact on the election. On February 9 the ninety-one members of Pennsylvania's Know-Nothing caucus convened to pick nominees for the Senate; because the Know-Nothings were in the majority, their nominee would be the next senator from Pennsylvania. Cameron led on the first four ballots, but on the fifth ballot, which Cameron won, a total of ninety-*two* votes were cast.

This threw the caucus into an uproar, and as a result, twenty-nine members stormed out of the room, leaving sixty-two caucus members. On the next ballot, Cameron received a majority of the votes (forty-four), out-polling his nearest rival, Andrew G. Curtin, by a ratio of 4 to 1. On motion, the vote was made unanimous, and Cameron became the nominee. His triumph however, was bittersweet: it engendered a lasting feud with Curtin, for reasons that are not entirely clear. Some sources claim that Cameron said something to or about Curtin that offended the latter, while others claim that the two men had struck a bargain by which each would help the other achieve political office (the secretaryship of the commonwealth for Curtin and the Senate for Cameron). In this version, Curtin failed to uphold his end of the bargain, enraging Cameron.[55] Whatever its cause, the dispute quickly turned vicious. One of Curtin's most ardent supporters, journalist Alexander K. McClure, had attacked Cameron in the press mercilessly since the late 1840s. Now, McClure stepped up his attacks, publicly denouncing Cameron as "a mere instrument of corrupt and designing politicians."[56] Meanwhile, the twenty-nine Know-Nothings who bolted the nominating convention circulated a handbill titled "To the Public," which excoriated the nomination proceedings and attacked Cameron personally.

On February 15 the legislature convened to elect a senator. While Cameron had received a majority of the Know-Nothing votes in the caucus, his total represented less than a third of the total members of the legislature, so his election was not assured. Cameron carried the first ballot with nearly half of the total members of the legislature and more than double the total of his next closest rival, Charles R. Buckalew. On the second ballot, Cameron was only five votes away from victory, and it became obvious that none of his other rivals could beat him. As a last-ditch effort to prevent his election, Cameron's political enemies moved to adjourn the proceedings for two weeks, which squeaked by with a narrow margin of four votes (66 to 62). The various factions opposed to Cameron hoped to use the recess to marshal their strength and settle upon a compromise candidate who could beat Cameron. Supreme Court Justice Jeremiah S. Black gleefully reported the results to Buchanan, who was then serving as U.S. Minister to Great Britain. According to Black, "Cameron was nominated for Senator by a system of secret voting inside the secret order [the Know-Nothings]— the cheats were cheated."[57]

The Pennsylvania House of Representatives even appointed a committee to investigate charges of bribery in relation to the election. The day before the scheduled resumption of voting, the committee reported that it had questioned twenty-five witnesses and was unable to find a few others. Many years later, Cameron received a letter from a former member of the legislature named Samuel F. Gwinner, who claimed two other members had offered him "consideration" if he would vote for Cameron. When Gwinner refused, the two men offered to increase the "consideration," so it would appear that there was some truth to the allegations, though whether Cameron knew about the attempted bribe is unclear.[58] Nevertheless, the final report concluded that the allegations of bribery were vague and unsubstantiated, but the committee's chairman (one of the twenty-nine Know-Nothing bolters) refused to sign it. Yet, despite all the sound and fury over the intervening fortnight, when the legislature reassembled on February 27, little had changed: on the first ballot, Cameron still led, though he received four fewer votes than the last ballot. Over the succeeding two ballots, Cameron received fifty-four and fifty-five votes, respectively, and it again became clear that none of the other nominees was strong enough to win. The legislature again voted to adjourn, this time until October 2. Practically, this signaled Cameron's defeat because it allowed Governor Pollock to appoint a temporary senator until another election could be held. Cameron intimated to the governor that he would be willing to withdraw from the contest in exchange for the governor's help in preventing Curtin from getting the seat, but Pollock (who was friendly with Curtin) demurred.[59] Effectively, this ended Cameron's candidacy for the Senate in 1855, and in mid-January 1856 the legislature elected former governor Bigler to the U.S. Senate. As one historian remarked, "The Senatorial struggle produced no result but bad will."[60]

Following Cameron's defeat, his enemies carped that his long career was over. Cameron's opponent in the 1845 Senate campaign, George W. Woodward, rejoiced at Cameron's loss, crowing, "Heaven be thanked for his defeat. I trust he is extinct. After Whigs or Know-Nothings have spit a creature out of their mouths, no democrat I trust can be . . . willing to swallow him."[61] The *Democrat and Sentinel* crowed, "His political career, as a leader of influence, has closed forever, and like the fallen Wolsey he may exclaim: 'Farewell! A long farewell to all my former greatness.'" The paper delighted in pointing out that Cameron, who owed his election in 1845 to bolting Democrats, had been checked by bolting Know-Nothings.[62] In May, the newspaper reminded voters that the next legislature would be responsible for electing a senator, and advised, "This is an important fact which the people would not forget when selecting their candidates for members of [the Pennsylvania State Senate]. [Those elected] should be men of sterling honesty, who if elected will faithfully carry out the instructions of their constituents, and steadily resist the approaches of that wily Know-Nothing demagogue, Simon Cameron."[63] That being said, the abortive run for the U.S. Senate in 1855 helped solidify Cameron's political machine, which was "ostensibly Democratic in substance but whose members swore liege loyalty to him."[64] As Cameron biographer Lee F. Crippen has noted, "by the summer of 1855, his correspondents began referring to the political 'machine' and asking Cameron to tell them what he wanted done in specific cases. They were now looking to him as the directing genius of the organization."[65]

In addition by 1856, the Know-Nothing Party was in decline. After a string of electoral victories in 1854, the party looked poised to replace the Whigs as the other major political party in the United States. The party's momentum, however, was checked by one thing: slavery. At its national convention in Philadelphia in late February 1856, the Northern and Southern wings of the party could not come to a consensus about slavery; Northern Know-Nothings were predominantly opposed to the expansion of slavery while the Southerners demanded a pro-slavery platform. As a result, delegates from Pennsylvania, Ohio, Iowa, Illinois, and the New England states bolted the convention. Calling themselves the North Americans, these delegates convened their own convention on June 12 in New York. The split in the party assured that it could not muster enough strength to defeat the Democratic presidential nominee, Buchanan, and it was clear that the Know-Nothing Party had no real future in national politics.

As a result of the Know-Nothings' collapse, anti-slavery Northerners of all stripes began casting about for a new party, and most found a home in the new Republican Party. The Republican Party began coalescing in 1854 just as the Know-Nothings reached the zenith of their influence. The Republicans represented a broad coalition of Northern whites opposed to both the Kansas-Nebraska Act specifically and the expansion of slavery generally. In February 1856, delegates met in Pittsburgh to plan the party's national nominating convention, to be held that summer. The organizers put out a call for a "Union Party," thereby ensuring the attendance of a diverse group of people opposed to the Kansas-Nebraska Act: Free Soilers, Whigs, Anti-Masons, and nativists. Michael Holt has aptly described the emerging Republican Party as "the sectional party of the North through which disgruntled citizens could express hostility to slavery, to the South, and to the Pro-Southern Democracy."[66] One historian has called the "torment and turmoil of the late fifties . . . a god-send for Simon Cameron" because the political upheavals that reshaped America's party system allowed Cameron to quickly establish himself as a leader of the state's Republican Party.[67] He became chairman of the Dauphin County chapter in August 1856, and he was soon invited to meetings of the party's national committee. In October 1856, Cameron was listed among the sponsors of a newspaper advertisement advocating a state convention to "settle a Union Electoral Ticket . . . [as] the most effective way to defeat Mr. Buchanan."[68]

In 1856 there were four main Republican candidates for the party's presidential nomination: Ohio governor Salmon P. Chase, U.S. Supreme Court Justice John McLean, and Senators William Seward (New York) and John C. Fremont (California). Strongly opposed to the extension of slavery, McLean wrote one of the two dissenting opinions in the Dred Scott case, which was the basis of his appeal to the Republicans. Another potential nominee, Salmon P. Chase, was also closely identified with the abolitionist movement. Having recently left the Senate to serve as Ohio's twenty-third governor, Chase had been an outspoken abolitionist since the 1830s, eventually earning himself the title "Attorney General for Fugitive Slaves." Chase actively campaigned against the "slave power" and was instrumental in articulating the supposed danger slave owners posed to republicanism. By far, the most radical candidate, at least on the issue of slavery, was New York senator William H. Seward. Seward entered the Senate in March 1849, in the midst over a heated fight over slavery caused by the Mexican-American War and the Wilmot Proviso. The following year, he opposed parts of the Compromise of 1850. In a bracing speech, he referred to a "law higher than the Constitution," a phrase that instantly made him one of the leading voices of the anti-slavery movement. Meanwhile, Fremont's appeal lay in his comparative lack of a record; only two years into his Senate term, Fremont had only registered his opinion on slavery by supporting the abolition of the slave trade in Washington DC, but his views on other issues were more obscure. He was selected by the first National Republican Convention as the party's presidential nominee in June 1856.

As always, Pennsylvania's electoral votes were crucial to any successful run for the White House, but the state's importance to the emerging Republican Party went even deeper. Many party leaders considered success in Pennsylvania as proof of a candidate's electability. Fremont ardently desired a Pennsylvanian on the ticket, if only for political reasons. Due to their radicalism on slavery, neither Wilmot nor former governor William F. Johnston would do. This left Cameron as the only Pennsylvanian with national reputation in the party, seemingly making him a shoo-in for the nomination. However, Francis P. Blair, the man Cameron had ousted from the *Washington Globe* a decade before, intrigued against the Pennsylvanian, and the second spot on the ticket instead went to William L. Dayton. Wilmot chaired the committee that wrote the Republicans' 1856 platform, and his radicalism on slavery, which prevented him from being seriously considered for the vice presidential nomination, now found expression in the party's platform. As a result, it advocated the Wilmot Proviso and decried slavery as a "relic of barbarism."[69]

In retrospect, the presidential election of 1856 was a portent of the sweeping changes reshaping American politics. Pierce hoped to be renominated, but anti-slavery Democrats abandoned the party over the administration's policies, and it soon became clear the president could not be reelected. At the party's nominating convention in June, the Democrats' "ducked" the issue of slavery in 1856, instead writing a national platform that emphasized foreign policy, making Buchanan (with his experience as minister to Russia and the United Kingdom and as secretary of state) the ideal candidate. Buchanan received the highest number of delegates' votes (135.5), with Pierce in second place (122), followed by Stephen Douglas (33) and Lewis Cass (5). Eventually, Buchanan was nominated, but only after Pierce and Douglas removed their names from consideration. The anti-slavery Know-Nothings held a national convention the following week, and (in an attempt to create a fusion party with the Republicans) nominated Fremont. However, the Know-Nothing convention selected Pennsylvania Governor William F. Johnston for its vice presidential nominee, which resulted in conflict between the two parties that weakened both. A splinter group of Know-Nothings, who objected to attempts to fuse with the Republican Party, held *their* own nominating convention and put forth former New Jersey governor Robert F. Stockton for president. Finally, the remnant of the Whig Party nominated former president Millard Fillmore, who had ascended to the presidency in 1850 following President Zachary Taylor's death.

The Republican Party's platform allowed the Democrats to cast themselves as the true party of union. Democrats asserted that Republican hostility to the South and to slavery would inevitably provoke a civil war.[70] Buchanan won a commanding victory in the electoral college, sweeping almost all of the slave states and capturing Pennsylvania, California, Indiana, and Illinois. Fremont, by contrast, won the remaining Northern states. Despite the defeat, there was a silver lining: while the electoral college made it seem as though Buchanan had won a decisive victory, the popular vote told a different story: the president-elect managed to eke out a plurality of the votes (45.3 percent), thereby besting his two opponents, Fremont (33.1 percent) and Fillmore (21.5 percent). Combine Fremont's total with Fillmore's (17.8) and you had an election that hinged on .2 percent of votes. Moreover, though Fremont had only captured 32.1 percent of Pennsylvania's popular vote, Buchanan was the commonwealth's favorite son, and *he* had only received 50.1 percent of the popular vote. Thus, the key for winning Pennsylvania in 1860, and with it the presidency, was finding a way to fuse Pennsylvania's Republicans with the commonwealth's Know-Nothings.[71]

Following Fremont's defeat, Cameron's attention shifted to his own political future. In March 1857, Senator Richard Brodhead's term in the Senate would end. Brodhead and Cameron were friends, and it appears that Cameron personally asked Brodhead not to run for reelection in the belief that he (Cameron) would win the seat. In the 1856 election, Democrats won a slim three-vote majority in the Pennsylvania House of Representatives, though in the Senate all of the anti-Democratic forces combined outnumbered Democrats. In order to win, Cameron would have to build a broad coalition of dissident Democrats and members of other parties just as he had done in 1845. He had a good start; Cameron's former rivals Wilmot and Congressman Thaddeus Stevens announced their intention to back him for the Senate, and both worked hard to secure the votes of their local legislators. Stevens wrote to one Pennsylvania state senator and endorsed Cameron, writing, "If you tender the nomination to S. Cameron I have reason to believe that he can get enough of his old friends to elect him. I opposed him before because I did not think him true to freedom. . . . He is now a genuine Republican as his late acts have shown. It is clear that we can elect no one else, and I submit to you whether it would not be better to elect him than be defeated."[72]

Cameron was not the only one scheming for the Senate seat; Democratic journalist John W. Forney wanted it as well. Forney was one of Buchanan's strongest and most consistent defenders. Unfortunately, what Forney possessed in pugnacious loyalty he lacked good sense, which was demonstrated by the fact that he demanded Buchanan repay his years of support with a lucrative government job. A cabinet post was simply out of the question for Forney, as was allowing him to continue as editor of Washington's *Union*, where he had already alienated influential Southerners. That was fine with Forney, because he thought he had found the perfect office: senator from Pennsylvania. Forney's former paper, the *Pennsylvanian*, published an editorial in early January urging Pennsylvania's Democrats to support a candidate for the U.S. Senate who had been loyal to the party, even singling Cameron out by name, arguing, "Certain it is that no honest man, of any political organization, whether Abolitionist, Know-Nothing, or Democrat, can contemplate without a blush of shame rising to his cheeks, the idea that he belongs to a political organization, weak enough and base enough, for any purpose, to make such a man as Simon Cameron its candidate for the office of United States Senator."[73] Forney asked the president-elect to write a letter to Pennsylvania's Democratic legislators pressuring them to vote for him. Buchanan was hesitant, thinking Forney erratic and unpredictable and therefore poorly suited for the Senate, though in the end he wrote the letter, which soon became public. Cameron learned of Buchanan's letter from a friendly reporter and in return shared that there were at least three Democratic legislators who refused, under any circumstances, to support Forney. As a result, Cameron confided that Buchanan's letter had likely decided the election by pushing those three Democrats to vote for him.[74]

The full legislature met in early January to elect Pennsylvania's new senator. On the first ballot, Cameron received a majority of the legislators' votes. As Cameron expected, three Democrats voted for him. These men were roundly condemned by the party for doing so; they were even expelled from their hotels and later lost their bids for reelection.[75] The democracy of Cambria County passed a series of resolutions condemning Cameron's election, going so far as to call it "a foul blot upon the fair fame of our gallant State."[76] Not to be outdone, the Buchanan Club of Schuylkill County condemned the three Democrats who voted for Cameron, calling their actions "the crime of a most gross and flagrant betrayal of the known wishes of the Party."[77] Allan Nevins called Cameron's return to the Senate a "sharp rebuff" to Buchanan because it was widely known that the president-elect had tried to engineer Forney's election. Consequently, Buchanan suffered an embarrassing political setback before even taking office![78]

However, that was far from the end of the matter. Cameron's enemies in the Pennsylvania Senate passed a resolution in mid-February 1857 demanding the creation of a joint committee to investigate reports of "undue and corrupt influences . . . used to control the election of a United States Senator."[79] Over the next five weeks, the joint committee interviewed fifty witnesses, collecting testimony about alleged bribery. The allegations were shadowy and impossible to prove; one witness, John F. Herr, claimed that David G. Eshelman told him that he had been offered money to procure votes for Cameron. When Herr asked Eshelman if he planned to bribe him, Eshelman replied in the negative. Herr also repeated a conversation with Benjamin Musser in which Musser allegedly claimed that, "Mr. Cameron would make a strong effort to secure his election. [Musser] stated, or his son in his presence, that Cameron wouldn't scruple to expend fifty thousand dollars, and stated that [Cameron] had written [Musser] a letter and his son also, to induce him to operate in his, Cameron's, favor."[80] Musser later confirmed his statement to Herr, but said it was "only common rumor that if money would elect him, it wouldn't be spared. I did not derive any knowledge of that kind from Gen. Cameron, directly or indirectly." Musser's son reported that "I do not know of any influence used by Gen. Cameron to secure his election to the U.S. Senate, except what I have stated."[81] In other words, just as with the Winnebago fiasco, the charges against Cameron were based on hearsay, rumor, and innuendo. As a result, the majority ultimately concluded that "there is no evidence calculated to implicate the canvas for this high and honorable office."[82] However, this did not satisfy two members of the committee, who issued a minority report that claimed, "Although somewhat conflicting, and not very direct, [the minority] have been able to disregard the [allegations against Cameron]. They do not desire to give it more importance than its character warrants; but are not prepared to join in the conclusions of fact so positively stated by the majority."[83] Thus, just like the Winnebago debacle, Cameron was more or less cleared of any impropriety but the controversy left a lasting odor of corruption that became impossible for him to shake.

On March 6, Senator Bigler presented the U.S. Senate a protest bearing the signatures of fifty-nine members of the Pennsylvania legislature regarding the circumstances of Cameron's election. Cameron welcomed the investigation, telling his Senate colleagues, "I hope the Senate will indulge my colleague in having the papers referred to the Committee of the Judiciary at the very moment committees are composed, and if he does not make such a motion I shall do so myself."[84] Within two days, the Committee on the Judiciary asked to be relieved of its investigation because there was no proof to support the protest's allegations. Cameron had managed to defy the odds (and the state Democratic Party) in order to win election to the Senate, just as he had done twelve years before. While Cameron saw the Committee on the Judiciary's action as a personal vindication, his return to power was bittersweet: the Senate was a far less congenial body than the one he had left in 1849. In a letter of congratulations following the election, Brodhead had hinted at the poisonous atmosphere in the capitol: "You requested my seat and I gave it to you . . . but I do not think you will be pleased with it. You may not be able to act politically with those about you."[85] Cameron himself noted the change in the Senate's character. Writing to a friend, he noted, "The South of today is not the South of Calhoun, Dixon, Lewis, and their compeers," though he continued to socialize with Southerners and considered many to be close friends.[86]

The changed tone in Congress was due entirely to tension over slavery. When Buchanan entered the White House, the most vexing (and most potentially explosive) issue was Kansas. At the time, Kansas had two territorial governments: a pro-slavery one headquartered in Lecompton that worked with the "official" governor and an anti-slavery one that met in Topeka and worked with *its* governor. Buchanan believed that he could weaken the incipient Republican Party by immediately admitting Kansas to the union as a slave state, but this was a major miscalculation: in reality, the Kansas issue was splitting the Democrats, driving some of them *into* the Republican ranks. In May 1858, Edwin D. Morgan, then serving as chairman of the Republican National Committee, gloated in a letter to Cameron that "this 'wise administration' will have left us in a better position politically than we could have left ourselves."[87] Buchanan was not helped by the fiery speeches given by Southerners demanding admission of Kansas as a slave state and threatening secession if they did not get their way. South Carolina's Senator James H. Hammond argued that the South could chart its own destiny as a separate nation, provocatively declaring, "You dare not make war on cotton . . . cotton is king."[88] In the words of Michael Holt, "If 1860 witnessed the perfection of the Republican organization, it also witnessed the final splintering of the Democratic Party into Buchanan and Douglas wings."[89]

To head off further confrontation, Cameron's friend Senator John J. Crittenden of Kentucky proposed that the Kansas constitution be submitted to the territory's voters through referendum. If it was voted down, the Kansans could elect a new convention to write another, more acceptable constitution. Crittenden was universally regarded as fair and impartial. Thus, if anyone was in a position to craft a compromise acceptable to all parties, it was Crittenden. His compromise was submitted to the floor on April 1 despite Buchanan's threat to veto it; while the president was fine with the constitution being submitted to the voters, he was adamantly opposed to a new constitutional convention. Cameron vigorously championed Crittenden's proposal, asserting that he daily received "by every mail, a large number of letters" indicating that his constituents supported the compromise.[90]

The House version of Crittenden's compromise passed by a narrow margin (120 to 112), but the Senate ultimately rejected it. In an attempt to compromise, an anti-Lecompton Democrat from Indiana, Representative William H. English, sponsored a new bill that attempted to bribe Kansans into accepting a proslavery constitution: under English's bill, if Kansans accepted four million acres of federal land and 5 percent of the proceeds from the sale of two million more acres, the state would automatically enter the union under the Lecompton constitution. If, however, the voters rejected this agreement, Kansas would be forced to wait until its population had significantly expanded before it could reapply for statehood. Illinois senator Stephen A. Douglas, who had emerged as the leader of the anti-Buchanan Democrats, opposed the bill, though it passed both the Senate and the House. Unfortunately for Buchanan, Kansas's voters rejected the land grant by a ratio of more than 6 to 1.[91]

In the wake of the English Bill's passage, a jubilant David

Wilmot wrote to Cameron predicting "it must break the prestige and power of the administration through out the state + the country. Its influence is already seen here."[92] Wilmot proved prescient: reaction in Pennsylvania to controversy over Kansas was generally negative. One Pennsylvania state senator introduced a bill instructing Senators Cameron and Bigler to fight any constitution not approved by the majority of voters in Kansas, and the *Union County Star and Lewisburg Chronicle* railed against Buchanan's "tyrannical policy . . . to force upon the people of Kansas a fraudulent Slavery Constitution in opposition to the known and oft expressed sentiments of the Freemen of the territory."[93]

Even issues seemingly unrelated to slavery—like those over the tariff—quickly became proxies for the sectional battle over the South's "peculiar institution." For instance, a Senate debate over federal government bonds segued first into an argument over the tariff and then a heated fight over slavery. Cameron jumped into the fray with a short speech that both defended Pennsylvania and viciously attacked the South.

> In the North, every man is a laborer, and every man is proud of his pursuit. Every man there produces something for the benefit of the whole, and every man is a portion of the community. It is not so in the cotton States. There they have two classes—one the free and the rich, and other the slaves, who do the labor. I make these remarks because it is constantly said by southern gentlemen that we of the North are oppressing them with taxation for our own benefit. I have been told, too, that my State was a beggar here—that she came asking for alms. Sir, I reject these assertions with scorn.[94]

Though Cameron frequently referenced his sincere desire to maintain the Union, his tone during this tense period was sometimes combative, and he was unflinching in protecting Pennsylvania's interests. In responding to a memorial presented by the other senator from Pennsylvania, William Bigler, praying for the adoption of the Crittenden Compromise, Cameron said,

"I do not think there are any offending States. I am sure the State of Pennsylvania has not offended her sister States. She has done nothing but what she would do again in the exercise of her constitutional rights. I look upon it this way: the North have won the battle on the great question of free and slave labor; they are the strong party, and they can afford to make concessions to the weaker, if concessions be desired."[95] His friends and political advisors urged confrontation rather than conciliation. Former Kansas Territory governor Andrew H. Reeder, who had seen the violence of "Bleeding Kansas" firsthand, advised Cameron on January 11 that there was "one great consolidated party [in Pennsylvania] in favor of a fight and especially in favor of blotting out the city of Charleston," widely seen as the center of Southern radicalism.[96] Cameron's friend and political ally, newspaper editor Russell Errett, advised that in Pittsburgh "the public mind is so inflamed against Compromise and so bitter at all efforts at concession . . . [you] can have no idea of the fierceness of the sentiment here in opposition to anything that looks like Compromise. It amounts almost to a fury."[97]

Overheated rhetoric like this provoked a number of physical altercations in Congress during the late 1850s. Though violence in the House and the Senate was not unheard of in earlier periods—Cameron himself had a run-in with another senator in 1849—the frequency and viciousness of the confrontations seemed greater. The most infamous incident of congressional violence occurred on May 22, 1856, when Representative Preston Brooks of South Carolina beat Massachusetts Senator Charles Sumner unconscious with a cane. Cameron himself was involved in an altercation with Missouri's James S. Green early on the morning of Tuesday, March 15, 1858. The Senate had been in session all night and tempers were understandably frayed. At one point, Green claimed that Cameron had lied in a speech, and the Pennsylvanian replied by calling Green a liar. Enraged, Green called Cameron a "damned liar," and Cameron replied by asking Green to step outside and "discuss" the matter. Eventually, cooler heads prevailed, and the following day, both men apologized to the Senate and to each other.[98]

As a result of confrontations like this, Cameron formed a compact with Michigan's Zachariah Chandler and Ohio's Benjamin F. Wade. Both Wade and Chandler were aggressive abolitionists and therefore the target of Southern anger. In 1874 the three men signed a memorandum describing their reasons for forming this pact.

> During the two or three years preceding the outbreak of the slaveholders' rebellion, the people of the free states suffered a deep humiliation because of the abuse heaped upon their representatives in both houses of congress by their colleagues from the slave states.
>
> This gross personal abuse was borne by many because the public sentiment of their section would have fallen with crushing severity upon them if they had retorted in the only manner in which it could be effectively met and stopped, by the personal punishment of their insulters. . . .
>
> We consulted long and anxiously, and the result was a league by which we bound ourselves to resent any repetition of this conduct by challenge to fight, and then, in the precise words, the compact" to carry the quarrel into a coffin."
>
> Only one method of stopping the . . . unendurable outrage was open, and that method required us to submit (because of the sentiment against dueling at home) to an ostracism if we defended ourselves, as galling as the endurance of the insults we encountered in the pursuit of our public duties. Nevertheless this arrangement produced a cessation of the cause which induced us to make it, and when it became known that some northern senators were ready to fight for sufficient cause, the tone of their assailants were at once modified.[99]

Clearly, as Brodhead had warned Cameron, the Senate was not the same collegial institution it had been in the 1840s.

Yet the pull of old friendships remained strong for Cameron. On March 23 Cameron chose not to vote on a controversial bill regarding Kansas. Cameron's old friend Jefferson Davis was quite ill but determined to vote on bill, against the advice of his physician and his family's wishes. A mutual friend wrote to Cameron in the hope that the Pennsylvanian could persuade Davis not to leave his sick bed. When Davis made clear his resolve to go to the Senate, Cameron suggested that he and Davis both absent themselves from the vote; since Cameron was going to vote against the bill, his absence would cancel out Davis's. Davis agreed and neither man cast a vote on the bill. Shortly before the vote, however, Cameron made a short speech registering his opinion on the matter and explaining his failure to vote.

Cameron's decision to "pair off" with Davis provoked calls for the state legislature to censure him. Cameron defended his decision by noting in a letter to George Bergren intended for publication that "I had been on intimate terms with [Davis] since I entered the Senate in 1845, and I could not hesitate to do an act of grace to a friend, knowing that the result could in no manner be affected by the loss of a vote on each side, while my refusal might endanger his life; and believing too, that I had character enough, won in the contest thus far, to do a good act without incurring the censure of good men. While I have omitted no exertion to defeat this [bill] and while I shall faithfully and zealously act with my party for the common good of our country, I will not permit myself to be one inch behind my opponents in courtesies and civilities which deprive politics of their harshness, and invite men of kindly feelings into the service of the State, where such courtesies produce no injury to the public."[100]

That being said, sectional tension intruded on Cameron and Davis's friendship. In his retirement, Cameron recalled how he and Davis had boarded together up until 1859, when the Pennsylvanian moved to new lodgings. Thereafter, he saw little of his old friend until a chance encounter with Davis's wife resulted in an invitation for Cameron to join them for breakfast. The following day, Cameron arrived at the Davises' house and, following the meal, retired to the library, where the two men discussed politics. The discussion quickly turned to slavery and became heated, with Davis claiming that Northerners were "stealing our negroes." Cameron "resented [Davis's comment] in words hardly more conciliatory than were Mr. Davis'." Eventually, the tension in the room abated, but not before Davis prophesied that a war was coming. Though they parted as friends, Cameron later claimed, "From that day on, I was convinced that war, and a desperate war, was not to be avoided."[101]

Cameron's own thinking about slavery during this period had not changed much since his first term in the Senate; he believed that Congress was powerless to do anything about slavery where it existed but he did not want to see it expand, believing that the spread of slavery threatened Pennsylvania's interests. He noted,

> I abhor slavery in every shape, but I am not willing to enter upon a crusade to liberate the slaves where they exist under the constitution. That must be left where it belongs. It will be sufficient for me if I can aid in keeping the blighting influence of slavery from land now free, and prevent its toleration in my own State, where the decision of the present Supreme Court would carry it in the next step after the Dred Scott decisions. I want to keep the black race from encroaching upon the white man, knowing that he must be depressed wherever the Negro is his competitor in the field or the workshop. It is this depressing influence of the blacks, that enables the four hundred thousand slave holders to keep in bondage three million of white men who now do their voting to control the politics of the Union and when they expect to do their fighting in case of separation. These poor white men of the South, are our brothers and our natural allies, [and] must be taught by our moderation and firmness that we are battling for their rights.[102]

Cameron's assertion that he abhorred slavery aside, his actual concern seems to have been the negative effect that slavery had on free white labor, an issue he had raised as far back as the early 1830s. In campaign literature for his 1860 presidential run, Cameron's views on slavery were described as follows:

Recognizing all the compromises of the Constitution, and willing to concede to the South all the rights guaranteed to her by them, he cannot and will not lend himself to slavery beyond the requirements of those compromises. Entertaining these views, he recognizes the power of the Federal Government to restrict slavery within the limits in which it now exists, and deems it expedient to exercise that power should there by an occasion for it. . . . True to the old fashioned Democratic faith of his native State, as he has ever proven himself on all other subjects, . . . [he] voted in accordance with his own honest convictions and the well known and undoubted sentiments of the people of the State which he represented.[103]

Clearly, Cameron was no abolitionist, though he remained deeply concerned about the effect of slavery on America's whites.

That being said, Cameron believed that at least some African Americans were equal to white men. For instance, sometime around 1859, Cameron employed an escaped slave named Tom Chester as a servant. According to a profile written about Chester in 1884, which was based on Chester's own recollections, "by faithfulness he secured {Cameron's] interest. While working [for Cameron], [Chester] showed a great love for papers and books and through Mr. Cameron's generosity he was liberally educated." Chester eventually left the United States for Liberia, where he served as the country's minister to Russia before becoming president of a railroad.[104] On the one hand, it is easy to make too much of this anecdote, especially given the fact that Cameron left few definitive statements about his attitudes toward blacks during this period. On the other hand, instances like this and his fight for civil rights during the 1870s indicate his advanced attitudes on race despite his conservativism regarding slavery.

In the Senate, Cameron remained a dogged protectionist. In 1857 Congress responded to a budgetary surplus by passing the Tariff of 1857, which lowered most of the rates established by the Walker Tariff a decade earlier. These reductions made the Tariff of 1857 the lowest in more than forty years.[105] However, the booming economic times that created the Treasury surplus did not last long; the Panic of 1857 caused a financial recession that led to renewed cries for protection. The downturn was caused by declining U.S. exports to Europe, which forced down the price of land and caused banks to cut back on lending. This left farmers and industrialists without cash to refinance the debts they had incurred during the boom years of the mid-1850s, and set off a cascade of defaults that rippled throughout the economy. In retrospect, the worst aspect of the panic was its sectional nature; the South's economy, fueled by cotton exports, continued growing. Southern congressmen used this as an opportunity to point out to their Northern counterparts the superiority of slavery, which did nothing to lessen sectional tension.[106] Congressmen from the South and the Northwest colluded to keep tariff rates low, enraging Northeastern businessmen. Buchanan blamed bankers and land speculators for the collapse, but vetoed public works bills and funding to land-grant colleges that might have eased the economic distress.

In June 1858, Cameron complained to the Senate that "nothing has been done for Pennsylvania" and that "there has never been a time, in the history of the iron business of Pennsylvania, when there was so much real distress among the laboring men of my State."[107] In January 1859, Cameron tried to shift the onus of passing a higher tariff onto President Buchanan and his congressional allies, saying, "Now, all I ask is, that he and other gentlemen who represent the President here shall act in good faith. Let me repeat, that on this subject the Opposition has no power. This revenue question is [in] the hands of the Administration, through its confidential agents in the House. They will pass a bill or not, as they think proper."[108] He returned to this theme in May 1860, saying, "The good people of my State are told that if they do not get an alteration in the tariff this year, it will be the fault of the Republicans of the Senate, and probably of a want of good faith on my part. I desire to say, sir, that I intend to press this question so that everybody here shall have an opportunity of showing how he stands upon it."[109]

Even in these turbulent times, when national events often took center stage, Cameron kept a close watch on political developments in Pennsylvania. Former Whig editor Alexander McClure, who had been recently elected to the Pennsylvania legislature, wanted to be Speaker of the Pennsylvania House of Representatives. Shortly before the legislative session opened, William C. A. Lawrence, who represented Cameron's district, asked McClure to appoint him chairman of the Pennsylvania House's Ways and Means Committee, but McClure refused to make any commitments. As a result, Lawrence approached Cameron, who quietly polled members of the legislature and discovered that Lawrence could defeat McClure's bid to be Speaker of the Pennsylvania House of Representatives. Shortly before the vote, Cameron met with McClure and offered to support McClure in exchange for a promise that, as speaker, McClure would assign Cameron's allies to powerful committees. McClure agreed, but insisted that Lawrence be told of this agreement. Cameron, apparently insulted by McClure's impertinence, decided to engineer Lawrence's election. With the hindsight of decades, McClure reflected, "Cameron thus had the speakership while I had the experience and in many conferences and arrangements which I made with Cameron during a score of years of political hostility I never repeated the role of political tenderfoot."[110]

Meanwhile, all was not well in Cameron's home: in July 1859 his daughter Rachel's husband, Judge James Burnside, was thrown from his horse and immediately died. His son Simon, who was born in 1844, suffered from some kind of mental disability and was committed to the Pennsylvania Training School for Feeble-Minded Children for a brief time. During Simon's commitment, the Camerons actively supported the institution; Margaret was listed as one of the "Life Subscribers and Donors," and Cameron donated a Shetland pony for the residents' use.[111] Cameron's concern over his son's future can be gleaned from a letter he sent his wife apparently after the boy eloped from the institution. "The teacher wrote me the other day, with little Simon's bill, and said he has not returned. . . . It does not seem as if he has made much progress. He will have to be looked after, and I wish you would write to him, if he has gone, or send for him to Middletown."[112] Eventually, it appears that the boy moved back to his father's house, where he lived until Cameron died in 1889. Under the terms of Cameron's will, the younger Simon (who never married) was "to have a home in the mansion house at Donegal," suggesting that he was incapable of supporting himself.[113]

Despite these personal setbacks, politically things could not have been better for Cameron. The fight over Kansas and the tariff as well as the generally poor economy took their toll on Buchanan. The 1858 midterm elections were a disaster for the Democrats, who lost thirty seats in the House and three in the Senate. In Pennsylvania the results were even worse: the Keystone State's Democratic congressional delegation was decimated, accounting for more than half the Republicans' gains in the House. The upset of 1858 fell most heavily on those Democrats closest to the president. "Throughout the North the Republicans were swept into governorships, the Senate, and the House. Southern secessionists were pleased, Unionists were appalled, and the president was temporarily reduced to a state of near hysteria."[114] Cameron had played an important role in this defeat, writing letters of encouragement to anti-Buchanan candidates and voters across the state. In addition, he crisscrossed Pennsylvania, encouraging voters to repudiate Buchanan's administration at the ballot box.[115] More important was Buchanan's interpretation of the results. Rather than seeing the election as a moment for introspection and course correction, to Buchanan "the election of 1858 meant that the Northern people had opted for the antislavery side of . . . [the] conflict, and he was determined to protect the South in any way he could."[116]

Following the midterm elections, Republicans flexed their muscle by using their new power to attack Buchanan and his administration. Representative "Honest" John Covode, an abolitionist and former Whig representing a northwestern Pennsylvania district, doggedly pursued allegations that members of the administration had offered lucrative government printing contracts to newspaper owners in exchange for editorial support of administration policy, and the president himself was implicated in offering political offices to congressmen and their supporters in exchange for their votes. Though Buchanan's use of patronage in this regard was hardly unique, the "overall effect [of Covode's investigation] was to brand the Buchanan administration as 'the Buccaneers,' more interested in spoils than in principle."[117] Many of the administration's most vocal opponents saw the midterms as a forecast of the 1860 presidential election, and eagerly began plotting their campaigns. Among them was Simon Cameron.

5

"What They Worship Is the God of Success," 1860–61

As Buchanan's unhappy term ground to a close, Democrats of all stripes scrambled to succeed him. The most likely candidate was Illinois senator Stephen A. Douglas. The "Little Giant," as he was popularly known, had pursued the Democratic nomination in 1856, but withdrew when it became clear that neither he nor Buchanan had the political strength to secure it while the other was in the race. Douglas's withdrawal allowed Buchanan to secure the nomination and, with it, the presidency, but any goodwill this might have engendered quickly evaporated when Douglas opposed Buchanan's Kansas policies. In addition, Douglas was convinced (probably correctly) that Buchanan intentionally distributed patronage to men hostile to him, so the senator worked to frustrate the administration. As a result, in the words of Buchanan's biographer, "hatred for Douglas had become an integral part of Buchanan's daily life."[1]

In the lead-up to the 1860 presidential election it became clear that the main issue would be slavery. In attempting to "split the difference" on slavery, Douglas responded to the Dred Scott decision by arguing in 1858 that territorial governments could skirt the decision by not passing laws that defined slaves as property. This argument, which came to be called the "Freeport Doctrine," advocated using legal sleight of hand to protect what Southerners saw as their constitutionally guaranteed right to own slaves. In the overheated political environment of the late 1850s, Southerners were appalled; Douglas opposed their interests in Kansas and now he advocated working around the Dred Scott decision rather than making a full-throated assertion of slave owners' rights. Douglas was the only Democrat capable of carrying Northern states in the 1860 presidential election, but as Elbert B. Smith has noted, "For Southerners . . . the suppression of Douglas was more important than rebuilding the strength of the Democratic party."[2] Buchanan, whose antipathy toward Douglas was legendary, surely needed no prodding from his Southern friends to throw the entire weight of his administration behind the goal of frustrating the Little Giant's ambitions, and he did so with relish.

Seeing the Democrats' disarray, Cameron predicted that "the Republican Party is strong in its principles, and no earthly force can prevent it from controlling this government after 1860."[3] Believing that the next president would be a Republican, Cameron pursued the party's presidential nomination, believing that he could leverage the Keystone State's electoral strength at the Republican convention to secure the presidential nomination. Shortly after returning to the Senate in 1857, he began lining up influential men whose support he needed to first secure the presidential nomination. In June, William P. Seymour, a supporter from Norristown, Pennsylvania, informed Cameron that his "position in the State is as good with reference to 1860, if we can succeed in building an American Democracy. . . . I have addressed you in the hope that our views may be identical and that with some moderate movement with <u>local men</u> we may place you head + shoulders above any man in the North for the Presidential race in '60."[4] In April 1859, John Cowan of the American Emigrant Aid and Homestead Society (an organization that helped abolitionists move to Kansas) assured Cameron that "everything seems to look bright for 1860. The North-West and New England are all right."[5] In March 1860, R. M. McAllister suggested that Cameron could secure John W. Forney's (who was by now alienated from Buchanan over patronage) support by promising him Cameron's Senate seat. McAllister wrote, "[Forney's] ambition seems to culminate in the United States Senate, and if you were President, there would be two Senators to elect next summer, and I see no reason, especially if you did not object, in the arrangement why Forney's Senatorial aspirations could not be gratified in the event just named."[6]

The second prong of Cameron's strategy was securing newspaper support, which he did with gusto. In October of 1858, the *Democratic Sentinel* reported that the *Tyrone Star* had "raised to the mast-head . . . the name of Simon Cameron as the *People's* candidate for President in 1860," a notion that the *Sentinel's* editors ridiculed.[7] The following year the *Franklin Repository* claimed that most of the papers in Pennsylvania opposed to the Buchanan administration "have spoken out in favor of Gen. Simon Cameron as the anti-Democratic candidate for president."[8] In February 1860 one man even approached Cameron for $600 to buy a newspaper, promising, "I would then come out fearlessly and boldly, and strongly urge your claims upon the Chicago Convention."[9] Cameron's response is lost, but it is likely that he replied to this letter the way he had to a similar request the year before: "Many applications have been made to me for pecuniary aid to newspaper[s] and their editors, since my name has been associated with the office you connect with it. I have given but one answer and that is, I can not with a sense of propriety give any money to aid my own political advancement."[10]

Of course, having important political backers and influential newspapers in one's corner was essential to securing the nomination, but the most important element was winning votes. Newspaper editor Russell Errett, Cameron's friend and supporter, toured the Midwest in the autumn of 1859 trying to drum up support for Cameron's presidential ambitions, while supporters organized clubs with the sole purpose of arousing public support for Cameron's nomination and election. In

May 1859 a group of supporters threw a "Cameron Festival" in Mount Joy, Pennsylvania, that Cameron attended.[11] The following month Charles Leib (who oversaw Cameron's political interests in Chicago) wrote to Cameron and informed the candidate that he was "quietly yet surely making interest for you, and I assure you that in the city of Chicago I could get up quite a respectable 'Cameron Club.'"[12] Three months later, in September 1859, Leib wrote the candidate and requested copies of his various speeches dealing with the tariff, which he intended to distribute in Chicago to build support for Cameron's nomination.[13] Leib was far from the only Cameron supporter laying the groundwork for Cameron's nomination: in late 1859 the "People's Club" of Philadelphia was organized, and it adopted a constitution that included the article "Any person may become a member of this Club by signing the Constitution, but in so becoming a member, he shall be regarded as pledged to use all his influence and exertions in favor of Gen. Cameron as the People's candidate for the Presidency."[14] Cameron was so popular in Pennsylvania that the state legislature even created a new county and named it for the senator!

Thus, going into the 1860 Pennsylvania presidential nominating convention, Cameron looked like the prohibitive favorite for the Keystone State's nomination. In widely circulated campaign literature, Cameron spelled out his platform: "maintaining the right of petition" (a slap at the "gag-rule," by which Southern congressmen and their Northern supporters prohibited debate over slavery in Congress), "the abolition of flogging in the Navy," "a system of cheap postage," and raising the tariff. He presented himself as "an advocate of progress, yet conservative."[15] Naturally, not all Republicans in Pennsylvania supported Cameron.[16] Writing to Cameron in March 1860, one supporter noted, "The trouble seems to be in the impression made or manufactured at Washington . . . that there is great antagonism there against you and that nearly any other Republican candidate named would reconcile matters and run better in Pennsylvania than yourself."[17] One of Cameron's sup-

1. Simon Cameron, c. 1860.

2. "Lochiel," home of the Hon. Simon Cameron,
Harrisburg. Source: *The Homes of America,*
ed. Martha J. Lamb.

3. (*Opposite top*) The Seventy-Ninth Regiment
(Highlanders), New York State Militia, c. 1861.
Source: *Harper's Weekly,* May 25, 1861, 329.

4. (*Opposite bottom*) Cabinet at Washington, July 13,
1861. Source: *Harper's Weekly,* July 13, 1861, 437.

5. The Committee on Foreign
Relations of the Senate, February
11, 1871. Source: *Every Saturday*,
February 11, 1871, 140.

porters, William S. Roland, went so far as to claim "there are Judases" in Pennsylvania's Republican Party.[18] One man in particular seems to have actively worked against Cameron at the convention: McClure. McClure's antipathy toward Cameron was stoked by the latter's move to defeat McClure's bid to be Speaker of the Pennsylvania House of Representatives. Cameron's role in McClure's defeat was widely known and it understandably angered McClure's supporters. McClure himself had written an angry letter to Cameron, complaining that "I have been advised from several quarters that you are opposing me; and that you are calling to concentrate on any other candidate who promises to be sufficiently strong to defeat me."[19] Though Cameron denied any role in opposing McClure, the latter was not mollified, and the convention was as good an opportunity as any to take his revenge.

A few weeks before the convention, a rumor began circulating to the effect that Cameron was engaged in some form of political skullduggery with Pennsylvania's Democrats. This rumor, which was undoubtedly spread by McClure or some of his close associates, made it back to Cameron in the form of a letter from one of his Philadelphia supporters: "There is now great danger of serious difficulty with a considerable portion of our delegation to Chicago, in consequence of a report, very freely circulated, of language used, by you, at an interview between yourself and McClure. . . . This report ascribes to you the expression of treasonable sentiments as to our success here at the election, and a personal wish to have us defeated, etc. I do, of course, not pretend to give the language or sentiments, or even the substance, ascribed to you, but it is such as to be calculated to do serious harm, and has, I know, had the effect of causing difficulty already with some of the delegates."[20]

Even more damaging were the rumors that Cameron's candidacy was nothing more than a stalking horse for William Seward's nomination. In a December 1859 letter to newspaperman Louis Blanche, an anonymous correspondent claimed,

You are aware that great efforts are being made by the friends of Gen'l Simon Cameron to organize Cameron clubs throughout the State for the ostensible purpose of bringing his name prominently before the public for the Presidency. This I assure you is merely a ruse for an ulterior purpose, Gen'l Cameron himself having no such aspirations, but he is acting as the secret and paid agent of Thurlow Weed, of New York, from whom he has already received fifteen thousand dollars to assist in organizing the State and to control the delegates to the State Convention, who are to be sold at the proper time to Wm. H. Seward.[21]

This impression resulted from a visit Seward paid to Cameron in April 1859. In a letter to Thurlow Weed, Seward claimed that Cameron "was for me, and Pennsylvania would be. It might want to cast a first ballot for him—or might not—but he was not in. He brought the whole legislature of both parties to see me—feasted me gloriously and they were in the main so free, so generous, as to embarrass me."[22] Seward even claimed that Cameron promised to raise funds for the New Yorker's campaign.

Addressing the rumor that Cameron was not really interested in the presidency, one correspondent wrote, "It is whispered that the late visit of Gov. Seward to Harrisburg was for the purpose of making some arrangement by which the support of this state could be obtained for him, to the [unreadable] of another and more worthy son of Pennsylvania than now occupies the Presidential chair."[23] Perhaps the most conclusive evidence to support the assertion that Cameron was working for Seward's nomination is that, in mid-1858, the senator was actively distributing German translations of Seward's speeches under his senatorial frank.[24]

While Seward's reconstruction of his visit is certainly plausible, the fact that it was widely known that he had little support in Pennsylvania calls it into question. Seward's well-known abolitionism made him anathema to a large portion of Pennsylvania's voters, who tended to be more conservative about slavery. David Wilmot claimed in an April 1860 letter to Cameron, "Although it grows of no demerits on his part . . . [my] clear belief [is] that Mr. Seward cannot carry the vote of our state, nor New Jersey, or Indiana."[25] Later noting his relief at Lincoln's nomination, Wilmot claimed that Seward would have lost Pennsylvania because the New Yorker "had occupied positions of such mark in the conflicts of the past ten years, that the Conservative & American elements in this State were irrevocably committed against" him.[26] The "Conservative & American elements in the State" that Wilmot described were Cameron's core supporters, making it somewhat unlikely that Cameron would have risked his political future promoting a candidate that his own followers would not have supported. Furthermore, he also courted Ohio governor Salmon P. Chase, who stayed at Cameron's house in the summer of 1859. It is more likely that Cameron was attempting to "cover the bases" by befriending the two most likely Republican presidential nominees and thereby place himself in the role of kingmaker in order to extract concessions from the eventual nominee, though this is purely speculation. Certainly, it seems unlikely that an ambitious man like Cameron would have turned down the Republican presidential nomination had it been offered to him, especially in what seemed likely to be a good year for the party, though he later claimed that "[I] never believed that I was qualified for [the presidency]."[27]

One man closely watching Cameron's campaign for the Republican nomination was Abraham Lincoln, who was also contemplating a run for the presidency in 1860. At that point Lincoln's claim to fame amounted to an undistinguished term in the House of Representatives and a widely reported campaign against Stephen A. Douglas for the latter's Senate seat in 1858. The fact that Lincoln had won the popular vote in 1858 (though was not awarded the seat by the legislature) catapulted him to prominence among Republicans and transformed him into a serious contender for national office. In response to Cameron ally William E. Frazer's letter in November 1859 soliciting his pledge to support Cameron's candidacy in 1860, Lincoln hedged—he only promised to support Cameron *if* the Pennsylvanian was nominated by the Republican Party.[28] Later that month, following a chance meeting with Cameron, Lyman Trumbull observed in a letter to Lincoln that "[Cameron] is earnest in getting the PA delegation for himself, & I reckon will succeed."[29] Early in 1850 the *Chicago Tribune*'s Joseph Medill noted in a letter to Lincoln that Cameron was "busy as the d—l" in pursuing the Republican nomination.[30] In February, just after the Iowa convention for selecting Republican delegates to that summer's National Democratic Convention in Chicago, Hawkins Taylor informed Lincoln, "If a vote had been taken by the Delegates when appointed, a large Maj of them with the lights then before them . . . would have voted for Cameron for President and Yourself for Vice President. This vote would have been given under the impression that Cameron Could Carry PA and that probably no other Person could."[31]

That Pennsylvania was a crucial state for the Republicans to carry is indicated in a letter sent to Lincoln by one of his supporters. "We must have Pennsylvania or we are almost certainly defeated. . . . I was of opinion for some time since, that it was so all important to carry Penna."[32] One sure way to carry Pennsylvania was to have a Pennsylvanian on the ticket, and there was simply no one in the Keystone State with as much political clout and national prominence as Simon Cameron. In November 1859, Henry P. H. Bromwell, a lawyer in Charleston, Illinois, forwarded Lincoln a handbill that was in circulation calling for a Cameron/Lincoln ticket.[33] Former Iowa State House of Representatives member Hawkins Taylor also noted the sentiment for a Cameron/Lincoln ticket, noting that while he preferred Lincoln to all other presidential candidates, he was "willing to see Cameron & You the candidates."[34] Charles Leib, writing to Cameron in March 1860, informed the Pennsylvanian that Lincoln was in Chicago, claiming that he was "evidently anxious for the Vice Presidential nomination."[35]

Leib miscalculated; Lincoln was determined to have the presidential nomination or nothing.[36] When a supporter asked if

Lincoln would accept the vice presidential slot if it was offered, Lincoln responded simply and emphatically: "No!"[37] In February of 1860, Zaccheus Beatty, a delegate to the Illinois State Republican nominating convention, advised Lincoln, "If Mr. Cameron will be content with the Vice Presidency, many of your friends suppose there will be but little difficulty in forming a ticket— Lincoln and Cameron. Hurrah!"[38] A few days later, another supporter wrote to Lincoln and expressed his belief that "Cameron or Reed for Vice Pres & yourself would give [the ticket] certain success."[39] Another correspondent asserted, "I am now fully of the opinion that the Strongest ticket we can get is Abraham Lincoln for President and Simon Cameron for Vice P."[40] Thus, by the beginning of 1860, Lincoln's supporters seriously discussed adding Cameron to the ticket, clearly recognizing that it was essential to carry Pennsylvania and that Cameron was one of the few Republicans able to do that. Apparently, Cameron's supporters were open to this possibility as well. Three days before the Republican nominating convention opened in Chicago, Mark Delahay advised Lincoln that he had spoken with members of Cameron's delegation who were attempting to create a slate of delegates from Illinois, Pennsylvania, and New Jersey committed to a Lincoln/Cameron ticket. Delahay opposed this, fearing that "such a move would appear like a 'Slate' and Seward is too potent here to attempt such a meeting. His friends would probably Slate us, if it were done."[41]

Though the convention did not officially open until Wednesday, May 16, by Sunday, May 13, Chicago was abuzz with activity and political intrigue. The candidates' supporters came by the trainload, ready to convince wavering delegates that their man had the popularity to win. By a special arrangement with Thomas A. Scott of the Pennsylvania Railroad, nearly four hundred of Cameron's supporters and two large bands traveled by train to Chicago free of charge.[42] On the convention's second day, the delegates turned to crafting a platform. Having learned their lesson in 1856, the platform's framers substantially toned down the party's anti-slavery proposals. Pennsylvania and New Jersey's delegation zealously demanded a strong and unambiguous plank committing the party to protectionism. Given the party's recent vintage and diverse collection of individuals united mostly in their alienation from the Democrats over slavery, this issue threatened to split the convention. Eventually, the pro- and anti-protection forces developed a compromise plank that committed the party to "such an adjustment of those imposts as to encourage the development of the industrial interests of the whole country."[43] It was a hodgepodge platform that reflected the Republican Party's hodgepodge makeup.

On Friday the convention took up selecting its presidential nominee. When the convention opened, Seward had the most committed delegates, holding nearly one-third of the votes. To many observers, when the doors opened at ten o'clock that morning, the nomination was Seward's to lose. In fact, Seward's men were so confident of victory that they canvassed the other candidates' supporters for names of acceptable vice presidential candidates. Yet despite Seward's apparent strength, there was an undercurrent of discontent with the prospect of the New Yorker's nomination due to his radicalism on the slavery issue. In March, R. M. McAllister wrote to Cameron and asserted, "The Democrats are rejoicing in the prospect of Seward's nomination as they consider his defeat certain."[44] Following the convention, one prominent Pennsylvanian confided to Lincoln that he was relieved that Seward was not the nominee, describing the delegation's feeling as "All that we really asked, was not to be burthened by Seward."[45] Seward's campaign manager, newspaper editor Thurlow Weed, made a serious mistake in avoiding Cameron during the lead-up to the convention, apparently out of fear that the Pennsylvanian sought the promise of a cabinet seat in exchange for his support.[46] Thus, Seward was actually far weaker than many people assumed, particularly with the crucial delegation from Pennsylvania.

Lincoln's men were not above political trickery to secure the nomination: in the lead-up to Friday's nomination contest, David Davis (called by one historian a "calculating deal maker") ordered the printing of one thousand counterfeit convention tickets that he had surreptitiously distributed to Lincoln supporters.[47] Davis cleverly ensured that the Pennsylvania and New York delegations were separated by pro-Lincoln delegations, preventing Cameron and Seward's men from brokering a deal that might rob Lincoln of the nomination.[48] More important, and despite Lincoln's expressed preference that his lieutenants "make no contracts that will bind me," Davis promised cabinet positions and other appointments in exchange for delegates' votes. One such promise was made to journalist and former representative Caleb B. Smith, who later became Lincoln's secretary of the interior. Late Thursday night, Davis met with the Pennsylvania delegation at the Tremont Hotel and, around midnight, got a commitment that the delegates would vote for Lincoln on the second ballot in exchange for a cabinet position for Cameron.[49] Weed recounted Leonard Swett's version of these events in his autobiography: "The efforts of [Lincoln's] friends, therefore were directed to getting for Mr. Lincoln the strength of [Chase, Cameron, and Bates], after their personal hopes should be abandoned. Everybody who knows politicians knows that what they worship is the god of success. . . . In the small hours of Friday morning, in a room at the Tremont House, two of Mr. Lincoln's friends and two of Mr. Cameron's being present[,] . . . the Cameron men agreed to come to us on the second ballot. They did so right nobly and gave us forty-eight votes."[50] In a letter to Lincoln following the election, Leonard Swett confessed, "The truth is, at Chicago we thought the Cameron influence was the controlling element & tried to procure that rather than the factions."[51] Swett and Davis later repeated their pledges to Cameron at a meeting in July in Saratoga, New York, apparently promising him the Treasury Department.[52]

Thus, when balloting began at noon on Friday, there had been a tectonic shift in the convention's dynamics of which Seward's men were blissfully unaware. The first man nominated was Seward, followed by Lincoln; here, Davis's trick of packing the convention hall with supporters worked its magic as the crowd burst into sustained and raucous cheering for the man from Illinois. Next, it was William L. Dayton's turn to be nominated, followed by Cameron, then John McLean and Salmon P. Chase. Following the first vote, but before the totals were announced, Reeder again stood, this time to withdrawal Cameron's name from nomination. The senator's fight for the nomination was over, and his state was firmly in Lincoln's column. Yet despite Pennsylvania's migration into Lincoln's camp, Seward still held the lead. On the third ballot, an avalanche of support flowed Lincoln's way, pushing him into the lead. Lincoln was now two votes away from the nomination, when one of Ohio's delegates jumped up and announced that the delegation was changing four of its votes to Lincoln, giving him the nomination.[53]

Cameron's supporters' bargain with Lincoln's men became common knowledge almost immediately; on Saturday, at least one paper reported that Cameron's support had been traded for an assurance that Lincoln would appoint him secretary of the Treasury.[54] In a letter to Cameron, one supporter wrote, "The Chicago battle is over and although you have not turned out triumphant, you have not lost but gained ground. The Illinois delegation as well as most of the New England delegation give you the credit of making the nomination and you have only to [illegible] heartily in the support of Lincoln to insure you an exalted and enviable position with old Abe's administration either in the shape of influence for your friends, or office for yourself or both."[55]

Though such assurances were obviously contingent upon Lincoln winning the election, "Honest Abe's" prospects looked good. In May, delegates to the Democratic National Convention nominated Stephen Douglas for president. This, and the relatively moderate platform adopted by the delegates, enraged a sizable group of pro-slavery zealots, who bolted the convention. The Democrats held a second national convention six weeks later, during which Douglas was again nominated. Again a number of delegates left the convention, convening their own nearby, and nominating Vice President John C. Breckenridge. There were now *two* Democratic presidential candidates running (eventually a third entered the field), which split the party and all but guaranteed Lincoln's victory.

Leaving nothing to chance, Cameron zealously supported Lincoln's candidacy. Shortly after Lincoln's nomination, Cameron wrote a letter to Charles Leib pledging to give the nominee his "hearty support."[56] Speaking a few weeks after the convention, Cameron endorsed the nominations of Lincoln and Hannibal Hamlin "in a most cordial and emphatic manner."[57] In August, Cameron wrote to Lincoln promising to work so that "beyond the shadow of a doubt," Lincoln would win Pennsylvania. Cameron also boasted, "The state is for you and we all have faith in your good intentions to stand by her interests."[58] Cameron supported Lincoln's campaign financially as well, sending $800 to Lincoln's campaign manager, David Davis, and promising more money if necessary.

Pennsylvania's Republican apparatus was still in flux during the campaign, and the party chose to call itself the People's Party because many Pennsylvanians perceived the Republicans to be too radical on slavery. This was the message Lincoln received from Francis Blackburn, a Philadelphian who had attended the Chicago convention as a delegate and voted for Lincoln. Blackburn claimed, "The [People's] Party in Pennsylvanian are thoroughly <u>Anti</u> Abolitionists and it is with difficulty that we can keep them solid with the <u>Republican</u> Party, [the People's Party] are Anti-Slavery, but are desirous of showing the South that while opposed to its Extension they will respect the rights of the slave holding States."[59] Consequently, Lincoln's campaign in Pennsylvania emphasized that he was no "ultra"—in this case meaning abolitionist—but rather a "conservative" on slavery. This meant that, while he may not have personally approved of slavery, he had no plans to do anything about it in the states where it already existed, a position identical to Cameron's.

As always, the tariff remained the most important issue in Pennsylvania.[60] Pennsylvanians had successfully demanded a pro-tariff plank at the Republican convention, much to Lincoln's distress, because he feared it would lose him votes in other regions of the country. However, a pro-tariff platform was the only way to win Pennsylvania. A reporter in Harrisburg suggested as much when he wrote in September 1859, "The opposition [anti-Democratic] politicians here say you may cry 'nigger, nigger,' as much as you please, only give us a chance to carry Pennsylvania by crying 'tariff.' Without this you can not elect your *President*."[61] No one better understood the importance of the tariff to electoral success in Pennsylvania than Simon Cameron, who in a speech before the Senate earlier that year called the tariff question "our 'nigger.'"[62] In August, David Davis toured Pennsylvania and met with Cameron. Describing the meeting to Lincoln, Davis noted that Cameron was "exceedingly anxious to have [Lincoln's] views on the tariff, & that he wanted them to assure the people of the State that they were Satisfactory to him [Cameron]."[63] By way of a response, the following day Lincoln forwarded scraps of a speech on the tariff he had written in the late 1840s. In the accompanying letter, Lincoln enjoined Cameron that "nothing about [the speech] must get into the newspapers," fearing that if it did he would lose the support of low-tariff voters in other regions.[64]

Though he campaigned vigorously for Lincoln, and despite presidential secretary John Hay's later assertion that "there has never been the slightest unkindness or distrust between [Cameron] and the President," Lincoln and Cameron had a complex relationship.[65] Over the course of their correspondence, the ever-genial Cameron was friendly and even a little casual with Lincoln. In one exchange, he forwarded the president-elect a number of letters from office seekers, facetiously noting, "As you have not many letters to read, these may help to pass the time."[66] Lincoln's reaction to Cameron was, by contrast, more complicated. On the one hand, Lincoln seems to have liked Cameron's soft-spoken amiability. The president-elect was, as he was with almost everyone, usually polite both in person and when he corresponded with Cameron. However, Lincoln was also close to Pennsylvania governor Andrew G. Curtin, and he seems to have resented the fact that Cameron was "forced" on him. Consequently, Lincoln frequently said or did things seemingly designed to antagonize and embarrass Cameron. At one point, Pennsylvania congressman Thaddeus Stevens, Cameron's sometime political opponent, allegedly responded to Lincoln's question regarding Cameron's honesty by saying, "I don't think he would steal a red hot stove." Later, Lincoln tactlessly repeated this remark to Cameron. Cameron, not surprisingly, was not amused by Stevens's remark, and demanded that the congressman retract it. When he next saw the president, Stevens asked why Lincoln had repeated the remark to Cameron. The president said he thought it was a good joke and did not expect it to anger Cameron. Stevens reported that the remark had offended Cameron and that the congressman had promised a retraction, saying, "I apologize. I said Cameron would not steal a red hot stove. I withdraw that statement," which only further delighted Lincoln.[67] During the crisis over Cameron's appointment, which Lincoln perpetuated through his vacillation, the president-elect seems to have thought the discomfort he caused Cameron was good sport; journalist Henry Villard, who had tremendous access to the president-elect, noted "that [Lincoln] laughed over [Cameron's discomfiture] until the tears coursed down his face."[68] In later years Cameron drew a stark contrast between Ulysses S. Grant and Lincoln, which gives some impression of his feelings toward the sixteenth president. According to Cameron, Grant was a man "of simple honesty—not cunning like . . . Lincoln."[69]

Nor was Lincoln the only strange bedfellow for Cameron during the 1860 campaign. The Pennsylvanian donated $800 of his own money to Lyman Trumbull's reelection campaign, despite the fact they disliked each other; Trumbull later repaid the favor by aggressively opposing the Pennsylvanian's appointment to Lincoln's cabinet.[70] Cameron even promoted Andrew

Curtin's gubernatorial candidacy, at least publicly.[71] In late July, Cameron gave a speech in Philadelphia in which he declared, "I see you have placed on your banners the names of Lincoln, Hamlin, and Curtin. That is all very well. Lincoln's name should be first, as it is national and perhaps most important, but the position and policy of our own State is hardly of secondary importance, and therefore I want to turn your attention to the election of Col. Curtin first, not only because of its great value to ourselves, because if that be secured the rest is surely to follow."[72] Cameron's support for Curtin had its limits; privately, he confided to John Z. Goodrich that he "would have preferred some other candidate to Mr. Curtin for Governor. But from the first he told me [Curtin] must and should be elected; that his election was too important in its influence upon the Presidential election to be hazarded, & it should not be." Based on Cameron's efforts, Goodrich concluded that "no man's influence was more potent in securing a Republican victory at the Penn. Election in Oct. than his.[73] In June, Curtin's close political ally McClure wrote to Cameron, assuring him that his record in the Senate over the past three years "should obliterate all political hostility to you in our ranks. I have so felt & acted and shall continue to do so."[74]

McClure was just being polite; in reality, old antagonisms had not disappeared. In a June 1860 letter to Lincoln, James E. Harvey confided, "Let me say just here, there is a rivalry springing up between [Cameron] & Curtin, our Candidate for Governor, which you would do well to ignore entirely. It will be bad enough by & by when we win."[75] There were at least two factions struggling for control of the state party—Cameron's and Curtin's—and the battle seems to have been waged over campaign tactics. Cameron resented the fact that McClure was chairman of the state party committee, and his supporters in Philadelphia complained that McClure was misusing campaign funds. McClure himself later admitted that he was unable to raise enough money for the campaign, though he blamed this on New York governor Edwin D. Morgan, who was then serving as chairman of the national committee.[76] One supporter claimed in a letter to Cameron that "unless McClure is forced out [of the campaign] . . . Curtin cannot be elected. In Phila, where he was strong, the feeling is very bitter and it all grows out of this McClure matter."[77] In an attempt to find a solution, most of the state party's central committee met in Cresson, Pennsylvania, in mid-July. Fearing his position would be undermined by Cameron's supporters, McClure arranged for a lavish feast the night before the meeting, complete with copious amounts of alcohol. As expected, when McClure called the meeting to order the following morning, most of Cameron's men were still in bed or nursing hangovers and therefore absent. The meeting was quickly adjourned and, because only the chairman (i.e., McClure) had the authority to convene meetings, it was the last one.

Cameron and his supporters responded to McClure's maneuvers at Cresson by creating their own committee, ostensibly for fundraising and supposedly ancillary to the state committee. McClure's supporters claimed that this move proved that Cameron's men were trying to engineer a coup, while Cameron's men claimed they were simply trying to overcome McClure's general incompetence when it came to fundraising and organization.[78] McClure's supporters retaliated by circulating a rumor that Cameron's fundraising committee was an attempt to "hedge their bets" and support one of the Democratic candidates. After speaking with Cameron's supporters, Davis learned that the fundraising committee was nothing of the kind; it merely reflected "a want of confidence in the pecuniary honesty of the head of the regular committee [McClure]."[79] In short, while the party presented a unified face to the voting public, in reality it was deeply divided by personal antagonisms, some of which went back years. Though the various factions were able to come together to elect both a governor and a president, the persistent factionalism had a profound effect on Pennsylvania's role in the first year of the Civil War.

Despite these political intrigues, Curtin was elected governor in October 1860. In recognition of Cameron's efforts on behalf of his candidacy, Curtin reluctantly appointed one of the Senator's cronies, former congressman Samuel Purviance, attorney general. Meanwhile, President Buchanan did everything possible to ensure Douglas's defeat in 1860. More than eight in ten eligible voters cast ballots that year, but Lincoln managed to garner only 39.7 percent of the popular vote. His three rivals split the other 60.1 percent, with Douglas garnering 29.5 percent, Breckenridge winning 18.2 percent, and Bell capturing 12.6 percent. And for the first time in U.S. history, a president was elected without a single electoral vote from the South. Lincoln won 54 percent of the popular vote in the North, but only 2 percent in the South, a signal of just how fragmented the country had become.[80]

Once he won the election, Lincoln turned to the difficult but important task of doling out the spoils. In this case it was especially important, providing a much-needed adhesive for binding the new party together.[81] In order to cement their control over the state party, Cameron's political enemies sought to undermine his standing with Lincoln and thereby deprive the Pennsylvanian of a cabinet position. Though previous historians have spent a great deal of energy exploring the controversy surrounding Cameron's appointment as a way of implying he was unqualified for the job, it is important to note that his was not an isolated case. Seward's enemies (including Salmon P. Chase, soon to go into the cabinet as secretary of the Treasury), vociferously attacked the prospect of *his* entering the cabinet, and denounced him in terms not dissimilar to those used to smear Cameron. To take both Seward *and* Cameron into the cabinet would have aroused Chase's faction of the party due to the two senators' close political alliance. In fact, Chase's wrote to Lincoln and vilified Cameron not because they objected to the Pennsylvanian, but because they wanted to ensure that Chase's influence was not checked by the combined efforts of Seward and Cameron.[82]

Given this state of affairs, it is understandable that Lincoln hesitated to appoint Cameron to the cabinet. Former congress-man George N. Eckert, who served in Congress with Lincoln, wrote a scathing letter to his former colleague in which he said, "I wish to say to you that under no circumstances or contingency will it answer to even dream of putting Simon Cameron in the Cabinet. He is corrupt beyond belief. He is rich by plunder—and can not be trusted any where."[83] In their campaign to dis-suade Lincoln from offering Cameron a place in the cabinet, the Pennsylvanian's enemies even resurrected the Winnebago controversy. Lincoln's friend James Churchman, who claimed to have been in Prairie du Chien in 1838, told the president-elect, "From watching the whole proceeding, I left with the strong impression, never since erased, that Cameron was a dis-honest man."[84] Newspaper editor Joseph J. Lewis wrote to Lin-coln and conceded, "I do not verify the charge [that Cameron bribed Pennsylvania senators to vote for his election to the U.S. Senate in 1854] for I have no personal knowledge on the sub-ject; but I trust it is enough for you to know that his character is subject to the most serious suspicions of the want of politi-cal integrity."[85] It is important to note that, in both cases, these critics reference Cameron's *reputation* for corruption, rather than any proof, as evidence that the Pennsylvanian was not fit for a cabinet position.

Cameron's supporters responded to these attacks by flooding Lincoln and his associates with letters demanding Cameron's nomination. One historian has called the barrage of letters on Cameron's behalf a "grist" that included support from impor-tant Pennsylvania Republicans like David Wilmot, the recently converted John W. Forney, and state senator John P. Sander-son. Cameron's supporters pulled no punches, bluntly remind-ing Lincoln's people of the commitments they had made on their man's behalf. A Cameron delegate named Joseph Casey reached out to Leonard Swett to remind the Lincoln man of the agreement that had been struck in Chicago. Casey was con-cerned that Lincoln not renege on the bargain Swett and Davis struck with Cameron's men at the convention.

From some things that occurred when I was at Springfield, my mind has since been in doubt, as to whether Mr. Lincoln has been made <u>fully acquainted</u> with the conversations and understandings between you & Judge Davis on the one side, & myself, on the other, at the Tremont House, the night before the nomination. That understanding of course, I was compelled to communicate to a few of Genl. Cameron's most intimate and confidential friends, in order to counteract other schemes, and overcome other inducements, proceeding from different quarters. Should the assurances I then gave fail to be realized I should be utterly ruined, in the estimation of many of my most valuable friends. As some of them would probably prefer to believe that I had deceived them, instead of being disappointed in my own expectations. Feeling, as you may suppose, a nervous anxiety on this matter, I submit it, to the better judgment of yourself and Judge Davis, whether it would not be better, that Mr. L is he is not now, should be in possession of the whole matter before he finally acts in the premises.[86]

Former Pennsylvania governor James Pollock wrote to the president-elect and recommended Cameron on the grounds that the Pennsylvanian "would be a safe counselor—conservative—National & true to all the great interests of the Country."[87] Behind the scenes, Swett pushed the president-elect to honor the promises made to Cameron in Lincoln's name at Chicago, especially after news of Seward's appointment to the State Department became public.

On December 30, Cameron traveled to Springfield and met with Lincoln and Edward Bates, whom the president-elect had invited to the meeting. Years later, Cameron recalled:

After the election, I made a trip to the West at Mr. Lincoln's request. . . . When I went to see him he said that he had concluded to make Mr. Seward Secretary of State and he wanted to give a place to Mr. [Salmon] Chase. 'Salmon Chase,' said he, 'is a very ambitious man.' 'Very well,' said I, 'then the War Department is the place for him. We are going to have armed conflict over your election, and the place for an ambitious man is in the War Department. There he will have lots of room to make a reputation. These thoughts of mine, that we were to have war, disturbed Mr. Lincoln very much, and finally he seemed to think I was entirely too certain about it.[88]

Cameron's words must have made an impact on Lincoln: before Cameron left Springfield, Lincoln gave the Pennsylvanian a letter offering appointment to either the War or Treasury departments.

The day after Cameron departed, McClure and Curtin arrived in Springfield to dissuade Lincoln from taking the senator into the cabinet. Except for McClure's recollections, no record of this meeting exists, but apparently, Lincoln demanded proof of Cameron's corruption. McClure later claimed that he handed over evidence so compelling that it "took Lincoln's breath away."[89] No one knows what McClure showed the president-elect, and we have only McClure's recollection of this story, but the following day, Lincoln sent Cameron a terse letter withdrawing the offer of a cabinet appointment. Lincoln wrote,

> Since seeing you things have developed which make it impossible for me to take you into the cabinet. You will say this comes of an interview with McClure; and this is partly, but not wholly ~~true~~ true—The more potent matter is wholly outside of Pennsylvania; and yet I am not at liberty to specify it. . . . And now, I suggest that you write me declining the appointment, in which case I do not object to its being known that it was tendered you. Better do this at once, before things so change, that you can not honorably decline, and I be compelled to openly recall the tender. No person living knows, or has an intimation that I write this letter. . . . P. S. Telegraph me instantly, on receipt of this, saying "All right."[90]

Almost immediately, McClure added insult to injury by gleefully spreading the news that Cameron would not be going into Lincoln's cabinet.

In reality, Lincoln's decision was far from final. On January 7

Lincoln wrote to Senator Lyman Trumbull and confided, "Gen. Cameron has not been offered the Treasury and I think will not be. It seems to me not only highly proper but a *necessity* that Gov. Chase shall take that place. . . . But then comes the danger that the protectionists of Pennsylvania will be dissatisfied; and to clear this difficulty, Gen. C. must be brought to cooperate. He would readily do this for the War Department."[91] In addition, news reached Lincoln that his friend and campaign manager David Davis was "quite huffy" over Lincoln's behavior, undoubtedly because he felt the president-elect's failure to honor promises made in his name reflected poorly on Davis.[92]

Lincoln's abrupt withdrawal of the appointment caught Cameron by surprise and angered him. Cameron never responded to Lincoln's request, but on January 8 he met with Leonard Swett and complained at length about Lincoln's letter. As Swett, who was sympathetic to the Pennsylvanian's position, told the story in a letter to Lincoln, Cameron complained "he has been badly treated [and] says he only consented to take the place to please his friends. He complains of the form of your letter. He thinks it contains an imputation upon his character and mortifies him."[93] After a long talk, Swett and Cameron apparently agreed that the Pennsylvanian would let it be known that he no longer wished to go into the cabinet, as Lincoln had suggested in his letter of January 3.

Instead of following up on his conversation with Swett, Cameron went about his business as if nothing was amiss. Lincoln's friend Swett reported to the president-elect that both Cameron and Seward, though not yet appointed, were doing their utmost to smooth the new administration's path.[94] For instance, because Lincoln had asked Cameron to investigate precautionary measures to prevent violence at the inaugural, the Pennsylvanian journeyed to Washington.[95] Cameron met with General Winfield Scott, the Commanding General of the United States Army to examine preparations for the inauguration and assess Scott's loyalty to the Union. In a letter to Lincoln, Cameron cheerfully reported that the general said "he will be glad to act under your orders, in all ways to preserve the Union," and that President Buchanan ordered Scott to preserve order during the inauguration. Cameron shared his impression of the situation in the capital. "Our friends are hopeful, but there is much trouble and some danger. . . . You will, I am sure, be satisfied that your friends are doing good service."[96] The senator even arranged for the Pennsylvania Railroad's "Director's Car" to be made available to the president-elect, free of charge, for Lincoln's trip from Springfield to Washington for the inauguration.[97]

While Cameron chose to pretend nothing was amiss, behind the scenes Cameron's friends made it clear to Lincoln how angry the Pennsylvanian was at the president-elect's about-face. Former congressman Joseph Casey wrote to Cameron in mid-January and informed Cameron that he was actively stirring up antagonism toward Lincoln among influential Republicans about the tone of Lincoln's withdrawal of the cabinet nomination.[98] Meeting with Lincoln on January 12, John P. Sanderson and Edgar Cowan (whose election to the Senate Cameron had helped engineer) conveyed Cameron's disappointment with Lincoln's actions and asked the president-elect to draft a new letter that to the Pennsylvanian that put the withdrawal in a more favorable light. On January 13 Lincoln did this, writing, "I learn . . . that your feelings were wounded by the terms of my letter. . . . I wrote that letter under great anxiety. . . . I intended no offense. My greatest object was to have you act quickly. . . . I say to you now that I know you would perform the duties of a Department ably and faithfully."[99]

If Lincoln thought his letter to Cameron would salve the Pennsylvanian's wounded pride, he was wrong; according to Thaddeus Stevens, in mid-January, Cameron said "that no earthly contingency could induce him to go into Mr. Lincoln's cabinet," apparently because the Pennsylvanian was offended by the tactless way in which the president-elect had behaved.[100] Worse, according to Seward, Cameron now demanded that Lincoln appoint no one from Pennsylvania or New Jersey and demanded that the president-elect "put before the public . . .

some explanation . . . [that would place him] in a position as strong as he was before he was invited to go to Springfield."[101] On January 21, Lincoln again met with Cameron's supporters, this time Pennsylvania Representative James K. Moorhead and *Philadelphia Evening Bulletin* founder Alexander Cummings. They vigorously pressed Lincoln to appoint Cameron to the cabinet, and managed to extract a letter from the president-elect to the senator and an invitation for Cameron to visit Lincoln in Springfield. Six days later, Moorhead returned the letter unopened and relayed Cameron's refusal to go to Springfield.

At this point Lincoln appears to have been vacillating about Cameron's appointment, and he was still not committed either way while en route to his inauguration in Washington DC. In Pittsburgh the president-elect was buttonholed by a group of Cameron supporters who pressed the Pennsylvanian's claims to a cabinet appointment. Writing afterward to Cameron, one supporter noted, "I am happy to say to you that your friends are much encouraged with the prospect that you go into the Cabinet," but he warned "it is important that many of your friends see the President at Harrisburg on the 22d. inst. By all means let this not be neglected, you should be there yourself."[102] When Lincoln stopped in Philadelphia, a delegation of Curtin's supporters met the president-elect and announced that the governor-elect had dropped his opposition to Cameron's going into the cabinet, removing one of the last remaining roadblocks to the Pennsylvanian's nomination.[103] Yet even then the situation remained fluid; as late as two weeks before the inaugural, Seward confessed to friends that his own place in the cabinet, let alone Cameron's, was not yet secured.[104]

However, Cameron's prospects had certainly improved over the preceding three weeks. By February 2, Thaddeus Stevens wrote to McClure, claiming, "Cameron himself asserts with entire confidence to his friends that he will be in the cabinet." Upon reaching Washington, Lincoln was surprised to receive word that some of Cameron's most ardent opponents, including Curtin, wished to rescind their earlier letters in opposition to the senator's appointment. On the evening of February 27, Lincoln and Cameron again met to discuss the Pennsylvanian's place in the cabinet. Lincoln told Cameron he could not have the Treasury Department and instead offered him the Department of the Interior, which the senator declined. Cameron recalled that the meeting became heated, mostly because he was angry about Lincoln's behavior since the election. "At Washington had a talk with him he asked me what I wanted—told him I didn't want anything. He might take the offices and keep them. I spoke pretty sharp. He offered to make me Atty. Genl. Or give me the Interior. I told him I was no lawyer; I didn't want anything if he couldn't give me what he had offered."[105] When he and Lincoln met again on March 1, just three days before Lincoln's inauguration, the president-elect again offered Cameron the War Department, saying that he had decided to appoint Chase to the Treasury. Initially, Cameron rejected the offer but, later that day, he returned to Lincoln's hotel suite and accepted the nomination.[106]

Cameron's decision to accept the War Department was momentous because it would place him squarely at the center of the war he saw coming. Ironically, the political skills that had secured for him a place in the cabinet—a large political following based on personal attachment and judicious distribution of patronage—worked against him as secretary of war. In accepting Lincoln's offer, Cameron embraced a job for which he was temperamentally unsuited. Though never as incompetent or as corrupt as his critics (and historians) maintained, it is nonetheless true Cameron was far from effective. Yet Cameron both laid the groundwork for later military success and pushed the administration to make the destruction of slavery a war aim, both of which contributed to the government's ultimate victory.

6

"Then Profit Shall Accrue," 1861–62

The new war secretary faced daunting and unprecedented challenges when he took office in March 1861: Cameron had to navigate the contradictory demands of an administration that desired peace but had to plan for war and he had to balance the often incompatible desires of cabinet members, the military, Northern state and border state governors, and the president. His failure to meet these challenges has been vastly overstated by historians; when he left the War Department in January 1862, it and the army were better organized and provisioned than a year before.

The Senate approved Lincoln's cabinet nominations on March 5, and a week later Cameron was sworn into office by his old friend Supreme Court Justice Robert C. Grier at the War Department.[1] The reason for the delay was that Cameron was in Pennsylvania, a fact that some historians cite as evidence that the new war secretary did not take his position seriously, especially given the worsening situation in South Carolina, where Confederate forces were preventing the government from reinforcing or resupplying U.S. troops at Fort Sumter. But if Cameron failed to take the deteriorating situation in Charleston seriously, he was not the only one: when the cabinet convened for its first meeting on March 6, Lincoln did not mention what he knew about Fort Sumter's rapidly worsening condition. Though the president invited senior military personnel to brief the cabinet, Navy Secretary Gideon Welles described the meeting itself as "uninteresting," implying that the cabinet discussed nothing of substance.[2] Clearly, if Cameron was not taking the conflict seriously, neither was Lincoln.

In fact, it was not until the evening of March 9 that Lincoln shared the truth about Sumter with the cabinet. Cameron did not attend this meeting because he was in Harrisburg, but he soon made his way to Washington. On March 15 Lincoln asked the cabinet if he should provision Sumter. Cameron attended this meeting and opposed provisioning the fort out of fear that doing so would provoke a wider confrontation. The secretary of war asserted that even if Sumter could be successfully provisioned, it could not be held indefinitely, so he reasoned it was better to abandon it now than abandon it later. The following day he presented his recommendations in writing, arguing that while it may have once been possible to resupply the fort, "it would be unwise to now make such an attempt," an impression "greatly influenced by the opinions of the Army officers who have expressed themselves on the subject."[3]

The confrontation over Sumter electrified the country. On Monday, March 18, Cameron ate dinner with a number of senators and prominent Republicans. When discussion turned to Sumter, Cameron claimed to be ignorant of Lincoln's plan, though at least one attendant thought the secretary was lying. Things were moving very quickly, and on Thursday, March 28, Senator Lyman Trumbull offered a resolution that asserted "that it is the duty of the President of the United States to use all the means in his power to hold and protect the public property of the United States and to enforce the laws thereof."[4] That night, following Lincoln's first state dinner, the president told the cabinet that Scott advocated evacuating Sumter. The cabinet, perhaps recognizing that congressional Republicans demanded action, condemned Scott's advice.[5] On Friday, March 29, Lincoln convened the cabinet at noon, though Cameron did not attend. The following day, Lincoln wrote a note to Cameron ordering the secretary to ready an expedition to resupply Sumter that could sail by April 6. A few days later, Lincoln was shocked when he read a letter from Fort Sumter's commander, Major Robert Anderson. According to Anderson, even with "sharp economy," Sumter's commander estimated he could hold out only a week. Lincoln instructed Cameron to order Major Anderson to hold out as long as possible and to inform Sumter's commander that a resupply expedition would be sent immediately.[6]

Meanwhile, at Lincoln's instruction, Cameron dispatched State Department clerk Robert S. Chew to meet with South Carolina governor Frederick W. Pickens and pass along the message that the federal government intended to supply Sumter with food but not additional men, weapons, or ammunition. Chew met with Governor Pickens and the commander of Confederate military operations in the area, General P. G. T. Beauregard. Chew passed along Cameron's message to both men and left soon after.[7] On April 11, Beauregard demanded that Anderson surrender the fort. Anderson refused, so the following day Confederate batteries began a heavy bombardment of the fort that lasted thirty-four hours. Finally, on April 13, Anderson surrendered and evacuated Fort Sumter. Less than twenty-four hours later, Lincoln's cabinet met to develop a plan for dealing with the crisis. Cameron offered an elaborate strategy based on the British approach to subduing the colonies during the American War for Independence. Under Cameron's plan, the first step was to fortify and protect the capital so as to use it as a supply base for future operations. Next, Cameron argued that the government had to retake Sumter because failure to do so would send the message that "we are not a Government." The third step was to occupy major ports like Charleston and New Orleans, thus preventing Southern states from exporting cotton or importing necessities. Having accomplished all this, Cameron argued that the president should then simply let the Confederacy suffocate.[8] No one in the cabinet seems to have supported the plan; its scope rendered it impracticable and it could take months or even years for the Confederacy to crumble.

Though opposed to Cameron's plan, the cabinet reached no consensus about what the next steps should be, so it met the next day for a marathon session that stretched from late morning into the early evening. Despite Seward's desire for a nonconfrontational solution, Lincoln called up seventy-five thousand members of state militias for three months' service. The president also called Congress back into session, asking members to convene on July 4. Almost immediately, Cameron telegraphed governors their recruitment quotas, usually calling for one regiment (composed of 37 officers and 743 men). Larger states like Ohio, Pennsylvania, and New York were asked to send thirteen, sixteen, and seventeen regiments, respectively.[9] Though several Southern states refused to send troops, Northern state governors responded enthusiastically, with most offering more men than their states' quotas mandated, and often more than they could clothe or provision. Pennsylvania sent five companies of militia armed with a grand total of thirty-four muskets and no ammunition.[10] While Seward and other cabinet members believed the conflict would be over quickly, Cameron predicted that it would be long and protracted. Cameron was in the minority, and most of his colleagues—Lincoln included—dismissed the secretary of war's predictions as alarmist and overly pessimistic.[11] Cameron, who was later criticized for the decision to call up only seventy-five thousand men, claimed after leaving the War Department that he pushed the president to ask for five hundred thousand, but he was overruled. Nevertheless, the new secretary of war intended to defeat the secessionists, a point he made clear a few weeks later when, during a social call, one of his acquaintances ridiculed the idea that Northerners would actually fight because Yankees "always made [war] pay or left it alone." Cameron's response was simple and unequivocal: "Then profit shall accrue."[12]

Alarmingly, Washington DC itself seemed threatened: Virginia seceded on April 17, and the following day, secessionists burned the federal arsenal at Harper's Ferry. Three days later, the Union Navy yard at Gasport, Virginia, went up in flames. Perhaps most concerning was the riot that broke out in Baltimore on April 19. Baltimore was not only a violently pro-Southern city (Lincoln had received fewer than one in twenty Baltimoreans' votes), it was also home to a large free black population, which exacerbated racial tensions. When the war broke out, pro- and anti-secession whites organized forces called "National Volunteers" and "Minute Men," respectively, and Governor Thomas H. Hicks refused the War Department's request for troops.

Because Baltimore was a major railroad hub, recruits headed to Washington had to pass through the city. On Thursday, April 18, nearly five hundred Pennsylvania volunteers arrived in Baltimore via the Northern Central Railroad and marched toward Fort McHenry. In response, several hundred "National Volunteers" mobilized to confront the Pennsylvanians, stoning the soldiers and injuring at least one man, a black recruit named Nick Biddle. The city's police only narrowly prevented a larger riot. Things did not go as well the next day when the Sixth Massachusetts Militia arrived at the city's President Street Station. Originally the plan was to decouple the train cars, hitch them to horses, and pull them through the city to Camden Station to continue the journey to Washington. Pro-secession mobs blocked the transfer by dumping sand and anchors on the tracks, preventing the Massachusetts troops from transferring to the Camden Station. In an attempt to get across the city, the soldiers detrained and marched toward Camden Station. They were quickly surrounded by a mob and attacked with bricks, stones, and pistols. The troops fired into the mob, igniting a riot. Before it was over, four soldiers had been killed and three dozen more were injured, with even more civilians killed or injured. Once the troops arrived in Washington, Lincoln and Cameron went out to greet them, and the president thanked the men for their "promptitude."[13]

Shortly after the riot, the governor of Maryland and the mayor of Baltimore telegraphed both the Baltimore & Ohio (B&O)

and the Northern Central and asked the railroads to stop any troop trains en route to Washington. The normally soft-spoken war secretary exploded and promised to "hang [the mayor] and his whole posse upon the trees around the War Department."[14] Cameron denied their requests, saying that neither the mayor nor the governor had the power to divert federal troops, and he ordered the troops to fight their way through the city if necessary.[15] That evening, a group of Baltimore's city officials, who expected more federal troops to arrive in the city at any time, met with Maryland governor Hicks and persuaded him to let them burn the bridges leading into the city, causing more than $100,000 in damage.[16] State militia and police forces, under the command of Police Marshal George P. Kane and former U.S. Army Lieutenant Isaac R. Trimble, managed to destroy at least four bridges. Fearing more violence, Baltimore mayor George William Brown and a small contingent of city leaders (Lincoln's personal secretary called them "the whining traitors from Baltimore") met with the president and, after an impassioned plea from B&O president Garrett, Lincoln countermanded Cameron's orders, instructing that troops in Cockeysville, Maryland, return to Harrisburg and then travel to Washington via a route outside Maryland.[17] Cameron vigorously disagreed with this move and told Pennsylvania Railroad (PRR) president J. Edgar Thomson that Lincoln's order was "one of the most painful acts I have witnessed."[18]

Given the upheaval in Baltimore, it was imperative to devise alternative transportation between the capital and the Northern states. Pennsylvania governor Curtin, Cameron, Thomson, and the leadership of other local railroads agreed that the best way to connect the capital to the Northern states was to run trains to Perryville and then use ferries to get to Annapolis; though this was more expensive and time-consuming, it had the advantage of bypassing Baltimore entirely. This was only a temporary expedient; long-term, the federal government needed to find a dependable railroad connection between the north and the capital, so Major General Robert Pattison, then commanding the Department of Washington, ordered Brigadier General Benjamin F. Butler to create a path from Annapolis to Washington. Upon arriving at Annapolis, Butler found the railroad tracks had been torn up for several miles, making it impossible to commute further. Out of necessity, on April 23 Butler seized a subsidiary of the B&O, the Annapolis & Elk Ridge, and began repairs so that it could be used to transport troops and supplies, a move he made without authorization. Four days later, Thomas Scott took over the work, eventually opening a rail route from Annapolis to Washington.[19]

As far as Cameron was concerned, the best and most reliable line to the capital was the Northern Central, so he dispatched to Harrisburg the new assistant adjutant general of the army, Major Fitz-John Porter, with a mandate to muster Pennsylvania militiamen into federal service and use them to protect the railroad. Porter arrived in Harrisburg on April 19 and immediately met with Governor Curtin, Thomas A. Scott of the PRR, and Cameron's son J. Donald, representing the Northern Central. The following day, the First, Second, and Third Regiments of Pennsylvania volunteers were dispatched via the Northern Central toward Washington. However, they got only as far as Cockeysville, Maryland, because of the destroyed railroad bridges. On April 21 Winfield Scott ordered Porter to return the men to Harrisburg, and the following day the secretary of war authorized troops to protect the Northern Central and the Philadelphia, Wilmington & Baltimore (PW&B). Soon a small army of Pennsylvania carpenters had begun repairing the Northern Central's damaged bridges under protection of Pennsylvania troops.[20] By early summer, all U.S. troops moving from New York to Baltimore were routed through Harrisburg via the Northern Central, which cut transit costs by one-third. While Cameron was quick to note this saved the federal government money, it nonetheless *looked* like war profiteering, boosting the Northern Central's profits by more than 40 percent.[21]

Naturally, the Northern Central's competitors were quick to criticize what they saw as discrimination. Samuel M. Felton, president of the PW&B, proved the loudest critic of this policy. The PW&B, in conjunction with the Camden & Amboy, had a much shorter route between Pennsylvania and Baltimore than did the Northern Central, which ran from Harrisburg to Baltimore. The major upside of the Northern Central from the War Department's perspective was that it was a continuous route, whereas troops or supplies would need to be transferred to two ferries on the PW&B and the Camden & Amboy. Eventually, the War Department relented and began using the PW&B. By contrast, no government freight was shipped over the B&O during Cameron's tenure as secretary. In 1859 B&O president Garrett had called the railroad a "southern line" and had threatened that in case of conflict between the states it would "prove the great bulwark of the borders, and a sure agency for home defense."[22] More damning, on April 15 Ohio governor William Dennison Jr. arranged to send eight hundred militiamen via the B&O to Washington in response to Lincoln's call for seventy-five thousand troops. Two days later, however, the flood of troops from the Northeast that descended on Baltimore taxed the B&O's capacity to its limit, and Garrett was forced to tell Dennison he would be unable to transport the Ohio men. Dennison distrusted Garrett's motives, and informed the War Department that the railroad had refused to carry troops.[23] Though B&O officials later claimed that they had not been disloyal, and therefore deserved government transportation contracts, Cameron refused, citing Dennison's telegram.

Cameron used his authority as secretary of war to establish a rate schedule for transportation that had largely been dictated by a convention of railroad company executives who met in Harrisburg in July.[24] Though Cameron later claimed that the War Department's circular only established *maximum* rates that quartermasters were authorized the pay, nothing in the circular indicated that. It is undeniable that the war benefited the Northern Central and devastated the B&O, though, as historian Brooks M. Kelley has noted, the Northern Central made more money from government contracts in the years *after* Cameron left the War Department, implying that the war secretary cared less about profiteering than about ensuring the smooth and timely movement of men and material.[25] Cameron later claimed that much of the charges of corruption against him came from men who were hurt economically by these moves.[26] Nevertheless, it is true that Cameron offered Lincoln the chance to buy Northern Central stock, which, the war secretary assured the president, "would make him all the money he ever wanted." Much to Cameron's shock, Lincoln declined.[27]

One of the most serious challenges facing Cameron was the abysmal state of America's military, which historian Allan Nevins described as "hardly strong enough to deal with a sizable Indian [uprising]."[28] As of Lincoln's inauguration, the U.S. Army numbered approximately sixteen thousand men, many of which were in the West fighting Native Americans. The army was stretched so thin that there were only about fifty soldiers in Washington at the time, and most of them were senior officers, not combat troops.[29] Following Lincoln's inauguration, more than a dozen forts in Texas surrendered to the Confederacy, while the state of Louisiana gave the rebels $500,000 held at the mint in New Orleans. On July 1 Cameron described the situation: "Government arsenals [including] . . . the ordinance depot at San Antonio and other Government works in Texas, which served as the depots of immense stores of arms and ammunition, have been surrendered by commanders or seized by disloyal hands. [Forts] have been successively stolen from the Government or betrayed by their commanding officers [and] customs houses . . . containing vast amounts of Government funds, have been treacherously appropriated to sustain the cause of rebellion. In like manner [several] branch mints have been illegally seized, in defiance of every principle of common honesty and of honor."[30]

In addition, almost one-third of the army's officers defected to the Confederacy.[31] Cameron took the officers' resignations personally, wondering if there was some "radical defect" in the education at West Point that could explain what he called this "extraordinary treachery."[32] For their part, the regular army officials reciprocated Cameron's antipathy, as Lincoln's Register of the Treasury Lucius E. Chittenden noted in his *Recollections of President Lincoln and His Administration*. According to Chittenden, Cameron and his clerks encountered "one obstruction which [they] could not overcome. It was the contempt of the officers of the regular army for the appointments from civil life. At that time every head of a bureau in the War Office was an officer of the regular army, with a very limited experience in the field. They sincerely believed that all good things came out of West Point, and that four years there, followed by twenty-five years of theoretical service in the army, were the indispensible qualifications of a bureau officer. These men never openly opposed efforts at improvement. . . . But, somehow, it always happened that when it was proposed to carry a new rule into practice . . . it could not be done."[33]

Worse was the War Department's confused chain of command: Cameron shared power with the general of the army (then Winfield Scott), a vague position whose relationship to the secretary of war was poorly defined.[34] Chase this as one of the key reasons for the military setbacks early in the war, saying, "Gen. Scott gives an order, Mr. Cameron gives another. Half of both are executed, neutralizing each other."[35] Add to that the "bungling and contradictory orders" issued by the War Department in an attempt to satisfy its many masters (the president, Congress, the various state governors), and confusion was inevitable.[36] Compounding the problem was the fact that the War Department was divided into eight bureaus: Adjutant General, Engineer, Medical, Ordinance, Paymaster, Quartermaster, Subsistence, and Topographical Engineer, all of whom were more or less independent of one another. Heading each bureau was a senior military officer who was often unaware of the challenges facing the heads of the other bureaus.[37] Andrew Carnegie, who worked with Assistant Secretary of War Thomas Scott, described the bureau chiefs as "martinets who had passed the age of usefulness." He went on to note that this sapped the War Department's effectiveness because "days would elapse before a decision could be obtained upon matters which required prompt action. Long years of peace had fossilized the service."[38] Frustrated by the confusion, Pennsylvania governor Curtin wrote to Cameron and testily noted, "It would be well for me to understand how authority is divided so that we can move with certainty."[39]

The War Department had only ninety employees when Lincoln won the 1860 presidential election, and the rash of secessions eroded that number. By the summer of 1861, Cameron had only fifty-six employees managing the largest military expansion in the nation's history up to that point. In an attempt to keep up with the worsening crisis, Cameron went on a hiring spree, packing the War Department with clerks and typists until they were sitting nearly elbow-to-elbow. Despite working in twenty-four-hour shifts, the War Department's staff was simply unable to keep up with the war's demands.[40] Shortly after leaving the cabinet, Cameron reflected, "I toiled in that Department as no man ever toiled before; I have told you that in my youngest years I worked for twenty hours out of twenty-four for successive months! That labor was nothing in comparison with the overpowering toil which I underwent at Washington."[41]

The War Department was a white building on 17th Street, just off the White House grounds, described by one historian as a "miserable tenement."[42] Cameron worked from a fifteen-by-twenty-foot corner office on the second floor with a sweeping view of the White House.[43] Cameron was no executive; as a backslapping, glad-handing politician, he was used to charming legislators in order to get their votes but he was totally unable to switch gears into being an administrator. He delegated little to subordinates and failed to create procedures for protecting his time and maximizing his effectiveness, a fact he conceded to a group of prominent Republicans in mid-1862. Cameron said, "The doors of my private dwelling were besieged from daylight to the latest hours of the night; the department was surrounded on all hands, and at all hours. Certain members of Congress . . . were ever besieging my doors, often patiently waiting for hours to catch a part of the drippings from the War Department."[44]

Making matters worse, Cameron was disorganized, frequently losing papers. When Cameron asked one caller what steps they had discussed in their prior meeting, the man replied, "You borrowed my pencil, took a note, put my pencil in your pocket, and lost the paper."[45] Cameron's disorganization frustrated military and civilian officials alike and made him a target of their anger, which was frequently expressed in rumors about his corruption. An acquaintance of George McClellan's complained to the general about Cameron, saying, "[He] is unfit for the place. Apart from the reputation for corruption, he is always 'too busy' to attend to military matters. Officers on the most important business are kept cooling their heels day after day in his lobby while d—d politicians get every access to him."[46] Recalling Cameron's tenure as secretary of war in 1893, one former clerk claimed, "After [Cameron] came into office, he was so engrossed with the patronage of his own and every other department into which he could reach that I don't think he found out there was a great war on hand till it had been going on some time. . . . He had some good points. He was amiable with such of his victims as called upon him, and when asked if there was any cause for removal, would pleasantly answer, 'None in the world; we just wanted your place, that is all.' . . . As a politician I would call him a very able man."[47]

This was an unfair accusation, and it reinforced the preexisting narrative of the "Winnebago Chief": namely, that Cameron saw government service as an opportunity to enrich himself and reward loyal supporters. In reality, Cameron was no guiltier of playing politics with the War Department than was Chase with the Treasury or Lincoln with the presidency, a fact reflected in Representative Henry Dawes's complaint in mid-July about the "corruption with which every Department seems reeking here."[48] Cameron actually fired a smaller percentage of his department than either Chase or Seward did in theirs; for this reason, historian Brooks M. Kelley has called Salmon Chase, rather than Cameron, the "greatest spoilsman of all" Lincoln's cabinet members.[49] Unquestionably, the new secretary of war rewarded some of his political cronies (J. P. Sanderson became a clerk in the department while a Democratic Pennsylvania legislator who had voted to elect Cameron to the Senate was appointed to General Henry Halleck's staff) and Cameron undoubtedly showed favoritism toward Pennsylvanians in hiring War Department employees (more than a quarter of whom hailed from the Keystone State). In addition, Cameron used his office to punish enemies (Ethan A. Hitchcock, the man who in the late 1830s claimed Cameron defrauded the Winnebagos, asserted that the new war secretary blocked his promotion to general).[50]

However, Cameron knew that the appearance of cronyism would lead to controversy. For instance, though he personally supported hiring pension agents who would be responsible for directing government funds to wounded soldiers or the families of those killed, he refused to do it, noting "'there would be a howl' about increasing the patronage of the department," which led one Republican to conclude, "I don't know whether Cameron is corrupt or not, but is certainly a most cowardly caitiff."[51] Thus, despite one congressman's observation that "Pennsylvania has so few privates in the army since she furnishes so many officers," Cameron never enjoyed the carte blanche in military appointments that his critics claimed.[52] In reality, Pennsylvania actually received *fewer* commissions in the army than the commonwealth was entitled to, a point that Cameron raised in a letter to Seward when the secretary of war complained that he had only interfered in military appointments on a single occasion "when I asked the President to select one and only one [general] from Pennsylvania." In a mid-July letter to Chase, Cameron asserted, "I am desirous that no Pennsylvanian shall receive the highest military office in the gift of the Government, except as a reward of merit achieved in the field."[53]

By contrast, Chase used his influence to reward generals from his home state, most notably Irvin McDowell and George B. McClellan, while Seward successfully convinced Cameron to appoint his son Augustus a paymaster, which was an extremely desirable position; paymasters entered the service as majors and had little fear of being killed or wounded in battle.[54] Nor was the president immune from pressuring the war secretary to appoint friends and supporters to key positions. At one point Lincoln requested that Cameron assign his former law clerk Elmer E. Ellsworth to special duty as adjutant and inspector general of the militia for the United States; for a variety of legal reasons, Cameron was unable to comply with this request, and Ellsworth was killed soon after in house-to-house combat in Alexandria.[55] Lincoln's request demonstrates that the president sought to reward his friends and political allies with plum military appointments, a point reinforced in June when Lincoln justified the appointment of a paymaster general because "we owe Rhode Island & Gov. Sprague a good deal because they give us such good troops & no trouble."[56] Even First Lady Mary Todd Lincoln pressured Cameron into appointing her friends to high rank in the military. This fact was not lost among influential Republicans and friends of the administration, who frequently tried to use their access to the president and his cabinet to gain military appointments.[57] Political appointments became so common that at one point Lincoln requested that Cameron forward to the Senate blank nominations because the president could not remember all his appointees' names. The expectation was that, once commissioned, these officers would use their political influence to recruit large numbers of volunteers who might not otherwise enlist to serve. As historian Thomas J. Goss noted, "The administration fully comprehended the potential benefits of such spokesmen for the Union cause and was more than willing to risk the dangers of military inexperience for the known dividends of political support."[58]

Moreover, when Cameron did hire his friends and political supporters, it was because they had the skills and knowledge to improve the War Department's effectiveness. For instance, in late April, Cameron hired his ally from the PRR, Thomas A. Scott, to oversee government traffic on the Northern Central. Politically savvy, Scott cultivated close friendships with the leaders of both the Curtin and Cameron factions of Pennsylvania's Republican Party.[59] When Scott arrived in the capital on April 26, he was almost immediately detailed to oversee the repair of railroad and telegraph lines between the capital and Annapolis. By the end of May, Cameron had expanded Scott's portfolio to include oversight of all government railroads and telegraphs.[60] Over the next few months, Scott became one of the war secretary's most trusted advisors, though some members of the cabinet objected to Scott's presence on Cameron's staff, largely for political reasons. The House Contracts Committee singled out Scott's appointment as "the single greatest mistake, if not an act of intentional fraud" on Cameron's part, which is odd given that Scott was generally regarded as the most competent man at the War Department during Cameron's tenure.[61]

Though the army's shortcomings and the confused chain of command undoubtedly made the war secretary's job difficult, by far the biggest problem Cameron faced in the first days of the war was the fact that the force eventually put into the field was a hodgepodge composed of three categories of soldiers: regular or career army, volunteers (individuals who enlisted directly into federal military service), and state militia. Northern state governors, rather than the federal government, were responsible for recruiting volunteers, so from the beginning, Lincoln's call for troops was problematic because of the ambiguous status of state militias. State militia units were overseen, drilled, and commanded by governors but subject to being called into federal service by the president. Once called into federal service, state militia units came under regular army authority and were transferred to the federal payroll.[62] Added to this were independent units formed in the "border states" (i.e., the slave states—Delaware, Maryland, Missouri, and Kentucky—that did not secede) whose governors did not respond to Lincoln's call for men. Volunteers were paid recruits raised by the individual states but put into federal service. One key difference between volunteers and the state militias was that the former were not legally prohibited from serving outside their states or for long periods of time, as the state militias typically were. One consequence of this fit of action was that the federal government went through a period of uncertainty and confusion, resulting in a series of missteps that laid the groundwork for later criticisms of Cameron.

The governors frequently accepted more troops than their quotas mandated, straining their abilities to train and equip the men. Lincoln's call for three-year troops in May had asked for fifty-five regiments, but by early July the federal government had accepted nearly four times that number into service. Recruits' enthusiasm was so intense that some even paid for the privilege of joining favored units. The flood of new recruits quickly overwhelmed state authorities' ability to provision the militiamen, and governors tried to pass this problem onto the federal government. The rapidly swelling army became a bureaucratic nightmare for the already strained War Department, which was in no position to accept seventy-five thousand men let alone the extras sent by the state governors, making the war secretary appear incompetent. The federal government was simply not capable of equipping, clothing, or feeding the recruits flocking to enlist. One witness described scenes of troops in Philadelphia on the brink of starvation, while those in Ohio took to begging in the streets for food.[63] Half of the federal government's five hundred thousand or so muskets were antiques that would never survive the rigors of battle, and the states' armories were not much better: when Pennsylvania tried to arm its volunteers, officials discovered that some of the commonwealth's weapons actually dated back to the American War for Independence.[64] The federal government owned a single armory, and its maximum production capacity was three thousand weapons per month. More alarming, the federal government did not own a single foundry, so all cannons had to be purchased from private companies, and the War Department purchased all uniforms from a single company in Philadelphia that lacked the capacity to produce thousands of additional pieces in such a short period of time.[65]

Throughout this period, the War Department was flooded with telegrams from the various governors requesting (sometimes demanding) uniforms, weapons, and other materials to equip their men. Most of the time, Cameron was simply unable to accede to the governors' wishes, which irritated them. Some governors dispatched agents across the country to buy weapons and uniforms, inflating prices and making these items even scarcer, a move that annoyed Cameron and hampered the federal government's ability to supply recruits.[66] In a move to avoid competing with the states for material, Cameron directed the governors to equip recruits and bill the War Department, a decentralized approach that ensured war profiteering on an immense scale. As early as July, Cameron estimated that the states were due $10 million for money they had already spent, and within a year Congress appropriated another $15 million to reimburse the states for additional costs.[67] During the war's first year, military procurement was decentralized and therefore disorganized, a function of American's pervasive fear of powerful central government.[68] It took the War Department nearly two years to gain control of the system and get to a point where it had enough weapons to effectively arm its troops.[69]

The war secretary relied heavily for procurement on Alexander Cummings, a prominent Philadelphia editor who founded both the *Philadelphia Evening Bulletin* and the *New York World* and who had pressed Lincoln to appoint Cameron to the cabinet. Cummings was probably the biggest embarrassment to Cameron; he was totally unqualified for the job and his brief term in office was characterized by a bizarre spending spree that ultimately embarrassed the War Department. At one point, Cummings spent $21,000 for, among other things, straw hats and linen pantaloons, despite the fact that neither item was typically issued to U.S. army personnel. He overpaid for shoes, and he used government funds to buy alcohol, herring, and pickles. By the end of the summer, he had spent $250,000 of the government's money, and while he did not personally receive any pay, in at least one case he directed business to a firm whose owners had occasionally lent him money.[70] By far, the most infamous example of procurement malfeasance was the infamous Hall Carbine Affair. In June 1861 Cameron approved the sale of five thousand obsolete Hall carbines to Arthur M. Eastman for $3.50 each. Eastman made minor alterations that cost between 75 cents and $1.25 per gun, and then sold them to Simon Stevens for $12.50 each. Stevens was personal friends with powerful congressman Thaddeus Stevens, and sold the modified guns back to the War Department for $22 each, apparently with Cameron's approval.

That being said, it is important to note that Cameron and his clerks were not the only ones who inked questionable deals in the war's chaotic first year; prominent Republicans including Thurlow Weed, New York governor Edwin Morgan, General Fremont, and others were linked to shady contracts. For instance, the administration delegated authority to spend $2 million on its behalf to a group of three prominent New Yorkers: former secretary of the Treasury John A. Dix and former New York state legislators Richard M. Blatchford and George Opdyke. This was in addition to another such committee closely allied with Governor Morgan, which exercised "practically the full authority of the War and Navy Departments" in recruiting, organizing, and provisioning troops.[71] Governor Curtin was accused of war profiteering by Pennsylvania's Democratic press and was forced to appoint a committee to investigate the charges; while the final report vindicated his integrity, it nonetheless criticized mismanagement and questionable appointments.[72] The heads of the War Department's various bureaus were accustomed "to make contracts without regard to the ability of the Treasury to meet their payments[, which] more than once brought the Treasury to the verge of bankruptcy."[73] The procurement effort was so decentralized and confused that in November 1861 Cameron begged Lincoln to prevent Joshua F. Speed (one of the president's closest friends) from purchasing arms in New York because, as the war secretary noted, "the only result of his efforts to purchase, is to enhance the price and to defeat the endeavors of the government to procure arms."[74]

As historian Mark R. Wilson, who wrote the most comprehensive study of federal government purchasing during the war, has noted, state officials typically went out of their way to buy from local firms, often without bothering to advertise for bids. Federal officials got in on the action, using their influence to direct lucrative contracts to their friends and supporters, and Cameron was no exception. In August, Quartermaster of the Army Montgomery Meigs sent Cameron a stinging response to a note from the War Department. "The enclosed note *from the President* [my emphasis] and yourself 'recommends' the purchase of eastern mules at a price of $8 per head higher than is to be paid for many thousands now collecting in Kentucky. . . . If political considerations connected with the situation of Kentucky it should be plainly ordered and not left to my discretion."[75] The following month, Cameron followed Meigs's request and ordered the quartermaster general to purchase one thousand cavalry horses from two Pennsylvanians at more than double the prevailing price. Even the president's wife, Mary Todd Lincoln, got into the act, pressuring both the War Department and Quartermaster Meigs personally in October to purchase a sizable number of horses from a friend of hers in Kentucky.

Finally, many of the complaints about corruption arose from people denied contracts. Lincoln's personal secretary John Hay cited one instance: "A leather dealer who came here the other day, full of righteous indignation that no contract had been awarded him, and profoundly impressed with the belief that there was cheating around the board, after several days of diligent investigation, having learned that every contract had been let on lower terms than he could afford to work for, went back to his tan-yard, and has not since called Cameron a thief."[76] When a group of businessmen from New York and Boston called on the president in late autumn and demanded Cameron's removal because of corruption, the president responded, "Gentlemen, if you want General Cameron removed, you have only to bring me *one proved* case of dishonesty, and I promise you his 'head.' But I assure you I am not going to act on what seems to me the most unfounded gossip."[77] In part, Lincoln's action was about protecting the integrity of his cabinet; had he given into these demands in Cameron's case, his other cabinet members' enemies would not be long in demanding other removals as well.[78] On the other hand, the businessmen's inability to produce any actual proof of War Department corruption supports the conclusion that Cameron, while overwhelmed and out of his depth, was not a crook.

In addition, in their zeal to meet their states' initial quotes, governors and state legislatures often passed laws that contradicted administration directives.[79] On May 3, Lincoln called for volunteers to enlist for three-year terms, which caused new problems. In the first place, Lincoln's call for troops deviated from the state militia system that had been in place since the Militia Act of 1792; under his new call, volunteers would augment U.S. regulars directly, as opposed to being mustered into the state militias. Shortly thereafter Cameron communicated to the various governors that he wanted ninety-day recruits to be converted into three-year commitments, which caused a new batch of problems. New York, Maine, and Vermont had passed laws authorizing two-year enlistments; when the War Department responded to the governors' appeals by saying the federal government only wanted men who enlisted for three years, the governors balked, saying they were not legally allowed to extend the terms an extra year. Vermont governor Erastus Fairbanks informed the war secretary that if the federal government did not see fit to accept the two-year volunteers, he would have to call an extra session of the legislature to comply with the War Department's requests.[80] In mid-May, Pennsylvania's legislature passed a law that prohibited volunteers that had not been accepted by the governor from leaving the state, a clear attempt to prevent the War Department from usurping Governor Curtin's authority.[81]

However, there was an important sop to the governors: under the terms of Lincoln's May 3 call, these new troops would not elect their own officers as had been the practice under the militia system. Instead, the state governors would appoint the new officers. Naturally, politics heavily shaded who was appointed, a fact that led Buchanan's former attorney general to claim that military appointments were "bestowed on persons whose only claim was their Republicanism."[82] Governors jealously guarded their right to name officers. Governor Samuel J. Kirkwood of Iowa complained about the fact that recruits from his state were fighting under officers from Illinois, and he and governors Andrew G. Curtin of Pennsylvania and William Dennison Jr. of Ohio tried to dictate the selection of department commanders in their respective states. Cameron tried to assert federal government control over the appointment of officers by promulgating an order on July 25 mandating all regimental officers to be examined by a board established by the War Department. This order was unpopular with both the governors, who objected to losing the ability to appoint officers, and the professional military men, who desperately wanted to take officer selection out of the realm of politics. In the end, Cameron won; though the board's rejections were sometimes overturned due to political pressure, in general the war secretary's order diminished the number of "political generals."[83] In addition, on December 3, the war secretary finally managed to seize control of recruitment from the governors, which laid the groundwork for a more orderly process. The new system, which had barely been adopted when Cameron left the War Department, assured that existing units were supplemented with new recruits, which facilitated continued battle readiness.[84]

Another challenge Cameron faced was the president's informal management style. Frustratingly, Lincoln often ignored the chain of command, tacitly encouraging subordinates to do the same.[85] Taking their cues from the president, some of Cameron's cabinet colleagues felt entitled to intrude on War Department matters. Without a doubt, the most consistent meddler was Secretary of State William Seward, who considered himself Lincoln's "prime minister." Charles Francis Adams, who knew Seward personally, claimed that the secretary of state considered Lincoln a "clown" and sought to keep the new president separated from the rest of the cabinet by holding as few cabinet meetings as possible. Then, Seward would "overawe and browbeat [Secretary of the Navy Gideon] Welles and Cameron" in order to get their departments under his control, at which point Seward would be the de facto president. Reflecting on Seward's behavior years later, Welles claimed, "The understanding that existed between Mr. Seward and Cameron at the organization of the Cabinet and not a very high appreciation of the abilities of Mr. Cameron led Mr. Seward to believe he might make himself familiar with the War Department, and assume as occasion required some of the duties of the Secretary of War, an assumption that was not entirely satisfactory to that officer."[86]

The most egregious example of Seward's meddling occurred in late March, when the secretary of state—without consulting the secretaries of war or the navy—implemented a plan to resupply Fort Pickens, a fort in Pensacola, Florida. On March 29, unbeknown to either Cameron or Welles, Seward met with the president and introduced Lincoln to Captain Montgomery C. Meigs, a thirty-four-year-old member of the Corps of Engineers. In January, Meigs had accompanied reinforcements dispatched to the area, so he seemed the ideal person to plan and lead an expedition to resupply Fort Pickens. Lincoln hesitated but, on March 31, ordered that the expedition proceed, without informing either Cameron or Welles. At about this time, Meigs telegraphed the Brooklyn Navy Yard and ordered the commandant to make ready the steam frigate USS *Powhatan*, which was followed by an order not to mention anything about the operation to the Navy Department.

The problem with Meigs's move was that Cameron and Welles expected to use the *Powhatan* to resupply Sumter, which was scheduled for the same time as the secret mission to Pickens. When Lincoln green-lit the Sumter operation, Welles ordered Captain Samuel Mercer to command the resupply fleet and to use the *Powhatan* as his flagship, and the commander of the Brooklyn Navy Yard, thoroughly confused by the contradictory orders, referred the matter to Seward who, enraged, confronted Welles. The two men immediately went to see the president to have Lincoln settle the matter, which he did by ordering that the *Powhatan* be made available to the Sumter mission. Seward, unhappy with the outcome, sent the order over his own signature, which Porter refused to obey because Lincoln had signed the original order. Thus, in the end, Seward got the *Powhatan*, but at the cost of thoroughly alienating Cameron and Welles.[87] Welles wrote later, "I was unwilling to believe that my colleague Mr. Seward could connive at, or be party to, so improper and gross an affair as to interfere with the organization of my department, and jeopardize its operations at such a juncture. What then were the contrivances which he was maturing with two young officers, one of the army and the other of the Navy, without consulting the Secretary of War or the Secretary of the Navy? . . . Mr. Cameron was greatly incensed; complained that Mr. Seward was trying to run the War Department, had caused Captain Meigs to desert."[88] Cameron was so angered by Seward's behavior that he threatened to court-martial Meigs for being absent without leave and for spending War Department funds without the secretary's approval. This event permanently damaged Cameron's relationship with Seward and left a lasting bitterness that the secretary of war made little effort to hide.[89]

In another instance, Cameron issued to his acquaintance Henry Johnston a pass to cross the Union lines, which Johnston used numerous times to go to Richmond. In October, Johnston crossed the lines but, upon trying to return to the North, was arrested and detained on Seward's order. When Cameron heard the news, he was furious, and he immediately ordered Johnston released. Seward, however, countermanded Cameron's order.[90] Eventually the matter was sorted out, but not without permanently damaging Cameron's esteem for Seward. On one occasion, the normally soft-spoken Cameron flew into a rage at Seward's meddling, yelling at the secretary of state, "You are always meddling in that which does not concern you!"[91] Chase later concluded that had Cameron not had to suffer all this interference, "I am confident there would have been comparatively little complaint [with Cameron's work at the War Department]."[92]

Because Cameron was visibly overwhelmed by these gargantuan challenges, Lincoln increasingly delegated responsibility to Secretary of the Treasury Chase, which the secretary of war seems to have appreciated; by May, Cameron had asked Chase to assume full responsibility for the department when he (Cameron) was out of Washington.[93] Chase drafted the War Department's orders for enlarging the regular army and the creation of a volunteer army in early May, and he was partially responsible for McClellan's ascension to general-in-chief of the army. Moreover, Chase also took on the responsibility of overseeing the recruitment of new regiments and of handling the War Department's correspondence with the governors.[94] As a result, congressmen and administration officials concerned about military matters frequently wrote to both Cameron *and* Chase.[95] Because they worked so closely together, Cameron was swept into Chase's orbit, further alienating him from his erstwhile ally, Seward.

Despite Chase's assistance, War Department operations remained chaotic throughout 1861. Voices in and out of the cabinet pressured Cameron and Lincoln to bring some order to the government's procurement procedures by filling the now vacant quartermaster generalship, and the leading candidate quickly became Seward's favorite, Montgomery C. Meigs. Meigs was not the only candidate, but he had Seward's backing at a moment when the secretary of state exercised considerable influence in the cabinet.[96] Beginning with the Fort Pickens expedition, Seward boosted Meigs for promotion and never missed an opportunity to bring the young officer to Lincoln's attention. Cameron strongly opposed Meigs's promotion to quartermaster general, in part because he saw him as Seward's agent. Moreover, Cameron was still angry about the Fort Pickens debacle, and while there was little he could do to Seward, he could frustrate Meigs's ambition. Welles recalled that "Mr.

Cameron sometimes complained of interference with the War Department and army matters by the Secretary of State, and on one occasion, when [Seward] was commending Meigs, as he often did, for great ability, Cameron proposed to transfer that officer to the State Department, where his talents were most used and highest appreciated."[97] It was not until several months later, after much back and forth, that the secretary of war offered the younger man the quartermastership, which Meigs quickly accepted.[98]

Over the next few months, a semblance of order was established over federal procurement, in large part because both Cameron and Meigs were able to centralize and regularize purchases. As historian Mark W. Summers noted, "After the end of the first year [of the war], the complaints about procurement of supplies diminished as [soldiers] found themselves newly clad."[99] While Meigs is certainly due some credit for formalizing and regularizing army procurement, his reforms were not universally applauded. Many depot quartermasters, who faced unique challenges in provisioning troops in their commands, found that formal contracting often cost the government more money than it saved.[100] Nor were the depot quartermasters the only ones concerned about Meigs's reforms; state governors, who feared that the new quartermaster would stop spending money in their states, vigorously contested the centralization of procurement, telling the War Department they preferred to continue purchasing locally and have the federal government reimburse them. Even after the governors were told in the fall of 1861 to stop spending money, some continued purchasing supplies and submitting the bills to the War Department for reimbursement. Both Israel Washburn and Oliver P. Morton, the governors of Indiana and Maine, respectively, resisted Meigs's repeated attempts to curtail their spending. As late as December 16, Cameron was writing letters to recalcitrant governors, demanding that they adhere to the new policies for procurement. They did not go down without a fight: Washburn claimed it was his "right" to outfit the troops, while

Morton appealed to Seward for help, but in both cases Meigs eventually succeeded in gaining control of most of the army's procurement spending.[101]

The war posed challenges that the federal government and the War Department were initially poorly equipped to meet. Added to those challenges were complications due to rivalries within the cabinet and the competition for war contracts, all of which fostered intense opposition to Cameron. Even if the secretary of war had been an efficient and capable executive, it was inevitable that his conduct would have been heavily criticized. For all his missteps, the War Department was far more capable of meeting these challenges at the end of Cameron's tenure than when he arrived. As late as October 28, Lincoln expressed unqualified support of Cameron's judgment, noting in a letter to the war secretary about a proposal for managing the military telegraph system, "I have not sufficient time to study and mature an opinion on this plan. If the Secretary of War has confidence in it, and is satisfied to adopt it, I have no objections."[102] Within a few months, Lincoln would force Cameron from office, but it was because the war secretary had touched the "third rail" of Civil War politics—slavery—not due to incompetence or corruption.

7

"Gentlemen, the Paragraph Stands," 1861–62

O n Independence Day 1861, Cameron's job got even harder because Congress convened in a special session. The war was no longer Lincoln's alone; he now had to negotiate with Congress, and a significant number of congressmen wanted to manage the war. As late as 1862, Republican Benjamin Franklin Wade believed, "It does not belong to the President to devise a policy for the country. His duties are well performed when he has caused the laws to be faithfully executed. . . . It devolves upon Congress to devise a policy."[1] Members of both houses pressured Lincoln and Cameron to take decisive action against the Confederacy. Adding their voices to those of the Northern governors, whose bloodlust and demands for battle had "become an indomitable, deafening roar," Congress pushed the administration into a corner, particularly after a series of skirmishes in June seemed to augur a decisive Union victory.[2] Speaker of the House Galusha A. Grow bluntly threatened Cameron, telling the secretary of war to prosecute the war more vigorously or "you will be as powerless in thirty days as you are now powerful."[3] On July 11, Illinois senator Lyman Trumbull tried to push a resolution through the Senate demanding that the army move to occupy Richmond no later than July 20; though it failed, at least fifteen senators backed the resolution, and many of Lincoln's friends counseled that sooner or later it would pass.[4] The pressure contributed to one of the Union's worst defeats and made the abolition of slavery one of the war's aims.

Despite commander of the Army of Northeastern Virginia General Irvin McDowell's vigorous protestations that he could not possibly organize, discipline, and equip his men while at the same time marching and fighting, the pressure on him and the administration to fight was simply too great to be ignored. On July 16 McDowell decamped from Washington with about thirty-five thousand men—the largest field army in North America up to that point—with an eye toward relieving the threat of a Confederate invasion of Washington.[5] McDowell planned to attack the Confederates at Bull Run with two columns while a third attacked the Confederates' southernmost flank, hopefully pushing the Confederates back to the Rappahannock River. Everything presaged a victory, a sentiment that Cameron likely expressed on the evening of July 20 when he met with Lincoln to brief the president.[6]

Things did not go nearly so well when McDowell and Johnston's men met in battle the following morning. Initially, the four-hour battle seemed to be going the Union's way, and the president was pleased by the encouraging telegrams he received about it. By 11:30 a.m. McDowell had collapsed the Confederate line, and the rebels were retreating. Reforming, however, the Confederates managed to capture the Union's cannons, which turned the tide of the battle, and by 4 p.m. McDowell's forces were in a panicked retreat. Worse, his troops' inexperience quickly manifested itself; men became separated from their officers and, in the confusion, federal troops fired upon one another. However, the decisive factor was the appearance of fresh Confederate troops under the command of Brigadier General Joseph E. Johnston. Johnston commanded the approximately twelve thousand men of the Army of the Shenandoah. Seeing an opportunity, Johnston headed for Bull Run, where he joined with Beauregard, eliminating McDowell's advantage in numbers and turning the tide of battle.

The loss of what was, up to that point, the largest and bloodiest battle in U.S. history was bad enough but it was made worse by the fact that spectators from Washington had seen the whole disgraceful thing. The ghosts of Bull Run haunted the country for months to come. McDowell's defeat ensured that the general would have to be replaced, and on July 22, Cameron telegraphed General George B. McClellan, telling him, "Circumstances make your presence here necessary," and ordering him to come to Washington as soon as possible.[7]

Yet even that was not the worst of it: one of the 460 U.S. soldiers killed at Bull Run was Cameron's brother James. Almost exactly a year younger than Simon, James had accepted the colonelcy of the Seventy-Ninth New York Volunteer Infantry Regiment in late June and was killed leading his men in a charge to recapture the federal cannon at Henry House Hill. The regiment itself lost nearly two hundred men, almost half of the Union men who died.[8] That evening, Cameron joined the president and Seward at General Scott's house, where an aide read telegrams from the War Department as they were delivered. At one point the aide announced that Colonel Cameron was among the dead.[9] The war secretary managed to remain stoic for the rest of the day, but on his way home that evening, he ran into Ohio senator John Sherman. When Sherman asked about the events at Bull Run, Cameron "hurried me into his house and said: 'Our army is defeated, and my brother killed.' He then gave way to passionate grief."[10]

The day after Bull Run, Congress—"shocked but determined"—passed a bill authorizing the president to raise a volunteer army of up to five hundred thousand men for three years, followed by a supplementary bill a few days later that raised the total to one million.[11] Lincoln and Cameron interpreted Congress's authorization to raise five hundred thousand troops as a mandate to accept volunteers *directly* into federal service, bypassing the governors, rekindling the simmering conflict between governors and the War Department. Curtin wrote an angry letter decrying the War Department's policy as setting the federal government "in competition with . . . the State[s]. The consequence has been much embarrassment, delay, and confusion."[12] In September, Massachusetts governor John Andrew dispatched two men to meet with Cameron and extract a promise from the secretary of war that the government would stop granting authority for individuals other than governors to recruit volunteers, at least in his state. These complaints forced the president to backtrack, and he and Cameron devised a new policy whereby individuals who received authority to recruit volunteers would have to first report to the governor. Once a unit was ready to be mustered into service, the governors were authorized to "reorganize them and prepare them for service in the manner he may judge most advantageous for the interests of the General Government."[13] As a result the governors were largely responsible for mobilization of the Union army well into the early part of 1862.[14]

The defeat at Bull Run dampened enthusiasm for military service; rather than exceeding their quotas, governors now found it difficult to meet them. Attempts to get three-months men to reenlist for three years or the duration of the war were unsuccessful, despite the relatively large bounties offered by state officials. By late August, Missouri governor Hamilton R. Gamble tried to spur recruitment by suggesting that, if the state failed to meet its quota through volunteers, he might resort to a draft. A few weeks later other governors made similar threats in a variety of subtle ways. The threat of a draft became so pervasive that Cameron actually issued a statement forbidding the governors from undertaking such an action.[15] Tension over reenlisting the three-month men contributed to a riot in Harrisburg in July. Because many of the three-month men refused to reenlist, they were discharged but their pay was not immediately available, so they were basically told to support themselves until it arrived. Not surprisingly, this was hardly the news the men wanted to hear, and they demanded immediate payment. The soldiers' demands reflected a pervasive rumor that the federal government lacked the money to pay the them; in a letter to Jay Cooke, Cameron claimed that "from the beginning of the war, attempts from various quarters have been made to induce the soldiers to believe that there would be delay and difficulty on the part of soldiers to get their pay. Sometimes these efforts arose from ignorance of the ability of the Government, but oftener from a wish to speculate on the hard earned pay of the soldier."[16]

The lone paymaster in Harrisburg quickly became a target of the soldiers' abuse, and he telegraphed to Washington, frantically asking for money to pay the men. The War Department sent two additional paymasters, but on July 27 a mob of disgruntled soldiers surrounded the paymasters' hotel in an attempt to get their back wages, even going so far as to burn the paymasters in effigy. Apparently, some among the mob planned to seize weapons from the local armory and force local officials to pay their back wages. Consequently, the War Department mobilized the Twelfth Regiment of Pennsylvania Reserves to put down the mob, and Cameron dispatched his nephew Bruce to Harrisburg, where the men were paid in notes drawn on the Middletown Bank. Some historians have seen this as yet another financial swindle, but the reality is far different: it was a stopgap measure necessitated by the federal government's utter lack of preparation for war. If Cameron had not paid the troops in Middletown Bank notes, it is possible the soldiers would have rioted.

Events like this reinforced some congressmen's beliefs that they, rather than the president, should direct the war. One way Congress exercised control over the administration's conduct of the war was through investigative committees, which proliferated between 1861 and 1865. The Thirty-Seventh (1861–63) and Thirty-Eighth (1863–65) congresses formed substantially more special committees (19 and 16) than the average for the congresses of the 1850s (11.2), and many of these committees were charged with oversight or investigation of the war effort.[17] One reason for this explosion of special committees was that committee work in Congress provided lawmakers a number of opportunities: it allowed them to establish a reputation, gave them bona fides on relevant issues, and provided a measure of restraint on the executive's power.[18] Secession magnified the power of the radical Republicans—those committed to the immediate and unconditional abolition of slavery—and while these were men of high principle, they often ignored important military and political considerations. Historian Bruce Tap, the foremost expert on the most important of these committees, the Committee on the Conduct of the War, describes the members this way: "[They] believed that the Union war effort would benefit if directed by officials with staunch antislavery credentials. Regarding military science as superfluous, committee members believed that military skill was largely derived from common sense. Further, they attempted persistently to use political ideology as the measure to evaluate the army's principle leaders, believing that battlefield success inevitably followed from correct political beliefs."[19] As a result, conflict between Congress and the president, who was trying to avoid making the war about slavery, was inevitable.

Within days of convening in special session, the House of Representatives created a committee to investigate federal government procurement. Chaired by New York's Charles H. Van Wyck, the committee held hearings for nearly a year and then deliberated until July 1863 before releasing its report, which heavily criticized the government's procurement procedures.[20] Because federal law prohibited further actions against anyone who testified, the committee did not call Cameron to testify, thereby depriving him of the opportunity to defend himself.[21] The war secretary later claimed that Van Wyck's conclusions were heavily influenced by a fight the two men had over the War Department furnishing weapons to a certain regiment; the confrontation ended with Cameron ordering Van Wyck to leave the War Department.[22]

That something other than economy in government animated Van Wyck can be inferred from administration and congressional reaction to the committee's work. Lincoln's personal secretaries, John Hay and John Nicolay, described the committee's work as "often hasty and unjust in its judgments."[23] Congressman Thaddeus Stevens, himself a vocal and acerbic critic of the administration, nonetheless compared the Van Wyck committee to the Jacobins during the French Revolution, condemning them for rejoicing "in feeding upon the mangled carcasses of their fellow citizens." Cameron was mortified by the rash of investigations, at one point saying, "What are we to think of a party that, within sixty days after going into power, appoints a committee to investigate the frauds of its own members?"[24]

Senator Lyman Trumbull, always looking for an opportunity to attack the secretary of war, claimed, "Cameron ought to be removed forthwith for incompetency, to say nothing of the rumors of jobbing."[25] In a letter to philanthropist and prominent abolitionist John M. Forbes, *New-York Evening Post* editor William Cullen Bryant asserted:

> Mr. Cameron's retirement, instead of being impolitic, would be the most politic thing that could be done, by way of giving firmness and strengthening the administration with the people. The dissatisfaction here is as great as with you, and I hear that at Washington it is expressed by everybody, except Cameron's special friends and favorites, in the strongest terms. If I am rightly informed, there is nothing done by him with the promptness, energy, and decision which the times demand, without his being in a manner forced to it by the other members of the Cabinet, or the President. A man who wants to make a contract with the government for three hundred mules, provided he is a Pennsylvanian, can obtain access to him, when a citizen of East Tennessee, coming as the representative of the numerous Union population of that region, is denied. There are bitter complaints, too, of Cameron's disregard of his appointments and engagements in such cases as I have mentioned.[26]

Two things are immediately apparent about Bryant's criticism of Cameron: first, they are entirely based on rumor and, second, those rumors reflect complaints by individuals angered by the fact that the War Department did not award them contracts. Samuel F. Du Pont wrote to his wife and claimed that many of the claims against Cameron were politically motivated, designed to force moderates out of the cabinet to make way for abolitionists.[27] Cameron's supporters vigorously fought the attacks on his character and the calls for his removal, but they became so ubiquitous that Chase was forced to defend his colleague, telling one correspondent, "Of course Cameron makes mistakes. . . . But he is administering his department vigorously, patriotically, and honestly, I am quite sure."[28] While Van Wyck's committee turned up some mistakes and fraud, in general it yielded a relatively small number of either. With regard to Cameron specifically, Lincoln thought many of the committee members "each had a good-sized axe to grind" with the secretary of war and therefore took their charges with a sizable grain of salt.[29]

A related challenge concerned public opinion in both the United States and Europe. In early May, one correspondent warned Cameron not to "underrate the importance of the English press," and later that month both the president and the secretary of war met with New York representative F. B. Cutting to discuss strategies for massaging European public opinion.[30] The fact that the administration was so concerned about public opinion disgusted New York Republican George T. Strong, who denounced the war secretary as "wanting in moral courage, [because] the first question he asks about any measure is 'What will the newspapers say?'"[31] Cameron had good reason to worry what the newspapers said; as one of his friends noted, "You are said to be rich, but your general reputation is that of an inordinate lover of gain. . . . If there is truth to these reports, change your tactics, for it is nearly as public as the report of the retreat at Bull Run."[32] A few days after Bull Run, one critic even went so far as to write, "Your cursed ambition has been the cause of the death of your amiable brother. You have pushed yourself into [a] position for which God and nature never intended and you will meet your reward by the midnight howls of your conscience."[33]

Worse, bad news kept coming. On August 10 Confederates routed a small force under General Nathaniel Lyon, a well-known and popular abolitionist, at Wilson's Creek, outside Springfield, Missouri. Lyon was killed, and many in the press blamed Cameron for the defeat.[34] A fresh wave of criticism of the cabinet erupted in August, and though Seward and Welles were also targets, Cameron caught the lion's share. One of Lincoln's friends passed along rumors that "Mr. Seward is drunk, daily; and it is universally believed that Cameron is a thief—All men believe you, upright—but know you lack experience and fear you lack nerve," while a prominent Republican complained of the perception that "the army is a mere mob, War Department, paralyzed by corruption; Navy Department, ditto, and so forth."[35] Senator Lyman Trumbull denounced the war secretary's alleged corruption, while prominent Illinois Republican Ebenezer Peck told the president that Cameron should be replaced.[36] Even soldiers criticized the war secretary. Brigadier General John Pope, then serving under Fremont in the Department of the West, claimed in a letter, "Everybody in this wide land knows [Cameron] to be corrupt and dishonest, a public plunderer and an unprincipled politician[,] . . . a man notoriously plundering the Govt and betraying his trust and neglecting every vital interest under his charge."[37] One of Salmon Chase's friends wrote to the Treasury secretary, claiming, "The Western public are nearly unanimous in believing [Cameron] a bad man, and distrust a whole administration that retains such a man in its counsels. He may be guiltless of the charges made against him, but the people cannot be made so to believe *now*, nor will they confide, as they should, in a government in which he enacts so important a part. Innocent or guilty, he is a stumbling block, and so far as outsiders can see, should be removed."[38] The attacks on his character, like those following the Winnebago scandal, irritated and hurt Cameron. Cameron defended himself by asserting, "If I have any ability whatever, it is the ability to make money. I do not have to steal it. I can go into any street on any day, and as the world goes, make all the money I want."[39]

Faced with eroding public support and hounded by members of Congress both demanding more vigorous prosecution and investigating the administration's conduct of the war, Lincoln and Cameron took radical steps to end the rebellion. In April the president told Major General Robert Patterson that he was authorized to suspend habeas corpus if he considered it necessary in the course of his duties.[40] In December, Cameron ordered the U.S. Post Office to send any letters addressed to anyone in a seceded state to the Dead-Letter Office.[41] On May 25 General George Cadwalader arrested John Merryman under Lincoln's suspension order. Merryman, a lieutenant in the Maryland state militia, used his office to recruit and train Confederate soldiers. Some of these recruits had been responsible for burning the bridges into Baltimore in April. United States Supreme Court Chief Justice Roger Taney traveled to Baltimore and personally issued a writ of habeas corpus, which Cadwalader ignored. Taney's participation made things worse for Merryman; he was to have been released, but when he applied for a writ of habeas corpus, the Lincoln administration changed course and indicted him for treason, a capital offense.[42] Merryman was finally released from prison later in July, but Cameron again had him arrested in September, along with another group of legislators, editors, and other influential secessionists.

In another instance, Cameron ordered the arrest of Pierce Butler, a wealthy Philadelphian with family in South Carolina, over the latter's criticism of the Lincoln administration and strident support of the Confederacy. Butler claimed that the secretary of war had him arrested over a personal matter, rather than a legitimate war-related concern. The authorities found nothing incriminating, and were thus forced to release him the following month. Almost immediately he sued Cameron in state court, alleging "trespass, *vi et armis*, assault and battery, and false imprisonment."[43] Butler's suit threatened the extraordinary powers the administration had undertaken to prosecute the war, and Lincoln was forced to come to Cameron's defense, asserting that the war secretary had acted "under the President's directions . . . for the prompt suppression of the existing insurrection."[44] This was far from the only controversial arrest: in September, Cameron personally ordered the arrest of a crippled newsboy caught selling the *Daily News* (which was banned from the U.S. mail and later confiscated by federal authorities) and who had been overheard uttering treasonous sentiments.[45]

By far, the best-known instance of political repression during Cameron's tenure was the arrest of members of the Maryland legislature. In the aftermath of the Baltimore riot, Maryland's governor, Thomas Hicks, mobilized the state militia to keep order and called for a special session of the legislature to meet in Annapolis on April 26 to decide whether to secede. Lincoln, concerned by the threat of secession but equally wary of antagonizing a border state, had the War Department order General Benjamin F. Butler not to interfere with the legislators until they took overt action. Butler complied, though he did try to forestall secession by telling newspaper reporters that he would arrest the legislators if they voted for secession. His comments were widely reported, and though the legislature voted its sympathy with the Confederacy, it stopped short of seceding.[46] In early September, rumors began circulating that the Confederates intended to invade Maryland following the state legislature's passage of a secession ordinance. If this happened, Washington would be isolated from the Northern states, and Confederate capture of the capital city would simply be a matter of time. At about this time, Maryland state legislator S. Teackle Wallis, who chaired the body's Committee on Federal Relations, proposed a resolution condemning the Lincoln administration for what it claimed were the arbitrary arrests of the state's citizens. Both houses of the Maryland legislature passed the resolution, stoking the administration's fear that the Maryland legislature was planning to secede, an event the administration resolved to prevent.

On September 11 Cameron ordered General Nathaniel P. Banks to arrest "all or any part of the members" of the Maryland state legislature suspected of harboring secessionist views. That evening Allan Pinkerton and his detectives scoured Baltimore while federal troops were detailed to arrest Police Marshal George P. Kane at his home. That same day, Cameron ordered General John A. Dix to arrest six people and prevent them from communicating with anyone.[47] Early on the 12th, Dix and Banks carried out their orders, arresting a sizable number of legislators and newspaper editors. Summarizing the prevailing attitude, Attorney General Edward Bates famously remarked, "To keep them quiet we must make them conscious that they stand in the presence of coercive power."[48]

Meanwhile, the administration faced growing dissatisfaction in the West, where General John C. Fremont's August 30 proclamation of martial law throughout Missouri undermined Lincoln's kid glove treatment of the border states. According to Fremont, "Circumstances, in my judgment, of sufficient urgency, render it necessary that the commanding general of this Department should assume the administrative powers of the State. . . . The property, real and personal, of all persons, in the State of Missouri, who shall take up arms against the United States, or who shall be directly proven to have taken an active part with their enemies in the field, is declared to be confiscated to the public use, and their Slaves, if any they have, are hereby declared Free men."[49] Fremont's authority as commander of the Department of the West gave him control of the western part of Kentucky, and the proclamation stoked fears that the federal government intended to manumit the Bluegrass State's slaves, a feeling reinforced when Cameron congratulated the general via telegram.[50]

Lincoln was less enamored of Fremont's proclamation than Cameron because it seemingly made emancipation of slaves administration policy, a fact that alarmed slave owners in the border states. The president, as was his custom, tried to deal with the issue as diplomatically as possible: on September 2 he wrote to Fremont and asked the general to modify the proclamation to bring it into line with the Confiscation Act, which had become law on August 6. Fremont flatly refused, and Lincoln saw no other course but to publicly countermand the general, which the president did on September 11. Naturally, this enraged the Radicals, who all along sought to turn the war into an abolitionist crusade. Benjamin Wade of Ohio called the president "poor white trash," and the Radicals demanded that Lincoln make changes in the cabinet by appointing men committed to abolishing slavery.[51]

Fremont's proclamation of martial law was hardly the only issue with the general; in the words of one historian, Fremont "was out of control."[52] The general requisitioned supplies almost constantly, straining authorities' capacity for meeting his demands. Fremont saw in this a conspiracy, believing that members of the War Department wanted him to fail.[53] When Postmaster General Montgomery Blair and Quartermaster Montgomery Meigs went to St. Louis to investigate in September 1861, they found the general was "building fortifications about the City at extravagant cost. He has built more gunboats than directed. He is buying tents of bad patterns . . . at prices fixed by himself—not by the proper purchasing officers. The impression among the regular officers is that he is incapable, and that he is looking not to the Country but to the Presidency."[54] Added to that were a series of bad contracts for food, weapons, and transportation given under Fremont's direction to his personal friends. An informant claimed that "unless there is a change in [Fremont's] department . . . it will require double the number of men to do what could be done now with a proper man at the Head. I assert without fear of contradiction that there is less system and efficiency & more corruption in this department or in other words in St. Louis than in all the balance of the United States." More shocking, there were even rumors that Fremont was addicted to opium and he had become "really imbecile."[55]

Due to these alarming reports, the president conferred with Cameron on both October 4 and 7 about his options in dealing with Fremont. It appears that Cameron pressed Lincoln not to remove Fremont, at least not until they had all of the facts.

The issue was also likely raised in the cabinet meeting on October 10, because the following day the president dispatched his trusted personal secretary John Nicolay (under the ruse that Nicolay was going west due to ill health) to St. Louis to investigate conditions in Fremont's command.[56] Nicolay's report did little to clarify the matter, so the president dispatched first Montgomery Blair and Quartermaster Meigs and then later Cameron and Adjutant General Lorenzo Thomas to investigate the charges against Fremont. The war secretary carried Lincoln's order removing Fremont from command with him. Before Cameron departed Washington, Chase recommended that the general be retained if he displayed "vigor, capacity, and integrity," but if Fremont did not have those qualities, "let nothing prevent you from taking the bull by the horns."[57] Based on a telegram that Cameron sent to Lincoln on October 12, the secretary of war intended to give Fremont the president's order but the general pleaded with Cameron, begging for more time to deliver a victory, and the war secretary agreed. According to Cameron, Fremont "was very much mortified, pained, and, I thought, humiliated. He made an earnest appeal to me . . . I told him that I would withhold the order until my return to Washington, giving him the interim to prove the reality of his hopes as to reaching and capturing the enemy, giving him to understand that should he fail, he must give place to some other officer."[58]

Cameron's decision to retain Fremont fed divisions in the cabinet, with Chase and Seward supporting the secretary of war and Bates and Blair demanding that the general be relieved.[59] Bates confided to his diary that it was now "beyond all question that the removal must be made and instantly—the President seemed to think so, and said it was now clear that Fremont was not fit for the command. . . . Still, at the very pinch, the Sec of State, came again, as twice before, to the rescue—and urged delay—both Cameron and Chase gave in and timidly yielded to delay; and the President still hangs in painful and mortifying doubt."[60]

Fremont's failure to deliver the victory he had promised Cameron convinced Lincoln to draft a new order removing the general from command, which reached Fremont on November 3.[61] At Cameron's behest, Quartermaster General Meigs ordered that no contracts signed before October 14 (the day Fremont was officially removed from command) should be paid. Cameron also instructed Meigs to remove one of Fremont's aides, Justus McKinstry. On October 25 Lincoln appointed a committee to investigate the contracts Fremont had signed and empowered to refuse payment to those it deemed inappropriate. Though Congress supported the president's decision by retroactively authorizing the local disbursing agent to pay claims based on the committee's recommendations, Lincoln's removal of Fremont infuriated Radicals, who redoubled their efforts to make abolition of slavery the war's primary aim.[62]

Cameron's sympathy for Fremont was based in part on the fact that the secretary of war agreed with the general that abolition of slavery was a legitimate war aim. Shortly after the cabinet meeting on April 15, Cameron described the proceedings to a reporter named James R. Gilmore. During their meeting in Cameron's office, the war secretary related his unsuccessful call for five hundred thousand volunteers and claimed that he had suggested "the giving of freedom to all slaves who would desert their masters and join the Union armies."[63] This contradicted Lincoln's plan to avoid antagonizing the border states, but inevitably the issue of slavery bled into military and strategic decision making.

Events in the field eventually forced the administration's hand. Following his successful occupation of Baltimore, Benjamin F. Butler was transferred to Fort Monroe in Hampton, Virginia. Shortly after Butler's arrival on May 22, three escaped slaves reached federal lines. These particular slaves belonged to Colonel Charles K. Mallory of the 115th Regiment of the Virginia Militia, which presented a delicate legal issue: whether the federal government was bound to abide by the Fugitive Slave Law (which was still U.S. law) when the slave owner in question was a rebel. Butler resolved not to return the escaped slaves but rather to write out a receipt, which was standard procedure when seizing property, and forward it to Colonel Mallory. In the meantime Butler declared the fugitive slaves "contraband of war" and set them to work around the fort. Soon thereafter one of Colonel Mallory's men arrived and demanded the slaves be returned under the Fugitive Slave Act. Butler refused, citing the fact that Virginia had seceded from the Union and could therefore not demand the enforcement of federal law. The Virginian retorted that, because the federal government's position was that the state could not secede, Butler was legally bound to enforce the Fugitive Slave Act and return the slaves. Butler countered that the slaves were contraband of war and, as a result, he was within his rights to keep them. Perhaps less sure of the law then he let on to Mallory, Butler requested guidance on the issue from the War Department. Cameron (with Chase's assistance) promptly authorized Butler to use the fugitive slaves' labor but cautioned the general not to "interfere" with loyal citizens' property rights.[64]

News of Butler's action elated abolitionists, who saw it as the first step in transforming the war against secession into a war against slavery. The administration was more cautious. If not handled gingerly, Butler's actions threatened to antagonize the border states, so Cameron issued the following orders: "The government cannot recognize the rejection by any state of its Federal obligations, nor can it refuse the performance of the Federal obligations resting upon itself."[65] This half-step reflected the administration's lack of a coherent policy regarding Confederate slaves, and it meant that the federal government's approach to this issue was largely reactionary. In September, Cameron took another half-step, ordering Butler to send "all negro men capable of performing labor" (as well as their families) to General McClellan so they could be "usefully employed on the military works in this vicinity."[66] In mid-October, he ordered General Thomas Sherman, then occupying Port Royal, South Carolina, to accept fugitive slaves into his camp and organize them into labor squads. Cameron's orders including the follow-ing instruction: "And you will assure all persons held to invol-untary labor, who may thus be received into the service of the Government, that they will, under no circumstances, be again reduced to their former condition, unless at the expiration of their respective terms of service, they freely choose to return to the service of their former masters." Before Thomas Scott could send Cameron's letter, however, it came to the president's attention, and inserted a clause that made clear that, while fugi-tive slaves could be organized into work details, there would no "general arming of [escaped slaves] for military service."[67]

Meanwhile, the Radicals in Congress tried to force Lincoln's hand. Yet as 1861 closed, a growing number of congressmen demanded that blacks be allowed to serve. Increasingly, even moderates were questioning the logic of preventing blacks from volunteering, particularly when thousands of whites were dying. As one newspaper asked, "Shall we love the Negro so much that we lay down our lives to save his?"[68] On July 22 the House of Representatives passed a resolution asking the War Depart-ment if it had any information "whether the Southern Con-federacy, so-called, or any State thereof, has in their military service . . . any negroes"; Cameron responded three days later that the department had no information.[69] The point of the resolution was obvious: if the Confederacy enlisted slaves, the administration would have to recognize abolition as a legiti-mate war aim. In August, Congress passed and Lincoln (reluc-tantly) signed the Confiscation Act of 1861. The law allowed courts to confiscate slaves from owners who participated in the rebellion. However, the bill did not officially emancipate the slaves, so in practice escaped slaves who came into Union lines became property of the United States government. As Cam-eron noted in response to Butler's most recent query about War Department policy regarding escaped slaves, "Under these cir-cumstances, it seems quite clear that the substantial rights of loyal masters will be best protected by receiving such fugitives, as well as fugitives from disloyal masters, into the service of the

United States, and employing in such occupations as circumstances may suggest or require."[70] When prompted by Butler for clarification regarding how this new law affected contraband policy, Cameron responded, "It is the desire of the President that all existing rights, in all the States, be fully respected and maintained. The war now prosecuted on the part of the Federal government is a war for the Union, and for the preservation of all Constitutional rights of the States, and the citizens of the States, in the Union."[71]

Despite the fact that he toed the administration's line in public, behind the scenes Cameron advocated arming freed slaves to the president as early as the summer of 1861, but to no avail. Chase recalled, "In addition to certain Border state matters, the principle subjects of conference between General Cameron and myself were slavery and the employment of colored troops. We agreed very early that the necessity of arming them was inevitable; but we were alone in that opinion. At least no other member of the administration gave open support, while the President and Mr. Blair, at least, were decidedly averse to it."[72] By the end of the summer, Cameron broke with the administration. In August, the war secretary promised Massachusetts Senator Charles Sumner that he would issue an order declaring every escaped slave who made it to Union lines free.[73] Cameron's statement delighted the Radicals—in the autumn Sumner marveled that Cameron "goes beyond Fremont"—and a few weeks later he confided to a friend that *"the Secy of War & Secy of the Navy are both determined to make the war bear on slavery. . . .* I know it from their own lips."[74] On November 1 the secretary of war journeyed to New York with Colonel John Cochrane of the 65th New York Regiment, a "War Democrat." There, Cameron was serenaded at the Astor House and gave a short speech. What made the trip memorable, however, was the fact that after Cameron spoke, Cochrane delivered his own speech in which he called for arming blacks.[75] Cameron said nothing in response, leading many to conclude that he agreed with Cochrane's sentiments.

Cameron went even further two weeks later. On November 13 Cochrane delivered a fiery and provocative speech in which he called for arming slaves and "in God's name" bidding them to "strike for the human race."[76] Cameron heard the speech and, according to at least one newspaper, said, "I APPROVE OF EVERY SENTIMENT UTTERED BY YOUR NOBLE COMMANDER. All the doctrines he has laid down, I approve of, as if it were uttered in my own words. They are my sentiments, and the sentiments which will eventually lead to victory."[77] Cameron's endorsement of Cochrane's speech ruffled more than a few feathers, and on November 22 Lincoln's friend Joshua F. Speed forwarded a letter to the president he had received from James Guthrie. Guthrie complained that "the speech of John Cochrane endorsed by Secretary Cameron has given us much trouble [in Kentucky]. . . . The man must be demented or he would not be always throwing these stumbling blocks in the way of friends of the Union in the border states."[78] More than a decade later, Cameron was still bitter about Speed's letter, noting, "Lincoln complained that [Cameron's speech to Cochrane's men] would have hurt him in Kentucky—he was always afraid of Kentucky—he believed everything Speed told him about it. We didn't get any troops in KY."[79] At a cabinet meeting two days after Cochrane's speech, Cameron aggressively made the case for arming former slaves, which apparently made Lincoln unhappy, though the president said nothing. By contrast, Interior Secretary Caleb Smith and Attorney General Edward Bates vigorously attacked Cameron's recommendations, possibly with the president's approval.[80]

Cameron's advocacy of arming African Americans soon became public knowledge. Invited to a reception at John W. Forney's house for *Louisville Journal* editor George D. Prentice, Cameron became embroiled in a debate with Interior Secretary Caleb Smith over arming former slaves. Smith was so opposed to abolition that, when an acquaintance asked him how he would respond if Lincoln promulgated an emancipation proclamation, Smith claimed, "I will resign and go home and attack the administration."[81] (When Lincoln showed the draft of the Emancipation Proclamation to his cabinet, Smith was as good as his word; he resigned, leaving the cabinet on December 31, 1862, the day before the Emancipation Proclamation was officially promulgated.) When Cameron promised that he would arm any able-bodied man who wanted to serve, Smith ridiculed the idea, and the journalists in attendance published accounts of the argument. Prentice printed details of the confrontation in the *Louisville Journal,* denouncing Cameron for even broaching the topic of arming slaves.[82] Some members of the cabinet saw Cameron's increasingly vocal support of arming former slaves as a political ploy. For instance, Gideon Welles claimed that Cameron "was beguiled [by the belief he might be a candidate for the Presidency] and led to mount the nigger hobby," while Montgomery Blair joked to Cameron that the war secretary had "elbowed Fremont out of his place [among abolitionists], and himself quietly taken his seat in . . . [the] Abolition boat."[83]

By November 25, word of Cameron's anticipated recommendation appeared in the *New York Tribune.* John Cochrane later recalled, "[Cameron's] friends in Pennsylvania were startled with the rumor that he intended to [advocate arming slaves] and maintain the doctrine in his annual report, then preparing to be made to the President. A delegation of remonstrants visited him at his home in Washington. Chief among them was Col. John W. Forney. All night the angry debate raged against the obnoxious matter, till at length, as early day struggled through the curtained windows, the Secretary arose, walked to the sideboard, and filling a glass, said, '*Gentlemen, the paragraph stands,*' and drank off his whiskey and water.'"[84]

Cameron forwarded a copy of the report to Edwin Stanton for comment. Stanton was a successful attorney who had briefly served as Buchanan's attorney general. Years after the war, Cameron claimed that he "had hardly made a move in which the legality of any question could arise [until he received Stanton's advice]."[85] Stanton was a staunch unionist but he was also "a remarkably devious man" and an "unctuous double-dealer" who seems to have manipulated Cameron to effect the secretary's removal. Stanton "cordially indorsed [*sic*]" the paragraph that advocated arming of slaves, modifying only a few sentences of the report "so the lawyers will not carp at it."[86] Despite approving Cameron's recommendation, Stanton undermined the secretary of war by claiming to his friends that he did not want the war to become a crusade to abolish slavery. Stanton's brother-in-law even pressured New York's bankers not to loan the federal government any money until Cameron was removed from office.[87] As Stanton's biographer noted, "Wittingly or unwittingly, Stanton had prepared the way for Cameron's [firing] . . . which Stanton had long been advocating."[88]

The final report recommended, "If it shall be found that the men who have been held by the rebels as slaves are capable of bearing arms and performing efficient military service, it is the right, and may be the duty, of the Government to arm and equip them, and employ their services against the rebels, under proper military regulation, discipline, and command."[89]

In response to Cameron's report, Lincoln fumed, "This will never do! General Cameron must take no such responsibility. That is a question which belongs exclusively to me."[90] Lincoln's friend Joshua Speed, who had earlier expressed concern over Cameron's vocal support for arming slaves, defended the secretary of war by saying, "Mr. Cameron has exhibited the common weakness of talking in advance of action—Solomon says there is a time for all things. This is the time for action, not words—Many who condemn Mr. Cameron for what he said, would approve the conduct he invites when the case arises for it."[91] The president disagreed, and as late as August 1862, Lincoln refused units of African American volunteers, claiming it would turn "500,000 bayonets" in the border states against the Union.[92] When Lincoln raised the matter with Cameron, the secretary of war defended his action by (correctly) noting that Navy Secretary Gideon Welles had advocated the enlistment of fugitive slaves into the U.S. Navy in September.[93] The only cabinet member who came to Cameron's defense was Chase. Welles described the cabinet meeting:

On Saturday I learned [Lincoln] was displeased with portions of the report of the Secretary of War and quite as much displeased that it had been printed, and to some extent distributed without its first being submitted to him. He was especially dissatisfied with that part which assumed to state or enunciate the policy to be pursued by the administration in regard to slaves. . . . In the discussions that took place Cameron found a friend and supporter in the Secretary of the Treasury . . . No one condemned [Cameron's] views though there was general disapproval of his enunciation of a policy which if it were the policy of the administration properly belonged to the President to communicate to Congress and the country.[94]

On December 2 Montgomery Blair telegraphed postmasters across the country and ordered them to return Cameron's report, which only fueled rumors of a schism in the cabinet. The damage was done, however: some postmasters did not receive Blair's telegram, and both versions of Cameron's report were published in newspapers across the country. The editor of the *Daily Illinois State Journal* wrote to Cameron in order to tell him "how much pleasure your unmodified report has caused not only myself but <u>all the Republicans and many of the Democrats of Illinois</u>," a sentiment he expressed to his readers, calling the original report "a model of perspicacity, sound statesmanship, [and] shrewd, practical, common sense."[95]

On December 3 Lincoln sent his annual report to Congress without those of his cabinet secretaries. Thaddeus Stevens fanned the controversy's flames by attacking the president in a caustic speech that was widely reported in the newspapers. According to the *New York Times*, Stevens "declared that Gen. MCCLELLAN was trying to control the Legislative and Executive powers of the nation; that [McClellan] had threatened to resign unless the President should cause MR. CAMERON's report to be amended before received or reported to Congress. MR. STEVENS closed with some earnest and energetic declarations of his relentless purpose to overthrow the slave system, and sat down with applause from his side of the caucus."[96] On the other hand, the secretary of war's recommendations were not universally popular; in late December, Kentucky's state legislature passed a resolution calling upon the president to "dispense" with Cameron's services.

Cameron's recommendations have raised questions about how deep his convictions ran. Historian T. Harry Williams argued that the Radicals might have "winked at Cameron's peculation if he had been right on the issue of slavery," suggesting that Cameron's recommendations were driven by political, rather than military, considerations.[97] This ignores the fact that Cameron argued from the war's first shots that freeing the slaves of rebellious slave owners was a logical strategic move, and that by the summer of 1861 he had recommended enlisting African Americans. Senator Charles Sumner wrote in early June, he noted, "Nothing is more painful to me than this conflict, except that I feel it was inevitable, & that the result will be the extinction of Slavery. Our Secy of War, who is no enthusiast, admitted to me only a week ago, that it would 'wipe out Slavery.'" According to a letter Cameron wrote in mid-December, "The opinions upon the subject of slavery in that report are not of recent vintage, but have been entertained by me during nearly all my life; and I have acted, in accordance with them, upon all proper occasions."[98]

But Cameron did not stop at merely advocating enlisting slaves as a war measure; as previous chapters have illustrated, Cameron seems to have held pretty advanced attitudes on race, and these were reflected in his policies at the War Department. While secretary of war, Cameron retained a black clerk named Francis Datcher who had worked in the department for nearly forty years. Cameron knew Datcher for decades and seems to have genuinely respected the man. When Cameron resigned from the War Department, he wrote the following testimonial praising Datcher's service:

> More than forty years ago I came to Washington, a boy, on business connected with the War Department, and was kindly and courteously received by Francis Datcher, a colored man,

having the manners and deportment of a gentlemen, who ushered me into the presence of Mr. Calhoun, then Secretary of War. Almost every year since, in passing through the various grades of life open to every American, I have had occasion to visit the War Department, and I have always found Datcher at his post, as courteous and civil as when I first saw him. When I entered upon my duties as head of this Department, I was glad to have the opportunity to say: "Francis, while I am here, you will do me a great favour if you will remain, and extend to me the treatment which I have long received at your hands during our long years of acquaintance."[99]

Cameron's advocacy of arming African Americans, far from a political move, seems to have reflected both his commitment to win the war and his personal aversion to slavery.

Even as the controversy over Cameron's report raged, events in the winter of 1861–62 intensified calls for changes at the War Department. Congressman Henry Dawes captured the prevailing sense of despair when he noted in early January 1862, "Confidence in everybody is shaken to the very foundation. . . . The credit of the country is ruined—its army impotent, its Cabinet incompetent, its servants rotten, its ruin inevitable."[100] Quartermaster Meigs was at his wits' end: all of the money appropriated for expenses and supplies was gone, and he could only keep things going by appealing to the patriotism of suppliers to extend him generous credit.[101] Ominously, a group of New York bankers had informed the president that they would not subscribe to Chase's recent call for $100 million in bond sales unless Lincoln replaced Cameron.[102]

Worse, the military situation had not improved. As Bates noted to his diary, "The Sec of War and the President himself are kept in ignorance of the actual condition of the army and the intended movements of [McClellan]—if indeed they intend to move at all—In fact the whole administration is lamentably deficient in the lack of unity and coaction. There is no quarrel among us, but an absalute [sic] want of community of intelligence, purpose, and action."[103] Bates was not the only one frustrated about the administration's inability to command the army; writing to General Thomas W. Sherman around this time, Cameron confided, "I am constrained to believe that all the operations of our army have been too much delayed and there has been too great a desire to avoid responsibility rather than to force the enemy into early action. The fact seems to be overlooked that while we are preparing our enemy is also engaged in preparation, and that being in his own country, he can do so much more rapidly than ourselves."[104]

Following the controversy over Cameron's report, the president seems to have sidelined the war secretary, who played little or no part in meetings about the conduct of the war. Rumors that Cameron would resign from the cabinet circulated in Washington as early as the fall, and some expected him to leave in early November. Writing to diplomat John Bigelow in early September, army officer James Bowen claimed, "Cameron had expressed his readiness to leave the Cabinet. A week since it was probable that both he and Welles would vacate their offices."[105] That same month, Chase revealed to a friend that Cameron had expressed his willingness to leave the cabinet, suggesting that the war secretary left rather than being forced out.[106] By contrast, Navy Secretary Gideon Welles recalled that "it was determined that Mr. Cameron should retire from the office of Secretary of War,—not wholly for the reason given out, but for certain loose matters of contracts, and because he had not the grasp, power, energy, comprehension, and important qualities essential to the administration of the War Department, to say nothing of his affiliation with Chase." On the other hand, he also later claimed that "I had no doubt from the aspect of affairs after the first of December that Mr. Cameron was to leave the Cabinet," laying the blame chiefly on Cameron's report.[107]

Welles's contention that Cameron was forced out dovetails with an assertion by Mexico's ambassador to the United States, Matías Romero, who called Cameron's departure "often speculated," and noted "Cameron apparently did not even resign, but the president removed him." Romero believed that Cameron was forced out because the secretary of war and the president held "divergent views on the question of slavery" and the fact that Cameron had been "discredited because of the contracts he signed for armaments, clothing, and food for the army."[108] Cameron always maintained that he had resigned because the president needed a scapegoat and he was willing to "fall on his sword." In the 1870s Cameron told a reporter, "It was necessary for somebody to go out and attend to Fremont. [Montgomery] Blair went first and came back and equivocated. I told Lincoln, I understand this—Fremont has got to be turned out, and somebody will have to bear the odium of it—If I go and do It I will probably lose my place here. In that case, you must give me a foreign mission. That was the beginning of the Russian Mission."[109]

It is not at all surprising that Cameron tried to convince the public that he had left Lincoln's cabinet willingly and as a martyr to political necessity, but this version of events also appears in his private correspondence with his former colleagues in the cabinet officials. For instance, in a December 1862 letter to Chase, Cameron wrote, "To my mind, some change of men is necessary for the preservation of the country. I thought so, last winter, when the President said he needed a 'scape goat,' and I needed no second whisper to induce me to give place to another." If this was untrue, it was an odd statement to make to Chase given that the secretary of the Treasury would have known the actual circumstances behind Cameron's departure from the cabinet.[110]

In any event, on January 10 Lincoln convened a cabinet meeting, during which Bates complained that Lincoln needed to "act out the powers of his place, to command the commanders."[111] Following the meeting, Lincoln spoke with Thurlow Weed and asked the editor for his opinion about removing Cameron from the Cabinet. At some point in the day, Lincoln vented his frustration to Quartermaster Meigs about the general state of the war. Late that evening, the president called a council of war that included Seward and Chase, but *not* Cameron; Assistant Secretary of War Thomas Scott attended instead.[112] On January 11, Cameron received a note from Lincoln that read, "As you have, more than once, expressed a desire for a change of position, I can now gratify you, consistently with my view of the public interest. I therefore propose nominating you to the Senate, next Monday, as Minister to Russia."[113] Lincoln's note was uncharacteristically brusque and implied that the president offered Cameron the Russia mission because it had suddenly become available, but this was not the case; rumors that Cassius M. Clay, the U.S. Minister to Russia, would return home appeared in American newspapers at least two months before.[114] Offended by the note's tone, Cameron visited Chase later that evening. Cameron expressed uncertainty about whether he was leaving the cabinet, remarking to Chase that he was "determined to maintain himself at the head of his department if he remained, and resist thereafter all interference," to which the Treasury secretary replied that he would support the Pennsylvanian.[115] At Chase's suggestion, the two men went to Willard's Hotel to confer with Seward.[116] Both Chase and Seward told Cameron to see the president about the letter in the morning, a plan to which the Pennsylvanian agreed.[117] Later that evening, however, Cameron wandered over to Thomas A. Scott's house where, in the presence of both Scott and Alexander McClure, the secretary wept over the letter's abrupt tone, throwing it down in front of the two shocked men, and claiming that it signaled his personal and political ruination. By one account, Cameron was extremely intoxicated, and both men tried comforting him by claiming that the letter's tone probably reflected the fact that Lincoln was busy with the war.

The following day, Seward and Chase asked Lincoln to rescind the note and draft a new, more complimentary letter. Lincoln complied with their request, backdating the new letter to January 11. In it the president wrote, "Should you accept, you will bear with you the assurance of my undiminished confidence, of my affectionate esteem, and of my sure expectation that, near the great sovereign whose person and hereditary friendship for the United States, so much endears him to Americans, you will be able to render services to your country, not less important than those you could render at home."[118] Cameron responded with a face-saving letter of resignation that recounted the version of his cabinet career that he would tell for the rest of his life.

> When you invited me to Springfield, Illinois, and presented me the choice of one, of two places named in the list of your Constitutional advisors, I could not, for grave public reasons, and after great reflection, refuse a trust so trying and laborious. My life has been one of constant labor and excitement; . . . I have devoted myself, without intermission, to my official duties; I have given them all my energies; I have done my best. It is impossible, in the direction of operations so extensive, but that some mistakes happen and some complications and complaints arise. In view of these recollections, I thank you from a full heart, for the expression of your "confidence in my ability, patriotism, and fidelity to the public trust." . . . In retiring from the War Department, I feel that the mighty Army of the United States, is ready to do battle for the Constitution—-that it is marshaled by gallant and experienced leaders—that it is fired with the greatest enthusiasm for the good cause; and also, that my successor, in this department, is my personal friend, who unites to wonderful intellect and vigor, the grand essential of being in earnest in the present struggle, and of being resolved upon a speedy and overwhelming triumph of arms. I therefore, gracefully accept the new distinction you have conferred upon me, and as soon as important and long neglected private business has been arranged, I will enter upon the important duties of the mission to which you have called me.[119]

On the evening of January 13, Bates noted to his diary the news of Cameron's departure from the cabinet, which he heard from New York senator Ira Harris, caught him completely by surprise. Nothing about it had been discussed at the cabinet meeting the previous Friday and "stranger still, I have not been sent for by the Prest. Nor spoken to by any member."[120]

Lincoln's choice of Edwin Stanton to replace Cameron is also shrouded in contradictory reports. Cameron later claimed that he engineered Stanton's appointment. According to this version, Cameron met with Lincoln and convinced an initially skeptical president that Stanton was the best choice. Welles contradicted this narrative, arguing instead that Lincoln's nomination reflected Seward's influence. According to Welles, "It was a surprise, not only to the country but to every member of the Administration but the Secretary of State, that Stanton was selected."[121] According to Seward's most recent biographer, the president visited Seward's home one evening in early January. Apparently, Lincoln complained about Cameron's administration of the War Department, and the two men discussed replacements, eventually settling on Edwin Stanton.[122] According to Welles, Seward did this because Stanton had fed the secretary of state information about the Buchanan administration, so he "assumed he would have a trusty and reliable friend and supporter in the War Department in place of Cameron, who had left him for Chase."[123]

Whatever the real story behind Stanton's nomination, Cameron's political enemies delighted in his fall from power. Former secretary of war Joseph Holt wrote to Lincoln on January 15 to "express the desire that I feel as an American citizen to thank you—which I do from my heart—for the appointment of the present Secretary of War."[124] Lincoln's secretary John Nicolay called the change "a very important and much needed one," while General George Meade noted that "everyone seems relieved at the change in the War Department."[125] Worse, it was clear that the public did not entirely buy the story that Cameron had willingly resigned. In a letter to diplomat John Bigelow, Irish reporter W. H. Russell claimed that Lincoln had "sacrificed" Cameron as a sop to Democrats in the border states.[126] One correspondent wrote to Cameron in mid-January and referred to the suspicion "of it having been made so uncomfortable [for Cameron] that resignation was the only course left."[127] N. P. Sawyer, a dry goods merchant in Pittsburgh, wrote to Cameron and mentioned the widespread belief "that you have been removed from the cabinet because you advocated the use of all the means within our reach to put down this outrageous rebellion."[128] The War Department's clerks and army personnel were so unhappy to see Cameron go that they went to his house en masse to wish him well. Cameron's friends and supporters sent along consolatory letters. One correspondent perhaps captured it best when he said, "I don't care whether you are the Secretary of War, Minister to Russia, or his dispenser of patronage, I think you continue to be Simon Cameron."[129]

Though Cameron's term as war secretary ended on January 13, he stayed in the position until Stanton took the reins on January 20.[130] While Cameron's departure from the cabinet might have made Lincoln's life easier, it did little to quiet the Pennsylvanian's critics, who kept up a relentless assault against him. On January 13 Representative Henry L. Dawes of the Contracts Committee unleashed a verbal tirade against Cameron that culminated in a call for the outgoing secretary's censure. While the Senate Foreign Affairs Committee unanimously supported Cameron's nomination to be minister to Russia, Senator Lyman Trumbull objected, and the Senate went into executive session to discuss the matter. Matías Romero called the opposition to Cameron's appointment "violent," mentioning that it had the unique effect of giving Radical Republicans and Democrats something in common.[131] Despite Trumbull's best efforts, the Senate voted to confirm Cameron's appointment, 28 to 14, and that only with a great deal of effort on Charles Sumner's part.[132]

Meanwhile, the tone at the War Department changed dramatically following Cameron's departure. Stanton immediately decreed that the department would conduct public business on Mondays and meet with senators and representatives on Saturdays; all other days were reserved for issues dealing with military operations. In addition, he announced he would see no one, and transact no business, outside of his office.[133] When Chase arrived at the War Department on Cameron's last day, all he found was Stanton, a single clerk, and a detective. In a letter to his daughter, Chase noted, "After frauds already! Let the defaulters & thieves look out!!" Stanton appointed two commissioners to audit all pending claims against the department, and on April 1, Charles Leib was removed from his position as quartermaster due to misbehavior. Though Cameron had little to do with his onetime political lieutenant, he could not escape being tarred with Leib's disgrace, which was compounded a few months later when Leib published the salacious *Nine Months in the Quarter-Master's Department; or, The Chance for Making a Million*, which seemed to prove all of the vague charges of corruption swirling around army procurement. Stanton showed little of the loyalty to his subordinates that Cameron had shown, firing a few solely to satisfy the Committee on the Conduct of the War.[134] One of Cameron's former clerks wrote to him in February complaining of "a general moan around the walls of the department. . . . It appears in truth as if daily confusion grows worse. . . . We have orders upon orders, all seemingly predicated on the idea that everything heretofore was disorder and fraud."[135]

Though Cameron's brief tenure as secretary of war has made his name shorthand for profiteering, graft, and corruption, it is certainly worth noting that Stanton came in for criticism along similar lines. Postmaster Montgomery Blair called Stanton a "great scoundrel" and asserted (but offered no proof) that he made "all sorts of fraudulent contracts, to put money in his own pocket—that, in that way, 'Cameron was a fool to him.'"[136] After initially expressing enthusiasm at Stanton's appointment, within a month diarist George T. Strong complained that "Mr. Cameron promised and repromised us reforms, but nothing was done. . . . So with Lincoln. So with Stanton." By early summer he noted that "people talk against [Stanton] almost as freely as they did against Cameron. . . . They overrated him absurdly at first, and now condemn him a knave and a fool."[137]

Recognizing the incredible challenges facing the government during the war's first year, A. Howard Meneely wrote, "Only a Secretary of almost superhuman capacity could have satisfied the needs of the time, and Cameron soon proved he was not such a man."[138] Allan Nevins claimed that as secretary of war, Cameron "was honest and did his best. But he was a misfit . . . clumsy, forgetful, [and] unsystematic." Russell Weigley, whose biography of Montgomery C. Meigs is uniformly critical of Simon Cameron, nonetheless conceded that "despite many allegations to the contrary, Cameron was a careless administrator rather than a dishonest one, and that he received blame for a good deal of administrative chaos that was not of his making but unavoidable in the rapid expansion of his department and the Union armies."[139] Historian Geoffrey Perret has claimed that "Cameron was not a thief," noting, "For all its absurdities and failures, the mobilization of the Union Army was a success without precedent. It was so phenomenally successful at putting any men into the field quickly that no subsequent American mobilization could compare. Its failings were those mainly of success, and only partly those of Simon Cameron."[140] Cameron himself ruefully summarized his time at the War Department this way: "At first having no means at my command; then laughed at for predicting the war would be a long and bloody one; and all the time harassed by contractors and others who were bent on making all they could out of the crisis, I was certainly not in a place to be envied. Still, I held on, doing what I could, until, sincerely believing that it would be for the best, I recommended that the negroes of the South be armed and employed in the service of the Union. That idea was a trifle too advanced for the time, and the end of it was that I was out of the cabinet."[141]

8

"A Man Out of Office in Washington," 1862–67

Cameron's ouster from the cabinet was the nadir of his long political career, and in December 1862 Cameron complained, "A man out of office in Washington is greatly shorn of power."[1] Ironically, Cameron's removal from the cabinet actually strengthened his hand politically because it turned him into a martyr to the abolitionist cause while the Radicals were growing more powerful in the Republican Party. Over the five years between his resignation and his reelection to the Senate, Cameron rebuilt his relationship with Lincoln and then used his access to the president to secure a treasure trove of federal patronage for his supporters, thereby consolidating control over Pennsylvania's Republican Party.

Cameron's exit from the cabinet in no way sated his many enemies; if anything, it emboldened them. On April 15 Cameron was arrested at the behest of Pierce Butler while on a trip to Philadelphia.[2] Cameron's lawyer, Benjamin H. Brewster, managed to get his client released, while Governor Curtin and Pennsylvania attorney general William Meredith investigated ways to derail the case under state law. In a letter to U.S. district attorney George A. Coffey, Attorney General Edward Bates laid out the larger implications should Butler's case against Cameron proceed. According to Bates, "There are other actions pending of a somewhat similar character—especially one against Secretary Welles in this District—and no doubt they will greatly multiply unless met vigorously and carefully."[3] Meredith suggested to Chase and Senator Benjamin Wade that Congress pass an act of indemnity, or a statue that protects from prosecution an individual who has broken the law, in order to stop the criminal proceedings against Cameron.

Congress, however, seemed disinclined to help the disgraced former war secretary. In the House of Representatives, Indiana Democrat William S. Holman introduced a resolution "that Simon Cameron, late Secretary of War, by investing Alexander Cummings with the control of large sums of the public money, and authority to purchase military supplies, without restriction . . . and by involving the government in a vast number of contracts with persons not legitimately engaged in the business pertaining to the subject-matter of such contracts . . . adopted a policy highly injurious to the public service and deserves the Censure of the House." The resolution passed by a vote of 79 to 45 (a total that included more than a few Republicans) on April 30.[4] More galling was that some of Cameron's personal friends voted for the measure, a devastating blow to someone who valued loyalty above all other virtues. Yet there was a silver lining of sorts: Cameron's recommendation that African Americans be recruited into the army won him the favor of many Radical Republicans, and their support now became evident. For instance, Cameron's sometime antagonist Thaddeus Stevens worked to prevent the House from censuring Cameron, and in early May he wrote to the former war secretary to bemoan the fact that "some men who I thought your friends deserted [you]."[5]

In addition, the censure resolution forced Lincoln to defend Cameron, albeit reluctantly. Three weeks after the censure, Lincoln transmitted to Congress a defense of Cameron's tenure as war secretary, saying, "Congress will see that I should be wanting equally in candor and in justice if I should leave the censure . . . to rest exclusively or chiefly upon Cameron. The same sentiment is unanimously entertained by the heads of the departments, who participated in the proceedings, which the House of Representatives has censured. It is due to Mr. Cameron to say that, although he fully approved of the proceedings, they were not moved nor suggested by himself, and that not only the President, but all the other heads of departments, were at least equally responsible with him for whatever error, wrong, or fault was committed in the premises."[6] Cameron thanked Lincoln in a letter, saying he would "never cease to be grateful" for the president's defense, but all of these developments left Cameron "in no good humor with many people."[7]

Though Lincoln (tepidly) defended Cameron's actions as secretary of war, the president did little else to assist the Pennsylvanian. As he prepared to leave for Russia, Cameron tried to ensure that Lincoln would "take care of" his supporters and friends when it came to patronage; failure to do so would guarantee the destruction of his political machine in Pennsylvania. In late June, Chase responded to Cameron's complaints that the administration was not doing enough to provide for the Pennsylvanian's supporters by noting the challenges the Treasury secretary faced. "It is impossible to take a mere list and follow it implicitly, without regard to the views of others, you being thousands of miles away, while others were at hand and [the president] desirous that they might be gratified. You know doubtless that Mr. Lincoln had notes sent to members enquiring whom they wanted [appointed from] their respective district."[8]

That he was not particularly keen about going to Russia is evidenced by the fact that he tried to finagle his way back into the Senate. In mid-February, one supporter—clearly responding to Cameron's inquiries—confidently asserted, "I think I can get a party from the different districts that would insure you a good many democratic votes for the United States Senatorship."[9] Cameron laid the groundwork for a return to the Senate by purchasing the John Harris mansion in Harrisburg so that he could be close to the state capital. He even went so far as to inquire about the possibility of securing a diplomatic post for David Wilmot, whose departure from the Senate would create a vacancy that Cameron could fill. Wilmot was in poor health, but was willing to accept a diplomatic position provided he was posted in Southern Europe, where he thought the warm weather would help him recover. Chase agreed to prevail on Lincoln to appoint Wilmot, though rumor had it that the president opposed the plan and nothing came of it.[10] As a result Cameron resigned himself to taking up his diplomatic post in Russia.

Thus, publicly disgraced and obviously out of favor with Lincoln, on May 7, Cameron, his wife, Margaret, their son Simon, their daughter Maggie, his private secretary Kintzing Pritchett, and Secretary of the Legation Bayard Taylor departed New York for Liverpool aboard the *Persia*. The Camerons spent ten days touring Britain, shopping, and meeting with notables, including the irascible Henry Adams, son of Lincoln's minister to England. In a letter to his brother, the twenty-four-year-old Adams acerbically noted, "The last week we have had that whited sepulcher General Cameron here, and as were invited to have our first large dinner on Wednesday, he was invited to it. Then last night I took him to Monckton Milnes, where he was the object of considerable interest. I can't say that I was proud of my charge, nor that I like his style. . . . I hope he will vanish into the steppes of Russia and wander there for eternity. He is of all my countrymen one of the class that I most conspicuously and sincerely despise and detest."[11] From England the Camerons journeyed to France, where he dined with U.S. ambassador to France William L. Dayton. Then, it was onto Belgium, Holland, and Germany, finally arriving (after a thirty-two-hour train ride from Prussia) in St. Petersburg on June 15.[12]

U.S.-Russian relations at this particular moment were quite good, given that the two countries shared a common enemy: Great Britain. Less than a decade earlier, Russia had suffered a stinging defeat in the Crimean War at the hands of a British-led coalition that was determined to check Russian expansionism into areas controlled by the Ottoman Empire. Americans supported the Russians, and the United States aided Russia by supplying it and allowing Russian shippers to sail under American neutrality. The United States tried, unsuccessfully, to broker a peace between Russia and Great Britain's coalition, and private U.S. citizens skirted American neutrality by doing business with Russian firms, thereby aiding the Russian war effort. Though Russia lost the war, she "had not forgotten the touch of America's helping hand during the [war] and now was only too willing not to ally herself with Great Britain." The only issue of substance Cameron faced on his arrival was negotiating the construction of an intercontinental telegraph line between Russia and the United States across the Bering Strait. Leaving nothing to chance, Seward had instructed Clay to ensure that Cameron had "little to do" in Russia, perhaps the best evidence that Lincoln nominated the Pennsylvanian for reasons other than diplomatic skill.[13]

Upon arriving in Russia, Cameron was annoyed to find that he had to occupy the house Cassius M. Clay had rented at the exorbitant cost of $3,000 per year because the lease ran until September 1. Clay had only been ambassador for a year, but he had already made quite an impression. A wealthy planter who was related to Lincoln's hero Henry Clay, Cassius M. Clay was a well-known and vocal abolitionist who had served in the Kentucky House of Representatives and as a cavalry captain during the Mexican-American War. He was brash and outspoken and had survived an assassination attempt when (despite having been shot in the chest) he knifed his assailant and threw the man over an embankment. Rough around the edges, he was described as a "boisterous showman . . . [who] liked to sport his pearl handled . . . knife at the Czar's court." Clay, whom one historian has described as "unpredictable," had resigned his position in order to join the army (Cameron carried with him a major general's commission for Clay), but before Clay even returned to the United States he apparently had second thoughts, writing to Lincoln that Cameron would not remain long in St. Petersburg and asking to be reappointed to the ministership.[14]

On June 25 Clay presented Cameron and Bayard Taylor to Czar Alexander II. During the interview Cameron thanked the czar for the support he had shown to the U.S. government during the secession crisis and complimented Alexander on having promulgated the Emancipation Manifesto of March 3, 1861, which granted serfs all the rights of citizens. Cameron found his introduction to Alexander entirely satisfactory, claiming that the czar "took a liking to him." In a letter to the president, Cameron gushed to Lincoln about the czar's solicitude, noting that the entire court was out of St. Petersburg at that particular moment, so the Russian had made a special trip into the city to meet the new American minister.[15]

Despite the warmth of their reception, the Camerons were unhappy in Russia. In a letter to his daughter Rachel, Cameron noted, "This is a cold hard climate, and to us, the city [St. Petersburg] is very dull as we have no acquaintances and cannot speak so as to make them."[16] While Cameron was abroad, his brother William looked after the former war secretary's farm. On July 21 William wrote to his brother to assure him that Cameron's farm had produced a good harvest and to report that he had purchased more than 2,500 acres of land for coal mining, apparently a joint business venture for the two brothers.[17] Meanwhile, Cameron's son Donald looked after his father's political affairs. Over the summer of 1862, Donald met with Cameron's supporters and even began organizing financial support for a potential Senate campaign.[18] These efforts quickly bore fruit: in late June one supporter wrote to Cameron and claimed, "Your friends are in such high spirits that you will not be satisfied with the Senate but will turn your eyes to higher office. . . . I have no doubt that wherever your ambition may lead you will have thousands who will go with you and strive to make you triumphant."[19] During the fall of 1862, a number of Cameron's supporters wrote to Donald to share political intelligence and pressure the younger Cameron to get his father to come home.[20]

His supporters need not have worried: from the moment Cameron set foot in St. Petersburg, he began planning his return to

Pennsylvania. In a letter dated July 9, Cameron confided to one of his former clerks that he intended to return home immediately to rebut "the charges brought against my administration of the War Department."[21] The day after meeting the czar, Cameron wrote to Seward and Lincoln requesting an immediate furlough so that he could return to the United States, defend his reputation, and salvage his political career. "Going [at mid-September], will enable me to reach home in time before the Pennsa. [sic] election to be of some service to my country, for I think your troubles will soon be removed from the Army to Congress. I shall make this application to the State Department officially—but I ask it now, from your friendship"[22] In early August, the British North American Royal Mail-Steam Packet Company confirmed Cameron's room assignments on a steamer leaving from Liverpool in October, but Seward denied Cameron's June 26 request for a furlough, so the Pennsylvanian elected to accompany his wife back to the United States and planned to resign once he arrived. While he made preparations to leave, Cameron again asked for a furlough and requested both his son Donald and Chase to pressure Seward into granting it. On September 6 Seward did just that, but the news reached Cameron in Geneva on October 10 as he was en route to the United States.

A curious incident occurred during Cameron's trip from St. Petersburg to London. During a stopover in a small German town, Cameron saw a black man standing in the crowd. Working his way over to the man, whom he mistakenly assumed to be American, Cameron asked the man in German, "How are you, my friend?" Cameron was shocked when the man turned to face him, replying in Dutch, "I am no American; I am an African, and if you are an American I do not want to talk to you. I won't talk to any man who comes from a country professing to being free, in which human beings are held as slaves." At this, Cameron shrank away but later ran into the man again, who took the opportunity to upbraid the former war secretary for slavery, ending his rant with "Say, am I right, or am I wrong, answer me?"[23] Before Cameron could respond, his interrogator ambled away. The encounter was widely printed in American newspapers and seemed to confirm Cameron's liberal attitudes on race, which only further endeared him to the abolitionist wing of the Republican Party.

A committee of friends welcomed Cameron when his ship arrived in New York, and when he finally arrived at Lochiel, his country estate in Lancaster County, Pennsylvania, he discovered many letters of support. Cameron returned at a propitious moment. Clay had resigned his commission, and Lincoln was under enormous pressure to find a place for him. The Russia mission looked like an ideal solution to Lincoln's problem if Cameron planned on resigning it. Clay pressured Cameron to resign the Russia mission so that he (Clay) could have it back. The former ambassador even went so far as to see Lincoln in early September to persuade the president to allow Cameron to come home in the expectation that the Pennsylvanian would resign the Russian mission.[24] Lincoln told Cameron that he did not want to return Clay to Russia but that Clay's aggressive abolitionism was causing problems in Kentucky and, though Taylor was qualified for the position and doing well, the president's hands were tied.[25] Meanwhile, Clay exultantly, and rather tactlessly, bragged to Bayard Taylor that he would "return to Russia if Mr. Cameron returns and resigns as he promised me," a prospect that alarmed Taylor, who wanted the Russia mission for himself.[26]

Though back in the United States, Cameron stayed in regular contact with Taylor, frequently exchanging letters. Taylor proved himself adept at handling the mission's business, adroitly negotiating the proposed intercontinental telegraph line. Possibly in an attempt to give Taylor time to establish himself in the job, and thereby head off Clay's reappointment as minister to Russia, Cameron dragged his feet in resigning. As a result the president requested that Cameron come to Washington, which the Pennsylvanian did on December 14.[27] Yet Cameron did not resign, and met with the president (at Lincoln's request) again on January 6. This did not have the desired effect, and Lincoln anxiously telegraphed the Pennsylvanian in mid-February, saying, "Genl. Clay is here + I supposed the matter we spoke of will have to be definitely settled now. Please answer."[28] The former secretary of war did not actually resign until February 23, perhaps relishing the chance to cause Lincoln some political discomfort.[29] Despite his best efforts, Cameron was unable to fulfill the promise he had made to Taylor to engineer his ascension to the post, writing to Taylor that Clay was "making the most desperate effort to get back [to Russia]."[30] For his part Taylor refused to remain in Russia as Clay's assistant, and he returned to the United States in 1864.

Cameron's lingering bitterness over his departure from the cabinet was evident in a letter he wrote to Chase on Christmas Eve 1862. Writing about the fact that Seward had tendered, and then rescinded, his resignation, Cameron said, "In [Seward's] case, I would rather have lost my head than to have taken back my resignation—and yet, I knew he would do so."[31] Lincoln's promulgation of the Emancipation Proclamation on January 1, 1863, only stoked Cameron's resentment. When Chase wrote to Cameron and gloated, "At length the President and . . . Seward have come to the position we occupied a year ago," the former war secretary responded sarcastically, saying, "Well hurrah for Lincoln and the Emancipation Proclamation after the War Minister was deposed for the recommendation. Hurrah! Hurrah!"[32] Whatever Cameron's personal antipathy toward Lincoln, the Emancipation Proclamation burnished the Pennsylvanian's reputation and helped the former war secretary move past the lingering controversies from his time in the cabinet. In other words, Cameron's political rehabilitation had begun. There was even a widely circulated rumor that Cameron was organizing a black regiment to take the field, with himself in command. Though this was obviously not the case—at sixty-four Cameron was certainly in no shape for military service—it was credible enough that his friends and supporters volunteered to join.[33] One friend wrote to Cameron in mid-September, telling the former war secretary, "I hope you now see the power which you have with the Republican Party."[34]

With his fortunes radically changed from a year before, Cameron again thought seriously about being a candidate for the Senate when the Pennsylvania legislature convened in January 1863. He met with Pennsylvania's leading unionists, promising them that if they could deliver unanimous support he could find the necessary Democratic votes to ensure his election. One of the ways he pressured Democrats to "fall in line" was to ask Chase to have Stanton delay patronage appointments in Pennsylvania "for the reason that two or more men, who have votes, are seeking such places for friends."[35] The former war secretary asked for Chase's help and got it; the Treasury secretary approached various leaders of the iron and coal industries and asked them to support Cameron's candidacy, which they agreed to do.[36] Thomas A. Scott, Cameron's friend and former assistant, pressured acquaintances to support the former war secretary's senatorial ambitions, while Cameron himself traveled throughout the state drumming up support for his candidacy.[37]

Yet the outcome was hardly foreordained: at least four unionists pledged to McClure that they would *never* vote for Cameron, and at least one of Cameron's supporters wrote to dissuade the prospective candidate from running because of the "entire approbation of the people in this section of the State" for David Wilmot.[38] Cameron's supporters, undoubtedly with his knowledge, played a double-faced game: in public, they supported Wilmot while, at the same time, advanced Cameron's candidacy. As late as January 3, Wilmot sent Cameron a letter relating that he had (naively, as it later turned out) "assured all my friends that you would not be a candidate against me—That on this point we had a full understanding." Meanwhile, Cameron's allies solicited Democratic votes. Cameron reached out to an employee of the Northern Central Railroad, James L. Rightmyer, and asked him to approach T. Jefferson Boyer of Clearfield County and solicit his support. Boyer later claimed that Cameron personally offered him $10,000 and an appointment as paymaster in the army in exchange for his vote, and another legislator—P. Frazier Smith—indicated that he had not yet decided which way to vote but was very much in need of a $5,000 loan before he could make up his mind; Cameron obliged.[39]

Pennsylvania's Democrats, who had twice been burned by Cameron's deft political maneuvering, were determined not to be checked a third time. The party sent a trainload of armed thugs from Philadelphia and had them loiter menacingly around the Pennsylvania capitol. The message was clear: a Democrat who voted for Simon Cameron could expect to have an "accident" on his way out of the legislature.[40] In vain, Cameron appealed to his old enemy, Governor Curtin, to dispatch troops to protect Democrats who voted for him, but the governor, through McClure, claimed it would be inappropriate to "interfere" with the workings of a legislative assembly (the fact that the Democrats had imported people to do just that seemed not to have bothered him). In reality, it seems McClure refused in order to protect the party, which would have been split by the refusal of some Republicans to vote for Cameron if they believed he actually had a chance at "winning election to the Senate.[41] The night before the election, the Democrats nominated state senator Charles R. Buckalew, who was sure to unite their party.

The Pennsylvania legislature convened to vote for senator on January 13, 1863. Before the election, Republicans caucused and, on Cameron's assurances that he had Boyer's vote and therefore would be elected, nominated the former war secretary for senator. When the legislature convened for the election, however, Cameron was unable to deliver a single Democratic vote, and the seat went to Buckalew, who received sixty-seven votes to Cameron's sixty-five. Soon after the election, Cameron's friends cornered Boyer, who claimed that he was told that his vote was not necessary because two other Democratic votes had been found. Fearing for his safety, Boyer chose to remain at home.[42] Cameron blamed Wilmot, claiming in letters to Lincoln and Chase that one of Wilmot's friends had voted for William D. Kelley, thereby alarming Democrats pledged to vote for Cameron, who in turn voted for Buckalew.[43] McClure defended Wilmot, claiming that, even had Cameron managed to secure Democratic support, his enemies in the Republican Party would have voted for Buckalew rather than send Cameron back to the Senate.[44]

One Democrat, Albert Schofield, claimed that Cameron's supporters tried to bribe him, and the Democratic members of the Pennsylvania House of Representatives this allegation. Over the next three months, the investigating committee interviewed thirty-six witnesses during forty-three sessions, and the Democratic majority concluded that Cameron had employed "unlawful means" to win the seat.[45] At one point, four witnesses testified that Cameron met with Democratic state senator Jefferson Boyer at the State Capitol Bank or at the legislator's hotel room. Boyer later testified that he merely "played along" in the hope of protecting the Democratic Party and exposing Cameron's fraud.[46] Curiously, Cameron never testified, and the proceedings were an absolutely partisan affair, which resulted in the release of a minority report that attacked both Boyer's honesty and the majority's obvious unfairness. Nevertheless, the committee's Democratic majority directed Pennsylvania's attorney general to prosecute Cameron for bribery. The situation's direness forced Cameron to turn to Curtin and McClure for help. The Democratic victory in the 1862 midterm elections and the looming Pennsylvania gubernatorial election meant that more than Cameron's personal reputation and future were at stake; the entire party could be dragged down by an investigation into the election. McClure urged Attorney General William M. Meredith not to prosecute Cameron, and the state took no legal action against the former war secretary or any of the other parties involved.

Meanwhile, Cameron still faced the fallout from his tenure as secretary of war. In December 1862, Baltimore's police commissioners filed suit against Cameron and the Northern Central Railroad for damages arising from their arrests. Fortunately, Congress passed the Habeas Corpus Act, which retroactively protected government officials and military officers who arrested civilians as part of the effort to win the war. In addition, the act required that any lawsuits be transferred from state to federal courts, so the case was removed to federal court in Baltimore. The law did not, however, prohibit individuals who had been arrested for suing for damages, raising the prospect of expensive judgments against soldiers and other government officials. The former war secretary had lobbied hard for the Habeas Corpus Act, personally contacting his former colleagues in the Senate and pressing Lincoln to put the administration's weight behind it, due in no small part to the fact that he had a stake in its protections.

At that time, John Merryman, who had been arrested on Winfield Scott's orders, was suing General George Cadwalader in Maryland state court as well. In what could hardly have been a coincidence, the Northern Central Railroad, whose bridges Merryman had burned in April 1861, sued the Marylander and two other men for $200,000 in damages, likely to pressure Merryman to drop his suit against the former war secretary. Cameron was clearly involved in the case—Maryland's state attorney wrote to the former war secretary and advised him that the company could sue Merryman. In the fall of 1863, Merryman offered the railroad $2,600 but the Northern Central's management refused to settle. In addition, Cameron retained Thomas Alexander, the Northern Central railroad's former president, as his attorney. Alexander pushed for a vigorous defense, at one point suggesting to Cameron that the former war secretary might pressure the government to charge Merryman with treason, a crime that, if he were convicted, could cost the Marylander his life. Cameron forwarded Alexander's suggestion to Lincoln, and the former war secretary mentioned to Secretary of State Seward that the attorney showed "uncommon ability [and] great zeal and industry" in combating Merryman's case.[47] In mid-November, Alexander got Baltimore's police commissioners to drop their case against Cameron by stating in open court that Cameron had no role in their arrests. In the spring of 1865, Merryman dropped his suit against Cadwalader and the Northern Central dropped its suit against Merryman, likely as part of a quid pro quo arranged by the respective parties' attorneys.[48] Though it had taken nearly four years, Cameron managed to put Merryman's suit behind him.

Throughout 1863, Cameron worked behind the scenes to ease Curtin out of office, seeing the government as an impediment to his reelection to the Senate. The 1863 gubernatorial election was only a few months away, and Curtin was in poor health and was ambivalent about seeking another term as governor. Cameron wanted Representative John Covode, a prominent abolitionist who had served on the Joint Committee on the Conduct of the War, to succeed Curtin. In April, Cameron, along with McClure and John W. Forney, met with Lincoln at Curtin's suggestion, which resulted in a written promise from the president to tender the governor a first-class diplomatic post when the governor's term ended. After thanking the president, Curtin announced he would not run for a second term and acquiesced to Covode's nomination.[49] Unionists in Pennsylvania, however, strongly urged Curtin to run, particularly after the Democrats nominated Cameron's perennial antagonist, Pennsylvania Supreme Court justice George W. Woodward. In addition, Covode complained that Secretary of State Seward and Seward's wealthy patron, Thurlow Weed, were actively pushing Curtin to run.[50] By June, Cameron had guessed—correctly, as it later turned out—that Curtin would bow to public pressure and run again. In response, the former secretary of war set about derailing Curtin's chances.

Robert E. Lee's Gettysburg campaign temporarily interrupted Cameron's plans and brought the war to Pennsylvania, though it worked to the former war secretary's advantage by highlighting his unique access to the administration. Rumors of a Confederate invasion of Pennsylvania abounded in early June 1863, and Stanton ordered the creation of two new departments—the Monongahela and the Susquehanna—to organize the troops and coordinate a response. On June 10 Secretary of War Stanton sent Cameron a telegram informing his predecessor that Major General Darius Nash Couch had been given command of the newly created Department of the Susquehanna. In that telegram Stanton asked Cameron to "see [Couch] and give him what aid you can."[51] On June 12 Governor Curtin confirmed that a "large rebel force" threatened the state. At a meeting held at the Dauphin County Courthouse, Curtin, Cameron, Thomas A. Scott, and Couch urged their fellow citizens to help repel the invaders. Cameron, acting as the meeting's chairman, predicted that Lee would never be foolish enough to try to strike at the capital but, if the Confederate general did, the former war secretary pledged to grab a musket and join the militia under Curtin's command.[52] Cameron's enthusiasm was designed to spur local citizens to grab their guns and fight, a campaign that heretofore had not gone well. On June 9 Lincoln had called for one hundred thousand six-month volunteers from Pennsylvania and Maryland to help repel the Confederate forces, but only about a third of that number answered the call, in part due to the fact that these men would not receive the federal enlistment bounty. On June 16 Stanton sent a message to all Northern governors asking for more troops, and by June 26 Curtin was reduced to begging for sixty thousand men for ninety days or the duration of the emergency.[53]

By this point the Confederates were nearly on Pennsylvania's doorstep; on the very day that the Keystone State's Democratic Party nominating convention met—June 17—Confederate soldiers under Lieutenant General Richard S. Ewell crossed into Pennsylvania. Two weeks later, the Battle of Gettysburg prevented the Republicans from holding their party nominating convention, which was scheduled for July 1; it would now convene on August 5. McClure rushed to Philadelphia to try to raise troops to defend Harrisburg, but with disappointing results, and by June 30 he complained to Lincoln that "our people are paralyzed for want of confidence and leadership."[54] It all came to a head at Gettysburg, a little town approximately forty miles southwest of Harrisburg. Though a Union victory, the battle's toll was staggering: in three days of vicious fighting, nearly eight thousand soldiers died, and more than twenty-seven thousand others were wounded. Cameron's friend and former aide Bayard Taylor lost his younger brother at Gettysburg, a painful reminder of the war's growing cost.[55]

The Confederate retreat from Gettysburg allowed Cameron to resume his campaign against Curtin. At the Union State Convention in August, Cameron's lieutenants planned to nominate Covode in the hope of diluting Curtin's strength and thereby preventing the governor's renomination. The strategy apparently backfired by convincing many lukewarm Unionists that only Curtin could unite the party and win in October, and the convention renominated the governor on the first ballot. Even though Curtin's supporters had vigorously attacked the former war secretary in the lead-up to the fall campaign, Cameron fell into line and actively supported Curtin.[56] First he reined in newspaper attacks on Curtin—Russell Errett's *Cambria Tribune* went to far as to say, "The people know they may trust safely in [Curtin's] hands their dearest right"— and then he campaigned for the governor, though tepidly: in one speech, Cameron told his listeners, "I come not here to advocate the election of Andrew G. Curtin as Andrew G. Curtin; but I come here to aid in the election of the representative of the loyalty of Pennsylvania. This is not time for personal feelings, and I have none."[57] Writing to Cameron on October 9, one of the former war secretary's supporters said, "I am earnestly working for Curtin, and have contributed my means towards that end, and look upon the election of Woodward as a . . . calamity."[58] Woodward's refusal to resign from the bench hobbled his campaign, which relied on racial demagoguery and promises to sue for peace. Curtin defeated Woodward by fifteen thousand votes, only half of his margin of victory in 1860.[59]

Cameron was still angry at Lincoln over being forced out of the cabinet, a fact that led him to seek out alternative candidates for the Republican presidential nomination. In early

1863, Cameron discussed with General Benjamin F. Butler the idea of running for president. According to the former secretary of war, the next president would surely be a military man and, given Butler's prominence among abolitionists, Cameron reasoned that the general might have a realistic chance of winning the White House. Partially as a "trial run," Cameron invited Butler to Pennsylvania during the fall of 1863 to campaign for Curtin, but the general's ineptitude as a campaigner convinced the former secretary of war that Butler lacked the political skills to win the presidency, and by the end of the year Cameron resigned himself to Lincoln's renomination. Despite his disappointment, Cameron saw an opportunity: if he could play a significant role in Lincoln's renomination and reelection, he would gather crucial political capital that he could use to consolidate his control over Pennsylvania's Republican Party. So Cameron became an enthusiastic supporter of Lincoln's renomination and reelection, even quashing efforts to replace the president as the Republican's nominee. Years later, Cameron recalled that he traveled to Washington in late 1863 in response to an invitation from "a number of the most prominent gentlemen [who were undertaking] . . . a secret effort to bring about the ejectment of President Lincoln from the White House." According to Cameron, "I was asked for my advice. I gave it stating that it would be little short of madness to interfere with the administration."[60]

In a meeting with Cameron in January 1864, Lincoln expressed concern about running for a second term. Lincoln asked Cameron if the former secretary of war could engineer a letter on his behalf, as he had years earlier for Andrew Jackson to allow him to get around his pledge to serve only a single term, and the Pennsylvanian replied, "Yes, I think I might." Shortly after the New Year, Cameron "went to Harrisburg . . . [and represented to members of the legislature] the political situation, and advised them that such a letter as we had years before sent to Jackson should then be forwarded to Lincoln. They all agreed with me, and shortly afterward the letter was prepared and forwarded on behalf of all the Republican Senators and representatives of our State."[61] Cameron wrote Lincoln a letter grandiloquently declaring, "Providence has decreed your re-election and no combination of the wicked can prevent it."[62] The Pennsylvania legislature's letter to Lincoln galvanized the state's Radical Republicans, who saw the president as moving too slowly on the issue of slavery. The Radicals, led by Thaddeus Stevens, worked with McClure to postpone the Republican Nation Convention in order to find a candidate who could credibly challenge Lincoln for the nomination, but Cameron—working through various lieutenants—thwarted these efforts, defanging opposition to Lincoln and weakening the Curtin faction.

Cameron's efforts reaped the expected dividends, and he soon was welcomed back into Lincoln's orbit, though not in an official capacity. In early March 1864, Cameron escorted Ulysses S. Grant (newly promoted to lieutenant general) to a presidential reception at the White House, and the following month the president sent Cameron a note offering to see the Pennsylvanian "any time it is convenient for you to come."[63] By December, Lincoln's personal secretary John Nicolay (the man who, in early 1862, had called Cameron's removal from the War Department a "much needed" change) wrote to the Pennsylvanian and enthusiastically offered to "join you and others in the enterprise of buying and publishing the 'Baltimore Sun.'"[64]

Perhaps the best evidence of Cameron's political rehabilitation is the fact that Lincoln tasked his former war secretary with sounding out General Benjamin F. Butler's willingness to replace Hannibal Hamlin as the Republican Party's vice presidential nominee in 1864. The president was concerned about the fact that Radical Republicans were seriously considering challenging his renomination due to their frustration with the administration.[65] Lincoln had angered the radicals in the summer by pocket vetoing the Wade-Davis Bill, which set much higher standards for Confederate states to be readmitted to the Union than Lincoln's own plan, and the president hoped to offset that anger and broaden his political appeal by choosing a unionist Democrat to balance the ticket. Cameron later recalled:

> I had been summoned from Harrisburg the President to consult with him in relation to the approaching campaign. . . . Mr. Lincoln had been much distressed at the intrigues in and out of his cabinet to defeat his nomination; but that was now assured, and the question of a man for the second place on the ticket was freely and earnestly discussed. . . . Several men were freely talked of, but without conclusion as to any particular person. Not long after that, I was requested to come to the White House again. I went and the subject was again brought up by the President, and the result of our conversation was *that Mr. Lincoln asked me to go to Fortress Monroe and ask General Butler if he would be willing to run and, if not, confer with him upon the subject.*[66]

The allegation that Lincoln asked Cameron to act as his emissary to Butler has aroused a great deal of scholarly controversy, with some historians dismissing it outright.[67] As with so much about Cameron's political machinations, the truth is hard to get at because the documentary record is incomplete and marred by the self-serving impulses of the individuals involved. Cameron had toyed with seeking the vice presidency himself—the Pennsylvania legislature even passed a resolution endorsing a Lincoln/Cameron ticket—but, when he could not secure the needed support outside the state, gladly took on the role as Lincoln's emissary to Butler, or so the story goes. It is certain that Cameron visited Butler at Fort Monroe in March 1864, though this may have been Butler's idea rather than Cameron's. It was Butler who, on January 15, wrote to Cameron and asked him to "come down to Fortress Monroe and see me" about "matters of some moment and discretion."[68] On the other hand, Lincoln personally signed the pass that allowed Cameron to travel to Fortress Monroe on February 24, so it stands to reason that the former war secretary discussed the meeting with the president, as the Pennsylvanian later attested.[69]

Now nicknamed the "Beast of New Orleans" for issuing General Order 28, which stated his policy to treat any woman who disrespected soldiers under his command as whores, Butler recalled years later that he had facetiously (and somewhat tactlessly, given subsequent events) agreed to accept the vice presidential nomination only if Cameron could personally guarantee Lincoln's resignation or death within ninety days of being inaugurated. In a letter to Lincoln shortly after his meeting with Butler, Cameron reported in an almost offhand way that "I came from Ft. Monroe yesterday after spending three days there, during which time I had much pleasant conversation with Genl. Butler—part of which I would like to communicate to you."[70] Cameron later recalled that Lincoln seemed to "regret" Butler's decision, but the "Beast of New Orleans" was not the president's only option for a possible running mate: while Cameron had traveled to Fortress Monroe, Lincoln had reached out to former Tennessee governor and prominent war Democrat Andrew Johnson through General Daniel Sickles.

At the party's state convention, former state senator George V. Lawrence made Cameron chairman of the State Central Committee in spite of a memorial promoting McClure signed by a majority of the delegates. Cameron's allies ensured that Pennsylvania's fifty-two delegates to the Republican National Convention in Baltimore were bound to vote for Lincoln as a unit. As a sign of Cameron's return to the fold, Lincoln's secretary John Nicolay accompanied the Pennsylvanian to Baltimore.[71] Before the convention, the former secretary of war convened a meeting of the Pennsylvania caucus to select a vice presidential candidate; Andrew Johnson ranked third. Cameron orchestrated a complimentary vote for Hannibal Hamlin on the first ballot and then a switch to Johnson.[72] Cameron deliberately frustrated the convention's balloting by sending a written resolution to the clerk calling for a package nomination of Lincoln and Hamlin. Apparently, his goal was to hide the fact that the president wanted Hamlin off the ticket by making it appear that the convention demanded Johnson. The resolution had the desired effect, causing the convention to dissolve into a cacophony of "hurrahs" and angry objections, with Cameron standing "arms folded, grimly smiling, regarding with composure the storm he had raised."[73] Delegate and Kansas senator James H. Lane succeeded in having the motion withdrawn, claiming that it put him and the other members of his delegation (who were bound by instruction from their state committee to support Johnson) in an "awkward predicament."[74] Once a semblance of order had been restored, Cameron innocently agreed to withdraw his resolution if it was in the "best interests" of the party, initiating a roll call first for president and then vice president. The roll call for president went relatively smoothly—Lincoln received all but Missouri's twenty-two votes, which went to Ulysses S. Grant—but during the roll call for vice president, Pennsylvania first voted for Hamlin. However, before the vote could even be tallied, Cameron demanded recognition and, as chairman of the delegation, changed the state's vote to Johnson, setting off a crescendo of similar moves by state delegations throughout the convention that eventually left Hamlin with only nine votes.[75] Pennsylvania congressman Thaddeus Stevens fumed to McClure, "Can't you find a candidate for Vice-President in the United States without going down to one of those damned rebel provinces to pick one up?"

Cameron knew Johnson personally, having served in the Senate with him for more than three years, and seems to have admired the Tennessean. A few weeks after Johnson publicly repudiated secession on the Senate floor in December 1860, Cameron referred to his fellow senator as "lion hearted Johnson," describing the Tennessean as a "Union-loving man . . . [who] deserves and commends himself to our kindliest sympathies."[76] Yet, the former war secretary soon regretted Johnson's nomination, writing a few weeks after the convention to Treasury secretary William P. Fessenden, "Johnson will be a strong candidate for the people, but in the contingency of death, I should greatly prefer a man reared and educated in the North."[77] Allegedly, during the convention, Cameron told Representative

John Scull, "The Republican Party has made a grave mistake," and in August 1866, Cameron confided to his friend Charles Dana, "If [Thaddeus Stevens] had been listened to [at Baltimore] we would not be cursed with Johnson."[78]

The Democrats nominated George B. McClellan, who as a native Pennsylvanian posed a serious challenge to Lincoln's prospects in the ever-important Keystone State. The Emancipation Proclamation had alienated many of the Keystone State's white voters, who saw the war becoming an effort to free the slaves rather than one to save the union.[79] The president's fortunes in Pennsylvania were at low ebb in the summer of 1864, and Lincoln seemed unwilling or unable to do anything about it.[80] Newspaper editor Russell Errett, who was one of Cameron's most ardent supporters, repeated to the former war secretary a prominent Pennsylvania Republican's complaint that "Mr. Lincoln will do nothing. He refuses to change his cabinet or do anything else to promote his election."[81] Cameron shared this concern; in a letter to his future son-in-law Wayne MacVeagh, Cameron wrote, "Looking upon the re-election of Mr. Lincoln as the only solution for the country, I am painfully anxious for his success. . . . Let us rather sustain him, and unite together in urging upon him more rigorous measures, and the correction of such among his administration as are manifest."[82] In the early fall, Cameron worked to counter McClellan's popularity in Pennsylvania by arranging speaking tours for committed unionists, often in close consultation with the White House.[83]

Cameron recognized that it was absolutely essential to harness the soldiers' vote, which could decide the election. On August 31 one captain wrote to Cameron to report rising dissatisfaction among the men over the "the rulings of the War Department by which men are kept in service beyond the period of three years from their enlistment and by which officers of the volunteer force are required to renew the contract to serve for three years from the date of promotion."[84] Pennsylvania amended its constitution in August 1864 to allow soldiers from the Keystone State to vote from the field. The short time between the amendment and the fall elections depressed the vote totals, despite the fact that the party hired one hundred private commissioners to collect soldiers' ballots.[85] The former war secretary complained, "The Democratic leaders now oppose the enfranchisements of the soldier. In the olden times the Democratic leaders, such as Jefferson, Jackson, Snyder, and Shulze, insisted that the executive franchise followed the flag under which the soldiers fought. If that flag was potent on the sea and land, to protect a man in war, why should it not possess the other virtues of continuing his political franchises?"[86] Cameron even tried to halt the draft in close districts, though with mixed success. On November 8, due in large measure to Cameron's efforts, Lincoln defeated McClellan by twenty thousand votes in Pennsylvania, while nationwide he won a commanding 55 percent of the vote to McClellan's 45 percent. Cameron met with Lincoln the day after the president's second inauguration, and the two men engaged in friendly and "earnest conversation." According to White House doorman Thomas F. Pendel, Lincoln even showed Cameron his hand, every finger of which was blistered from shaking the hands of the throngs of well-wishers the previous day.[87]

Cameron's return to Lincoln's good graces made it possible for him to maintain the allegiance of his followers by providing access to Republican Party, federal, and military patronage. In February 1864 Cameron wrote to Lincoln's secretary John Nicolay in order to secure an appointment with the president for a "good friend," undoubtedly to secure a patronage position.[88] Cameron's success did not go unnoticed; in October 1863 the *New York World* groused, "Pennsylvania is open to peculiar temptations. No other state has profited so enormously by the war. Her farmers are enriched by the contracts for the supplies to the army; her coal is bought in immense quantities for the government vessels, while all her foundries are going day and night to supply governmental orders for guns, cannon, iron-plates, and machinery. Thus all the great material interests of the state are open to the corrupting influence of direct government patronage."[89]

Cameron succeeded and, by late 1864, "every one of the leading Cameron lieutenants occupied important posts."[90] Samuel Purviance, John P. Sanderson, and even Alexander Cummings all received lucrative positions, as did the editor of Cameron's Harrisburg newspaper, the *Telegraph*. Though Curtin's clique controlled state patronage, it simply could not compete with Cameron's access to federal patronage, leading both the governor and McClure to repeatedly complain about the Lincoln administration's favoritism toward the former war secretary.[91]

Cameron's political rehabilitation was not limited to the Lincoln administration; it extended to Congress as well. By the spring of 1865, federal military success made it possible for civilians to travel south, and Cameron joined his old friend Senator Benjamin Wade to inspect Savannah; the trip was subsidized by the War Department, and Stanton personally okayed paying Cameron's expenses.[92] On that trip Cameron had the opportunity to fulfill a promise he had made to his friend and former Senate colleague Jefferson Davis. According to Cameron, during an argument with Davis in late 1860 over secession, the Southerner claimed, "When the South seceded, such paralysis will fall upon Northern enterprise, that the grass will grow in the streets of your northern cities!" Irritated, Cameron retorted, "Mr. Davis, if the Southern States secede, utter ruin will fall on your section. Your slaves will be liberated, and will assist in your destruction. The North will not be ruined, but I will with my own hands, plant corn in the streets of Charleston, the cradle of treason." Whether this discussion actually took place or not, during his trip to South Carolina, Cameron planted corn in Charleston and paid a soldier to tend it. In August the local army commander sent Cameron four ears of corn, which he described as "poor . . . at best, probably owing to the soil."[93] Cameron displayed that corn in a cabinet in his study for all to see.

Another event occurred on this trip that offers a window into Cameron's thinking on race. He and his traveling companions visited Hilton Head Island in South Carolina, where hundreds of newly freed blacks had gathered and built a community. Cameron and his fellow visitors attended a church service on the island, after which the minister appealed to them for help in paying off his congregation's debt, which was approximately $300. Cameron was apparently quite moved by the minister's appeal, and canvassed his fellow travelers for contributions. The former war secretary donated the largest amount toward retiring the debt, and the congregation thanked him by naming their new chapel "St Simon's Chapel" in 1876. Nor was this the only time African Americans expressed their gratitude to him. In late 1865 a procession of black soldiers marched by Cameron's mansion, honoring the man whom they saw as making it possible for them to serve in the military. Cameron was heartened by the scene and delivered an impromptu speech, saying:

> I cannot let this opportunity pass without thanking the African soldiers for the compliment they have paid me, but more than all to thank them for the great service which they have been to their country in the terrible rebellion. I never doubted that the people of African descent would play a great part in this struggle, and I am proud to say that all my anticipations have been realized. Your services, offered in the early part of the war, were refused; but when the struggle became one of life and death, then the country gladly received you, and thank God, you nobly redeemed all you promised.[94]

The following spring, Lincoln was assassinated. Though Cameron was officially named one of Lincoln's civilian pallbearers, he did not attend the funeral, a reflection perhaps of the fact that they were never friends, merely two ambitious men who used each other to achieve their goals. Whatever grief Cameron may have felt over Lincoln's passing, the president's assassination was a very real threat to Cameron's political comeback. Relying heavily on his ready access to executive patronage in order to keep his political machine running, Cameron also needed to line up support for his bid to return to the Senate in 1867. Following Lincoln's death, Pennsylvania's Union Republican Party leaders met in Harrisburg and (likely at Cameron's behest) adopted resolutions complimentary to Andrew Johnson, the new president. They selected Cameron and a small delegation of Pennsylvania Republicans to journey to Washington and deliver the resolutions personally. Sensing an opportunity to ingratiate himself with the new president, Cameron met with Johnson and promised him the support of the Keystone State's Republicans. However, he *also* told Johnson that he believed that secessionists must be severely punished for their crimes, a position that would soon distance him from the new administration.

At the Republican State Convention in August 1865, fissures over Johnson's policies were already evident. In the lead-up to the convention, Thaddeus Stevens demanded and got a resolution calling for seceded states to be treated harshly, though the convention also passed a resolution supporting Lincoln's "fellow patriot and successor, Andrew Johnson," which Cameron promoted and to which Thaddeus Stevens acquiesced.[95] The price of Stevens's accommodation, however, was a series of resolutions supporting newly freed slaves' "just hopes of security, education, and elevation in intellectual and moral improvement" and calling on Johnson to "support all measures by which treason shall be stigmatized, loyalty recognized and the freedom, stability and purity of the National Union be secured."[96]

In early March 1866, Cameron tried to maneuver the state party into nominating his preferred candidate for governor, John W. Geary, a former Democrat whom Franklin Pierce had appointed governor of Kansas in 1856. Cameron and Geary corresponded during the latter's brief tenure as governor, so the two men were well acquainted, but the candidate also received John W. Forney's and Thaddeus Stevens's endorsement, a testament to his broad base of support among Pennsylvania's unionists. Cameron met with Geary in early 1866 and managed to extract a promise that, if Geary won the election, he would appoint Henry C. Johnson, a Cameron man, secretary of the commonwealth. According to McClure, "We were greatly surprised to learn, when the convention met, that it was absolutely a Cameron assembly. He had, for the first time, won absolute mastery of the Republican State convention and the organization, and his candidate for Governor was General Geary, who was especially objectionable to [Curtin's supporters]."[97] Curtin's faction, left rudderless by the governor's absence during December and January (he was in Cuba recuperating from a physical and mental breakdown) and by McClure's illness (he came down with a fever during the convention) scrambled to find their own candidate, settling on a disgruntled former Cameron supporter named Winthrop W. Ketcham. Cameron had managed to secure Ketcham an appointment as solicitor of Philadelphia's federal court of claims, but had not supported the latter's bid for the collectorship of Philadelphia.[98] Ketcham had no chance against Geary, who won the nomination.

The main issues of the 1866 campaign were Reconstruction and African Americans' rights, which reflected rising anger in Pennsylvania at President Johnson's lenient policies toward the South. On February 19, 1866, Johnson vetoed a bill funding the Freedman's Bureau, a federal government organization designed to aid former slaves making the transition to freedom. This move radicalized many former moderate Republicans and crystallized the party's opposition to the president, to the point that when a convention in Philadelphia was called for the purpose of endorsing Johnson's policies, it attracted mostly Democrats.[99] It was clear that Johnson's supporters had no future in the Republican Party, and by the summer of 1866 Cameron entered the fray against the president. In early November, Cameron made a speech in which he declared that, if he were in Congress, he would be the first to vote to remove the president from office.[100] Naturally, this speech alienated Cameron from the president, placing the former war secretary in the same position as the rest of the state's Republicans: largely excluded from federal patronage, the lion's share of which was now directed to Senator Edgar Cowan's supporters.

In that year's gubernatorial election, Geary bested the Democratic nominee, Heister Clymer, by seventeen thousand votes, while in the congressional elections Republicans won three-quarters of the seats, an increase of 20 percent from 1864. Many interpreted this as a rebuke of Johnson's policies, but Geary's election also represented a victory for Cameron, particularly after the new governor appointed Benjamin H. Brewster attorney general. Brewster, who had defended the former war secretary in the Butler case, was Cameron's personal friend and devoted supporter. Even better from Cameron's perspective was that Geary had long coattails, and Republicans achieved an insurmountable majority in the state legislature, ensuring that a Radical Republican would replace Edgar Cowan in the Senate.

Naturally, Cameron was not the only candidate; Cameron's chief rival was his longtime antagonist Andrew Curtin. At stake was more than just the Senate seat—Cameron and Curtin were vying for control of Pennsylvania's Republican Party. Curtin, wracked for years by ill health, could not compete with the energetic Cameron, and complained bitterly of the nondemocratic system by which the Pennsylvania legislature selected the senator. By contrast, on Christmas Day 1866, Cameron wrote to his friend Benjamin F. Butler, "I expect and intend to win."[101] In the lead-up to the election, Cameron courted a number of influential politicians, including former Chester County district attorney Wayne MacVeagh. Cameron worked closely with MacVeagh during the gubernatorial election in 1863 and the presidential election the following year.[102] As it turned out, Cameron had something MacVeagh wanted: Cameron's daughter Virginia. In 1866 Virginia married MacVeagh, and he soon became a trusted cog in Cameron's machine.[103]

On January 1, both houses of Pennsylvania's legislature convened to select their respective speakers. This was taken as a bellwether of the respective candidates' strength; if neither's supporters managed to win, many believed it would open the door to a compromise candidate like Stevens or Grow. First, Cameron managed to get Stevens's and Grow's supporters to align against Curtin's nominee for Speaker, Matthew Quay. Then, in an astonishing coup de grâce, Donald Cameron (who had been managing his father's Senate campaign) got four of Thaddeus Stevens's supporters to pledge their support to Cameron's candidate for Speaker of the Pennsylvania Senate, likely by arguing that Stevens was too weak to actually win.[104] This about-face, coupled with a late afternoon meeting with Donald Cameron, convinced Curtin's nominee for speaker to remove his name from consideration, and John P. Glass (the Cameron candidate) was elected.

Curtin's supporters tried to forestall Cameron's election by introducing a state senate resolution calling for an investigation into charges (that they themselves circulated) that Cameron had corruptly influenced caucus members' votes. Cameron's supporters used a variety of parliamentary maneuvers to ensure that the investigating committee was friendly to the former war secretary, checking Curtin's faction. In order to derail Cameron's path back to the Senate, leaders of the various anti-Cameron factions—Curtin, Stevens, Grow, and John W. Forney met in Forney's hotel room to plot strategy. Unable to find a suitable compromise candidate, someone floated the idea of bolting the caucus and voting with the Democrats, but Curtin refused, and that very evening Cameron won the caucus's nomination by forty-six votes, double Curtin's total. Cameron trounced Cowan, who had been nominated by the Democrats despite having been elected to the Senate in 1861 as a Republican, in the general assembly, winning eighty-one votes to Cowan's forty-seven on a party line vote. Cameron saw the election as vindicating his honesty "to my children and my friends."[105] Following his election, Cameron hosted a small party at a local hotel, during which he celebrated victory in what he called "the last struggle of my political life" and railed against Johnson, calling the president a traitor.[106] He committed himself to supporting military rule of the South and mentioned the tariff before finally noting that he wished to see suffrage extended to Pennsylvania's African Americans by excising the word "white" from the state constitution. In advocating political equality for African Americans, Cameron identified himself as among the most radical and progressive Republicans, at least on the issue of race.[107] Though Cameron's victory in the Senatorial election was far from the "last struggle" of his political life, it nonetheless represented a decisive turning point in Pennsylvania's political history. Cameron not only won the Senate seat, he also crushed Curtin and McClure's bid to control Pennsylvania's Republican Party. While Cameron still faced challenges to his power, moving forward he was generally recognized as the political "boss" of Pennsylvania.

9

"Nothing Can Beat You," 1867–77

Cameron's return to the Senate marked his arrival as the putative boss of Pennsylvania's Republican Party and his final defeat of both Curtin and McClure. While Cameron's power in Pennsylvania was not uncontested, by the late 1860s he had constructed a durable, powerful political machine that dominated the Keystone State until the New Deal.[1] Cameron's decade-long stint in the Senate displayed all of the characteristics of his earlier terms: passionate devotion to protectionism, a commitment to the Pennsylvania Railroad's interests, and a sociability that crossed party and sectional lines.[2] Now the Senate's oldest member, by 1870 he was the most senior member of both houses of Congress, having served for more years than any member of either house.[3]

Though described by one of his Senate colleagues as a "bitter and uncompromising Republican" because of his desire to remake the South following the Civil War, Cameron remained extremely social, often dining with those with whom he disagreed politically.[4] Because of his loyalty and fundamental generosity, he often pursued pardons for old friends and acquaintances who had served in the Confederate government and military. At various times he solicited a pardon for Joseph E. Johnston, and urged a commission for the son of a former

Confederate.[5] One of his colleagues in the Senate recalled an incident that occurred shortly before Cameron retired. Mary Long, wife of Confederate general Armistead Lindsay Long, approached Senator Robert E. Withers for assistance. Her husband was nearly blind and the family was on the verge of starvation. Mrs. Long had been led to believe that, if Tilden won the presidential election, she would receive a patronage job, but with Hayes's victory in the presidential election, it seemed unlikely that the wife of a former Confederate general could count on help. Withers said there was nothing he could do for her, but then he discovered that Mrs. Long had, as a child, been a playmate of Cameron's children. "I felt a little encouraged by what she had said, and replied, 'Mrs. Long, there is not a Senator who can aid you as much as General Cameron, if you can enlist him earnestly in your cause. It will be hard to get an interview with him, because he never pays attention to the cards of strangers, but you remain here, and I will go in and try my best to get him to come out, and if he does come, you tell him exactly they story you have told me, and I do not think he can refuse to aid you." Withers spoke to Cameron, who (after more than forty years) remembered the woman. After meeting with her, Cameron said to Withers, "Why Senator, that poor woman is in a h-ll of a fix . . . I will do anything I can for her."[6] Within two days, Cameron had (over the objections of some of his Republican colleagues in the Senate) gotten President Grant to appoint Mrs. Long postmaster at Charlottesville.

That being said, Cameron saw Reconstruction as a moment to reform Southern society and thereby alleviate the sectional tension that had caused the war. Naturally, this put him at odds with Johnson, so just as in the 1840s, Cameron bitterly opposed the policies of a president from his own party. This time, however, Cameron was not alone. In an attempt to circumscribe Johnson's authority, congressional Radicals began the Fortieth Congress on March 4, 1867, immediately after the close of the Thirty-Ninth instead of in December as prescribed in the Constitution. They did so to limit presidential control of Reconstruction, and more than anything else that had yet occurred, this demonstrated the breach between the executive and legislative branches and portended further confrontations. On March 3, 1867, the Thirty-Ninth Congress passed the Tenure of Office Act over Johnson's veto. The act prevented the president from removing any executive appointee whose appointment had been ratified by the Senate without the upper house's consent. The purpose of the measure was to restrict Johnson's control over Reconstruction by limiting his ability to remove cabinet officers like Secretary of War Edwin Stanton, who was far more radical than the president.

Though the Tenure of Office Act's constitutionality was debatable, the battle lines were clear, and when Johnson tried to remove Stanton during a Senate recess in August 1867, it ensured a showdown between the executive and legislative branches of the government. Johnson replaced Stanton with General Ulysses S. Grant, who became the secretary of war ad interim. However, when the Senate reconvened, it rejected Johnson's removal of Stanton, and on January 28 Grant resigned the office. Johnson then tried to get General William T. Sherman to accept the position, but Sherman refused, and the president next turned to Lorenzo Thomas. Once Thomas accepted the nomination on February 21, 1868, Johnson ordered Stanton removed from office. When Thomas delivered the president's dismissal order to the War Department, Stanton refused to obey, instead ordering Thomas arrested for violating the Tenure of Office Act. Stanton then barricaded himself in his office. Eventually, to prevent the courts from getting involved, Stanton had the charges against Thomas dropped, but it was clear that would not be the end of the conflict.

Three days after Johnson ordered Stanton's removal, the U.S. House of Representatives approved by a vote of 126 to 47 Thaddeus Stevens and John A. Bingham's resolution of impeachment. One week later, the House passed eleven articles of impeachment against Johnson, and the president's trial in the Senate began on March 30. Navy Secretary Gideon Welles complained,

"The managers conduct the trial as it was that of a horse thief."
He further claimed, "A shameless, brazen effrontery and vil-
lainy mark certain Senators," later singling Cameron out by
name. Most people expected the Senate to convict Johnson,
and Pennsylvania's legislature even passed a resolution recommending that, once that happened, his successor should
appoint Stanton secretary of the Treasury; Stanton eventually
wrote to Cameron declining such a nomination, but the legislature's action certainly expressed the widespread belief that
Johnson would soon be forced from office.[7]

The Constitution mandates that, to remove the president
from office, two-thirds of senators must vote to convict. In each
of three ballots, thirty-five senators voted to convict Johnson
for high crimes and misdemeanors, while nineteen consistently
voted to acquit the president. Seven Republican senators voted
for acquittal after receiving Johnson's assurances that he would
allow Congress to control Reconstruction. Two other factors
seem to have also motivated these men to keep Johnson in
office: hearings later conducted by Massachusetts representative Benjamin F. Butler generated vague evidence that Johnson secured at least some of these votes through promises of
patronage or money, while many of the Republicans who voted
for acquittal did so because the man who would have become
president—Senate president pro tempore Benjamin Wade—
supported women's rights and was therefore considered unsuitable for the presidency.[8] Johnson was thus able to serve out the
last few months of his term.

Given the Republicans' alienation from the sitting president,
there was no chance that the party would nominate Andrew
Johnson in 1868. The party's various factions settled on Ulysses
S. Grant as the man to unite the Republicans and lead it to victory in the presidential election, and he was nominated unanimously by the delegates at the national convention in Chicago
in mid-May. Behind the scenes, however, Cameron faced challenges to his power from the weakened Curtin faction, which
was trying to force the former governor on the Republican ticket

as Grant's running mate. At the state nominating convention in March, McClure managed to secure passage of a resolution disbarring delegate Donald Cameron from taking his seat, but he was later checkmated when the national convention seated Donald on the floor. Cameron's friend and ally Russell Errett repaid McClure's attack on Donald by nominating Ohio senator Benjamin Wade for vice president, causing an uproar that only subsided when the convention's delegates voted to separate balloting for the presidential and vice presidential nominations. Though the convention nominated Curtin, the vote was not unanimous, and the divisions in Pennsylvania's delegation to the national convention in Chicago doomed the former governor's chances at getting the vice presidential slot. Because Pennsylvania was so evenly split between Democrats and Republicans, Grant's supporters worked feverishly to raise funds to elect the former general. Jay Cooke, the so-called "financier of the Civil War," claimed to have "bled" for the cause, while the national committee spent at least $40,000 in Pennsylvania.[9] Cameron never doubted the outcome; on September 23 he wrote to Grant to say, "While in Washington, Monday and Tuesday, so many inquiries were made of me regarding the vote in Pennsylvania that I fear you, like others, may doubt our ability and intention to carry . . . it. I write, therefore, to say to you, that it is . . . certain for the republican ticket in October. . . . So, I think you may as well begin to think over your 'Inaugural.'"[10] In October the Republicans picked up twelve seats in the Pennsylvania legislature, and the following month Grant carried the state by twenty-nine thousand votes. Grant won the presidency, garnering 52.7 percent of the popular vote and receiving 214 electoral votes to Democrat Horatio Seymour's 80.

Grant quickly developed a close connection to Pennsylvania: prominent Republicans connected with Philadelphia's Union League contributed $50,000 to buy the former general a house in the city. The president became a regular visitor to the city, often socializing with Philadelphia's elite. Almost immediately, the various factions of Pennsylvania's Republican Party began jockeying for control over the new administration's patronage appointments. Curtin's supporters pressed Grant to appoint the former governor to his cabinet, but the new president surprised everyone by naming Philadelphian Adolph Borie secretary of the navy. Borie had two distinctions: he was aligned with neither Curtin nor Cameron and he was the biggest contributor to purchasing Grant's Philadelphia house.[11] Writing in his diary, Secretary of State Hamilton Fish explained the president's thinking. According to Fish, Grant believed that no man from Pennsylvania could be appointed "who would not be objectionable to either the Cameron or the anti-Cameron party . . . [and] Mr. Borie [was] the only man [from Pennsylvania] not identified with either."[12]

Borie was spectacularly unqualified for the job, holding it for only a few months, and this appointment failed to satisfy any faction of the Keystone State's Republican Party. In a clear attempt to curry favor with Curtin's faction, Grant appointed the former governor his minister to Russia, a position that virtually belonged to Pennsylvania (between 1834 and 1902 it was held by no fewer than nine Pennsylvanians, though usually for brief periods). Cameron's remarks on the appointment were hardly complimentary; he noted that Curtin was not his choice, or even the choice of Pennsylvania's voters, but out of deference to Grant's wishes, he would not block the nomination, though he certainly could have: Senate protocol gave senators an unofficial veto over appointments from their home states. Cameron later crowed in a letter to his son-in-law Wayne MacVeagh, "I *could have rejected him.*"[13] In truth, Curtin's going to Russia was politically the best thing that could have happened to Cameron because it ensured that the already weakened former governor's political strength eroded even further.

Despite his delight at Curtin's departure, Cameron's relations with the new president proved rocky. Grant had little political experience when he assumed the presidency in March 1869, and no feel for the deference that executives were expected to show to state congressional delegations when it came to federal appointments. Grant accidentally crossed Cameron by nominating Alexander L. Russell, Curtin's former adjutant general, to be minister to Ecuador, without first consulting the senator. Cameron successfully derailed the nominations, demonstrating the wisdom of Secretary of State Fish's advice that "there is no use in fighting Cameron," but at the cost of souring his relationship with the new president.[14] In an effort to improve relations between the president and the senator, Cameron's friend Thomas L. Kane invited Grant to visit Pennsylvania in August. Unbeknown to Grant, Kane invited Cameron as well, specifically for the purpose of healing the rift between the two men. Kane's plan worked to perfection, with Grant coming away much impressed with Cameron. Over the course of Grant's presidency, Cameron frequently joined the president at the White House and on trips, including on a visit to New England in August 1873.[15] Much like his father, Donald seems to have impressed Grant, who invited the younger Cameron to stay at the White House as his personal guest in early 1871.[16]

In addition, Cameron vigorously supported Republican attempts to ensure that African Americans had opportunities to participate in American life as equal citizens. In January 1869 he voted for the Fifteenth Amendment to the Constitution, which stipulates that the "right of citizens of the United States to vote shall not be denied or abridged by the United States or by any state on account of race, color, or previous condition of servitude." He committed himself to pursuing black suffrage, noting, "I thought clothing a black man in the American uniform clothed him with the rights of an American citizen, and I am sad to see that even Pennsylvania denies him the ballot, the only weapon whereby he can protect himself."[17] In 1881 Cameron predicted "that before thirty years from the close of the war have passed, you will find the great mass of the colored people of the South owning property and producing, if not the majority of the products of this section, yet a remarkable ration. If the situation in the South shows anything, it is that the future prosperity of that section depends . . . upon the industry and thrift of the colored man."[18] That Cameron believed this was reflected in the fact that he consistently used his power as senator to achieve equality of opportunity for African Americans.

For instance, in 1870 Mississippi's state legislature elected to the U.S. Senate Hiram R. Revels, a black minister who had organized two regiments of U.S. Colored Troops during the war. Southern Democrats vigorously tried to prevent Revels from taking his seat, arguing that, under the Dred Scott decision, no black man was a citizen until the ratification of the Fourteenth Amendment in 1868, meaning that Revels did not meet the Constitutional requirement that candidates be citizens of the country for at least nine years before they were eligible to serve in the Senate. During the debate, Cameron spoke in favor of seating Revels, claiming to have told Jefferson Davis shortly before the war "that one result of [secession] would be the emancipation of the slaves; that the freedmen would become soldiers, and then citizens, that citizens would receive office, and that then, so just was an overruling Providence, a negro would take the seat which Davis was about to vacate."[19] On a strict party line vote, the Senate voted to admit Revels on February 25, 1870, and three weeks later America's first black Senator gave his maiden speech, a plea for the reinstatement of the black members of Georgia's general assembly who had been illegally expelled by Southern Democrats. Following his speech, "Senator Cameron was the first to go and shake hands with Senator Revels, and congratulate him on his speech."[20]

That was not all: On May 28, 1873, the trustees of Lincoln University invited Grant to attend the school's commencement, scheduled for June 28. Described by one historian as "the first institution founded anywhere in the world to provide a higher education in the arts and sciences for youth of African descent," it was located in Chester County, Pennsylvania.[21] Apparently, Cameron was quite familiar with the school and its work—the invitation mentioned the fact that "Genl Cameron will no doubt tell you what is doing here"—and the senator himself wrote to Grant on June 2 and urged the president to accept the university's invitation. According to Cameron, "Dr. Dickey, the President, is an enthusiastic, learned and energetic man, of the Presbyterian church, & has accomplished wonders. His pupils are all Negros—and wile all shew as much ability as the same number of whites, some of them evince the very highest order of ability. I think you would be much interested in the great work of this Institution—and I am sure your presence would greatly cheer and encourage the good men engaged in the work."[22] Though the president did not attend the ceremony, this invitation highlights Cameron's continuing interest in education and his commitment to improving opportunities for African Americans.

Meanwhile, Grant's tin ear for politics strained his relationship with Congress, and the president came to view Cameron as a political ally who knew how to navigate the treacherous shoals of senatorial procedure and prerogatives. In a letter to Cameron, Grant vividly expressed his antipathy toward Congress, writing, "Your letter of yesterday asking me to name a day when I can meet Dawson Coleman, and other friends, at a dinner at your house, is received. Not before the meeting of Congress. After that unhappy event I would be willing to run away any Saturday from my natural enemy."[23] In particular, the president sparred with Charles Sumner, the venerable Massachusetts senator then chairing the Senate Foreign Relations Committee. Sumner had a well-earned reputation for pugnacious independence, and his frequent conflicts with the Grant administration led to the senator's deposition from the chairmanship of the Senate Foreign Relations Committee. Early in his presidency, Grant privately negotiated a treaty for the annexation of Santo Domingo (now known as the Dominican Republic). In doing so, he ignored the prerogatives of the Senate and the machinery of American diplomacy. On March 15, 1870, the foreign relations committee unfavorably reported the treaty to the whole Senate. Cameron signed the report but hedged his position, claiming that he was opposed to ratification *given the circumstances of the treaty's negotiation,* but would have voted for annexation under different circumstances. Two days later, Grant went to the Senate and met for two hours with fifteen senators, including Cameron, outlining the reasons they should vote for the treaty.

Apparently, Cameron found Grant's arguments convincing, because when the treaty came before the Senate on Thursday, June 30, the former war secretary voted for it. In the days leading up to the vote, Cameron had even counseled the president to use patronage to buy Louisiana's votes by replacing the collector of the Port of New Orleans.[24] Despite Grant's best efforts, and Cameron's vote, the Senate rejected the treaty, voting twenty-eight to twenty-eight. Grant's anger at the Senate's failure to ratify the treaty boiled over in a conversation with Ohio governor Rutherford B. Hayes, during which the president called Charles Sumner "unsound" and referred to Missouri senator Carl Schurz as "an infidel and atheist." On another occasion while passing Sumner's house, Grant shook his fist in rage and declared, "That man up there has abused me in a way I never suffered from any other man living."[25] The president made it known that he wanted Sumner disciplined for opposing the treaty, and on March 8, 1871, the Republican caucus voted twenty-six to twenty-one to remove Sumner from the foreign relations committee chairmanship. In his place, the caucus chose Cameron, whose friendship with the president was widely known, and the entire Senate voted thirty-three to nine to affirm the caucus's selection.[26]

When he got the news that the Republican caucus planned to remove Sumner, Cameron—who had not planned to be in Washington for the first few days of the congressional session—immediately made arrangements to return to the national capital. Journeying from Harrisburg to Washington, Cameron arrived in the Senate chamber just as Senator Schurz was ridiculing the Pennsylvanian's qualification to chair the foreign relations committee. Sarcastically, Schurz told his colleagues, "Nobody doubts . . . [that Cameron's] studies of international law have been profound, or that his long experience in the service of the country, especially as to our relations with foreign powers, eminently fits him for that place."[27] Schurz's statement belied the fact that Cameron already served on the committee and (unlike many of his predecessors, including Sumner) actually had experience as a diplomat (short as it was). Sumner's removal fomented dissension with the Republican ranks; one prominent Republican noted, "I hope that the disasters sure to follow this Sumner blunder, will make [Cameron and the other party leaders] pause and reflect. Otherwise, a new candidate, or defeat—perhaps, defeat in any event—awaits the Republican Party in 1872."[28] Cameron responded to these and other attacks on his ascension to the chairmanship by saying, "I did not rob [Sumner] of anything. I would rather now, much rather, add to his reputation than detract from it in any way."[29] As for Sumner, there were apparently no hard feelings; when the senator from Massachusetts left the Senate in March 1874, both he and Cameron wished each other well.

Cameron acquitted himself well in his new position. According to Grant, "The work of the committee when Mr. Cameron took charge was in a most deplorable state, due entirely to Mr. Sumner's obstructiveness and dilatoriness," but things changed under the senator from Pennsylvania.[30] As chairman of the foreign affairs committee, Cameron was heavily involved in work on the Treaty of Washington, which created international tribunals to arbitrate several claims the United States had against the United Kingdom. Specifically, the United States demanded retribution for damage done by ships that British companies had built and sold to the Confederacy, the most infamous of which was the css *Alabama*, which had boarded nearly five hundred ships, captured or burned sixty-five U.S. merchant ships, and taken more than two thousand prisoners during the Civil War. In addition, the treaty empowered the tribunal to settle American and British differences regarding the border of Oregon and fishing rights in the region. The Grant administration got most of what it wanted from the treaty, which the Senate ratified by a vote of fifty to twelve, a reflection of the improved relations between the administration and the Senate Committee on Foreign Relations.[31] On May 30, 1871, Secretary of State Fish wrote to Cameron, noting, "I beg to tender to you my very sincere and earnest thanks for the generous & very efficient & effective aid & support you have rendered to the various subjects which have gone from the Department of State to the Senate, since you have been at the head of the Committee on Foreign Relations. . . . Since you took charge in the Senate of the business from this Department, I have felt that important measures, & Treaties negotiated were no longer to be smothered, and pigeonholed in the Committee room."[32]

The foreign affairs committee room became the center of Cameron's political intrigues, where he continued the practice of entertaining friends and political allies, usually over a bottle or two of champagne.[33] Most of Cameron's colleagues enjoyed his amiable charm even if they disagreed with him politically. In addition, the president's respect and gratitude proved useful: Shortly after assuming the chairmanship of the Senate Foreign Relations Committee, Cameron managed to convince Grant to appoint John W. Forney to the lucrative collectorship of the Port of Pennsylvania and engineered the appointment of his son-in-law Wayne MacVeagh to a diplomatic mission. It was widely known that MacVeagh was traveling to Europe for health, rather than diplomatic reasons, and he took a meandering route through the United Kingdom, Germany, France, and Italy before arriving at his destination, whereupon he almost immediately sought a furlough from his diplomatic responsibilities. Aware of the political repercussions of what would appear to be a taxpayer-funded sightseeing tour of Europe, Cameron advised that he remain for a respectable interval, and MacVeagh took his father-in-law's advice.[34]

However, Cameron also used his power to help those who had little prospect of returning the favor. In the summer of 1870, Cameron proved decisive in helping former First Lady Mary Todd Lincoln get a pension from Congress. Following Lincoln's death, Mary struggled to make ends meet, in part due to her extravagant spending. Early in 1866 Cameron had solicited wealthy Republicans with a goal of raising $20,000 so that Mary could purchase and furnish a house, lest the nation be treated to the spectacle of the slain president's wife living in poverty. For reasons that are not entirely clear, and despite what appear to be Cameron's vigorous efforts, the plan fell through, and Mary Todd Lincoln remained in a precarious financial position.[35] In the summer of 1870, a bill to provide Mary Todd Lincoln a lifetime pension lay stalled in Congress. On the last day of the session, Cameron delivered an impassioned speech in support of the bill. Memorably, he ended the speech by saying, "I do not want to talk, and I say, let us vote."[36] Apparently, Cameron's words moved at least a few of his colleagues, because the Senate voted to approve the pension, and President Grant signed the bill that same day.

In an attempt to consolidate his control over federal patronage in the Keystone State, Cameron set about ensuring the election of a pliable candidate as Pennsylvania's other senator. Projecting an air of "standing above the fray," Cameron relied on his son Donald to take care of the details, a reflection of the younger Cameron's growing importance to his father's political machine.[37] Cameron's quest to control the election of Pennsylvania's junior senator brought him into conflict with another faction of the Keystone State's Republican Party, the Philadelphia-based Treasury Ring, which was closely allied to Curtin. At the ring's head were former Pennsylvania state treasurer William H. Kemble and Matthew S. Quay, who had distinguished himself in organizing Curtin's campaign in the western part of Pennsylvania during the gubernatorial election of 1860. The ring's goal was to elect Kemble, who as state treasurer had treated Pennsylvania's treasury as his own, enriching himself by investing the money in "pet" banks that surreptitiously paid the treasurer interest on the commonwealth's deposits. In addition, he and his cronies regularly used Pennsylvania's sinking fund to fund the ring's political activities.[38]

Cameron settled on railroad lawyer and Pennsylvania state

representative John Scott for the Republican Senate nomination. Scott was a neophyte when it came to politics (he had only been in the Pennsylvania House for a single year), and Cameron undoubtedly believed that Scott would follow his lead in dispensing federal patronage. Working through his son Donald, Cameron engineered Scott's ascension to the Speakership of the Pennsylvania House of Representatives on January 4, 1869, and then orchestrated his selection as the junior senator from Pennsylvania. Outgoing secretary of the navy Gideon Welles acidly noted, "The railroad controls Pennsylvania, and Cameron has had the adroitness to secure it."[39]

By this time, Cameron was at the apogee of his power and influence, finding positions for many of his most loyal followers, including Russell Errett, George Bergner, and his son-in-law Wayne MacVeagh. Cameron's biographer notes, "If consensus of opinion is to be relied upon, there can be little doubt of the influence exerted by Simon Cameron upon the Grant administration." In this regard Cameron was one of a number of Republican senators, each firmly in control of the political machines of his respective state, who used their closeness with Grant to channel and control patronage appointments back home. This "kitchen cabinet" included men like New York's Roscoe Conkling, Michigan's Zachariah Chandler, Indiana's Oliver P. Morton, and Massachusetts representative (and former Union general) Benjamin F. Butler. Governor Rutherford B. Hayes, a Republican whose program of civil service reform eventually brought him into conflict with Cameron, complained in 1871, "I fear that such advisors as Chandler, Cameron, and Conkling are too influential with Grant. They are not safe counselors."[40]

Hayes's statement reflected the pervasive factionalism that appeared as the Republicans looked toward the 1872 presidential election. It is worth remembering that the Republican Party was a coalition of individuals with diverse political beliefs held together largely by what they were *against*—the extension of slavery and the "slave power"—rather than what they supported. The Civil War, having resulted in the abolition of slavery and the hobbling of the South, seemed to some to make the party obsolete, while the corruption and spoilsmanship that seemed to characterize Grant's administration alienated many Republicans. An anti-administration group calling itself "Liberal Republicans" emerged in Missouri in January 1872. The national Liberal Republican organization called a convention of all anti-administration Republicans to meet on May 1. Frustrated by Cameron's control of federal patronage, old antagonist Alexander McClure (who with the aid of the Keystone State's Democrats had won election to the state senate) quickly assumed leadership of the state's Liberal Republican movement. In a letter printed in the *Philadelphia Bulletin*, McClure took aim not only at Grant but also at "the bad men" who had deceived the president, a thinly veiled jab at Cameron.[41] McClure traveled to the Liberal Republican convention, where he embarrassed himself and Curtin by trying to have the former governor (who was now serving as Grant's minister to Russia) nominated for president, which damaged his relations with the "regular" Republicans and contributed to his exit from Russia later that year. The convention eventually nominated Horace Greeley for president. Greeley was far from the ideal candidate; one observer called him "so conceited, fussy, and foolish that he damages every cause he wants to support." Yet Pennsylvania's Liberal Republicans and the Democrats undercut their chances by maintaining their individual state committees and failing to coordinate their campaigns. While Cameron's followers largely stayed loyal to the senator, he was pained by the defection of Thomas L. Kane, the man who less than four years earlier had arranged Cameron's rapprochement with Grant.

Nor were concerns over corruption limited to national politics; at the state level, voices criticized Pennsylvania's legislature, which was widely considered among the most corrupt in the nation. The reform movement posed a special challenge for Cameron; after all, "a struggle in Pennsylvania against Grant must include, as one of its goals, the overthrow of its adjunct within the state, the political machine of Simon Cameron."[42]

While many reformers were undoubtedly interested in purifying government, many others jumped on the bandwagon because they felt excluded from the patronage Cameron controlled. In fact, historian Frank B. Evans characterized the reform movement in Pennsylvania as "born of frustrated ambition and the desire for personal revenge against Simon Cameron."[43] That being said, it is undeniable that Pennsylvania's legislature was corrupt, a fact made plain by the scandals that rocked the Keystone State in the late 1860s and early 1870s.

The worst scandal by far involved irregularities at the state treasury that came to light in 1870, when Governor Geary called attention to the fact that the treasurer (one of Cameron's lieutenants) had grown rich in a job that only paid $1,700 per year. Geary went so far as to call for the legislature to reform the office by mandating that the treasurer invest the commonwealth's funds in Pennsylvania bonds instead of "pet" banks owned by political allies. Within a week, William Kemble and Robert W. Mackey (the former and current state treasurers) met to plot strategy. In a letter to President Grant, one prominent Republican summed up the matter, noting the perception "that Cameron had waged such relentless warfare on everybody in the party who would not bow down to him that there was a great disposition on the part of vast numbers of the best Republicans in the state to let the state ticket go by the board and to devote themselves to electing an anti-Cameron legislature— that Cameron, by his position in the Senate, controlled the patronage of the state, and no matter how good a Grant man and a Republican a man might be, yet if he was not a Cameron man he was marked for slaughter."[44] Thus, the contest was not between "clean" versus "corrupt" government; instead, it was a turf war between two rival factions of Pennsylvania's Republican Party, each vying for control of spoils.

The other great scandal that rocked Pennsylvania in the early 1870s also concerned money, in this case a debt collector's commission. In the late 1860s, it was widely believed that the federal government owed the Commonwealth of Pennsylvania $2 million, but that was a guess and few expected Evans to collect more than a fraction of that amount. Through diligent research and persistence, Evans discovered additional claims and by the middle of 1871 had collected nearly $3 million owed to Pennsylvania. Under the terms of Evans's employment, he was allowed to keep up to 10 percent of the money he collected, which he did, amassing a commission of $291,000. When this fact became public it fueled a backlash against Geary and the legislature, helpfully fueled by the Commonwealth's Democrats and elements of the Republican Party alienated from the governor. At one point, Evans was even arrested for embezzlement, though a judge found that he had kept his commission in good faith and ordered him released. To Geary's dismay, both Cameron and Curtin's factions accused the governor of malfeasance, charges that seemed credible when it became known that Auditor General John F. Hartranft had "borrowed" several thousand dollars from Evans. In April 1872 Pennsylvania's Republicans nominated Hartranft for governor, who was still mired in the Evans scandal. Though he had cultivated the nominee as a potential gubernatorial candidate for more than two years, Cameron initially questioned the wisdom of Hartranft's nomination given the ongoing scandal and the threat posed by the Liberal Republicans, but his doubts were assuaged by the fact that Hartranft commanded both Russell Errett's and Donald's allegiance.[45]

In addition, the always erratic John W. Forney—who was going through one of his periodic bouts of pique with Cameron—viciously attacked the nominee in the hope of damaging the former War Secretary's control over the state party. A few weeks before the election, Forney published Hartranft's account books, apparently showing that the auditor general had systematically under taxed the Northern Central Railroad, which was closely linked to Simon Cameron. The combined weight of Forney's attacks and the Liberal Republican-Democratic alliance raised concerns among some of Hartranft's backers, including Cameron. Over the summer, the senator called two conclaves to discuss the matter, fearing that a Liberal-Republican/Democratic victory in the governor's race might cost Grant the state in the presidential election. A less cataclysmic, but still worrisome, possibility was that the Liberal Republican/Democratic alliance would command a majority of representatives in the legislature, a terrifying prospect given that Cameron's Senate term ended in January 1873 and he wanted to be reelected. According to McClure (who was not present at either of the meetings), it was Donald Cameron who insisted that Hartranft remain the Republican nominee, an indication of the younger man's growing control over the family political machine.

In an attempt to buttress Hartranft, Cameron implored Grant to cut the editor off from all federal patronage, but the president refused to do so lest Forney start attacking him. Hartranft's supporters were reduced to bribing two convicted felons with promises of pardons in exchange for affidavits swearing to Hartranft's innocence. Hartranft won the election and, when he formed his cabinet early the following year, its composition "reflected complete control by the Cameron hierarchy."[46] Ironically, as a result of the widely held belief that he controlled the governor, Cameron made a conscious effort to distance himself from Hartranft and to give the governor a measure of independence; as the senator confided in a letter to President Grant, "The difficulties of [Hartranft's] position after his election, and the often repeated taunt he was entirely under my influence and control, cause me to form the resolution to leave him entirely untrammeled in all his acts."[47]

When the mainstream of the Republican Party assembled in Philadelphia for its national convention in June, the only real issue was who would join Grant on the ticket. The Republicans were casting about for a new vice president because the incumbent, Schuyler Colfax, was implicated in the Crédit Mobilier of America scandal. At the Republican national convention, both Cameron and his son Donald were mentioned as potential vice presidential nominees. Initially, the odds looked good for a Grant/Donald Cameron ticket but, despite strenuous efforts on his part, Cameron was unable to get his son on the ticket. The silver lining was that Cameron found the eventual nominee— Massachusetts senator Henry Wilson— acceptable due to the fact that, when he left the cabinet in 1862, the vice presidential nominee had been one of the few willing to defend him. According to Cameron's biographer, "There is hardly any doubt" that Cameron was instrumental in Wilson's nomination, though (as with so many of Cameron's political maneuvers over the years) he was careful not to leave a paper trail.[48]

Despite the scandals and the Liberal Republicans' challenge, Grant won a commanding 55.6 percent of the popular vote to Greeley's 43.8. In the electoral college, the results were even more one-sided: the president received 286 electoral votes to Greeley's 66, a landslide that effectively killed the Liberal Republican movement. Grant's reelection and the collapse of the Liberal Republican movement signaled that "the Cameron machine was more firmly entrenched in Pennsylvania than ever before."[49] Following a weak challenge from Philadelphia millionaire Charlemagne Tower, Pennsylvania's Republican Party nominated Cameron for the Senate, and on January 20 the legislature reelected him to another six-year term as the senior senator from Pennsylvania. Following the election, a supporter wrote to Cameron and gushed, "Nothing can beat you. You are invincible."[50] While Cameron did not go quite as far as claiming invincibility, he proudly noted that this was the first time he was elected to the Senate where the result was uncontested, a reflection of his control over the Republican Party in Pennsylvania.

Secure in his reelection and with Donald and his lieutenants Matthew Quay and Robert Mackey absorbing more of the day-to-day responsibilities of administrating the family's political machine, Cameron was able to devote more time to traveling. At the end of the congressional session in March 1873, Cameron and Margaret traveled to New Orleans, returning after an absence of four decades and inaugurating a series of annual visits to the Crescent City. It was on one of these sojourns in

1874 that Cameron had the misfortune of encountering the so-called Widow Oliver. This meeting laid the groundwork for one of the most humiliating episodes in Cameron's long public career, although he could not have known it at the time. In 1875 Cameron joined approximately a dozen other senators on a trip to the American Southwest and Mexico, seeing first-hand the land he had played a small part in wresting from the Mexicans thirty years before.[51]

Now in his mid-seventies, Cameron was generally in good health (with the exception of a minor stroke that temporarily paralyzed his right arm in the autumn of 1870 and a fall on the ice in the winter of 1871 that confined him to the house briefly), though he was undoubtedly aware that his generation was passing from the scene.[52] On May 7, 1873, Cameron's friend and former cabinet colleague Salmon P. Chase died. Just a little over a year later, Cameron's Senate colleague Charles Sumner died, and a few months later Cameron's friend and lieutenant George Bergner died. Most devastating were the losses that hit closest to home, and those came in rapid succession during the early 1870s. In August 1871 his daughter Rachel Burnside died, the sixth child Cameron and his wife Margaret lost during their long marriage. Devastating as well was Margaret's death on June 19, 1874. The family held her funeral at the house on Front Street in Harrisburg, and even the local Democratic papers conceded that she was a "most estimable lady."[53]

Despite his advancing age, Cameron actively pursued new business opportunities. In late 1870 Cameron joined a syndicate headed by Thomas A. Scott, his friend and former aid at the War Department, to lease the Western & Atlantic Railroad, then owned by the state of Georgia, and at various times during the 1870s he sat on the First National Bank of Sunbury's board of directors.[54] However, as Cameron's experience at the War Department a decade earlier demonstrated, the senator was no executive, preferring to leave the details to others. As he aged, this tendency became more pronounced, and Cameron ceded day-to-day responsibilities to those around him, especially his son Donald. In an article titled "The Clan Cameron," a reporter for the *Washington Post* summarized the differences this way: "Simon Cameron is endowed with strong common sense, and upon this foundation he reared the superstructure of experience and worldly wisdom that in the abstract almost any man might envy. . . . There were many, very many, who had been bound to Simon Cameron by the cords of personal kindness through a long course of years, and these were his main dependence. Don Cameron's strength lies in other directions. His is a mind of quick perceptions and prompt conclusions, but nevertheless cold, retentive, self-absorbed."[55]

When Congress came back into session in the spring of 1874, Cameron was drawn into the politically fraught conflict over monetary policy. In 1873 the price of silver crashed following the passage of the Coinage Act, which moved the United States from bimetallism (i.e., coining both silver and gold) to monometallism (i.e., coining only gold). The Coinage Act had a deflationary effect that spooked investors and caused a contraction of credit that ultimately bankrupted Jay Cooke & Company, a major U.S. banking firm heavily invested in railroads. Cooke's failure set off a cascade effect—the Panic of 1873—that resulted in catastrophic bank failures and the closure of the New York Stock Exchange for ten days. Unemployment skyrocketed, and the businesses that survived cut wages, which in turn lowered demand for goods and services, exacerbating the economic collapse.

Since the contractionary effects of the Coinage Act had set off the Panic of 1873, people demanded the federal government reverse course by flooding the market with money, in this case paper currency (or "greenbacks," so-called for the color of the currency emitted by the federal government during the Civil War). Doing so would have an inflationary effect, making it easier for those in debt to meet their obligations and freeing up money for investment. Treasury secretary William A. Richardson authorized the emission of $26 million in greenbacks, but when this failed to end the depression, Congress passed the Inflation Bill of 1874, which authorized the government to release another $18 million in paper currency. The bill badly divided Grant's cabinet and, despite vigorous lobbying by the country's business community, the president vetoed the bill on April 22, 1874. Cameron was aghast at the president's veto, predicting that it would cost the Republicans heavily in the midterm elections.[56] He was so incensed that he and a group of like-minded senators briefly considered releasing a manifesto denouncing Grant's actions; though they opted not to do this, Cameron nonetheless made it clear that he was determined to distance himself from what he saw as a political suicide.[57]

Cameron's prediction was prophetic: as a result of the depression, the Republicans suffered substantial losses in the midterm elections of 1874. Going into the elections, Republicans held a two-to-one advantage over the Democrats, but when Congress reconvened in 1875, Democrats held 169 seats to the Republicans' 109.[58] Democrats won a majority of seats in the Pennsylvania legislature and would therefore be in a position to choose a senator to replace John Scott, whose term was expiring. On the one hand, this was hardly unwelcome news: Scott had not proven quite as pliant as Cameron had hoped and had even occasionally run afoul of the senior senator on policy and patronage matters. Furthermore, the Democrats' control of the state legislature ensured that a Democrat would be elected to succeed Scott. As expected, the legislature selected a Democrat, William A. Wallace of Clearfield County, to be the state's new senator. While this may at first glance appear to have been a defeat for Cameron, it ensured that the Pennsylvanian would be the only dispenser of federal patronage in the Keystone State, as the president was going to do nothing to strengthen Wallace. In sum, Wallace's election was actually a boon for Cameron, enhancing his power and weakening any Republican faction in Pennsylvania that might challenge his political machine.

In the spring of 1875, Cameron succeeded in having the House of Representatives (by unanimous consent) adopt a resolution rescinding its censure of his conduct as secretary of war, an indication of his lingering bitterness over being forced out of Lincoln's cabinet more than a decade before. However, that vindication was leavened by the fact that Cameron's relationship with Grant had grown strained. Though Grant (undoubtedly at Cameron's behest) named two Cameron supporters to plum patronage, one thing seemed continually beyond the senator's reach: a cabinet post for Donald. As Cameron's biographer noted, the Pennsylvanian's "hope was to give [Donald] national stature by introducing him into the Grant cabinet and to keep him there into another administration until he [Simon Cameron] should choose to retire. Then, [Donald] would succeed him in the Senate."[59] Cameron had worked for years to secure Donald a seat in the cabinet. Shortly after Grant's second inauguration, the Pennsylvanian had publicly expressed his hope that Grant would seek a third term, a move that was widely interpreted as intended to push the president into taking Donald into the cabinet. Newspapers friendly to Cameron actively promoted Donald as a candidate for cabinet appointment. Cameron's efforts seemed to bear fruit when, in the spring of 1874, Grant suggested nominating either Donald or Joseph Patterson, a former Democrat, to be secretary of the Treasury. Clearly, Grant was aware of Cameron's desire to see his son named to the cabinet, but the breech between the two men over the inflation bill was deep. Unbeknown to Cameron, Grant discussed the matter with Secretary of State Fish, speaking "very highly of Don. Cameron's capacity and character but his relations to the Senator seemed to be an obstacle to his having [a cabinet] position," and the president ultimately did not appoint Donald, which strained their relationship.[60]

By the summer of 1875, Cameron was so frustrated at the fact that Grant had not taken Donald into the cabinet that he blustered "no Pennsylvanian with decent respect for himself would accept [a place in Grant's cabinet]." According to a report in the *New York Herald* in October 1875, "there is bad blood between the President and Simon Cameron. It seems that on last Saturday the ex-Secretary of War came down from Pennsylvania to [arrange an appointment for a friend]. The President, who was in no humor to see him, much less listen to the demand, snubbed him."[61] Cameron retaliated by letting languish a treaty that the Grant administration had negotiated, and by May, Grant was reduced to complaining that Cameron and other members of the Senate Foreign Relations Committee "have not treated him right."[62]

It was not until the last year of Grant's presidency that Cameron managed to finagle a cabinet seat for Donald. It turned out that, beginning in 1870, Secretary of War William W. Belknap had abused his power to award sutlers (suppliers of uniforms and other goods) exclusive contracts to operate at U.S. Army installations. Specifically, he gave the lucrative contracts to friends and political allies in return for kickbacks. On February 29, 1876, Congress began investigating Belknap, and on March 2 he resigned as secretary of war. Unsatisfied by his resignation, the House of Representatives voted to impeach Belknap. Following a trial in the Senate, Cameron voted to convict the former Secretary of War, though he was heard muttering, "Terrible, terrible. This comes from Grant's system of appointments."[63] Belknap was acquitted largely on the grounds that, now as a private citizen, conviction in the Senate was inappropriate. Initially, Grant appointed Ohio Supreme Court Justice Alphonso Taft to replace Belknap, but Taft served only three months before the president appointed him attorney general, leaving the War Department again vacant. So it was, after years of trying, Cameron finally achieved his goal: in the spring of 1876, Grant named Donald Cameron of secretary of war.

Because 1876 was an election year, Republicans around the country began jockeying to succeed Grant. Cameron did not attend the convention, and the machine's interests were represented by Donald, a sure sign that he was increasingly in command of Pennsylvania's Republican Party. At the convention, Donald offered to toss the Pennsylvania delegation's vote to Maine senator James G. Blaine in exchange for an iron-clad promise of a cabinet seat for Pennsylvania, assuming that Blaine would retain Donald as secretary of war. Blaine's campaign manager refused the offer, and that refusal Blaine the nomination: on the last ballot, Blaine was twenty-eight votes behind Ohio governor Rutherford B. Hayes, which was the exact number of votes Pennsylvania's delegation had to offer. Cameron's lieutenant, Matthew S. Quay, made this explicit when he cheekily wrote to Hayes the following year, "I am immediately responsible for the action of the Pennsylvania delegation [at the convention] which resulted in your nomination. Mr. Blaine will tell you this if ever the subject is discussed between you."[64]

Always the good party man, Cameron campaigned vigorously for Hayes, and Pennsylvania delivered the largest block of electoral votes for Hayes of any state. Cameron spent election night with President Grant at publisher George W. Child's house. Tilden clearly won the popular vote by more than 250,000, but the outcome in the electoral college was unclear. At first count, Tilden had won 184 electoral votes to Hayes's 165, with 20 in dispute, making it impossible to determine who won the election. Fearing the possibility of another civil war, in January 1877 Congress passed legislation that created a commission, composed of five members each of the House, the Senate, and the Supreme Court, empowered to decide the matter. Writing later, he criticized the outcome, claiming, "If any such bargain was made, it must have been negotiated by that new school of politicians who indulge in modish sentimentalism and cowardice calling them statesmanship, and go about sneering at obsolete courage and political conviction, calling them 'radicalism.'"[65] Cameron later explained his vote by saying, "It is not my custom as a victor to enter into compromises with those whom I have fairly defeated; nor do I permit any coward to do so if I can prevent it."[66] On January 22 Cameron took his concerns to the floor of the Senate, denouncing the bill as a ploy to give Tilden the presidency. Cameron voted against the bill, but it passed anyway. A few weeks later, the commission voted 8 to 7 along party lines to award Hayes the presidency, allegedly on the basis of his promise to withdraw federal troops from the South. Though no one has ever proved that such a bargain existed, before leaving office Grant removed troops from Florida and, shortly after his inauguration, Hayes removed U.S. troops from South Carolina and Louisiana, essentially ending Reconstruction.

Following Hayes's inauguration, Cameron's machine kicked into overdrive to persuade the new president to retain Donald in the cabinet. Hayes refused, saying that he had promised not to retain any of Grant's cabinet.[67] At a public meeting on March 6, 1877, Cameron expressed his bitterness over Hayes's decision, claiming that Pennsylvania had again made a president only to have the president forget that fact. Against his wishes, he voted for Hayes's nominees, but it was becoming increasingly clear that the next four years would be frustrating for Cameron if he stayed in the Senate. Cameron was out of step with President Hayes's program of civil service reform. Nearing the end of his presidency, Hayes boasted, "The end I have chiefly aimed at has been to break down congressional patronage, and especially Senatorial patronage. . . . I began by selecting a Cabinet in opposition to [the wishes of members of Congress], and I have gone on that path steadily until now I am filling the important places of collector of the port and postmaster at Philadelphia almost without a suggestion even from Senators or Representatives! Is not this a good measure of success for the Executive to accomplish almost absolutely unaided in Congress?"[68] Hayes's glee at attacking the basis of Simon Cameron's political influence reflected the basic philosophic chasm separating the two men. Whereas Hayes envisioned a government staffed by nonpartisan technocrats, Cameron was aghast at such a prospect, seeing the creation of a permanent federal bureaucracy as a threat to the republic. In 1887 Cameron dismissed civil service reform, claiming, "It is not a good thing in a republic to grow a large life office-holding class. We need new blood in the control of the business affairs of the nation, as well as in all other national concerns."[69] Cameron had complained, "A Republi-

can president ought to appoint Republicans," but there was little else he could do; it was clear he would have little influence
in Hayes's White House. In a certain sense, Cameron had out-
lived his era; though there would always be spoils to distribute,
increasingly civil servants hired without regard to party affiliation would replace patronage appointments.

On March 10, 1877, Cameron wrote Pennsylvania governor
John F. Hartranft a brief letter resigning from the Senate. In
public, the former war secretary claimed to be "tired of the
care and worry of office; of having to turn away good people
whom I would be glad to serve if I had the power, and of being
annoyed by bad people seeking to make use of me."[70] Most
observers interpreted Cameron's resignation as a protest against
Hayes's cabinet choices and as a last-ditch play to have Donald
succeed him in the Senate. This impression was cemented by
the fact that, on the very night that Cameron wrote his resignation letter, the Pennsylvanian and his son hosted a party at
Cameron's mansion in Harrisburg. At various intervals in the
evening, Donald took small groups of the notables aside and
broke the news of Cameron's impending retirement. Following
each announcement, Donald produced a register and asked the
state legislators in each group to sign it, thereby committing
themselves to vote for him to succeed his father in the Senate.
Within a few hours, a majority of the Republican legislators
had committed themselves to vote for Donald, and on March
13 he received 131 of 132 votes in the Republican nominating
caucus. A week later, Simon Cameron watched as every single
Republican in the legislature voted for Donald, electing him
the junior senator from Pennsylvania.

Cameron's resignation from the Senate did not mean he was
finished with politics, and Donald's place in the Senate gave him
a unique opportunity to embarrass Hayes. Pennsylvania's Republicans complained mightily that Hayes had failed to appoint a
Pennsylvanian to a cabinet post, and by the autumn of 1877
Hayes was tiring of the criticism. The president committed to
filling a first-class diplomatic post with a prominent Pennsylva-

nian, but could not come to a decision. Hayes elected to throw the choice to Pennsylvania's congressional delegation. He dispatched Secretary of State Evarts to meet with the delegation, and offered the position of U.S. ambassador to Great Britain—one of the most sought-after diplomatic appointments—if the Pennsylvanians could agree on a candidate. According to later reconstructions, Evarts explicitly committed the president to appointing whomever Pennsylvania's congressional delegation selected.

Shortly after this announcement, Donald Cameron convened a meeting of Pennsylvania's congressional delegation at his home in Washington DC and polled the members on their preferred candidates. Most of the members named Wayne MacVeagh, whom Hayes had already considered appointing, or former mayor of Philadelphia Morton McMichael. One congressman suggested Simon Cameron, and because no one was going to contest the suggestion in Donald's presence, Cameron became the congressional delegation's choice by default. All of the members present signed a petition to that effect, and a few days later, Donald himself presented the petition to Hayes, allegedly telling the president, "This is what Pennsylvania wants."[71] Hayes was flabbergasted and now faced a dilemma: embarrass himself by the subservience implied by appointing Cameron or incur the wrath of Pennsylvania's Republican machine by refusing to honor Evarts's pledge.

Ultimately, Hayes was saved from his dilemma the following day when members of Pennsylvania's congressional delegation visited the White House and told the president that they had been coerced into signing the petition asking that Cameron be appointed.[72] Feeling that he now had the political strength to defy Donald's wishes, Hayes instructed Evarts to let it be known to the press that the president considered the petition advisory only. A few weeks later, following a meeting with some prominent Pennsylvania businessmen, Hayes appointed Philadelphia merchant John Welsh, who had earned a reputation through his successful management of the Centennial Exhibition's finances. Rumor had it that New York senator Roscoe Conkling, a longtime Cameron ally, considered fighting the nomination but abandoned that plan when it became clear he lacked the political strength to succeed.[73] Yet, despite this setback and his alienation from the Hayes's administration, Cameron remained politically influential even in retirement.

10

"I'll Behave Myself as Long as I'm Here," 1877–89

Donald's confrontation with Hayes over appointing Cameron to represent the United States in Great Britain was hardly the only issue vexing Cameron's retirement. At age seventy-eight, Cameron was sued for $50,000 by a former Treasury Department employee named Mary S. Oliver, which the *New York Times* called "one of the greatest scandals that ever agitated Washington society."[1] According to Oliver, she had met Cameron at the Congressional Hotel in New Orleans in 1874 during one of his periodic sojourns to the Crescent City. The following year, she claimed, their acquaintance was "renewed," and the newly widowed Cameron (Margaret had died the year before) spent the night with her at the St. Charles Hotel, during which she claimed Cameron took "improper privileges."[2] Oliver further claimed that Cameron wrote to her a few months later, promising to "carry [her] to a better life" by making her his wife, and that sometime later he had sent her $300. When, after a year, Cameron failed to make good on his alleged promises, Oliver claimed she had no recourse but to file suit.[3]

A reporter described Oliver as "vivacious and attractive . . . though not precisely pretty, she still has charms enough left in the way of blue eyes, brown hair, round, full face, and plump figure."[4] The details of the "Widow Oliver's" background are hard to discern, in large part because her story changed. At one point, she claimed to be the granddaughter of Charles Stewart, a naval officer who rose to fame during the Barbary Wars and the War of 1812.[5] In another instance, she admitted to having given her name previously as "Mrs. General Sherman," conceding that she had not, in fact, even met William T. Sherman.[6] In an interview she gave in January 1878, Oliver claimed that she was born in Florida and that she did not know her parents' names, but that Cameron had known her mother and father. In this version of her story, she was adopted by Mrs. Alice Oliver of Louisville, Kentucky, and then married at the age of fourteen. She had a child the following year, but within five years she and her husband signed a contract of separation (but were not divorced). Soon after, she married her second husband, whose name she refused to give and who abandoned her during the Civil War.[7] In 1879 the "widow" claimed that the reporters had made up everything they printed (though she conceded that she had spoken to them).

Oliver testified under oath that she had told Cameron that she was born in Ireland but had immigrated to Montreal when she was twelve and that her father's name was Keefer. According to "Mrs. Oliver," she married a man named Stewart, with whom she moved to Virginia. Shortly thereafter, she met a man named Thomas M. Oliver, with whom she ran away to Raleigh, North Carolina, pretending to be his daughter. Their relationship ended when it turned out that Oliver's wife, who had been institutionalized in an asylum, was released, and he was forced to confess to "Mrs. Oliver" that he was not, in fact, a widower. At some point shortly thereafter, he abandoned "Mrs. Oliver," and she was forced to leave her daughter at a convent before moving to New Orleans to look for work.[8] Interestingly, Mr. Oliver's nephew, who lived with him at the time, could not recall meeting her before the family moved to Louisville, though he did confirm meeting her shortly before she decamped for New Orleans.[9]

It was here that she ran into Cameron in 1874, although at

times she claimed to have met him in Washington in 1865. When Cameron returned to New Orleans in 1875, she managed to extract from him a letter of recommendation addressed to Secretary of the Treasury Benjamin Bristow, which she used to secure a job in the department, though she soon lost that position. A short time after that, she secured a job at the Patent Office, but she lost that job after three weeks.[10] According to "Mrs. Oliver," she and Cameron began a romantic affair that culminated in December 1875 with his promise to marry her. "Mrs. Oliver" even described one particularly bizarre encounter when she and Cameron consummated their relationship for the first time. Apparently, Cameron asked "Mrs. Oliver" to visit him in his suite at the Congressional Hotel in Washington DC. When she arrived, the Senator locked the door, explaining that his daughter Virginia had come to Washington with her kids "and annoyed him, and he would not let them in. He told ["Mrs. Oliver"] that, should [Virginia and the kids] come to the door, for ["Mrs. Oliver"] to go to the back of the bed, and if they went to the window, for her to get behind the curtain, and that would prevent them from seeing her. [Virginia] and the children did come and knocked, but receiving no answer, went away. He then said that she must not leave the room alone, as it would look strange. Mr. Cameron had champagne in the room and invited her to drink, saying it would help her; she took a little of it." Eventually, he promised to marry her and she allowed him to take such "improper privileges."[11] Cameron was supposedly stopped from making good on this promise by the intercession of a woman named Annie Davis—variously described as Cameron's niece, his wife's cousin, and his friend—who apparently did not approve of the match.[12] Davis was so opposed to the relationship that, according to letters that Oliver sent to Cameron, she told Thaddeus Stevens's former housekeeper to assault Mrs. Oliver and "she sent a man to my very boarding house to injure me." In a letter to the octogenarian senator, Oliver complained, "Men accost me in the street and tell me Mr. Cameron sent them."[13]

Determining the only course of action available to her was to write to the senator, Mrs. Oliver repeatedly did so, proposing various solutions. In one letter she threatened, "If I cannot see you I will sue you, because that Annie Davis has separated us. . . . She does not love you; she only wants your money." "Mrs. Oliver" filed suit against Cameron in February 1877, alleging "the said defendant . . . undertook and faithfully promised to marry and take her, the said plaintiff, to wife in a reasonable time. . . . She avers that although a reasonable time for that purpose hath long elapsed . . . yet defendant hath not taken her to wife, although often requested to do so."[14] In a letter written shortly after she filed suit, she beseeched a mutual acquaintance to approach Cameron with a deal: "If Mr. Cameron will let me have his son Simon—because he has his name and is his child—to take care of, to live with me, I will live any place Mr. Cameron wishes. When I have something belonging to him to love I will be satisfied. As I now see that I cannot ever have Mr. Cameron, please do use influence on my behalf. If you can succeed with this proposition for me, I will drop all proceedings at once, and forever."[15] Somewhere along the way, she even wrote to Donald, promising to secure him a cabinet position "if you would make your father marry me."[16]

Knowing that his political enemies would be all too willing to embarrass him by repeating "Mrs. Oliver's" allegations, Cameron agreed to settle with the "widow" for $1,000 in September 1878.[17] The settlement was delivered to the "widow" through her attorney, former Ohio congressman Albert G. Riddle. "Mrs. Oliver" signed a receipt for the money, and Riddle considered the case closed, so he was surprised when, a week later, his client appeared asking about additional action against Cameron. Even more shocking was her appearance, which had changed drastically. When Riddle gave her the money a few days before, she was "thin as a walking stick;" now, she looked to be seven or eight months pregnant. "Mrs. Oliver" now claimed that Cameron had impregnated her and she demanded a much larger settlement. When Cameron spurned her renewed demands,

"Mrs. Oliver" increased the pressure, writing to the senator that she was pregnant: "I am going before the court next week *and swear to the truth that you are the father of my baby,* so that it will not come into the world unprovided for. You have forced me to do this because you would not agree to my proposition."[18] At one point, she even schemed to send a baby to the Senate floor to embarrass Cameron, but these plans did not pan out, and Riddle refused to represent her any longer. A few months later, he was visited by Belva Lockwood, who claimed to be representing "Mrs. Oliver" in her suit against Cameron. Lockwood was the first female attorney granted the right to argue before the U.S. Supreme Court and her practice dealt mostly with gender discrimination. Lockwood wanted to get some information from Riddle about the case. When Riddle passed along the signed receipt indicating that "Mrs. Oliver" had received a settlement, Lockwood turned down the case.

Not surprisingly, this salacious and titillating tale provided grist for endless gossip, much of it gleefully instigated by Cameron's political enemies. Once "Mrs. Oliver" filed suit, Cameron immediately ceased all contact with the woman, though for two years she tried unsuccessfully to see him. In one instance, she tried to convince one of the doorkeepers at the Capitol to admit her to Cameron's Senate committee rooms so that she could confront the senator, and she later wrote a letter purportedly from this doorkeeper to Cameron in the hopes that the senator would come and visit her.[19] These ploys failed, though "Mrs. Oliver" testified at various times that Cameron had procured an abortifacient that he persuaded (in some versions forced) her to drink, which is why she could not produce their love child.[20] She also claimed to have letters from Cameron proving they had an affair. When called upon to produce these letters, "Mrs. Oliver" could only provide three or four, claiming variously that Cameron had insisted that she reply to his letters on his, thereby ensuring that she did not keep them and that she had destroyed the hundreds of letters he had allegedly sent her.[21]

The case went to court in the spring of 1879, and the proceedings gave lie to Oliver's claims. In the two years since she filed suit, the press coverage was generally sympathetic to "Mrs. Oliver." Cameron was derided as the "Gay Deceiver," "A Fickle Lover," and "Sly Simon," while the *Washington Post* claimed in early 1878, "The fact is that the Cameron gang have tried to crush Mrs. Oliver by the methods they employ to wipe out an obnoxious political opponent in Pennsylvania. But fortunately for the cause of justice and the sanctity of female affections, the courts of the District of Columbia are not subject to the domination of the Cameron gang as are the courts of Pennsylvania."[22] Over the course of the thirteen-day trial, however, the tone of the coverage changed dramatically, in large part due to "Mrs. Oliver's" testimony, which was inconsistent, vague, and downright bizarre. Led by Cameron's friend Benjamin F. Butler, the senator's defense team carefully demolished each of "Mrs. Oliver's" claims. At one point the defense produced her husband, demonstrating that Cameron and "Mrs. Oliver" could not have been legally married regardless of what he might have promised her. Additionally, Butler produced a handwriting expert who testified that most of the letters Cameron allegedly sent to "Mrs. Oliver" were forgeries; the only letter the senator actually wrote, at least according to the witness, was the one to Treasury Secretary Bristow recommending "Mrs. Oliver" for a job.[23]

Adding even more intrigue to the case, the defense questioned a woman who insisted on wearing a veil that obscured her face. Identifying herself as Mrs. M. A. Henriques, she quickly became known as the "Veiled Woman," and her testimony decimated "Mrs. Oliver's" claims. According to the "Veiled Woman," she knew "Mrs. Oliver" during the latter's alleged affair with Simon Cameron and testified that no such relationship existed. Moreover, the "Veiled Woman" claimed that "Mrs. Oliver" had bragged of her plan to blackmail the senator.[24] On April 2 the case went to the jury at 1:00 p.m. Half an hour into its deliberations, the jury asked to see notes from the various reporters who had been covering the case, which the judge refused, saying, "Any twelve men who can't take that case and settle it on the testimony ain' fit to be jurors." Later he told a friend, "[The jury] should not have been out over twenty minutes." Initially, nine jurors found for the defense, and over subsequent ballots they wore down the three who believed "Mrs. Oliver." At exactly 3:00 p.m., the jury returned to the courtroom and delivered its verdict, finding for the defense.[25]

The cost of Cameron's vindication was high: $2,000 in attorney's fees and more than two years of embarrassing newspaper coverage. Moreover, as far as "Mrs. Oliver" was concerned, the case was far from over. A week after the verdict, "Mrs. Oliver" appeared before a crowd in Alexandria, Virginia, to present her side of the story. Approximately seventy-five people paid to hear what one reporter described as a "desultory talk," in which "Mrs. Oliver" claimed that "never in the history of the country had there been so many detectives and experts as had hunted her down. They had, in fact, brought the whole state of Pennsylvania, young and old, to perjure themselves, that Cameron might be acquitted. . . . Concluding, [she said] she was going to continue to fight Cameron in the courts just to show him she was as good as he was, and that she was going to rally her Irish friends and beat him in Pennsylvania."[26] Fight on she did, appealing the court's verdict on the grounds that her former lawyer, A. G. Riddle, should not have been allowed to testify against her. On May 22, 1880, the appeals court upheld the verdict, and "Mrs. Oliver's" breach of promise suit against Simon Cameron finally came to an end.

Even with these distractions, Cameron still took an active interest in politics and enjoyed playing the role of the "Sage of Donegal." He noted to one reporter, "I am not in politics right now, though I keep a pretty close eye on current events. The possession and use of political power is exceedingly fascinating, and I like to study the ebbs and flows of the tide as well as ever."[27] In retirement, Cameron remained well connected and influential. In April 1881 he called upon President James A. Garfield at the White House, and the following year he visited the Capitol, where his former colleagues gave him a standing ovation.[28] In May 1887 he visited Democratic president Grover Cleveland in the White House and the following year he even joined the first family on a trip to Florida.[29] Abraham Lincoln's son Robert invited Cameron to visit Chicago in May 1880, and in May 1888 Cameron traveled to Philadelphia, where he was feted by that city's "Cameron Club" on the occasion of its twenty-fifth anniversary.[30] In recognition of his enduring popularity, Pennsylvania's legislature appointed the former war secretary one of the commissioners charged with selecting prominent Pennsylvanians for inclusion in the National Portrait Gallery, and in 1880 one of Pennsylvania's congressional districts even nominated him for the House of Representatives (he declined).[31] All the while, he continued taking part in a variety of civic organizations, including service as a trustee for the State Hospital for Injured Persons of the Anthracite Coal Regions and as vice president of the Pottsville Fishing Party, and he raised funds for the Historical Society of Pennsylvania to construct a new building.

Cameron traveled across the South in an attempt to break the "solid South" by building effective Republican organizations in the states of the former Confederacy.[32] He and his son Donald tried to convince Grant to run for a third term in 1880 because Hayes had pledged to serve only a single term. For Donald, a Grant presidency would be a chance to return to the executive branch, which he enjoyed far more than the Senate. In February 1880, due to Cameron and Donald's machinations, Pennsylvania's Republican state nominating convention voted 133 to 113 to support Grant as a unit, meaning the former president would receive all of Pennsylvania's delegates' votes at the national convention in Chicago. Donald presided over the convention in his role as chairman of the Republican National Committee, but he was unable to keep control over Pennsylvania's delegation, which voted against Grant. In addition, the convention ousted some of Grant's delegates, and while the former president's supporters remained loyal to him, they simply could not garner enough votes to secure him the nomination.[33] Eventually, on the thirty-sixth ballot, the convention nominated Ohio congressman James A. Garfield for president and former collector of the Port of New York Chester A. Arthur for vice president. President Hayes rejoiced to his diary, "The unit rule (the corner-stone of the boss system) abolished—Cameron crushed—the Administration endorsed. . . . What other convention in all our history can show as much good and as little harm?"[34] Because the Democrats and the Republicans were nearly evenly matched (as the election of 1876 demonstrated), the Camerons perfunctorily supported Garfield's campaign, and the Ohioan squeaked to victory in November. In recognition of the Camerons' efforts, Garfield appointed Cameron's son-in-law Wayne MacVeagh attorney general of the United States, though Donald was left out of the cabinet.

A reporter who visited Cameron shortly before the former war secretary's eighty-eighth birthday left an indelible description, noting, "The general has a sallow complexion which is heightened by the shock of long white hair that covers his head and hangs down upon his shoulders, luxuriant around the edges but getting a trifle thin on top. The old statesman has a habit of running his fingers through his hair which makes it stand out in wild disorder. He has a long birch staff which comes up nearly to his shoulders, which he carries habitually in his hand as he walks about, even when in the hotel corridors or the house."[35]

Cameron's almost constant companion during his final years was his son Simon, whose disability made it impossible for him to live by himself. Cameron involved his son in the management of the Donegal estate, and following Cameron's death in 1889, his grandson James McCormick Cameron (Donald's son from his first marriage) looked after "Uncle Simon" until the latter's death in 1908.[36] In Cameron's later years, other family members—one of his brothers-in-law, and a granddaughter—lived with him both at his mansion in Harrisburg and his Donegal estate.[37] He woke every morning at about eight o'clock and ate a light breakfast. Afterwards, he retired to the porch or the library where he reviewed the newspapers and met with visitors. At about eleven o'clock the former war secretary typically drank a pint of champagne (down from a quart), after which he ate his lunch. Perhaps inevitably given his wine intake, Cameron napped in the afternoons and then ate a light supper at six (usually grits and oatmeal or cornmeal mush), spending the rest of the evening reading before going to bed at eleven o'clock or midnight. Cameron surrounded himself with mementos from his political life, and commissioned busts of himself and his wife, which he placed in alcoves along the staircase. He was generous with his time, spending hours reminiscing with visitors in his office or on the porch, where, surrounded by his dogs, he would recount humorous stories about his time in the Senate and the cabinet.[38]

Cameron remained as social as ever, frequently hosting dinner parties or picnics for his friends and neighbors. In 1886 Cameron invited nearly a dozen current and former senators to dinner at his Donegal estate, and two years later he hosted a similar party whose guest list included some of the most powerful men in American politics and industry, a sign of his enduring relevance even as he approached his nineties.[39] The former senator held a massive gathering for his neighbors at his Donegal estate to celebrate the one hundredth anniversary of U.S. independence, and he delighted the crowd by recounting the fact that, when his son Donald told him that he might not be able to attend, the old man had replied, "You'd better wait until you get an invitation—you ain't a Donegaler."[40] Donegal was his passion and he took a great deal of pride in its operations, boasting of its crops and showing it off to his constant stream of visitors.

As the political battles of the past receded into history, Cameron rebuilt his friendship with Benjamin H. Brewster, whom President Arthur appointed attorney general of the United States.[41] The result of their renewed friendship was a steady stream of lighthearted letters from Washington that kept Cameron up-to-date on events in the Capitol. At the same time, however, his circle of friends and family continued shrinking.

In 1877 Cameron's older brother William died of face cancer. Death claimed both Thomas A. Scott and John W. Forney in 1881, and Ulysses S. Grant (whom, despite their frequent disagreements, Cameron described as one of his closest and most intimate friends) died in 1885 after a prolonged battle with throat cancer.[42] Two years later, Cameron's younger sister Catherine died, leaving her brother to sort out the details of her estate.[43] Cameron's own mortality was much on his mind following a serious train accident in 1878. Returning to Harrisburg from Hot Springs, Arkansas, Cameron's train derailed, and though he was not seriously injured, for a time he was reported to have developed a fear of railroad accidents that temporarily curtailed his travel.[44]

Cameron was enormously financially successful in retirement, increasing his fortune by more than 50 percent through diverse investments in coal, railroads, oil, banks, and even a cattle ranch in Arizona, and he could count on an income of more than $50,000 from his land holdings, which were valued at more than $1 million.[45] Into his eighties Cameron personally oversaw the operation of a tobacco farm he owned near Lancaster.[46] In retirement his trips became longer and more exotic. Never a winter person, in February 1881, a few weeks shy of his eighty-second birthday, Cameron traveled to the West Indies, and the following year he spent time in Florida and Louisiana. Shortly after his eighty-fourth birthday, Cameron traveled through the American Southwest and into Mexico. In 1887, at the age of eighty-eight, Cameron took two extended trips: the first to Bermuda and the second to Europe. Astonishingly, following his trip to Bermuda in February, the octogenarian Cameron complained, "Life is altogether too slow in the Bermudas to suit me."[47] A few months later, Cameron traveled to Europe via the ocean liner *Britannic*, where he was able to meet his great-grandson who was born the same day the former war secretary arrived in London. While in London, Cameron was feted by British and American notables (including Buffalo Bill) before decamping for sightseeing and genealogical research in Scotland, where he stayed with steel magnate Andrew Carnegie.[48]

Donald, whose wife had died a few years earlier, remarried in the spring of 1878. His new bride, Elizabeth B. Sherman, was almost a quarter century younger than Donald, though the match was a happy one.[49] Cameron took a great deal of joy in his grandchildren, recalling in a letter to Wayne MacVeagh taking his grandson to the local grocer's store and indulging the boy's wish to be lifted into the grocery scale.[50] When he retired in 1877, Cameron had eighteen grandchildren, and in 1886 Donald and his new wife Eliza welcomed a baby girl whom they named Martha, and she quickly became the apple of her father's (and grandfather's) eye.[51]

Even in old age, Cameron remained generous, always looking for opportunities to help those in need. In 1883 his nephew Brewster wrote to Cameron expressing gratitude for all his uncle had done on his behalf, calling the older man a "friend and benefactor" and noting, "I am indebted to you for my start in life."[52] Nor was Cameron's generosity limited to family. In 1880 the former war secretary subsidized the printing of John Cuthbertson's diary for the Presbyterian Alliance.[53] That same year, Cameron donated the house standing on the site of the house in which he was born to a local Lutheran congregation for use as a parsonage. Six years later he sent $1,000 to aid those affected by a devastating earthquake in Charleston, South Carolina.[54] He even allowed a local family to use his Donegal estate as the site of their father's funeral because the man's family had owned the site decades before and he had been born in what became Cameron's house.

In July 1879 the citizens of Sunbury, Pennsylvania, dedicated a soldiers' monument. Cameron had agreed to raise $2,500 of the monument's cost and he was heavily involved in its planning and construction.[55] The forty-three-foot-tall base was crowned with a statue of Cameron's brother James, who had been killed at Bull Run. Cameron gave a speech at the unveiling, which was attended by the surviving members of the Highlanders.

Over the years, Cameron remained in touch with his brother's former troops, often making time to attend events the Highlanders scheduled. The Highlanders reciprocated Cameron's affection. In May 1864 one of the Highlanders wrote to Cameron following a celebration for the regiment's surviving veterans. Cameron was unable to attend, but sent a letter expressing his affection for the regiment and its men. The former soldier noted, "We expected you would have been present and the regiment and were really very sorry that you were not. Your kind and feeling letter was however read to [the men] and was fully appreciated by the brave Scotchmen."

In his later years, however, his generosity proved a costly virtue: constantly besieged for financial assistance, the former senator "lent" approximately $50,000, very little of which was ever repaid. He sank at least $14,000 into a ranching operation run by two of his grandsons, and his letters demonstrate that it became a pit into which he was constantly obligated to throw good money after bad. Another grandson, Thomas Burnside, disappointed Cameron by becoming a newspaper reporter and then an actor; one newspaper called him "a Bohemian of the most pronounced type."[56] It bothered Cameron, who once boasted that he did not need to steal because he could walk into the street and make all the money he could ever want, that his children and grandchildren lacked his business acumen. Even Donald came in for some criticism when, in 1889, he took an extended vacation in Europe. Cameron, who at the time was on his deathbed, wondered aloud how his son could abandon the Bank of Middletown at such a moment. In a widely reported comment, Cameron thought he had identified the main cause of his children and grandchildren's lack of business acumen: they had the advantages of Cameron's wealth and success. Speaking of Donald, Cameron is supposed to have said, "Yes, my son Don had many advantages, but I had one which overbalanced them all—poverty."[57]

The former secretary of war remained more or less healthy up to nearly the end of his life, though there were some serious illnesses in his last decade. One evening he awoke with a "peculiar sensation" and called for help. When none came, Cameron rose from his bed but fainted, falling to the floor. The noise awakened his son Simon, and the younger man came into his father's room. Seeing Cameron unconscious on the floor scared Simon, and he fled back to his own room without alerting anyone to what had happened. Fortunately, the noise woke one of the housekeepers, who found Cameron on the floor and revived him. A thorough examination proved this to be nothing more than a case of vertigo, and Cameron received a clean bill of health. Three years later, Cameron suffered a much more serious fall getting out of bed and lay on the floor for more than two hours before one of the housekeepers discovered him. This time, Cameron was confined to bed for a month due to the excruciating pain, and his condition was serious enough that Maggie and Virginia stayed at the house to sit at his bedside. Cameron felt his faculties ebbing at the time of his ninetieth birthday, saying, "I think I must be getting old. I can remember very clearly what happened fifty or sixty years ago, but am not so sure about things that happened within the last few months."[58]

In general, however, instances like this were the exception rather than the rule, and Cameron could be frequently seen walking five miles or more for pleasure. A devoted equestrian, Cameron frequently rode long distances on horseback until only a few months before his death.[59] For his ninetieth birthday, the Pennsylvania legislature passed a resolution of congratulations, and Cameron was flooded by visitors and well-wishers including the lieutenant governor, the speaker of the Pennsylvania House of Representatives, and most of the members of the state legislature. Seated as the men filed into his house on Front Street in Harrisburg, Cameron remarked, "Gentlemen, I am very glad to see you all and I am very much obliged for the honor done me. I don't know what more I can say, except that I'll behave myself as long as I'm here."[60] A week before, the "Cameron Club" of Philadelphia marched in Washington, each member dressed in a dark uniform that included black top hat, tan gloves, and a badge displaying Cameron's picture.[61]

Yet, for all the fanfare, Cameron was eager for the weather to warm so that he could return to Donegal. When spring finally arrived, the old man enjoyed spending the days sitting on the porch at his beloved estate, but shortly after he arrived, Cameron suffered what was described as a hemorrhage. Recovery was slow, though by June 10 he was able to leave his bedroom for short intervals. This recovery was short-lived, and in mid-June (fifteen years to the day from Margaret's death), one of Cameron's servants returned from a brief errand to find the former war secretary paralyzed by a stroke, though still conscious. The paralysis made it difficult for him to eat, which drained his strength, though he remained "quietly cheerful" and alert over the next few days. He died peacefully at about eight o'clock in the evening of June 26, 1889, surrounded by his family: his daughter Virginia and her husband Wayne MacVeagh, his son Simon, and a few of his grandchildren.[62] Cameron's grandson and namesake, Simon Brua Cameron, made the arrangements for the funeral. On the evening of June 27, Simon Cameron left his beloved Donegal for the last time, his body traveling by special train to Harrisburg. There, in the family mansion on Front Street, he was laid out in a parlor across from his library. The funeral service was conducted by a local minister on the afternoon of June 28 and, in accordance with his oft-expressed wishes, was a simple affair.[63] Clad in a black suit and placed in an oak casket, Cameron was buried next to his wife at the family plot, where he was joined in due course by his daughter Maggie and his son Simon.[64] The marker eventually placed at his grave was inscribed "Simon Cameron, Printer, Editor, Adjutant General of Pennsylvania, elected to four terms Senator of the United States, Secretary of War, Minister to Russia. Born in Donegal, Lancaster County, Penn, March 8, 1799. Died in Donegal, Lancaster County, Penn, June 26, 1889."[65]

Cameron's will was filed in early July, and estimates of his wealth varied widely; the San Francisco *Chronicle* asserted that his estate was worth $4 million, while the *Pittsburg Dispatch* put the figure at $1.7 million.[66] In death Cameron was as generous as he had been in life: he left $10,000 each to both the Harrisburg Hospital and the Harrisburg Home for the Friendless; he bequeathed his library and $5,000 to the YMCA of Harrisburg in order to create a library for journeymen and apprentices; he left $5,000 to the German Reformed Church of Maytown and the Donegal Church received $2,000. An old friend who had been kind to Simon received $5,000, while an old servant received $2,000. Cameron was extremely generous to his family, providing a trust fund for Simon and bequeathing the Donegal estate to Donald, whose daughters received $40,000 each.[67]

The press coverage of his death and funeral was sympathetic and adulatory, belying the controversies of his long political career. The War Department released a statement the day after Cameron died, ordering that "the offices connected with the Department of War will be draped in mourning for the period of thirty days and all business therein will be suspended on the day of the funeral. . . . [Furthermore,] upon the day after the receipt of this order at each military post seventeen guns will be fired at intervals of half an hour, commencing at meridian," an ironic tribute to a man who had been fired from the cabinet more than a quarter century before.[68]

Conclusion

"I Did the Best I Could and Was Never Untrue to a Friend"

Cameron's passing marked more than just the end of his life; it coincided with the end of an era. As the nineteenth century came to an end, the pressure to curb the abuses of the spoils system became irresistible. Hayes's civil service reforms laid the groundwork for sweeping changes in government hiring and procurement procedures that limited officeholders' discretion in rewarding their friends and supporters. Many civil service reformers looked on the Jacksonian era as the "bad old" days, and historians frequently repeated that judgment, depicting politicians like Cameron, who built political machines through the effective distribution of spoils, as unprincipled thieves. Meanwhile, the desire to finally "close the book" on the Civil War meant that Northerners and Southerners embraced a sanitized vision of the conflict that downplayed the role of slavery in causing the conflict. This, coupled with eight decades of scholarly consensus that viewed Reconstruction as a period of unmitigated greed and corruption, also did Cameron's historical reputation no favors.

In reality, Cameron was never the crook his enemies claimed. Surely, Cameron operated in the shadows of the American political system, forging backroom deals and trading quids for quos like the capitalist he was. Furthermore, it is unquestionable that he was among the most successful spoilsmen, effectively using patronage to build and operate a well-oiled political machine. Whether it was manipulating the Pennsylvania legislature into requesting that Lincoln run for a second term or using his wealth to punish David Taggart, Cameron never scrupled to use the considerable tools at his disposal to achieve his ends. A pro-business nationalist who saw political conflict as a form of winner-take-all combat, Cameron believed that what was good for him was good for Pennsylvania and good for the United States. What historians forget is that this was also the same man who consistently advocated political rights for African Americans. An acknowledged conservative, he became one of the leading Radical Republicans of his day, aggressively pushing the Lincoln administration to enlist blacks into the army and make the abolition of slavery a war aim. In short, if there is much to dislike about Cameron, there is also much to admire.

In assessing Cameron's complicated and often contradictory legacy, it is perhaps best to start with his own summation of his life. In 1866 Cameron wrote what he thought should be his epitaph: "I have made enemies because I had opinions and the courage to assert and defend them. I am an old man now, who has lived through the most wonderful days of our history, and when I am gone all I ask is that people may say that I did the best I could and was never untrue to a friend."[1]

NOTES

Introduction

1. Quoted in McClintock, *Lincoln and the Decision for War*, 122; Maury Klein, *Days of Defiance*, 258.

2. Cooper, *We Have the War upon Us*, 138; Randall, *Lincoln the President*, 1:204.

3. Kelley, "Fossildom, Old Fogeyism, and Red Tape," 93.

4. Meneely, *War Department*, 82–83.

5. John William Ward, *Andrew Jackson*.

6 James to Shunk, 15 August 1844, *Works of James Buchanan*, 6:68.

7. "The Next Pennsylvania Senator," *New York Times*, September 21, 1878.

8. Rufus Wilson, *Intimate Memories of Lincoln*, 357.

9. Cameron to Alison, 16 September 1861, Simon Cameron Papers, Library of Congress (hereafter LOC) MSS 14845.

10. Rufus Wilson, *Intimate Memories of Lincoln*, 344.

11. Bradley, *Simon Cameron*, 275.

1. "A Determined Will"

1. "Simon Cameron at Home," *New York Times*, June 3, 1878.

2. *Address of the People's Club*, 4.

3. Beck, "Camerons of Donegal," 86.

4. *Address of the People's Club*, 4.

5. "Simon Cameron, Printer," *Evening Star*, November 30, 1880.

6. *Banquet to the Hon. Simon Cameron*, 5.

7. Culver Smith, *Press, Politics, and Patronage*, 156; Elbert Smith, *Francis Preston Blair*, 69.

8. *Banquet to the Hon. Simon Cameron*, 5.

9. Eggert, *Harrisburg Industrializes*, 27.

10. Hendrick, *Lincoln's War Cabinet*, 68; McCormick, *Second American Party System*, 30.

11. McCormick, *Second American Party System*, 147.

12. McCormick, *Second American Party System*, 10.

13. Widmer, *Martin Van Buren*, 56.

14. McCormick, *Second American Party System*, 147.

15. Philip Klein, *President James Buchanan*, 45.

16. Grim, *Historical Sketch of the Doylestown Democrat*, 9.

17. "To the Public," *Bucks County Messenger*, January 2, 1821.

18. "To Your Tents, O Israel," *Bucks County Democrat*, October 9, 1821.

19. "Public Information," *Bucks County Messenger*, January 16, 1821.

20. "United States Bank," *Bucks County Messenger*, February 26, 1821.

21. "Valedictory," *Bucks County Democrat*, October 9, 1821.

22. "Simon Cameron, Printer," *Evening Star*, November 30, 1880.

23. McNair, *Simon Cameron's Adventure in Iron*; quoted in Beck, "Camerons of Donegal," 90.

24. "Pennsylvania Intelligencer," *Bucks County Messenger*, January 2, 1821.

25. *Address of the People's Club*, 5.

26. Snyder, *Jacksonian Heritage*, 13.

27. McNair, *Simon Cameron's Adventure in Iron*, 85; "Simon Cameron, Printer," *Western Christian Advocate*, December 1, 1880.

28. McNair, *Simon Cameron's Adventure in Iron*, 11–12.

29. Erasmus D. Keyes, who socialized with Cameron frequently during the latter's term as secretary of war, recalled that the Pennsylvanian once claimed "his health was poor, and that he derived benefit from the daily moderate use of champagne wine" (Keyes, *Fifty Years' Observation*, 349); Truman, "In the Convival Days of Old," 317.

30. "An Old-Time Landlord," *Washington Post*, May 8, 1880.

31. "The Webster Murder Case," *New York Times*, February 28, 1892.

32. Keyes, *Fifty Years' Observation*, 348.

33. Quoted in Niven, *Gideon Welles*, 47.

34. Cameron and David Krause to Henry Clay, 13 July 1825, *Papers of Henry Clay*, 4:563.

35. Cameron and David Krause to Henry Clay, 6 February 1826, *Papers of Henry Clay*, 5:87.

36. Cameron and David Krause to Henry Clay, 6 February 1826, *Papers of Henry Clay*, 5:797.

37. Cameron to Henry Clay, 15 October 1826, *Papers of Henry Clay*, 5:983.

38. Cameron to Henry Clay, 26 July 1827, *Papers of Henry Clay*, 6:821–22.

39. Muhlenberg to Polk, 6 August 1844, Simon Cameron Papers, LOC MSS 14845.

40. Cameron and David Krause to Henry Clay, 26 July 1827, *Papers of Henry Clay*, 6:1213.

41. Cameron to Bonsall, 26 June 1834, Dreer Collection, Historical Society of Pennsylvania (hereafter HSP).

42. Elbert Smith, *Presidency of James Buchanan*, 31.

43. Cameron to Buchanan, 15 May 1844, Buchanan Papers, HSP. Quoted in Crippen, *Simon Cameron*, 43.

44. Cameron to Buchanan, 15 May 1844, Buchanan Papers, HSP.

45. Crippen, *Simon Cameron*, 9.

46. Quoted in Crippen, *Simon Cameron*, 10.

47. Bartlett, *Chief Phases of Pennsylvania Politics*, 108.

48. *Banquet to the Hon. Simon Cameron*, 5.

49. Van Buren to Thomas Ritchie, 13 January 1827, Martin Van Buren Papers, LOC MSS 0091.

50. Quoted in Hailperin, "Pro-Jackson Sentiment," 200.

51. "Simon Cameron on Second Terms," *New York Times*, May 10. 1888.

52. Parton, *Life of Andrew Jackson*, 3:421.

53. Cameron to Buchanan, 29 December 1836, Buchanan MSS, HSP.

54. Howe, *What Hath God Wrought*, 328–33.

55. Culver Smith, *Press, Politics, and Patronage*, 156; and Elbert Smith, *Francis Preston Blair*, 100.

56. Cameron to Buchanan, 22 March 1835, Buchanan MSS, HSP.

57. Buchanan to Cameron, 7 September 1835, Simon Cameron Papers, LOC MSS 14845.

58. Hutchinson, *Chronicles of Middletown*, 127 and 146.

59. Cameron to Buchanan, 14 February 1837, Buchanan MSS, HSP.

60. Cameron to Buchanan, 20 March 1842, Buchanan MSS, HSP.

2. "The Great Winnebago Chief"

1. Buchanan to Jackson, 15 July 1834. Quoted in Kelley, "Machine Is Born," 6.

2. Lewis to Jackson, 25 July 1834, *Correspondence of Andrew Jackson*, 5 (1833–38): 276.

3. Cameron to Bonsall, 16 July 1834, Dreer Collection, HSP.

4. Jackson to Blair, 7 August 1834, *Correspondence of Andrew Jackson*, 5 (1833–38): 281. Van Buren to Bucke, 4 August 1834, Martin Van Buren Papers, LOC MSS.

5. Cameron to Buchanan, 10 February 1838, Buchanan MSS, HSP.

6. Waggoner, *"Neither White Men nor Indians,"* 1.

7. Cameron to Buchanan, 28 December 1837, 22 March 1838, 5 July 1838, Buchanan MSS, HSP.

8. Poinsett to Cameron, 21 July 1838, in *Reports to the House of Representatives*, 25th Cong., 3d Sess. (Doc. No. 229, 1839), 2.

9. Cameron to Coryell, 1 August 1838, Lewis Coryell Papers, HSP MSS 0151.

10. War Department to Cameron and Murray, 26 July 1838, in *Reports to the House of Representatives*, 25th Cong., 3d Sess. (Doc. No. 229, 1839), 6.

11. Cameron to Buchanan, 22 September 1838, Buchanan MSS, HSP.

12. Murray to Committee, in *Reports to the House of Representatives*, 25th Congress, 3d Sess. (Doc. No. 229, 1839), 20.

13. Murray and Cameron to T. H. Crawford, in *Reports to the House of Representatives*, 25th Congress, 3d Sess. (Doc. No. 229, 1839), 21.

14. Murray and Cameron to T. H. Crawford, in *Reports to the House of Representatives*, 25th Congress, 3d Sess. (Doc. No. 229, 1839), 16.

15. Cameron to Buchanan, 22 September 1838, Buchanan MSS, HSP.

16. Murray and Cameron to T. H. Crawford, in *Reports to the House of Representatives*, 25th Congress, 3d Sess. (Doc. No. 229, 1839), 18.

17. Murray and Cameron to T. H. Crawford, in *Reports to the House of Representatives*, 25th Congress, 3d Sess. (Doc. No. 229, 1839), 20.

18. Hitchcock to Crawford, 6 November 1838, in *Reports to the House of Representatives*, 25th Congress, 3d Sess. (Doc. No. 229, 1839), 7.

19. Hitchcock to Crawford, 6 November 1838, in *Reports to the House of Representatives*, 25th Congress, 3d Sess. (Doc. No. 229, 1839), 8.

20. Hitchcock to Crawford, 8 November 1838, in *Reports to the House of Representatives*, 25th Congress, 3d Sess. (Doc. No. 229, 1839), 11.

21. Hitchcock to Crawford, 8 November 1838, in *Reports to the House of Representatives*, 25th Congress, 3d Sess. (Doc. No. 229, 1839), 11.

22. Hitchcock to Crawford, 3 December 1838, in *Reports to the House of Representatives*, 25th Congress, 3d Sess. (Doc. No. 229, 1839), 13.

23. Hitchcock to Crawford, 5 December 1838, in *Reports to the House of Representatives*, 25th Congress, 3d Sess. (Doc. No. 229, 1839), 21.

24. Hitchcock to Crawford, 10 November1838, in *Reports to the House of Representatives*, 25th Congress, 3d Sess. (Doc. No. 229, 1839), 58.

25. Murray to Crawford, 28 December 1838, in *Reports to the House of Representatives*, 25th Congress, 3d Sess. (Doc. No. 229, 1839), 49.

26. C. A. Rogers to Crawford, 27 January 1839, in *Reports to the House of Representatives*, 25th Congress, 3d Sess. (Doc. No. 229, 1839).

27. Hartley to Poinsett, 28 January 1839, in *Reports to the House of Representatives*, 25th Congress, 3d Sess. (Doc. No. 229, 1839), 53.

28. Hartley to Poinsett, 28 January 1839, in *Reports to the House of Representatives*, 25th Congress, 3d Sess. (Doc. No. 229, 1839), 54.

29. Statement of John BT. Peon, 2 January, Hartley to Poinsett, 28 January 1839, in *Reports to the House of Representatives*, 25th Congress, 3d Sess. (Doc. No. 229, 1839), 57.

30. Statement of Joseph M. Street, in *Reports to the House of Representatives*, 25th Congress, 3d Sess. (Doc. No. 229, 1839), 55–57.

31. Statement of Joseph M. Street, in *Reports to the House of Representatives*, 25th Congress, 3d Sess. (Doc. No. 229, 1839), 57.

32. Cameron and Murray to Hartley, 16 February 1839, in *Reports to the House of Representatives*, 25th Congress, 3d Sess. (Doc. No. 229, 1839), 71.

33. Cameron and Murray to Hartley, 16 February 1839, in *Reports to the House of Representatives*, 25th Congress, 3d Sess. (Doc. No. 229, 1839), 73–73.

34. Murray to Poinsett, 24 February 1839, in *Reports to the House of Representatives*, 25th Congress, 3d Sess. (Doc. No. 229, 1839).

35. Cameron to Poinsett, 20 February 1839, in *Reports to the House of Representatives*, 25th Congress, 3d Sess. (Doc. No. 229, 1839), 75.

36. G. W. Featherstonhaugh to Cameron, 12 February 1839, in *Reports to the House of Representatives*, 25th Congress, 3d Sess. (Doc. No. 229, 1839), 76–77.

37. Weidman, *Rejoinder to the Defence* (1855), 54.

38. Buchanan to Cameron, 12 September 1839, Simon Cameron Papers, LOC MSS 14845.

39. Brodhead to Cameron, April 28 1840, Simon Cameron Papers, LOC MSS 14845.

40. Fleming to Cameron, June 10 1840, Simon Cameron Papers, LOC MSS 14845.

41. Weidman, *Rejoinder to the Defence* (1855), 54.

42. Cameron to Muhlenberg, 22 July 1844, quoted in Hensel, "Sidelights on an Early Political Campaign," 94–95.

43. Kelley, "Machine Is Born," 20.

44. Philip Klein, *President James Buchanan*, 151.

45. Snyder, *Jacksonian Heritage*, 171.

46. Bradley, *Simon Cameron*, 39.

47. Cameron to Buchanan, 23 January 1844, Buchanan MSS, HSP.

48. Richards, *Slave Power*, 112.

49. Van Buren to Hammet, 20 April 1848, http://www.nps.gov/mava/historyculture/upload/Hammett-Letter-1844.pdf, accessed May 30, 2014.

50. Quoted in Widmer, *Martin Van Buren*, 149.

51. Richards, *Slave Power*, 114.

52. Potter, *Impending Crisis*, 24.

53. Quoted in Crippen, *Simon Cameron*, 50.

54. Dodd, *Jefferson Davis*, 63.

55. James K. Polk quoted in Wilentz, *Rise of American Democracy*, 578.

56. Polk to Kane, 19 June 1844, quoted in Sellers, *James K. Polk: Continentalist*, 120.

57. *Pennsylvania North American*, 2 July 1844, quoted in Snyder, *Jacksonian Heritage*, 183.

58. Cameron to Polk, 18 October 1844, Polk Papers, LOC. Quoted in Crippen, *Simon Cameron*, 55.

59. Sellers, *James K. Polk: Continentalist*, 18.

60. Culver Smith, *Press, Politics, and Patronage*, 156; and Elbert Smith, *Francis Preston Blair*, 163.

61. Polk to Jackson, 17 March 1845, *Correspondence of Andrew Jackson*, 6 (1839–45): 382.

62. Jackson to Heiss, 8 April 1845, "Papers of John P. Heiss," 216.

63. This assertion is based on an unsourced claim that Heiss had either apprenticed with or worked for Cameron, and therefore should be taken with a grain of salt (Hudson, *Journalism in the United States*, 402).

64. Cameron to Muhlenberg, 22 July 1844, quoted in Hensel, "Sidelights on an Early Political Campaign," 94–95.

65. Donelson to Polk, 18 March 1845, *Correspondence of Andrew Jackson*, 6 (1839–45): 384.

66. Polk to Donelson, 28 March 1845, "Letters of James K. Polk and Andrew J. Donelson, 1843–1848," 63.

67. Brown to Polk, 7 January 1845, *Correspondence of James K. Polk*, 9:29–30.

68. Heiss to Polk, 21 February 1845, *Correspondence of James K. Polk*, 9:199.

69. Jefferson to William Short, 8 September 1823, Thomas Jefferson Papers, LOC MSS.

70. Polk to Donelson, 28 March 1845, "Letters of James K. Polk and Andrew J. Donelson, 1843–1848," 63.

71. Benton, *Thirty Years' View*, 651.

72. Cameron to Coryell, 31 March 1845, Lewis Coryell Papers, HSP MSS 0151.

73. Polk to Donelson, 28 March 1845, "Letters of James K. Polk and Andrew J. Donelson, 1843–1848," 64.

74. Bergeron, *Presidency of James K. Polk*, 175.

75. Cameron to Heiss, 27 May 1847, "Papers of John P. Heiss," 221; Coryell to Heiss, 12 December 1847, "Papers of John P. Heiss," 222.

76. Jackson to Polk, 7 April 1845, *Correspondence of James K. Polk*, 9:263.

77. Jackson to Blair, 7 April 1845, *Correspondence of Andrew Jackson*, 6 (1839–45): 395.

78. Polk to Donelson, 28 March 1845, "Letters of James K. Polk and Andrew J. Donelson, 1843–1848," 63.

79. Miller to Polk, 14 March 1845, *Correspondence of James K. Polk*, 9:194.

80. Snyder, *Jacksonian Heritage*, 355.

81. Buchanan to Shunk, 15 August 1844, *Works of James Buchanan*, 6:67.

82. Cameron to Buchanan, 20 January 1845, quoted in Snyder, *Jacksonian Heritage*, 344.

83. Snyder, *Jacksonian Heritage*, 189.

84. Crippen, *Simon Cameron*, 61.

85. Bradley, *Simon Cameron*, 47.

86. *Niles' Register* 67 (June 28, 1845): 264–65, quoted in Crippen, *Simon Cameron*, 58.

87. Sellers, *James K. Polk: Continentalist*, 293.

88. Cameron to Buchanan, 27 March 1845, Buchanan and Johnson Papers, LOC.

89. Cameron to Buchanan, 15 May 1844, Buchanan MSS, HSP.

90. Petrikin to Shunk, 21 April 1845, *Correspondence of James K. Polk*, 9:310–11.

91. Miller to Polk, 5 May 1845, *Correspondence of James K. Polk*, 9:344.

92. Quoted in *Works of James Buchanan*, 6:138.

93. "Address to the Democracy of Pennsylvania," *Niles' Register* 67 (June 28, 1845).

94. "Address to the Democracy of Pennsylvania," *Niles' Register* 67 (June 28, 1845).

95. *Bedford Gazette*, September 19, 1845, quoted in Blessing, "Life of Simon Cameron," 35.

96. Cameron to Buchanan, 27 March 1845, Buchanan and Johnson Papers, LOC.

3. "True-Hearted Pennsylvanian"

1. "Personal," *New York Tribune*, December 20, 1883.

2. Cameron to Buchanan, 20 October 1846, Buchanan and Johnson Papers, LOC.

3. Rothman, *Politics and Power*, 13–14.

4. Dallas to Richard Rush, 25 April 1846, Rush Papers, MSS LOC. Quoted in Sellers, *James K. Polk: Continentalist*, 356.

5. Webster to Franklin Haven, 5 August 1846, *Papers of Daniel Webster*, 6:194.

6. Bergeron, *Presidency of James K. Polk*, 142–43.

7. Nevins, *Ordeal of the Union*, 1:175.

8. Jackson to Blair, 4 April 1845, *Correspondence of Andrew Jackson*, 6 (1839–45): 394.

9. Bergeron, *Presidency of James K. Polk*, 144.

10. Belohlavek, *George Mifflin Dallas*, 106–7.

11. Horn to Polk, 15 March 1845, *Correspondence of James K. Polk*, 9:195.

12. Sellers, *James K. Polk: Continentalist*, 295.

13. Cameron to Buchanan, 13 March 1845, Cameron Papers, LOC. Cited in Crippen, *Simon Cameron*, 69.

14. Walker to Polk, 21 July 1845, *Correspondence of James K. Polk*, 9:85.

15. Quoted in Sellers, *James K. Polk: Continentalist*, 296.

16. At least, this was how McClure interpreted it. *Old Time Notes of Pennsylvania*, 1:99.

17. Cameron to Buchanan, 25 December 1845, in Buchanan Papers MSS, LOC. Quoted in Going, *David Wilmot, Free-Soiler*, 263.

18. The five who, in addition to Cameron, voted against Woodward's nomination were Missouri's Thomas Hart Benton, Arkansas's Ambrose H. Sevier and Chester Ashley, and Florida's David Yulee and James D. Westcott.

19. Polk, *Diary*, 1:184–85.

20. Polk, *Diary*, 1:46.

21. Polk, *Diary*, 1:183.

22. Polk, *Diary*, 1:190.

23. Polk, *Diary*, 1:191.

24. Polk, *Diary*, 1:202–3.

25. Polk, *Diary*, 1:216.

26. Polk, *Diary*, 1:216–17.

27. Polk, *Diary*, 1:216–17.

28. Polk, *Diary*, 1:218–19.

29. Bergeron, *Presidency of James K. Polk*, 185.

30. *Reports of the Secretary of the Treasury*, 5:1–6.

31. The American Presidency Project, http://www.presidency.ucsb.edu /ws/?pid=29486.

32. Sellers, *James K. Polk: Continentalist*, 453.

33. Polk, *Diary*, 1:109–10.

34. Snyder, *Jacksonian Heritage*, 196.

35. Roadman, "Daniel Sturgeon," 52.

36. Cameron to Polk, 18 October 1844, Polk Papers, LOC. Quoted in Crippen, *Simon Cameron*, 55.

37. *Niles' Register* 67 (June 28, 1845): 264–65, quoted in Crippen, *Simon Cameron*, 58.

38. "Memorial from Pennsylvania Miners," *Niles' Register*, July 18, 1846.

39. *Congressional Globe*, 29th Congress, 1st Sess., July 18, 1846, 1112.

40. *Congressional Globe*, 29th Congress, 1st Sess., July 27, 1846, 1141.

41. "Editorial on the Tariff Bill," *Papers of Daniel Webster*, 6:187.

42. Dallas to Henry Phillips, 28 July 1846, Dreer Collection MSS, HSP. Quoted in Belohlavek, *George Mifflin Dallas*, 113.

43. Quoted in Belohlavek, *George Mifflin Dallas*, 114.

44. Cameron to Buchanan, 26 September 1846, Simon Cameron Papers, LOC MSS 14845.

45. *Congressional Globe*, 29th Congress, 2d Sess., January 5, 1847, 111.

46. *Congressional Globe*, 29th Congress, 2d Sess., January 7, 1847, 128.

47. Cameron to Buchanan, 20 October 1846, Buchanan and Johnson Papers, LOC.

48. Coleman, *Disruption of the Pennsylvania Democracy*, 16.

49. "Correspondence," *Sunbury American and Shamokin Journal*, October 3, 1846.

50. Sellers, *James K. Polk: Continentalist*, 468.

51. *Congressional Globe*, 29th Congress, 1st Sess., *Appendix*, 1113. Quoted in Crippen, *Simon Cameron*, 105.

52. *Congressional Globe*, 29th Congress, 1st Sess., *Appendix*, 1133. Quoted in Bradley, *Simon Cameron*, 61.

53. Quoted in Bradley, *Simon Cameron*, 61.

54. Widmer, *Martin Van Buren*, 80.

55. Calhoun, *Works*, 5:331.

56. *Congressional Globe*, 29th Congress, 1st Sess., 95. Quoted in Bradley, *Simon Cameron*, 64.

57. Cameron to Buchanan, 18 May 1836, Buchanan MSS, HSP.

58. *Harrisburg Argus*, May 20, 1846. Quoted in Blessing, "Life of Simon Cameron," 38.

59. "Presentation of Swords," *Sunbury American and Shamokin Journal*, January 1, 1847.

60. W. B. Cameron to Buchanan, 17 March 1847; W. B. Cameron to Buchanan, 25 March 1847; W. B. Cameron to Buchanan, 5 April 1847; S. Cameron to Buchanan, 10 April 1847; W. B. Cameron, 10 April 1847, Buchanan and Johnson Papers, LOC.

61. *Whig*, August 15, 1846. Quoted in Potter, *Impending Crisis*, 23.

62. David Smith, *On the Edge of Freedom*, 40.

63. Earle, *Jacksonian Antislavery*, 10.

64. Sellers, *James K. Polk: Continentalist*, 24–25.

65. *Congressional Globe*, 29th Congress, 2d Sess., 551, 555–56. Quoted in Bradley, *Simon Cameron*, 64.

66. "Alarming if True," *Liberator*, August 25, 1848.

67. Shelden, "Messmates' Union," 457. Shelden further notes that Mangum was one of the city's most notorious "booze hounds," and that he counted Cameron among his drinking buddies (Shelden, *Washington Brotherhood*, 127).

68. "Exciting Debate in Congress—No Union with Slave Holders!," *Liberator*, April 20, 1848, 2.

69. *Congressional Globe*, 29th Congress, 2d Sess., 551. Quoted in Crippen, *Simon Cameron*, 86.

70. Potter, *Impending Crisis*, 25.

71. Quoted in Bradley, *Simon Cameron*, 63.

72. *Somerset Herald and Farmers' and Mechanics' Register*, April 14, 1846.

73. *Congressional Globe*, 29th Congress, 2d Sess., January 29, 1846, 274.

74. *Address of the People's Club*, 14.

75. Wilentz, *Rise of American Democracy*, 585.

76. Philip Klein, *President James Buchanan*, 187.

77. Cameron to Buchanan, 20 October 1846, Buchanan and Johnson Papers, LOC.

78. Cameron to Buchanan, 28 October 1849, Simon Cameron Papers, LOC MSS 14845.

79. *Somerset Herald and Farmers' and Mechanics' Register*, September 7, 1847.

80. "Taylor Meeting at Harrisburg," *Jeffersonian Republican*, July 7, 1847; "Presidency, 1848," *Niles' National Register*, July 10, 1847. According to Henry Mueller, Cameron's participation in the pro-Taylor boom was more about breaking Buchanan's hold on Pennsylvania's Democratic Party. However, as with many of Mueller's assertions, he offers no evidence to support this statement and it cannot be independently verified (Mueller, *Whig Party in Pennsylvania*, 143).

81. *Bradford Reporter*, May 26, 1847. Quoted in Blessing, "Life of Simon Cameron," 26.

82. Bauer, *Zachary Taylor*, 222.

83. James Cameron to Cameron, 1 April 1847, Cameron Papers, LOC. Quoted in Crippen, *Simon Cameron*, 101.

84. Taylor to R. C. Wood, 23 June 1847, *Letters of Zachary Taylor*, 109.

85. Davis to Cameron, 26 July 1847, *Papers of Jefferson Davis*, 3:196.

86. Bauer, *Zachary Taylor*, 226.

87. *Niles' Register* 73. Quoted in Mueller, *Whig Party in Pennsylvania*, 145.

88. Cameron to Buchanan, 18 December 1847, Buchanan and Johnson Papers, LOC.

89. Crippen, *Simon Cameron*, 102.

90. Weidman, *Rejoinder to the Defence*, xii–xiii.

91. Morrison, *Democratic Politics and Sectionalism*, 167.

92. Bradley, *Simon Cameron*, 84.

93. "Perseverance," *Christian Secretary*, February 11, 1848.

94. Cameron to Buchanan, 28 May 1839, Buchanan MSS, HSP.

4. "Exclude Him from the Ranks"

1. Myers, "Rise of the Republican Party," 6.

2. "The West Branch Insurance Company," *Democrat and Sentinel*, April 23, 1856.

3. "One of Nature's Gentlemen," *Omaha Daily Bee*, July 14, 1889.

4. Crippen, *Simon Cameron*, 112.

5. Churella, *Pennsylvania Railroad*, 1:238.

6. Churella, *Pennsylvania Railroad*, 1:210.

7. Churella, *Pennsylvania Railroad*, 1:239.

8. Eggert, *Harrisburg Industrializes*, 39.

9. Churella, *Pennsylvania Railroad*, 1:239.

10. Reaman to Cameron, 7 February 1859, Valley of the Shadow, http://etext .lib.virginia.edu/etcbin/civwarlett-browse?id=f8009, accessed July 11, 2014.

11. Loose, "Cholera in Lancaster and Columbia," 145. "Bell for the Courthouse," *Lewisburg Chronicle*, September 12, 1856.

12. Cameron, 14 January 1860, Cameron Family Papers, MG 500, Dauphin County Historical Society.

13. Frazer to Cameron, 8 June 1855, Cameron Family Papers, MG 500, Dauphin County Historical Society.

14. Davis to Lincoln, 5 August 1860, Abraham Lincoln Papers, http://memory .loc.gov/cgi-bin/query/r?ammem/mal:@field%28DOCID+@lit%28d0348000 %29%29, accessed June 14, 2014.

15. Hollinger to Cameron, 18 October 1853, Cameron Family Papers, MG 500, Dauphin County Historical Society.

16. On "Cameron Democrats," see letter to Cameron, 11 October 1854, Cameron Family Papers, MG 500, Dauphin County Historical Society. Nichols, *Democratic Machine*, 60.

17. King to Buchanan, 20 March 1850, *Works of James Buchanan*, 8:374.

18. Buchanan to Davis, 16 March 1850, *Works of James Buchanan*, 8:373.

19. Kidder to Buchanan, 11 May 1851, *Works of James Buchanan*, 8:416.

20. Buchanan to Kidder, 16 May 1851, *Works of James Buchanan*, 8:417.

21. Buchanan to Johnson, 22 December 1851, *Works of James Buchanan*, 8:430.

22. Bradley, *Simon Cameron*, 85.

23. Bradley, *Simon Cameron*, 86.

24. Crippen, *Simon Cameron*, 120.

25. Buchanan to Johnson, 30 March 1852, *Works of James Buchanan*, 8:448.

26. Nichols, *Democratic Machine*, 77.

27. Potter, *Impending Crisis*, 233.

28. Coleman, "Public Career of James Campbell," 28.

29. Crippen, *Simon Cameron*, 132.

30. Crippen, *Simon Cameron*, 133.

31. Nevins, *Ordeal of the Union*, 2:46.

32. Buchanan to Campbell, 22 April 1853, Simon Cameron Papers, LOC MSS 14845.

33. ? to Cameron, 25 February 1854, Simon Cameron Papers, LOC MSS 14845.

34. Butler to Cameron, 10 June 1854, Simon Cameron Papers, LOC MSS 14845.

35. Maury Klein, *Days of Defiance*, 47.

36. Lochman to Cameron, 21 January 1854, Simon Cameron Papers, LOC MSS 14845.

37. Fox to Cameron, 7 April 1854 and 13 April 1854, Simon Cameron Papers, LOC MSS 14845.

38. "The Barefoot Printer Boy," *Youth's Companion*, November 29, 1855.

39. Breten to Cameron, 8 December 1853, Simon Cameron Papers, LOC MSS 14845.

40. Carrigan to Cameron, 13 July 1857 and 19 July 1857, Cameron Family Papers, MG 500, Dauphin County Historical Society.

41. ? to Cameron, 7 October 1854, Cameron Family Papers, MG 500, Dauphin County Historical Society.

42. Anbinder, *Nativism and Slavery*, xiii.

43. Bradley, *Simon Cameron*, 368.

44. Potter, *Impending Crisis*, 157.

45. Crippen, *Simon Cameron*, 138.

46. Potter, *Impending Crisis*, 158.

47. Bradley, *Simon Cameron*, 108.

48. Kirkpatrick to Cameron 9, February 1854; Cameron to Kirkpatrick, 9 February 1854; Simon Cameron Papers, LOC MSS 14845.

49. For Cameron's statement that he "abhors" slavery, see Cameron to Bergren, 28 March 1858, Simon Cameron Papers, LOC MSS 14845. Cameron to Powell, 20 February 1855, Simon Cameron Papers, LOC MSS 14845.

50. Handbill dated 22 February 1855, Simon Cameron Papers, LOC MSS 14845.

51. Forney to Cameron, 22 February 1855, Simon Cameron Papers, LOC MSS 14845.

52. Cameron to White, 21 May 1854; Cameron to White, 26 June 1854; Cameron to White, 17 October 1854, Gilder Lehrman Collection 05891.

53. Weidman, *Rejoinder to the Defence*, 49.

54. Weidman, *Rejoinder to the Defence*, 53.

55. Kelley, "Machine Is Born," 14–15.

56. Russell, "Biography of Alexander K. McClure," 150.

57. Black to Buchanan, 17 February 1855, Buchanan MSS, HSP. Quoted in Philip Klein, *President James Buchanan*, 249.

58. Gwinner to Cameron, 1 August 1876. Quoted in Kelley, "Machine Is Born," 14.

59. Bradley, *Simon Cameron*, 100.

60. Russell, "Biography of Alexander K. McClure," 63.

61. Woodward to Rice, 5 March 1855, Simon Cameron Papers, LOC MSS 14845.

62. "United States Senator," *Democrat and Sentinel*, March 1, 1855.

63. "Important," *Democrat and Sentinel*, May 16, 1855.

64. Bradley, *Simon Cameron*, 77.

65. Crippen, *Simon Cameron*, 146.

66. Potter, *Impending Crisis*, 191.

67. Kelley, "Machine Is Born," 20.

68. *Lewisburg Chronicle*, October 10, 1856.

69. Crippen, *Simon Cameron*, 152.

70. Potter, *Impending Crisis*, 199.

71. Chadwick, *Lincoln for President*, 180.

72. Stevens to Gazzam, McPherson Papers. Quoted in Myers, "Rise of the Republican Party in Pennsylvania," 149.

73. Quoted in Crippen, *Simon Cameron*, 165, and Philip Klein, *President James Buchanan*, 160.

74. "Turned on Buchanan," *Washington Post*, July 5, 1908.

75. Crippen, *Simon Cameron*, 165, and Philip Klein, *President James Buchanan*, 265–66.

76. "The Slanderers Rebuked!!!," *Democrat and Sentinel*, February 4, 1857.

77. "The Pennsylvania Senator," *New York Daily Times*, January 20, 1857.

78. Nevins, *Emergence of Lincoln*, 1:80.

79. *Reports of Joint Committee of the Legislature of Pennsylvania.*

80. *Reports of Joint Committee of the Legislature of Pennsylvania*, 24.

81. *Reports of Joint Committee of the Legislature of Pennsylvania*, 27.

82. *Reports of Joint Committee of the Legislature of Pennsylvania*, 7.

83. *Reports of Joint Committee of the Legislature of Pennsylvania*, 8.

84. Quoted in Crippen, *Simon Cameron*, 165, and Philip Klein, *President James Buchanan*, 169.

85. Brodhead to Cameron, 28 January 1857, Cameron Family Papers, MG 500, Dauphin County Historical Society.

86. Quoted in Riddle, *Life of Benjamin F. Wade*, 250.

87. Morgan to Cameron, 27 May 1858, Cameron Family Papers, MG 500, Dauphin County Historical Society.

88. Elbert Smith, *Presidency of James Buchanan*, 44.

89. Potter, *Impending Crisis*, 270.

90. *Congressional Globe*, 36th Congress, 2d Sess., January 6, 1860, 351–52.

91. Elbert Smith, *Presidency of James Buchanan*, 45–46.

92. Wilmot to Cameron, 30 April 1858, Simon Cameron Papers, LOC MSS 14845.

93. "The State Convention," *Union County Star and Lewisburg Chronicle,* June 6, 1859.

94. *Congressional Globe,* 35th Congress, 2d Sess., March 2, 1859, 1564.

95. *Congressional Globe,* 36th Congress, 2d Sess., January 30, 1861, 634.

96. Reeder to Cameron, 11 January 1861, Cameron Papers. Quoted in Stampp, *And the War Came,* 87.

97. Errett to Cameron, 23 January 1861, Cameron Papers. Quoted in Stampp, *And the War Came,* 143.

98. *Congressional Globe,* 35th Congress, 1st Sess., March 16, 1858, 1133–34.

99. Quoted in Riddle, *Life of Benjamin F. Wade,* 250–51.

100. "Senator Cameron," *Sunbury American,* April 10, 1858.

101. "Simon Cameron at Home," *New York Times,* June 3, 1878.

102. Cameron to Bergren, 28 March 1858, Simon Cameron Papers, LOC MSS 14845.

103. *Address of the People's Club of Philadelphia,* 13–14.

104. "A Distinguished Colored Man," *Holt County Sentinel,* July 11, 1884.

105. Hofstadter, "Tariff Issue," 50.

106. Holzer, *Lincoln, President-Elect,* 129.

107. *Congressional Globe,* 35th Congress, 1st Sess., June 1, 1858, 2563, 2570.

108. *Congressional Globe,* 35th Congress, 2d Sess., January 24, 1859, 536.

109. *Congressional Globe,* 36th Congress, 1st Sess., May 21, 1860, 2206.

110. McClure, *Old Time Notes of Pennsylvania,* 1:224.

111. *Annual Report of the Pennsylvania Training School,* 6:27, 30.

112. Simon Cameron to Margaret Cameron, undated, Cameron Family Papers, MG 831, Historical Society of Dauphin County.

113. "Gen. Cameron's Will," *Pittsburg Dispatch,* July 10, 1889.

114. Elbert Smith, *Presidency of James Buchanan,* 81.

115. Crippen, *Simon Cameron,* 188–89.

116. Elbert Smith, *Presidency of James Buchanan,* 85.

117. Paludan, *Presidency of Abraham Lincoln,* 22–23.

5. "What They Worship"

1. Elbert Smith, *Presidency of James Buchanan,* 47.

2. Elbert Smith, *Presidency of James Buchanan,* 84.

3. Cameron to Bergren, 28 March 1858, Simon Cameron Papers, LOC MSS 14845.

4. Seymour to Cameron, 19 June 1857, Simon Cameron Papers, LOC MSS 14845.

5. Cowan to Cameron, 25 April 1859, Cameron Family Papers, MG 500, Dauphin County Historical Society.

6. McAllister to Cameron, 27 March 1860, Cameron Family Papers, MG 500, Dauphin County Historical Society.

7. "The Question Settled," *Democratic Sentinel*, October 27, 1858.

8. "The Next President," *Franklin Repository*, August 24, 1859.

9. Hysson to Cameron, 27 February 1860, Valley of the Shadow, http:// etext.lib.virginia.edu/etcbin/civwarlett-browse?id=f8033, accessed July 11, 2014.

10. Cameron to anonymous, 11 October 1859, Valley of the Shadow, http://etext.lib.virginia.edu/etcbin/civwarlett-browse?id=f8008, accessed July 11, 2014.

11. "Cameron Festival," Simon Cameron Papers, MG 33, Pennsylvania State Archives.

12. Leib to Cameron, 30 June 1859, Cameron Family Papers, MG 500, Dauphin County Historical Society.

13. Leib to Cameron, 2 September 1859, Cameron Family Papers, MG 500, Dauphin County Historical Society.

14. "The People's Club," *Alleghanian*, November 11, 1859.

15. *Address of the People's Club*, 25–27.

16. Cameron to White, 30 January 1860; Cameron to White, 15 March 1860, Gilder Lehrman Collection 05891.

17. McAllister to Cameron, 27 March 1860, MG 500, Dauphin County Historical Society.

18. Roland to Cameron, 16 May 1860, Simon Cameron Papers, LOC MSS 14845.

19. McClure to Cameron, 29 October 1858, Simon Cameron Papers, LOC MSS 14845.

20. Sanderson to Cameron, 4 May 1860, MG 500, Dauphin County Historical Society.

21. ? to Blanche, 1 December 1859, Simon Cameron Papers, LOC MSS 14845.

22. Seward to Weed, 11 April 1859, Weed Papers. Quoted in Stahr, *Seward*, 278.

23. Jones to Cameron, undated, MG 500, Dauphin County Historical Society.

24. Reeder to Cameron, 30 April 1858, Simon Cameron Papers, LOC MSS 14845.

25. Wilmot to Cameron, 16 April 1860. Quoted in Sprankling, "'Pennsylvania's for Lincoln,'" 18.

26. Wilmot to Lincoln, 11 July 1860, Abraham Lincoln Papers, http://memory.loc.gov/cgi-bin/query/r?ammem/mal:@field(DOCID+@lit(d0330500)), accessed August 6, 2014.

27. This was future secretary of the navy Gideon Welles's opinion of Cameron's candidacy, and many historians have agreed. Niven, *Gideon Welles*, 290; Sandburg, *Abraham Lincoln*, 2:45; Hendrick, *Lincoln's War Cabinet*, 70–71; Cameron to Allison, 16 September 1866, Simon Cameron Papers, LOC MSS 14845.

28. Frazer to Lincoln, 12 November 1859, Abraham Lincoln Papers, http://memory.loc.gov/cgi-bin/query/r?ammem/mal:@field%28DOCID+@lit%28d0205300%29%29, accessed June 16, 2014.

29. Trumbull to Lincoln, 23 November 1859, Abraham Lincoln Papers, http://memory.loc.gov/cgi-bin/query/r?ammem/mal:@field%28DOCID+@lit%28d0208100%29%29, accessed June 16, 2014.

30. Medill to Lincoln, 10 January 1860, *Lincoln Papers*, 1:228.

31. Taylor to Lincoln, 25 February 1860, Abraham Lincoln Papers, http://memory.loc.gov/cgi-bin/query/r?ammem/mal:@field%28DOCID+@lit%28d0244000%29%29, accessed June 18, 2014.

32. Hay to Lincoln, 27 March 1860, Abraham Lincoln Papers, http://memory.loc.gov/cgi-bin/query/r?ammem/mal:@field%28DOCID+@lit%28d0253300%29%29, accessed June 16, 2014.

33. Bromwell to Lincoln, 13 November 1859, Abraham Lincoln Papers, http://memory.loc.gov/cgi-bin/query/r?ammem/mal:@field%28DOCID+@lit%28d0205600%29%29, accessed June 16, 2014.

34. Taylor to Lincoln, 27 December 1859, Abraham Lincoln Papers, http://memory.loc.gov/cgi-bin/query/r?ammem/mal:@field%28DOCID+@lit%28d0218300%29%29, accessed June 16, 2014.

35. Leib to Cameron, 22 March 1860, Cameron Family Papers, MG 500, Dauphin County Historical Society.

36. This was a smart decision, because there were indications that Cameron's supporters would not have accepted Lincoln on the ticket. See Swett to Lincoln, 25 May 1860, Abraham Lincoln Papers, http://memory.loc.gov/cgi-bin/query/r?ammem/mal:@field%28DOCID+@lit%28d0289700%29%29, accessed June 28, 2014. Nevins, *Emergence of Lincoln: Prologue*, 241.

37. Nevins, *Emergence of Lincoln: Prologue*, 241.

38. Beatty to Lincoln, 3 February 1860, Abraham Lincoln Papers, http://memory.loc.gov/cgi-bin/query/r?ammem/mal:@field%28DOCID+@lit%28d0232500%29%29, accessed June 17, 2014.

39. Delahay to Lincoln, 6 February 1860, Abraham Lincoln Papers, http://memory.loc.gov/cgi-bin/query/r?ammem/mal:@field%28DOCID+@lit%28d0233100%29%29, accessed June 17, 2014.

40. Hay to Lincoln, 27 March 1860, Abraham Lincoln Papers, http://memory.loc.gov/cgi-bin/query/r?ammem/mal:@field%28DOCID+@lit%28d0253300%29%29, accessed June 16, 2014.

41. Delahay to Lincoln, 13 May 1860, Abraham Lincoln Papers, http://memory.loc.gov/cgi-bin/query/r?ammem/mal:@field%28DOCID+@lit%28d0264500%29%29, accessed June 16, 2014.

42. Nevins, *Emergence of Lincoln: Prologue*, 249.

43. Chadwick, *Lincoln for President*, 68; Nevins, *Emergence of Lincoln: Prologue*, 253.

44. McAllister to Cameron, 27 March 1860, MG 500, Dauphin County Historical Society.

45. Harvey to Lincoln, 21 Mary 1860, Abraham Lincoln Papers, http://memory.loc.gov/cgi-bin/query/r?ammem/mal:@field(DOCID+@lit (d0280700)), accessed August 6, 2014.

46. Stahr, *Seward*, 184.

47. Nevins, *Emergence of Lincoln: Prologue*, 256.

48. Chadwick, *Lincoln for President*, 68.

49. Nevins, *Emergence of Lincoln: Prologue*, 257.

50. Weed, *Life of Thurlow Weed*, 2:292.

51. Swett to Lincoln, 30 November 1860, Abraham Lincoln Papers, http://memory.loc.gov/cgi-bin/query/r?ammem/mal:@field(DOCID+@lit (d0473400), accessed June 27, 2014.

52. Pratt, "Simon Cameron's Fight for a Place," 4.

53. Nevins, *Emergence of Lincoln: Prologue*, 259–60.

54. Crippen, *Simon Cameron*, 234.

55. Purview to Cameron, 23 May 1860, MG 500, Dauphin County Historical Society.

56. Leib to Lincoln, 16 June 1860, Abraham Lincoln Papers, http://memory.loc.gov/cgi-bin/query/r?ammem/mal:@field%28DOCID+@lit %28d0301700%29%29, accessed June 18, 2014.

57. "Senator Cameron and Mr. Lincoln," *Raftsman's Journal*, May 30, 1860. Weed to Lincoln, 13 August 1860, Abraham Lincoln Papers, http://memory.loc.gov/cgi-bin/query/r?ammem/mal:@field%28DOCID+@lit %28d0351900%29%29, accessed June 18, 2014.

58. Cameron to Lincoln, 1 August 1860, Simon Cameron Papers, LOC MSS 14845.

59. Blackburn to Lincoln, 24 November 1860, Abraham Lincoln Papers, http://memory.loc.gov/cgi-bin/query/r?ammem/mal:@field%28DOCID+@lit %28d0463400%29%29, accessed June 18, 2014.

60. Cale, "Editorial Sentiment in Pennsylvania," 220.

61. *New York Herald*, September 13, 1859. Quoted in Luthin, "Abraham Lincoln and the Tariff," 615.

62. *Congressional Globe*, 36th Congress, 1st Sess., May 21, 1860, 2206.

63. Davis to Lincoln, 5 August 1860, Abraham Lincoln Papers, http://memory.loc.gov/cgi-bin/query/r?ammem/mal:@field(DOCID+@lit (d0348000)), accessed June 14, 2014.

64. Lincoln, Fragment of Speech on Protection, Abraham Lincoln Papers, http://memory.loc.gov/cgi-bin/query/r?ammem/mal:@field %28DOCID+@lit%28d0006000%29%29, accessed June 18, 2014. Lincoln to Cameron, 6 August 1860, Simon Cameron Papers, LOC MSS 14845.

65. Burlingame, *Lincoln's Journalist*, 189.

66. Cameron to Lincoln, 25 December 1860, Abraham Lincoln Papers, http://memory.loc.gov/cgi-bin/query/P?mal:1:./temp/~ammem_lBhp:, accessed August 6, 2014.

67. Sandburg, *Abraham Lincoln: The War Years*, 138.

68. Quoted in Holzer, *Lincoln, President-Elect*, 221; Hendrick, *Lincoln's War Cabinet*, 51–52.

69. Quoted in Bradley, *Simon Cameron*, 413.

70. Roske, *His Own Counsel*, 59.

71. Russell Errett, writing to Joseph Medill on July 24, 1860, claimed, "Everything in Pennsylvania depends upon the result of the first election. If we elect [Curtin], all will be will in November; if not, the November Contest will be doubtful, with the chances against us. There is a bare possibility of Carrying the November if we lose the October Election, but it is only a possibility." Abraham Lincoln Papers, http://memory.loc.gov/cgi-bin/query/r?ammem/mal:@field%28DOCID+@lit%28d0339200%29%29, accessed June 18, 2014.

72. "Speech of Gen. Cameron," *Raftman's Journal*, August 8, 1860.

73. Goodrich to Davis, 28 November 1860, Abraham Lincoln Papers, http://memory.loc.gov/cgi-bin/query/r?ammem/mal:@field%28DOCID+@lit%28d0468800%29%29, accessed June 18, 2014.

74. McClure to Cameron, 28 June 1860, Valley of the Shadow, http://etext.lib.virginia.edu/etcbin/civwarlett-browse?id=f8011, accessed July 11, 2014.

75. Harvey to Lincoln, 5 June 1860, Abraham Lincoln Papers, http://memory.loc.gov/cgi-bin/query/r?ammem/mal:@field%28DOCID+@lit%28d0300700%29%29, accessed June 18, 1860.

76. Kelley, "Machine Is Born," 27.

77. Russell, "Biography of Alexander K. McClure," 168–69.

78. Kelley to Lincoln, 7 August 1860, Abraham Lincoln Papers, http://memory.loc.gov/cgi-bin/query/r?ammem/mal:@field%28DOCID+@lit%28d0348900%29%29, accessed June 18, 2014; Pomeroy to Lincoln, 27 August 1860, Abraham Lincoln Papers, http://memory.loc.gov/cgi-bin/query/r?ammem/mal:@field%28DOCID+@lit%28d0361200%29%29, accessed June 18, 2014; Sanderson to Davis, 27 August 1860, Abraham Lincoln Papers, http://memory.loc.gov/cgi-bin/query/r?ammem/mal:@field%28DOCID+@lit%28d0361500%29%29, accessed June 18, 2014.

79. Davis to Davis, September 1860, Abraham Lincoln Papers, http://memory.loc.gov/cgi-bin/query/r?ammem/mal:@field%28DOCID+@lit%28d0384000%29%29, accessed June 18, 2014.

80. Paludan, *Presidency of Abraham Lincoln*, 3; McClintock, *Lincoln and the Decision for War*, xiii.

81. Holzer, *Lincoln, President-Elect*, 125; McClintock, *Lincoln and the Decision for War*, 187; Cooper, *We Have the War upon Us*, 82.

82. Geiger to Cameron, 7 February 1861, Simon Cameron Papers, LOC MSS 14845.

83. Eckert to Lincoln, 5 November 1860, Abraham Lincoln Papers, http://memory.loc.gov/cgi-bin/query/r?ammem/mal:@field(DOCID+@lit(d0426800)), accessed August 6, 2014.

84. Churchman to Lincoln, 1861, Abraham Lincoln Papers, http://memory.loc.gov/cgi-bin/query/P?mal:1:./temp/~ammem_Rj5A, accessed January 12, 2015.

85. Lewis to Lincoln, 9 January 1861, Abraham Lincoln Papers, http://memory.loc.gov/cgi-bin/query/r?ammem/mal:@field(DOCID+@lit(d0598600)), accessed August 6, 2014.

86. Casey to Swett, 27 November 1860, Abraham Lincoln Papers, http://memory.loc.gov/cgi-bin/query/r?ammem/mal:@field%28DOCID+@lit%28d0466600%29%29, accessed June 18, 2014.

87. Pollock to Lincoln, 19 November 1860, Abraham Lincoln Papers, http://memory.loc.gov/cgi-bin/query/r?ammem/mal:@field(DOCID+@lit(d0456200)), accessed August 6, 2014.

88. Quoted in Browne, *Everyday Life of Abraham Lincoln*, 371. Cameron told a similar story in 1878 when interviewed by a reporter from the *New York Times*. "Simon Cameron at Home," *New York Times*, June 3, 1878.

89. Potter, *Lincoln and His Party*, 201.

90. Lincoln to Cameron, 3 January 1861, Abraham Lincoln Papers, http://memory.loc.gov/cgi-bin/query/r?ammem/mal:@field(DOCID+@lit(d0568300)), accessed August 1, 2014.

91. Pratt, "Simon Cameron's Fight for a Place," 8.

92. Meneely, *War Department*, 72.

93. Swett to Lincoln, 8 January 1861, Abraham Lincoln Papers, http://memory.loc.gov/cgi-bin/query/r?ammem/mal:@field(DOCID+@lit(d0595900)), accessed June 27, 2014.

94. Eckley, *Lincoln's Forgotten Friend*, 87.

95. Potter, *Lincoln and His Party*, 263.

96. Cameron to Lincoln, 3 January 1861, Abraham Lincoln Papers, http://memory.loc.gov/cgi-bin/query/r?ammem/mal:@field(DOCID+@lit(d0568600)), accessed June 27, 2014.

97. Scott to Cameron, 4 January 1861, Abraham Lincoln Papers, http://memory.loc.gov/cgi-bin/query/r?ammem/mal:@field(DOCID+@lit(d0574800)), accessed June 27, 2014.

98. Casey to Cameron, 11 January 1861, Simon Cameron Papers, LOC MSS 14845.

99. Lincoln to Cameron, 13 January 1861, Simon Cameron Papers, LOC MSS 14845.

100. Stevens to Washburne, 19 January 1861, *Selected Papers of Thaddeus Stevens*, 1:178–79.

101. Seward to Lincoln, 13 January 1861, Abraham Lincoln Papers, http://memory.loc.gov/cgi-bin/query/r?ammem/mal:@field(DOCID+@lit (d0616500)), accessed June 27, 2014.

102. Purviance to Cameron. Quoted in Pratt, "Simon Cameron's Fight for a Place," 9.

103. "Hostility . . . to Gen. Cameron," *Conversations with Lincoln*, 77.

104. Quoted in Nevins, *War for the Union*, 22.

105. Maury Klein, *Days of Defiance*, 278; "Conversation with Gen. Cameron—Feb. 20th 1875," in Nicholay, *Oral History of Abraham Lincoln*, 42.

106. Maury Klein, *Days of Defiance*, 310.

6. "Then Profit Shall Accrue"

1. "Oath of Office Administered to Secretary Cameron," *Sunbury American*, March 16, 1861.

2. Cooper, *We Have the War upon Us*, 228; Hendrick, *Lincoln's War Cabinet*, 153.

3. Perret, *Lincoln's War*, 15–18; Cameron to Lincoln, 16 March 1861, Abraham Lincoln Papers, http://memory.loc.gov/cgi-bin/query/r?ammem/mal :@field(DOCID+@lit(d0817600)), accessed September 17, 2014.

4. Quoted in Nevins, *War for the Union*, 55.

5. Nevins, *War for the Union*, 55.

6. Nevins, *War for the Union*, 65.

7. Cameron to Chew, 6 April 1861, Abraham Lincoln Papers, http://memory .loc.gov/cgi-bin/query/r?ammem/mal:@field(DOCID+@lit(d0883500)), accessed September 17, 2014; Chew to Lincoln, 8 April 1861, Abraham Lincoln Papers, http://memory.loc.gov/cgi-bin/query/r?ammem/mal :@field(DOCID+@lit(d0882800)), accessed September 17, 2014.

8. Meneely, *War Department*, 177.

9. Hesseltine, *Lincoln and the War Governors*, 146.

10. William Harris, *Lincoln and the Union Governors*, 16; Rawley, *Politics of Union*, 21.

11. Perret, *Lincoln's War*, 117.

12. Bradley, *Simon Cameron*, 183. This recollection is somewhat disputed; according to Gideon Welles, the actual numbers discussed ranged between fifty thousand and one hundred thousand. Meneely, *War Department*, 101; Woodward, *Mary Chesnut's Civil War*, 87; Browne, *Everyday Life of Abraham Lincoln*, 372.

13. Burlingame, *Abraham Lincoln*, 2:140.

14. Macartney, *Lincoln and His Cabinet*, 41.

15. Meneely, *War Department*, 1861, 116.

16. Everett, "Pennsylvania's Mobilization for War," 170.

17. Burlingame, *Inside Lincoln's White House*, 6.

18. Meneely, *War Department*, 117; Kamm, "Civil War Career of Thomas A. Scott," 37.

19. Nevins, *War for the Union*, 85.

20. Everett, "Pennsylvania's Mobilization for War," 170.

21. Bradley, *Simon Cameron*, 201.

22. Quoted in Festus Summers, "Baltimore and Ohio—First in War," 240.

23. Toomey, *War Came by Train*, 61–63.

24. Kamm, "Civil War Career of Thomas A. Scott," 69–70.

25. Kelley, "Fossildom, Old Fogeyism, and Red Tape," 109.

26. *Banquet to the Hon. Simon Cameron*, 9.

27. Macartney, *Lincoln and His Cabinet*, 37.

28. Nevins, *War for the Union*, 194.

29. Nash, *Stormy Petrel*, 73.

30. Quoted in David Miller, *Second Only to Grant*, 75.

31. Perret, *Lincoln's War*, 51.

32. Goss, *War within the High Command*, 15.

33. Chittenden, *Recollections of President Lincoln*, 169–70.

34. Gurowski, *Diary*, 55.

35. Quoted in Randall, *Lincoln the President*, 1:361.

36. Meneely, *War Department*, 157.

37. Meneely, *War Department*, 25; Kelley, "Fossildom, Old Fogeyism, and Red Tape," 94–96.

38. Carnegie, *Autobiography*, 93.

39. Curtin to Cameron, 6 May 1861. U.S. War Dept., *War of Rebellion*, 196.

40. Nevins, *War for the Union*, 90.

41. *Banquet to the Hon. Simon Cameron*, 6.

42. Kelley, "Fossildom, Old Fogeyism, and Red Tape," 94.

43. Nevins, *War for the Union*, 194; Thomas and Hyman, *Stanton*, 162–63.

44. *Banquet to the Hon. Simon Cameron*, 5.

45. Nevins, *War for the Union*, 397.

46. Quoted in Kelley, "Machine Is Born," 47.

47. "Secretaries of War," *Washington Post*, November 5, 1893.

48. Nicklason, "Civil War Contracts Committee," 232.

49. Nevins, *War for the Union*, 227; Kelley, "Fossildom, Old Fogeyism, and Red Tape," 98–100.

50. "Rewarding His Friends," *Clearfield Republican*, December 4, 1861; Hitchcock, *Fifty Years in Camp and Field*, 473.

51. Strong, *Diary of the Civil War*, 188.

52. Bradley, *Simon Cameron*, 182.

53. Cameron to Chase, 17 July 1861, Simon Cameron Papers, LOC MSS 14845.

54. Hearn, *Lincoln, the Cabinet, and the Generals*, ix; Stahr, *Seward*, 257; Burlingame, *Abraham Lincoln*, 164.

55. Lincoln to Cameron, 18 March 1861, Abraham Lincoln Papers, http://memory.loc.gov/cgi-bin/query/r?ammem/mal:@field(DOCID+@lit (d0820400)), accessed September 17, 2014.

56. Lincoln to Cameron and Stanton, 27 March 1861, Abraham Lincoln Papers, http://memory.loc.gov/cgi-bin/query/r?ammem/mal:@field (DOCID+@lit(d1024200)), accessed September 17, 2014. On at least four other instances—July 18, August 22, November 13, and November 30—Lincoln asked Cameron to appoint friends and supporters to military or War Department positions (Miers and Powell, *Lincoln Day by Day*).

57. Du Pont to Du Pont, 15 July 1861, and Du Pont to Du Pont, 12 December 1861, *Selection from His Civil War Letters*, 1:104, 277; Lincoln to Cameron, 16 November 1861, Simon Cameron Papers, LOC MSS 14845.

58. Goss, *War within the High Command*, 40, 55.

59. Kamm, "Civil War Career of Thomas A. Scott," 8.

60. Cameron to Whom It May Concern, 23 May 1861, Simon Cameron Papers, MG 33, Pennsylvania State Archives.

61. David Miller, *Second Only to Grant*, 113; Meneely, *War Department*, 199–200; Kamm, "Civil War Career of Thomas A. Scott," 46, 81.

62. Everett, "Pennsylvania Raises an Army," 83.

63. Tucker to Cameron, 14 May 1861. Cited in Meneely, *War Department*, 149.

64. Nevins, *War for the Union*, 343–46.

65. Meneely, *War Department*, 149; Winkle, *Lincoln's Citadel*, 169.

66. Nevins, *War for the Union*, 349; Perret, *Lincoln's War*, 105; Hendrick, *Lincoln's War Cabinet*, 265.

67. Shannon, *Organization and Administration of the Union Army*, 1:54.

68. Mark Wilson, *Business of Civil War*, 5.

69. Nevins, *War for the Union*, 359.

70. Shannon, *Organization and Administration of the Union Army*, 1:61–62.

71. Meneely, *War Department*, 119.

72. Stanton Davis, "Pennsylvania Politics," 225.

73. Chittenden, *Recollections of President*, 170.

74. Cameron to Lincoln, 5 November 1861, Abraham Lincoln Papers, http://memory.loc.gov/cgi-bin/query/r?ammem/mal:@field(DOCID+@lit (d1284300)), accessed September 17, 2014.

75. Quoted in David Miller, *Second Only to Grant*, 110.

76. Burlingame, *Lincoln's Journalist*, 108.

77. Sandburg, *Abraham Lincoln: The War Years*, 143.

78. Beatie, *Army of the Potomac*, 2:132.

79. Meneely, *War Department*, 114.

80. Fairbanks to Cameron, 7 May 1861. Cited in Meneely, *War Department*, 155.

81. Bradley, *Simon Cameron*, 185.

82. Stanton to Dix, 11 June 1861. Quoted in Meneely, *War Department*, 171.

83. Meneely, *War Department*, 195.

84. Kelley, "Fossildom, Old Fogeyism, and Red Tape," 103.

85. Perret, *Lincoln's War*, 72.

86. Burlingame, *Abraham Lincoln: A Life*, 98; Meneely, "Three Manuscripts of Gideon Welles," 486.

87. Meneely, *War Department*.

88. Welles, *Diary*, 21–25.

89. Weigley, *Quartermaster General*, 146.

90. Glenn, *Between North and South*, 43.

91. Quoted in Bradley, *Simon Cameron*, 177.

92. Quoted in Kelley, "Fossildom, Old Fogeyism, and Red Tape," 111.

93. Bradley, *Simon Cameron*, 181; Meneely, "Three Manuscripts of Gideon Welles," 487.

94. Shannon, *Organization and Administration of the Union Army*, 1:27; Perret, *Lincoln's War*, 44–45.

95. Sherman to Chase, 24 September 1861, *John Sherman's Recollections*, 263; "June 13, 1861," Miers and Powell, *Lincoln Day by Day*.

96. Risch, *Quartermaster Support of the Army*, 334.

97. Welles, *Diary*, 38.

98. Quoted in David Miller, *Second Only to Grant*, 94; Weigley, *Quartermaster General*, 162–64.

99. Mark Summers, "Spoils of War," 14.

100. Mark Wilson, *Business of Civil War*, 136–37.

101. Mark Wilson, *Business of Civil War*, 27–30.

102. "October 28, 1861," Miers and Powell, *Lincoln Day by Day*.

7. "Gentlemen, the Paragraph Stands"

1. Quoted in Perret, *Lincoln's War*, xiii.

2. Meneely, *War Department*, 183.

3. Brichford, "Congress at the Outbreak of the War," 158.

4. Meneely, *War Department*, 186.

5. T. Harry Williams, *Lincoln and the Radicals*, 29.

6. "July 20, 1861," Miers and Powell, *Lincoln Day by Day*.

7. Quoted in Sears, *George B. McClellan*, 94.

8. Beatie, *Army of the Potomac: Birth of Command*, 434.

9. Perret, *Lincoln's War*, 67.

10. Sherman, *John Sherman's Recollections*, 261.

11. Quoted in William Harris, *Lincoln and the Union Governors*, 29.

12. Quoted in William Harris, *Lincoln and the Union Governors*, 31.

13. Quoted in William Harris, *Lincoln and the Union Governors*, 32.

14. William Harris, *Lincoln and the Union Governors*, 38; Meneely, *War Department*, 152.

15. Shannon, *Organization and Administration of the Union Army*, 1:273–74.

16. Everett, "Pennsylvania's Mobilization for War," 191–92; Cameron to Cooke, 5 August 1861, Simon Cameron Papers, LOC MSS 14845.

17. Bogue, *Congressman's Civil War*, 63.

18. Bogue, *Congressman's Civil War*, 61.

19. Tap, *Over Lincoln's Shoulder*, 2.

20. Weigley, *Quartermaster General*, 195–96.

21. Nicklason, "Civil War Contracts Committee," 241–42; Kelley, "Fossildom, Old Fogeyism, and Red Tape," 107.

22. *Banquet to the Hon. Simon Cameron*, 7.

23. Quoted in Tap, *Over Lincoln's Shoulder*, 3; Bogue, *Congressman's Civil War*, 60.

24. Quoted in Mark Wilson, *Business of Civil War*, 156; quoted in Macartney, *Lincoln and His Cabinet*, 36.

25. Quoted in Randall, *Lincoln the President*, 2:55.

26. Bryant to Forbes, 21 August 1861, *Letters of William Cullen Bryant*, 4:228.

27. Du Pont to Du Pont, 25 July 1861, *Selection from His Civil War Letters*, 1:110–12.

28. Chase to Potter, 8 July 1861, Simon Cameron Papers, LOC MSS 14845.

29. Bogue, *Congressman's Civil War*, 86; Burlingame, *Abraham Lincoln: A Life*, 185.

30. Miers and Powell, *Lincoln Day by Day*.

31. McClintock to Cameron, 9 May 1861, Abraham Lincoln Papers, http://memory.loc.gov/cgi-bin/query/r?ammem/mal:@field(DOCID+@lit (d0981500)), accessed September 17, 2014. Strong, *Diary of the Civil War*, 187.

32. Thortaurse to Cameron, 25 July 1861, Simon Cameron Papers, LOC MSS 14845.

33. Dougherty to Cameron, 26 July 1861, Simon Cameron Papers, LOC MSS 14845.

34. Tap, *Over Lincoln's Shoulder*, 16.

35. Crawford to Lincoln, 10 August 1861, Abraham Lincoln Papers, http://memory.loc.gov/cgi-bin/query/r?ammem/mal:@field(DOCID+@lit (d4209000)), accessed September 17, 2014. Strong, *Diary of the Civil War*, 183.

36. Meneely, *War Department*, 232.

37. Pope to Horton, 22 August 1861. Quoted in Nevins, *War for the Union*, 322.

38. Mellen to Chase, 1 August 1861, *Salmon P. Chase Papers*, 3:84.

39. Quoted in Perret, *Lincoln's War*, 116; Rufus Wilson, *Intimate Memories of Lincoln*, 380.

40. Tucker, *Major General Isaac Ridgeway Trimble*, 112–13.

41. Winkle, *Lincoln's Citadel*, 206.

42. White, *Abraham Lincoln and Treason*, 45–46.

43. Bell, *Major Butler's Legacy*, 350.

44. Sprague, *Freedom under Lincoln*, 151.

45. Sprague, *Freedom under Lincoln*, 168–69.

46. Nash, *Stormy Petrel*, 93.

47. Sprague, *Freedom under Lincoln*, 188.

48. Bates to Banks, 16 June 1861. Quoted in White, *Abraham Lincoln and Treason*, 44.

49. Fremont, "Order of Martial Law."

50. Perret, *Lincoln's War*, 85–86; Cameron to Fremont, 30 August 1861, Simon Cameron Papers, LOC MSS 14845.

51. Parrish, "Fremont in Missouri," 10; T. Harry Williams, *Lincoln and the Radicals*, 40–41.

52. Paludan, *Presidency of Abraham Lincoln*, 86.

53. T. Harry Williams, *Lincoln and the Radicals*, 39.

54. Quoted in David Miller, *Second Only to Grant*, 106.

55. Hall to Cameron, 18 September 1861, Abraham Lincoln Papers, http://memory.loc.gov/cgi-bin/query/r?ammem/mal:@field(DOCID+@lit(d1178300)), accessed September 17, 2014; Shaffer to Cameron, 22 September 1861, Abraham Lincoln Papers, http://memory.loc.gov/cgi-bin/query/r?ammem/mal:@field(DOCID+@lit(d1194300)), accessed September 17, 2014; Lee to "Phil," 19 October 1861, in Lee, *Wartime Washington*, 86.

56. Miers and Powell, *Lincoln Day by Day*.

57. Chase to Cameron, 7 October 1861, *Salmon P. Chase Papers*, 3:100.

58. Cameron to Lincoln, 12 October 1861, Abraham Lincoln Papers, http://memory.loc.gov/cgi-bin/query/r?ammem/mal:@field(DOCID+@lit(d1243100)), accessed September 17, 2014; Cameron to Lincoln, 14 October 1861, Abraham Lincoln Papers, http://memory.loc.gov/cgi-bin/query/r?ammem/mal:@field(DOCID+@lit(d1244800)), accessed September 17, 2014.

59. Niven, *Salmon P. Chase*, 281.

60. Bates, *Diary*, 198. In a letter to a friend, Chase essentially corroborated Bates's narrative, insofar as he (Chase) counseled delay (Chase to Smith, 11 November 1861, *Salmon P. Chase Papers*, 3:107–9).

61. Parrish, "Fremont in Missouri," 44; Tap, *Over Lincoln's Shoulder,* 83.

62. Murray, "Fremont-Adams Contracts," 518–19.

63. Gilmore, *Personal Recollections of Abraham Lincoln,* 24.

64. Shannon, *Organization and Administration of the Union Army,* 2:147–48; Schuckers, *Life and Public Services of Salmon Portland Chase,* 420.

65. Cameron to Butler, 30 May 1861, Simon Cameron Papers, LOC MSS 14845.

66. Quoted in Winkle, *Lincoln's Citadel,* 237.

67. Cameron to Sherman, 14 October 1861, quoted in Meneely, *War Department,* 342.

68. Rawley, *Politics of Union,* 79.

69. *Congressional Globe,* 37th Congress, 1st Sess., July 27, 1861.

70. Cameron to Butler, 8 August 1861, in Butler, *Private and Official Correspondence,* 1:201.

71. Cameron to Butler, 9 August 1861, Simon Cameron Papers, LOC MSS 14845.

72. Schuckers, *Life and Public Services of Salmon Portland Chase,* 420. Quoted in Hendrick, *Lincoln's War Cabinet,* 272–73.

73. Sumner to Phillips, 8 August 1861, *Selected Letters of Charles Sumner,* 2:75.

74. Sumner to Martineau, 29 October 1861, *Selected Letters of Charles Sumner,* 2:81–82.

75. Beatie, *Army of the Potomac: McClellan Takes Command,* 124.

76. Thomas and Hyman, *Stanton,* 132.

77. *Covington Journal,* November 23, 1861.

78. Guthrie to Speed, 22 November 1861, Abraham Lincoln Papers, http://memory.loc.gov/cgi-bin/query/r?ammem/mal:@field(DOCID+@lit (d1307000)), accessed September 18, 2014.

79. "Conversation with Gen. Cameron—Feb. 20th 1875," in Nicolay, *Oral History of Abraham Lincoln,* 43.

80. Niven, *Gideon Welles,* 392.

81. Rufus Wilson, *Intimate Memories of Lincoln,* 379.

82. Bates, *Diary,* 203.

83. Quoted in Macartney, *Lincoln and His Cabinet,* 43; quoted in Harschlip, "Simon Cameron and the War Contracts Committee," 29; Bates, *Diary,* 203–4.

84. Cochrane, *Arming the Slaves,* 11–12.

85. Quoted in Browne, *Everyday Life of Abraham Lincoln,* 372.

86. Nolan, *Benjamin Franklin Butler,* 120; Weigley, *Quartermaster General,* 212.

87. Thomas and Hyman, *Stanton,* 126; Paludan, *Presidency of Abraham Lincoln,* 106.

88. Thomas and Hyman, *Stanton,* 134.

89. Quoted in *Selected Papers of Thaddeus Stevens*, 1:230.

90. Sandburg, *Abraham Lincoln: The War Years*, 145–46.

91. Speed to Lincoln, 22 December 1861, Abraham Lincoln Papers, http://memory.loc.gov/cgi-bin/query/r?ammem/mal:@field(DOCID+@lit (d1352100)), accessed September 18, 2014.

92. Quoted in Rawley, *Politics of Union*, 78.

93. Meneely, *War Department*, 349.

94. Meneely, "Three Manuscripts of Gideon Welles," 487.

95. Baker to Cameron, 10 December 1861, Simon Cameron Papers, LOC MSS 14845.

96. Quoted in *Selected Papers of Thaddeus Stevens*, 1:230.

97. T. Harry Williams, *Lincoln and the Radicals*, 37; Burlingame, *Lincoln's Journalist*, 189.

98. Cameron to Gilmore, 15 December 1861, Simon Cameron Papers, LOC MSS 14845.

99. "Francis Datcher," *Friends' Review*, May 3, 1862.

100. Quoted in Thomas and Hyman, *Stanton*, 135.

101. Weigley, *Quartermaster General*, 210.

102. Hearn, *Lincoln, the Cabinet, and the Generals*, 91.

103. Bates, *Diary*, 220.

104. Quoted in Kelley, "Fossildom, Old Fogeyism, and Red Tape," 113.

105. Bowen to Bigelow, 4 September 1861, in Bigelow, *Retrospectives of an Active Life*, 362–63.

106. Meneely, *War Department*, 232.

107. Welles, *Diary*, 1:57; Meneely, "Three Manuscripts of Gideon Welles," 487–88.

108. Romero, *Mexican View of America*, 96.

109. "Conversation with Gen. Cameron—Feb. 20th 1875," in Nicolay, *Oral History of Abraham Lincoln*, 43.

110. Cameron to Chase, 24 December 1862, *Salmon P. Chase Papers*, 3:344–45.

111. Bates, *Diary*, 223–24.

112. Miers and Powell, *Lincoln Day by Day*.

113. Lincoln to Cameron, 11 January 1862, Abraham Lincoln Papers, http://memory.loc.gov/cgi-bin/query/r?ammem/mal:@field(DOCID+@lit (d1393200)), accessed September 17, 2014.

114. Sumner to Lincoln, 26 October 1861, Abraham Lincoln Papers, http://memory.loc.gov/cgi-bin/query/r?ammem/mal:@field(DOCID+@lit (d1268800)), accessed September 17, 2014.

115. Burlingame and Ettlinger, *Inside Lincoln's White House*, 60.

116. Arnold, *History of Abraham Lincoln*, 250.

117. Chase, *Inside Lincoln's Cabinet*, 60; Burlingame and Ettlinger, *Inside Lincoln's White House*, 62–63.

118. Lincoln to Cameron, 11 January 1862, Abraham Lincoln Papers, http://memory.loc.gov/cgi-bin/query/r?ammem/mal:@field(DOCID+@lit (d1393400)), accessed September 17, 2014.

119. Cameron to Lincoln, 11 January 1862, Abraham Lincoln Papers, http://memory.loc.gov/cgi-bin/query/r?ammem/mal:@field(DOCID+@lit (d1394000)), accessed September 17, 2014.

120. Bates, *Diary*, 226.

121. Welles, *Diary*, 1:57.

122. Stahr, *Seward*, 325.

123. Meneely, "Three Manuscripts of Gideon Welles," 491–92.

124. Holt to Cameron, 15 January 1862, Abraham Lincoln Papers, http://memory.loc.gov/cgi-bin/query/r?ammem/mal:@field(DOCID+@lit (d1400900)), accessed September 17, 2014.

125. Thomas and Hyman, *Stanton*, 141; Meade to ?, 16 January 1862, in *Life and Letters of George Gordon Meade*, 1:243.

126. Russell to Bigelow, 16 January 1862, in Bigelow, *Retrospectives of an Active Life*, 1:448.

127. Nichols to Cameron, 14 January 1862, Simon Cameron Papers, LOC MSS 14845.

128. Sawyer to Cameron, 14 January 1862, Simon Cameron Papers, LOC MSS 14845.

129. Forney to Cameron, 14 January 1862, Simon Cameron Papers, LOC MSS 14845.

130. Meneely, *War Department*, 370.

131. Romero, *Mexican View of America*, 97.

132. Sumner to Lieber, 19 January 1861, *Selected Letters of Charles Sumner*, 2:98.

133. Meneely, *War Department*, 371.

134. Kelley, "Fossildom, Old Fogeyism, and Red Tape," 111.

135. Pritchett to Cameron, 17 February 1862, Simon Cameron Papers, LOC MSS 14845; quoted in Thomas and Hyman, *Stanton*, 161–62.

136. Bates, *Diary*, 291; quoted in Hendrick, *Lincoln's War Cabinet*, 460.

137. Strong, *Diary of the Civil War*, 207, 228.

138. Meneely, *War Department*, 110.

139. Nevins, *War for the Union*, 410; Weigley, *Quartermaster General*, 89–90.

140. Perret, *Lincoln's War*, 105.

141. "Simon Cameron at Home," *New York Times*, June 3, 1878.

8. "A Man Out of Office"

1. Quoted in White, *Abraham Lincoln and Treason*, 121.

2. "News from Washington," *New York Times*, April 22, 1862.

3. Quoted in Libhart, "Simon Cameron's Political Exile," 200.

4. Quoted in Libhart, "Simon Cameron's Political Exile," 200.

5. Stevens to Cameron, 2 May 1862, *Selected Papers of Thaddeus Stevens*, 1:297.

6. *Journal of the House of Representatives*, 1861–62, May 27, 1862.

7. Cameron to Lincoln, 26 June 1862, quoted in Bradley, *Simon Cameron, Lincoln's Secretary of War*, 196. Cameron to Chase, 3 May 1862, Chase MSS, HSP, quoted in Bradley, *Simon Cameron*, 218.

8. Chase to Cameron, 23 June 1862, quoted in Kelley, "Machine Is Born," 55.

9. Rice to Cameron, 16 February 1862, Simon Cameron Papers, LOC MSS 14845.

10. Blue, *Salmon P. Chase*, 361; Bradley, *Simon Cameron*, 214; Kelley, "Machine Is Born," 52.

11. Quoted in Libhart, "Simon Cameron's Political Exile," 202.

12. Libhart, "Simon Cameron's Political Exile," 206.

13. Libhart, "Simon Cameron's Political Exile," 205, 206.

14. Libhart, "Simon Cameron's Political Exile," 204.

15. Cameron to Lincoln, 26 June 1862, Abraham Lincoln Papers, http://memory.loc.gov/cgi-bin/query/r?ammem/mal:@field(DOCID+@lit(d1664900)), accessed December 13, 2014.

16. Cameron to Cameron, 7 July 1862, Cameron Family Papers, MG 831, Historical Society of Dauphin County.

17. Cameron to Cameron, 21 July 1862, Simon Cameron Papers, LOC MSS 14845.

18. ? to Cameron, 18 April 1862; Scott to Cameron, 19 July 1862; Simon Cameron Papers, LOC MSS 14845.

19. Forney to Cameron, 11 June 1862, Simon Cameron Papers, LOC MSS 14845.

20. Purviance to Cameron, 1 November 1862; Casey to Cameron, 3 November 1862; Cameron Family Papers, MG 831, Historical Society of Dauphin County.

21. Cameron to Lesley, 7 July 1862, Simon Cameron Papers, LOC MSS 14845.

22. Cameron to Lincoln, 26 June 1862, Abraham Lincoln Papers, http://memory.loc.gov/cgi-bin/query/r?ammem/mal:@field(DOCID+@lit(d1664900)), accessed December 13, 2014.

23. "Minister Cameron and the African," *Friend's Review*, December 6, 1862.

24. Clay to Cameron, 6 September 1862, Simon Cameron Papers, LOC MSS 14845.

25. Taylor to ?, 23 December 1862, in Prahl, "Bayard Taylor's Letters," 417.

26. Quoted in Bradley, *Simon Cameron*, 224.

27. Bradley, *Triumph of Militant Republicanism*, 191.

28. Lincoln to Cameron, Simon Cameron Papers, LOC MSS 14845.

29. Bradley, *Simon Cameron*, 222; Taylor to Cameron, 1 March 1863, Simon Cameron Papers, LOC MSS 14845.

30. Taylor to ?, 23 December 1862, in Prahl, "Bayard Taylor's Letters," 413.

31. Cameron to Chase, 24 December 1862, *Salmon P. Chase Papers*, 3:344–45.

32. Chase to Cameron, 16 August 1862, quoted in Bradley, *Simon Cameron*, 226; Cameron to Chase, Chase MSS, HSP, quoted in Bradley, *Simon Cameron*, 235.

33. Cumming to Cameron, 24 February 1863; Kane to Cameron, 5 February 1863, Simon Cameron Papers, LOC MSS 14845.

34. Forney to Cameron, 19 September 1863, Simon Cameron Papers, LOC MSS 14845.

35. Cameron to Chase, 4 December 1861, Chase MSS, HSP, quoted in Bradley, *Simon Cameron*, 227.

36. Kelley, "Machine Is Born," 62; Chase to Cameron, 26 November 1862, Cameron Family Papers, MG 831, Historical Society of Dauphin County.

37. Berriman to Cameron, 14 December 1862, Cameron Family Papers, MG 831, Historical Society of Dauphin County.

38. Stanton Davis, "Pennsylvania Politics," 270; Young to Cameron, 7 August 1862, Simon Cameron Papers, LOC MSS 14845.

39. Kelley, "Machine Is Born," 65.

40. Bradley, *Simon Cameron*, 228.

41. Russell, "Biography of Alexander K. McClure," 285.

42. Kelley, "Machine Is Born," 73.

43. Cameron to Lincoln, 13 January 1863, in Bradley, *Simon Cameron*, 229.

44. Bradley, *Simon Cameron*, 232.

45. "Report on the Committee on Frauds," quoted in Bradley, *Simon Cameron*, 231.

46. Bradley, *Simon Cameron*, 231.

47. Quoted in White, *Abraham Lincoln and Treason*, 102.

48. White, *Abraham Lincoln and Treason*, 102–3.

49. Stanton Davis, "Pennsylvania Politics," 291.

50. Covode to Cameron, 11 February 1863, Cameron Family Papers, MG 831, Historical Society of Dauphin County.

51. Stanton to Cameron, 10 June 1863, Simon Cameron Papers, LOC MSS 14845.

52. Crist, "Highwater 1863," 161.

53. Coddington, "Pennsylvania Prepares for Invasion," 159–60.

54. Quoted in Russell, "Biography of Alexander K. McClure," 290.

55. Taylor to Cameron, 3 August 1863, Cameron Family Papers, MG 831, Historical Society of Dauphin County.

56. Hall to Cameron, 17 September 1863, Cameron Family Papers, MG 831, Historical Society of Dauphin County.

57. Quoted in Albright, "Civil War Career of Andrew Gregg Curtin," 36.

58. Chambers to Cameron, 9 October 1863, Abraham Lincoln Papers, http://memory.loc.gov/cgi-bin/query/P?mal:12:./temp/~ammem_PlUC, accessed December 18, 2014.

59. Quoted in Stanton Davis, "Pennsylvania Politics," 300; Beers, "Andrew Gregg Curtin," 20.

60. "Simon Cameron at Home," *New York Times,* June 3, 1878.

61. "Simon Cameron at Home," *New York Times,* June 3, 1878.

62. Quoted in Bradley, *Simon Cameron,* 238.

63. Bradley, *Simon Cameron,* 239; Lincoln to Cameron, 7 April 1864, Simon Cameron Papers, LOC MSS 14845; *Lincoln Day by Day.*

64. Nicolay to Cameron, 23 December 1864, Simon Cameron Papers, LOC MSS 14845.

65. Flood, 1864, 122.

66. Quoted in Butler, *Butler's Book,* 634–35.

67. Fehrenbacher, "Making of a Myth"; Horowitz, "Benjamin Butler"; Donald, *Lincoln.*

68. Butler to Cameron, 15 January 1864, Cameron Family Papers MG 831, Historical Society of Dauphin County.

69. "Pass—Honorable Simon Cameron and Friends," February 24, 1864, Simon Cameron Papers, LOC MSS 14845.

70. Cameron to Lincoln, 29 March 1864, Abraham Lincoln Papers, http://memory.loc.gov/cgi-bin/query/r?ammem/mal:@field(DOCID+@lit(d3193000)), accessed December 14, 2014. Fehrenbacher, "Making of a Myth," 28; Horowitz, "Benjamin Butler," 201.

71. Flood, 1864, 24.

72. Bradley, *Simon Cameron,* 242.

73. Bradley, *Simon Cameron,* 243.

74. *Papers of Andrew Johnson,* 7 (1864–1865): 661.

75. Bradley, *Triumph of Militant Republicanism,* 202.

76. Quoted in *Papers of Andrew Johnson,* 4 (1860–61): 291–92.

77. Cameron to Fessenden, 15 June 1864. Quoted in Hamlin, *Life and Times,* 463.

78. Hamlin, *Life and Times,* 484; Cameron to Dana, quoted in Tinkcom, *John White Geary,* 114.

79. Neely, "Civil War Issues," 397.

80. Bradley, *Simon Cameron,* 245.

81. Errett to Cameron, 25 August 1864, Simon Cameron Papers, LOC MSS 14845.

82. Cameron to MacVeagh, 26 August 1864, MacVeagh Family Papers (Collection 1616), HSP.

83. Nicolay to Cameron, 4 September 1864, Simon Cameron Papers, LOC MSS 14845.

84. Boyd to Cameron, 31 August 1864, Simon Cameron Papers, LOC MSS 14845.

85. Kelley, "Machine Is Born," 110.

86. "Pennsylvania Politics," *New York Times*, July 10, 1864.

87. Pendel, *Thirty-Six Years*, 36–37.

88. Cameron to Nicolay, 26 February 1864, Abraham Lincoln Papers, http://memory.loc.gov/cgi-bin/query/P?mal:1:./temp/~ammem_ixYt::, accessed December 18, 2014.

89. *New York World*, October 9, 1863, quoted in Kelley, "Machine Is Born," 93.

90. Bradley, *Simon Cameron*, 247.

91. Bradley, *Simon Cameron*, 249.

92. Bradley, *Simon Cameron*, 251.

93. "General Cameron and Jeff. Davis," *Raftsman's Journal*, August 16, 1865; "Cameron's Corn," *New York Times*, July 28, 1873.

94. "Reception of the Colored Services at Harrisburg," *Liberator*, November 24, 1865.

95. Bradley, *Simon Cameron*, 255.

96. *Selected Papers of Thaddeus Stevens*, 2:93.

97. Quoted in Tinkcom, *John White Geary*, 113.

98. Bradley, *Simon Cameron*, 261.

99. Bradley, *Simon Cameron*, 265.

100. Bradley, *Simon Cameron*, 269.

101. Bradley, *Simon Cameron*, 278.

102. MacVeagh to Cameron, 21 September 1863, Cameron Family Papers, MG 831, Historical Society of Dauphin County.

103. Kelley, "Machine Is Born," 146.

104. Bradley, *Simon Cameron*, 278.

105. Quoted in Kelley, "Machine Is Born," 154.

106. "Middle States," *New York Times*, January 16, 1867.

107. Cashdollar, "Andrew Johnson and the Philadelphia Election," 371.

9. "Nothing Can Beat You"

1. Bradley, *Triumph of Militant Republicanism*, 211.

2. Withers, *Autobiography of an Octogenarian*, 329.

3. "Facts about Congressmen." *Clearfield Republican*, January 19, 1870.

4. Blaine to Blaine, 15 May 1872, *Letters of Mrs. James G. Blaine*, 1:125–28.

5. "Congress," *Memphis Daily Appeal*, March 29 1876; *Anderson Intelligencer*, February 16 1882.

6. Withers, *Autobiography of an Octogenarian*, 331.

7. "Domestic," *New York Observer and Chronicle*, April 16, 1868; "Domestic," *New York Observer and Chronicle*, April 23, 1868; Stanton to Cameron, 14 April 1868, Simon Cameron Papers, loc mss 14845.

8. Stewart, *Impeached*, 284–99.

9. Bradley, *Triumph of Militant Republicanism*, 297.

10. *Papers of Ulysses S. Grant*, vol. 19: *July 1, 1868–October 31, 1869*, 285–86.

11. Bradley, *Triumph of Militant Republicanism*, 302–3.

12. *Papers of Ulysses S. Grant*, vol. 26: *1875*, 108n.

13. Cameron to MacVeagh, 18 April 1869, quoted in Bradley, *Simon Cameron*, 297.

14. *Papers of Ulysses S. Grant*, vol. 19: *July 1, 1868–October 31, 1869*, 403.

15. Grant to Cameron, 18 December, undated; Fish to Cameron, 15 March 1877; Grant to Cameron, 30 March 1876, Simon Cameron Papers, loc mss 14845. *Maine Farmer*, August 16, 1873.

16. Bradley, *Simon Cameron*, 310–11.

17. "Cameron—He Makes Speech," *Green County Republican*, January 23, 1867.

18. *Interior Journal*, March 11, 1881.

19. *Zion's Herald*, March 3, 1870. Davis denied that Cameron had ever made such a prophecy, and the two men's supporters fought about the veracity of Cameron's claims for years ("A Bad Memory," *Post*, April 28, 1870).

20. "A Woman's Letters from Washington," *Independent*, March 31, 1870.

21. Bond, *Education for Freedom*, 3.

22. *Papers of Ulysses S. Grant*, vol. 24: *1873*, 410–11.

23. *Papers of Ulysses S. Grant*, vol. 24: *1873*, 234–35.

24. Nevins, *Hamilton Fish*, 369.

25. Hesseltine, *Ulysses S. Grant, Politician*, 205; Robert and Leona T. Rienow, *Of Snuff, Sin, and the Senate*, 42.

26. *Saturday Evening Post*, March 18, 1871.

27. Quoted in Bradley, *Simon Cameron*, 310–17.

28. Quoted in Bradley, *Simon Cameron*, 330.

29. Quoted in Bradley, *Simon Cameron*, 310–18.

30. *Papers of Ulysses S. Grant*, vol. 28: *November 1, 1876–September 30, 1878*, 258.

31. Nevins, *Hamilton Fish*, 493.

32. *Papers of Ulysses S. Grant*, vol. 21: *November 1, 1870–May 31, 1871*, 362–63n.

33. Withers, *Autobiography of an Octogenarian*, 331.

34. Bradley, *Simon Cameron*, 321; MacVeagh to Cameron, 26 December 1870, Simon Cameron Papers, LOC MSS 14845.

35. Baker, *Mary Todd Lincoln*, 266.

36. Justin Turner and Linda Turner, *Mary Todd Lincoln*, 572.

37. Bradley, *Simon Cameron*, 300.

38. Kelley, "Machine Is Born," 236.

39. Quoted in Bradley, *Simon Cameron*, 303.

40. Bradley, *Simon Cameron*, 330.

41. Bradley, *Simon Cameron*, 332.

42. Bradley, *Simon Cameron*, 331.

43. Evans, *Pennsylvania Politics*, 37.

44. *Papers of Ulysses S. Grant*, vol. 23: *February 1–December 31, 1872*, 238.

45. Bradley, *Simon Cameron*, 336.

46. Bradley, *Simon Cameron*, 348.

47. *Papers of Ulysses S. Grant*, vol. 24: *1873*, 234–35.

48. Bradley, *Triumph of Militant Republicanism*, 403.

49. Evans, *Pennsylvania Politics*, 45.

50. Anthony to Cameron, 9 October 1872, Simon Cameron Papers, LOC MSS 14845.

51. "Personalities," *Independent*, April 1, 1875.

52. Kelley, "Machine Is Born," 268; ? to Cameron, 3 February 1871, Simon Cameron Papers, LOC MSS 14845.

53. Bradley, *Simon Cameron*, 353.

54. Kelley, "Machine Is Born," 268; "Election of Bank Directors," *Sunbury American*, January 27, 1872; *Sunbury American*, February 2, 1875.

55. "The Clan Cameron," *Washington Post*, May 13, 1878.

56. Hesseltine, *Ulysses S. Grant, Politician*, 337.

57. Jones, *John A. Logan*, 76.

58. Cherny, *American Politics in the Gilded Age*, 57.

59. Bradley, *Simon Cameron*, 356–57.

60. *Papers of Ulysses S. Grant*, vol. 25: *1874*, 173n.

61. *Papers of Ulysses S. Grant*, vol. 26: *1875*, 353n.

62. *Papers of Ulysses S. Grant*, vol. 27: *January 1–October 31, 1876*, 295n and 395n.

63. *The Colombian*, June 18, 1875; *Papers of Ulysses S. Grant*, vol. 27: *January 1–October 31, 1876*, 55n.

64. Quoted in Bradley, *Simon Cameron*, 373.

65. Quoted in Bradley, *Simon Cameron*, 379.

66. "The Electoral Commission," *New York Times*, May 25, 1877.

67. Evans, *Pennsylvania Politics*, 310.

68. Hayes, *Diary and Letters*, 3:612.

69. *Eaton Democrat*, February 17, 1887.

70. *New Northwest*, March 16, 1877.

71. Quoted in Bradley, *Simon Cameron*, 392.

72. Hayes, *Diary and Letters*, 3:514.

73. Hoogenboom, *Presidency of Rutherford B. Hayes*, 107.

10. "I'll Behave Myself"

1. "St. Stephen's Guild," *New York Times*, September 5, 1889.

2. Quoted in Bradley, *Simon Cameron*, 405.

3. Quoted in Bradley, *Simon Cameron*, 405.

4. "Old Simon's Love," *San Francisco Chronicle*, February 19, 1877.

5. "The Oliver-Cameron Suit," *New York Times*, March 25, 1879.

6. "Mrs. Oliver's Third Day," *Washington Post*, March 21, 1879.

7. "Old Simon's Fiancee," *Washington Post*, January 28, 1878.

8. "Up Rises Mr. Oliver," *Washington Post*, March 19, 1879.

9. "A Very Bad Woman," *Washington Post*, March 25, 1879.

10. "The Widow Oliver Ousted," *Washington Post*, July 18, 1878.

11. "Surprising Mrs. Oliver," *New York Times*, March 19, 1879.

12. "Suing for Fifty Thousand," *New York Times*, March 18, 1879; "Mary's Wounded Heart," *Washington Post*, March 18, 1879; "Surprising Mrs. Oliver," *New York Times*, March 19, 1879.

13. "Surprising Mrs. Oliver," *New York Times*, March 19, 1879.

14. "Breach of Promise Suit," *New York Times*, February 9, 1877.

15. "Surprising Mrs. Oliver," *New York Times*, March 19, 1879.

16. "S.C.'s Love Letters," *New York Times*, January 31, 1878.

17. "The Oliver-Cameron Suit," *New York Times*, March 25, 1879.

18. "Mrs. Oliver under Fire," *Washington Post*, March 20, 1879.

19. "Mrs. Oliver's Story Ended," *New York Times*, March 21, 1879.

20. "Mrs. Oliver's Third Day," *Washington Post*, March 21, 1879.

21. "Suing for Fifty Thousand," *New York Times*, March 18, 1879; "Mary's Wounded Heart," *Washington Post*, March 18, 1879.

22. "Simon as a Fickle Lover," *Sun*, February 10, 1877; "Sly Simon," *Daily Globe*, March 18, 1879; *Washington Post*, January 15, 1878.

23. "Simon Cameron's Defense," *New York Times*, March 26, 1879.

24. "Her Ninth Husband," *Evening Star*, January 1, 1884.

25. "A Great Case Ended," *Washington Post*, April 2, 1879.

26. "Mary Ann M'Caffrey," *Washington Post*, April 10, 1879.

27. Quoted in Kelley, "Machine Is Born," 324–25.

28. "Washington Facts and Gossip," *Cambria Freedman*, May 26, 1882.

29. "Callers at the White House," *Washington Post*, April 21, 1881; "The Federal Government," *Washington Post*, May 5, 1887; "On the Way to Florida," *New York Times*, February 22, 1858.

30. Lincoln to Cameron, 27 May 1880, Simon Cameron Papers, LOC MSS 14845; "Simon Cameron on Second Terms," *New York Times*, May 10, 1888.

31. Swayne to Cameron et al., 13 August 1878, Simon Cameron Papers, LOC MSS 1484; "Minor Notes," *Vermont Phoenix*, September 24, 1880.

32. Withers, *Autobiography of an Octogenarian*, 386–87.

33. Hoogenboom, *Presidency of Rutherford B. Hayes*, 198.

34. Hayes, *Diary and Letters*, 3:605.

35. "Sturdy Old Simon Cameron," *Rock Island Daily Argus*, April 20, 1887.

36. Bradley, *Simon Cameron*, 413.

37. "The Cameron Clan," *San Francisco Chronicle*, April 13, 1879.

38. "Simon Cameron's Home at Harrisburg," *Highland Weekly News*, June 1, 1876.

39. "Simon Cameron's Guests," *New York Times*, May 8, 1866, "Entertaining Statesmen," *Washington Post*, July 1, 1888.

40. Bradley, *Simon Cameron*, 403.

41. Brewster to Cameron, 10 October 1869; Cameron to Brewster, 20 October 1869; Kane to Cameron, 29 October 1869; Kane to Grant, 29 October 1869, Simon Cameron Papers, LOC MSS 14845; "Koons-Brewster," *Washington Post*, February 7, 1883.

42. "Col. Scott's Funeral," *Sun*, May 25, 1881; "Death of Col. Forney," *Stark County Democrat*, December 15, 1881; "Gen. Simon Cameron's Tribute," *Sun*, July 24, 1885.

43. "Mrs. Catherine Bobbs' Will," *Indiana State Sentinel*, May 4, 1887.

44. "A Wrecked Train," *Sedalia Weekly Bazoo*, April 2, 1878; "Condensed Views," *Northern Tribute*, June 1, 1878.

45. Bradley, *Simon Cameron*, 411; Kelley, "Machine Is Born," 329.

46. "Simon Cameron's Last Purchase," *New York Times*, June 13, 1883; "Personal," *Washington Post*, June 2, 1879.

47. "Back from the Bermudas," *New York Times*, February 2, 1887.

48. Bradley, *Simon Cameron*, 409.

49. Joyce C. King, "Dining Elegantly in History," *Reading Eagle*, June 6, 1982.

50. Kelley, "Machine Is Born," 323.

51. "Personal," *Harper's Bazaar*, May 26, 1877; "Three Noted Babies," *Los Angeles Times*, May 22, 1887.

52. Cameron to Cameron, 1 May 1883, Simon Cameron Papers, LOC MSS 14845.

53. Bourne to Cameron, 3 December 1880, Simon Cameron Papers, LOC MSS 14845.

54. "Other Churches," *Christian Advocate*, October 25, 1880; "Charleston Rising Again," *New York Times*, September 17, 1886.

55. "Gift By General Cameron," *New York Times*, July 23, 1878.

56. "After Some of Simon Cameron's Money," *Salt Lake Hearld*, December 18, 1891.

57. Bradley, *Simon Cameron*, 416; "Rich Men's Sons," *Ladies' Home Journal*, December 1889.

58. "Simon Cameron," *Bismarck Weekly Tribune*, March 22, 1889.

59. "Clinging to Life," *Pittsburg Dispatch*, June 25, 1882.

60. Bradley, *Simon Cameron*, 415.

61. "From the Quaker City," *Washington Post*, March 3, 1889.

62. "Simon Cameron's Death," *New York Times*, June 27, 1889.

63. "Simon Cameron's Funeral," *Washington Post*, June 30, 1889.

64. Bradley, *Simon Cameron*, 417.

65. "Personal Gossip," *New York Times*, September 19, 1893.

66. "Gen. Cameron's Will Filed," *New York Times*, July 6, 1889; "Personal Notes," *San Francisco Chronicle*, July 7, 1889; "Gen. Cameron's Will," *Pittsburg Dispatch*, July 10, 1889.

67. "Washington Girls," *Los Angeles Times*, January 12, 1890.

68. "The Sage of Donegal," *New York Times*, June 28, 1889.

Conclusion

1. Quoted in Bradley, *Triumph of Militant Republicanism*, 422.

BIBLIOGRAPHY

Archival Sources

Gilder Lehrman Institute of American History, New York.
　　Letters from Simon Cameron to Robert G. White (GLC 05891.01-.17).

Historical Society of Dauphin County, Harrisburg PA.
　　Cameron Associated Collections (MG-831).
　　Cameron Family Papers (MG-500).

Historical Society of Pennsylvania.
　　Ferdinand J. Dreer Collection (MS 0175).
　　James Buchanan Papers (MS 0091).
　　Lewis Coryell Papers (MS 0151).

Library of Congress, Washington DC.
　　Abraham Lincoln Papers. http://memory.loc.gov/ammem/alhtml
　　　　/malhome.html. Accessed February 25, 2015.
　　James Buchanan Papers.
　　James Buchanan and Harriet Lane Johnson Papers.
　　Martin Van Buren Papers.
　　Simon Cameron Papers.
　　Thomas Jefferson Papers.

Millersville University–McNairy Library, Millersville PA.
　　Maggie Cameron Diaries, 1857–62.

Pennsylvania State Archives, Harrisburg.
　　Simon Cameron Collection (MG-33).

University of Pennsylvania–Rare Book and Manuscript Library, Philadelphia.
　　Simon Cameron, 1799–1889; Letters, 1848–75.

U.S. Army Heritage and Education Center, Carlisle PA.
　　Cameron Family Papers, 1854–94.

The Valley of the Shadow: The Eve of War: Letters and Diaries. http://valley
.lib.virginia.edu/VoS/letterspl.html. Accessed February 23, 2015.
The Valley of the Shadow: The Eve of War: Newspapers. http://valley.lib
.virginia.edu/VoS/newspaperspl.html. Accessed February 23, 2015.
The Valley of the Shadow: The War Years: Letters and Diaries. http://valley
.lib.virginia.edu/VoS/lettersp2.html. Accessed February 23, 2015.
The Valley of the Shadow: The War Years: Newspapers. http://valley.lib.virginia
.edu/VoS/newspapersp2.html. Accessed February 23, 2015.

Published Sources

*Address of the People's Club of Philadelphia in Favor of Gen. Simon Cameron for the
Next Presidency of the United States.* Philadelphia PA: People's Club, 1859.
Albright, Rebecca Gifford. "The Civil War Career of Andrew Gregg Curtin,
Governor of Pennsylvania." *Western Pennsylvania Historical Magazine* 48,
no. 1 (January 1965): 1–18.
Alotta, Robert I. *Stop the Evil: A Civil War History of Desertion and Murder.* San
Rafael CA: Presidio Press, 1978.
Alton, Edmund. *Among the Law-makers.* New York: Charles Scribner's Sons,
1886.
Ambacher, Bruce I. "George M. Dallas and the Bank War." *Pennsylvania
History* 42, no. 2 (1975): 116–35. JSTOR. Accessed February 21, 2015.
————. "The Pennsylvania Origins of Popular Sovereignty." *Pennsylvania
Magazine of History and Biography* 98, no. 3 (1974): 339–52. http://www
.jstor.org/stable/10.2307/20090871?ref=no-x-route:2a1cb3630745a1e
afb1bf45347a09c6e. Accessed February 21, 2015.
Anbinder, Tyler. *Nativism and Slavery: The Northern Know Nothings and the Pol-
itics of the 1850s.* New York: Oxford University Press, 1992.
Annual Report of the Pennsylvania Training School for Feeble-Minded Children.
Vol. 6. Philadelphia PA: Henry B. Ashmead, 1859.
Arnold, Isaac N., Mary Todd Lincoln, and Robert Todd Lincoln. *The History
of Abraham Lincoln, and the Overthrow of Slavery.* Chicago: Clarke, 1866.
Atlee, John L. *Cholera in Lancaster and Columbia in 1854.* Lancaster PA: Lan-
caster County Historical Society, 1958.
Auchampaugh, Philip G. "John W. Forney, Robert Tyler and James
Buchanan." *Tyler's Quarterly Historical and Genealogical Magazine* 15
(1933): 71–90.
Axelrod, Alan. *Political History of America's Wars.* Washington DC: CQ Press,
2007.
Baker, Jean H. *James Buchanan.* New York: Times Books, 2004.
————. *Mary Todd Lincoln: A Biography.* New York: Norton, 1987.
*Banquet to the Hon. Simon Cameron, Given at the Jones' House, May 2d, 1862, by the
People of Harrisburg.* Harrisburg: Printed at "Telegraph" Job Office, 1862.

Baringer, William E. *A House Dividing: Lincoln as President Elect*. Springfield
    IL: Abraham Lincoln Association, 1945.

Bartlett, Marguerite Gold. *The Chief Phases of Pennsylvania Politics in the Jack-
    sonian Period*. Pennsylvania: H. R. Haas, 1919.

Bates, David Homer. *Lincoln in the Telegraph Office; Recollections of the United
    States Military Telegraph Corps during the Civil War*. New York: Century, 1907.

Bates, Edward. *The Diary of Edward Bates: 1859–1866*. Edited by Howard Ken-
    nedy Beale. Vol. 4. Washington DC: Government Printing Office, 1933.

Bauer, K. Jack. *Zachary Taylor: Soldier, Planter, Statesman of the Old Southwest*.
    Baton Rouge: Louisiana State University Press, 1985.

Beatie, Russel H. *Army of the Potomac*. Vol. 1: *Birth of Command, November
    1860–September 1861*. Cambridge MA: Da Capo, 2002.

———. *Army of the Potomac*. Vol. 2: *McClellan Takes Command, September
    1861–February 1862*. Cambridge MA: Da Capo Press, 2002.

Beck, Herbert J. "The Camerons of Donegal." *Papers of the Lancaster County
    Historical Society* 56, no. 4 (1952): 85–112.

Beers, Paul B. "Andrew Gregg Curtin." *Civil War Times Illustrated* 62, no. 2
    (February 1967): 12–20.

Bell, Malcolm. *Major Butler's Legacy: Five Generations of a Slaveholding Family*.
    Athens: University of Georgia Press, 1987.

Belohlavek, John M. *George Mifflin Dallas: Jacksonian Patrician*. University
    Park: Pennsylvania State University Press, 1977.

Benton, Thomas Hart. *Thirty Years' View; or, A History of the Working of the Amer-
    ican Government for Thirty Years, from 1820 to 1850. Chiefly Taken from the
    Congress Debates, the Private Papers of General Jackson, and the Speeches of
    Ex-Senator Benton, with His Actual View of the Men and Affairs: With Histor-
    ical Notes and Illustrations, and Some Notices of Eminent Deceased Contempo-
    raries: By a Senator of Thirty Years*. Vol. 2. New York: D. Appleton, 1854.

Bergeron, Paul H. *The Presidency of James K. Polk*. Lawrence: University Press
    of Kansas, 1987.

Bigelow, John. *Retrospections of an Active Life*. Vol. 1. New York: Baker & Tay-
    lor, 1909.

Birkner, Michael J. "James Buchanan and the Political Crisis of the 1850s: A
    Panel Discussion." *Pennsylvania History* 60, no. 3 (July 1, 1993): 261–87.

Blaine, James G. *Twenty Years of Congress: From Lincoln to Garfield; with a Review
    of the Events Which Led to the Political Revolution of 1860*. Norwich CT:
    Henry Bill, 1884.

———. *Twenty Years of Congress: From Lincoln to Garfield; with a Review of the
    Events Which Led to the Political Revolution of 1860*. Vol. 2. Norwich CT:
    Henry Bill., 1886.

Blaine, James G., and Harriet S. Blaine Beale. *Letters of Mrs. James G. Blaine*.
    Vol. 1. New York: Duffield, 1908.

Blair, William Alan. "A Practical Politician: The Boss Tactics of Matthew Stanley Quay." *Pennsylvania History* 56, no. 2 (April 1, 1989): 77–92.

Blair, William Alan, and William Pencak. *Making and Remaking Pennsylvania's Civil War.* University Park: Pennsylvania State University Press, 2001.

Blessing, Ruth Elizabeth. "A Life of Simon Cameron: Pennsylvania Politician, 1799–1889." PhD diss., Lehigh University, 1939.

Bloom, Robert L. "Kansas and Popular Sovereignty in Pennsylvania Newspapers, 1856–1860." *Pennsylvania History* 14, no. 2 (April 1, 1947): 77–93.

———. "Newspaper Opinion in the State Election of 1860." *Pennsylvania History* 28, no. 4 (October 1, 1961): 346–64.

Blue, Frederick J. *No Taint of Compromise: Crusaders in Antislavery Politics.* Baton Rouge: Louisiana State University Press, 2005.

———. *Salmon P. Chase: A Life in Politics.* Kent OH: Kent State University Press, 1987.

Bogue, Allan G. *The Congressman's Civil War.* Cambridge: Cambridge University Press, 1989.

———. *The Earnest Men: Republicans of the Civil War Senate.* Ithaca NY: Cornell University Press, 1981.

Bond, Horace Mann. *Education for Freedom.* Princeton NJ: Princeton University Press, 1976.

Bordewich, Fergus M. *America's Great Debate: Henry Clay, Stephen A. Douglas, and the Compromise That Preserved the Union.* New York: Simon & Schuster, 2012.

Bowers, Douglas E. "From Caucus to Convention in Pennsylvania Politics, 1790–1830." *Pennsylvania History* 56, no. 4 (October 1, 1989): 276–98.

———. "From Logrolling to Corruption: The Development of Lobbying in Pennsylvania, 1815–1861." *Journal of the Early Republic* 3, no. 4 (December 1, 1983): 439–74.

Bradley, Erwin Stanley. *Simon Cameron, Lincoln's Secretary of War: A Political Biography.* Philadelphia: University of Pennsylvania Press, 1966.

———. *The Triumph of Militant Republicanism: A Study of Pennsylvania and Presidential Politics, 1860–1872.* Philadelphia: University of Pennsylvania Press, 1964.

Brandt, Dennis W. *From Home Guards to Heroes: The 87th Pennsylvania and Its Civil War Community.* Columbia: University of Missouri Press, 2006.

Brichford, Maynard J. "Congress at the Outbreak of the War." *Civil War History* 3, no. 2 (1957): 153–62.

Brodie, Fawn McKay. *Thaddeus Stevens: Scourge of the South.* New York: Norton, 1966.

Browne, Francis F. *The Everyday Life of Abraham Lincoln: A Narrative and Descriptive Biography with Pen-Pictures and Personal Recollections by Those Who Knew Him.* Minneapolis: Northwestern Pub., 1887.

Bryant, William Cullen. *The Letters of William Cullen Bryant*. Edited by William Cullen Bryant II and Thomas G. Voss. Vol. 4: *1858–1864*. New York: Fordham University Press, 1975.

Buchanan, James. *The Works of James Buchanan: Comprising His Speeches, State Papers, and Private Correspondence*. Edited by John Bassett Moore. Vol. 6: *1844–1846*. New York: Antiquarian Press, 1960.

———. *The Works of James Buchanan: Comprising His Speeches, State Papers, and Private Correspondence*. Edited by John Bassett Moore. Vol. 8: *1848–1853*. New York: Antiquarian Press, 1960.

Burlingame, Michael. *Abraham Lincoln: A Life*. Vol. 2. Baltimore MD: Johns Hopkins University Press, 2008.

———, ed. *Lincoln's Journalist: John Hay's Anonymous Writings for the Press, 1860–1864*. Carbondale: Southern Illinois University Press, 1998.

Burlingame, Michael, and John R. T. Ettlinger, eds. *Inside Lincoln's White House: The Complete Civil War Diary of John Hay*. Carbondale: Southern Illinois University Press, 1997.

Burton, William L. *Melting Pot Soldiers: The Union's Ethnic Regiments*. Ames: Iowa State University Press, 1988.

Butler, Benjamin F. *Butler's Book: Autobiography and Personal Reminiscences of Major-General Benj. F. Butler: A Review of His Legal, Political, and Military Career*. Boston: A. M. Thayer, 1892.

———. *Private and Official Correspondence of Gen. Benjamin F. Butler during the Period of the Civil War in Five Volumes*. Vol. 1: *April 1860–June 1862*. Norwood MA: Privately Issued by the Plimpton Press, 1917.

———. *Private and Official Correspondence of Gen. Benjamin F. Butler during the Period of the Civil War in Five Volumes*. Vol. 2: *June 1862–February 1863*. Norwood MA: Privately Issued by the Plimpton Press, 1917.

Cale, Edgar B. "Editorial Sentiment in Pennsylvania in the Campaign of 1860." *Pennsylvania History* 4, no. 4 (October 1, 1937): 219–34.

Calhoun, John C. *The Papers of John C. Calhoun*. Edited by Robert Lee Meriwether, William Edwin Hemphill, and Clyde Norman Wilson. Vols. 21–26. Columbia: Published by the University of South Carolina Press for the South Caroliniana Society, 1993–2001.

———. *The Works of John C. Calhoun*. Vol. 5: *Reports and Public Letters*. New York: D. Appleton, 1904.

Cameron, Simon. *Report of the Secretary of War*. Vol. 2. Washington DC: Government Printing Office, 1861.

Carl, Sandburg. *Abraham Lincoln: The War Years*. Vol. 2: *1861-1864*. New York: Dell, 1926.

———. *Abraham Lincoln: The War Years*. Vol. 3: *1864–1865*. New York: Dell, 1926.

Carlson, Robert E. "James Buchanan and Public Office: An Appraisal." *Pennsylvania Magazine of History and Biography* 81, no. 3 (July 1, 1957): 255–79.

Carnegie, Andrew, and Van Dyke John Charles. *Autobiography of Andrew Carnegie*. Boston: Houghton Mifflin, 1920.

Carpenter, F. B. *The Inner Life of Abraham Lincoln: Six Months at the White House*. Lincoln: University of Nebraska Press, 1995.

Cashdollar, Charles D. "Andrew Johnson and the Philadelphia Election of 1866." *Pennsylvania Magazine of History and Biography* 92, no. 3 (July 1968): 365–83.

Chadwick, Bruce. *Lincoln for President: An Unlikely Candidate, an Audacious Strategy, and the Victory No One Saw Coming*. Naperville IL: Sourcebooks, 2009.

Chadwick, French Ensor. *The Relations of the United States and Spain, Diplomacy*. New York: C. Scribner's Sons, 1909.

Chase, Salmon P. *Inside Lincoln's Cabinet: The Civil War Diaries of Salmon P. Chase*. Edited by David Herbert Donald. New York: Longmans, Green, 1954.

———. *The Salmon P. Chase Papers*. Edited by John Niven, James P. McClure, Leigh Johnsen, and Kathleen Norman. Vol. 2: *Correspondence, 1823–1857*. Kent OH: Kent State University Press, 1997.

———. *The Salmon P. Chase Papers*. Edited by John Niven, James P. McClure, and Leigh Johnsen. Vol. 3: *Correspondence, 1858–March, 1863*. Kent OH: Kent State University Press, 1996.

———. *The Salmon P. Chase Papers*. Edited by John Niven, James P. McClure, Leigh Johnsen, and Kathleen Norman. Vol. 4: *Correspondence, April 1863–1864*. Kent OH: Kent State University Press, 1997.

———. *The Salmon P. Chase Papers*. Edited by John Niven. Vol. 5: *Correspondence, 1865–1873*. Kent OH: Kent State University Press, 1993.

Chase, Salmon P., and George S. Denison. *Annual Report of the American Historical Association for the Year 1902: In Two Volumes*. Vol. 2: *Diary and Correspondence of S. P. Chase*. Washington: Government Printing Office, 1903.

Cherny, Robert W. *American Politics in the Gilded Age, 1868–1900*. Wheeling IL: Harlan Davidson, 1997.

Chesnut, Mary Boykin Miller. *Mary Chesnut's Civil War*. Edited by C. Vann Woodward. New Haven CT: Yale University Press, 1981.

Chidsey, Donald Barr. *The Gentleman from New York: A Life of Roscoe Conkling*. New Haven CT: Yale University Press, 1935.

Chittenden, Lucius E. *Recollections of President Lincoln and His Administration*. New York: Harper & Brothers, 1891.

Churella, Albert J. *The Pennsylvania Railroad*. Vol. 1: *Building an Empire, 1846–1917*. Philadelphia: University of Pennsylvania Press, 2013.

Clark, Martha Bladen. *Donegal Church: Colin McFarquhar, a Landmark of Presbyterian History*. Lancaster PA: Lancaster County Historical Society, 1913.

Claussen, E. Neal. "Hendrick B. Wright and the "Nocturnal Committee." *Pennsylvania Magazine of History and Biography* 89, no. 2 (April 1, 1965): 199–206.

Clay, Cassius Marcellus. *The Life of Cassius Marcellus Clay: Memoirs, Writings, and Speeches, Showing His Conduct in the Overthrow of American Slavery, the Salvation of the Union, and the Restoration of the Autonomy of the States.* New York: Negro Universities Press, 1969.

Clay, Henry. *The Papers of Henry Clay.* Edited by James Franklin Hopkins and Mary Wilma Massey Hargreaves. Vol. 4. Lexington: University Press of Kentucky, 1972.

———. *The Papers of Henry Clay.* Edited by James Franklin Hopkins and Mary Wilma Massey Hargreaves. Vol. 5. Lexington: University Press of Kentucky, 1973.

———. *The Papers of Henry Clay.* Edited by James Franklin Hopkins and Mary Wilma Massey Hargreaves. Vol. 6. Lexington: University Press of Kentucky, 1981.

———. *The Papers of Henry Clay.* Edited by Melba Hay. Vol. 10. Lexington: University Press of Kentucky, 1991.

Cochrane, John, and Henry O'Reilly. *American Civil War: Memories of Incidents Connected with the Origin and Culmination of the Rebellion That Threatened the Existence of the National Government . . . including the Proposition Made in a Speech at the Astor House, in New York, in November, 1861, When . . . John Cochrane . . . First Publicly Advocated the Arming of the Slaves in the War for the Union . . .* New York: Rogers & Sherwood, 1879.

———. *Arming the Slaves in the War for the Union: Scenes, Speeches, and Events Attending It . . . Extract from a Private Memoir concerning the War.* New York: Rogers & Sherwood, 1875.

Coddington, Edwin B. "Pennsylvania Prepares for Invasion, 1863." *Pennsylvania History* 31, no. 2 (April 1, 1964): 157–75.

———. "Prelude to Gettysburg: The Confederates Plunder Pennsylvania." *Pennsylvania History* 30, no. 2 (April 1, 1963): 123–57.

Coleman, John F. *The Disruption of the Pennsylvania Democracy, 1848–1860.* Harrisburg PA: Pennsylvania Museum and Historical Commission, 1975.

———. "The Public Career of James Campbell." *Pennsylvania History* 29, no. 1 (1962): 24–39. http://www.jstor.org/stable/10.2307/27770079?ref=no -x-route:44263ce1c1854be16edc0aeea385f3cb. Accessed February 21, 2015.

Collins, Bruce. "The Democrats' Loss of Pennsylvania in 1858." *Pennsylvania Magazine of History and Biography* 109, no. 4 (October 1, 1985): 499–536.

Cooper, William J. *We Have the War upon Us: The Onset of the Civil War, November 1860–April 1861.* New York: Alfred A. Knopf, 2012.

Crawford, Samuel Wylie. *The Genesis of the Civil War: The Story of Sumter, 1860–1861.* New York: C. L. Webster, 1887.

Crippen, Lee Forbes. *Simon Cameron: Ante-bellum Years.* Oxford: Mississippi Valley Press, 1942.

Crist, Robert Grant. "Highwater 1863: The Confederate Approach to Harrisburg." *Pennsylvania History* 30, no. 2 (April 1, 1963): 158–83.

Crouthamel, James L. "Three Philadelphians in the Bank War: A Neglected Chapter in American Lobbying." *Pennsylvania History* 27, no. 4 (1960): 361–78. http://www.jstor.org/stable/10.2307/27769984?ref=no-x-route :6cd420d5862a6e40c250e8929e691a87. Accessed February 21, 2015.

Curran, Daniel J. "Hendrick B. Wright: A Study in Leadership." PhD diss., Fordham University, 1962.

Curry, Earl R. "Pennsylvania and the Republican Convention of 1860: A Critique of McClure's Thesis." *Pennsylvania Magazine of History and Biography* 97, no. 2 (April 1, 1973): 183–98.

Davis, David Brion. "Some Ideological Functions of Prejudice in Ante-Bellum America." *American Quarterly* 15, no. 2, pt. 1 (July 1, 1963): 115–25.

Davis, Jefferson, Lynda Lasswell Crist, Mary Seaton Dix, and Kenneth H. Williams. *The Papers of Jefferson Davis.* Vol. 3. Baton Rouge: Louisiana State University Press, 1971.

———. *The Papers of Jefferson Davis.* Vol. 4. Baton Rouge: Louisiana State University Press, 1971.

———. *The Papers of Jefferson Davis.* Vol. 5. Baton Rouge: Louisiana State University Press, 1971.

———. *The Papers of Jefferson Davis.* Vol. 6. Baton Rouge: Louisiana State University Press, 1971.

Davis, Rodney O. "Dr. Charles Leib: Lincoln's Mole?" *Journal of the Abraham Lincoln Association* 24, no. 2 (July 1, 2003): 20–35.

Davis, Stanton L. "Pennsylvania Politics, 1869–1863." PhD diss., Western Reserve University, 1935.

Davis, W. W. H. *A Genealogical and Personal History of Bucks County, Pennsylvania.* Baltimore: Genealogical Pub., 1975.

———. *History of Doylestown, Old and New: From Its Settlement to the Close of the Nineteenth Century, 1745–1900.* Doylestown PA: Intelligencer Print, 1904.

Dennison, Eleanor Elizabeth. "The United States Senate Committee on Foreign Relations." PhD diss., Leland Stanford Junior University, 1940.

Dodd, William Edward. *Jefferson Davis.* Philadelphia: G. W. Jacobs, 1907.

Downey, Matthew T. "Horace Greeley and the Politicians: The Liberal Republican Convention in 1872." *Journal of American History* 53, no. 4 (March 1, 1967): 727–50.

Du Pont, Samuel Francis. *Samuel Francis Du Pont: A Selection from His Civil War Letters.* Edited by John D. Hayes. Vol. 1: *The Mission, 1860–1862.* Ithaca NY: Published for the Eleutherian Mills Historical Library by Cornell University Press, 1969.

————. *Samuel Francis Du Pont: A Selection from His Civil War Letters*. Edited by John D. Hayes. Vol. 2: *The Repulse: 1863–1865*. Ithaca NY: Published for the Eleutherian Mills Historical Library by Cornell University Press, 1969.

Earle, Jonathan H. *Jacksonian Antislavery and the Politics of Free Soil: 1824–1854*. Chapel Hill: University of North Carolina Press, 2004.

Ecelbarger, Gary L. *The Great Comeback: How Abraham Lincoln Beat the Odds to Win the 1860 Republican Nomination*. New York: Thomas Dunne Books, 2008.

Eckley, Robert S. *Lincoln's Forgotten Friend, Leonard Swett*. Carbondale: Southern Illinois University Press, 2012.

"Economic Change and Political Realignment in Antebellum Pennsylvania." *Pennsylvania Magazine of History and Biography* 113, no. 3 (July 1, 1989): 347–95.

Eggert, Gerald G. *Harrisburg Industrializes: The Coming of Factories to an American Community*. University Park: Pennsylvania State University Press, 1993.

————. "The Impact of the Fugitive Slave Law on Harrisburg: A Case Study." *Pennsylvania Magazine of History and Biography* 109, no. 4 (October 1, 1985): 537–69.

————. "'Seeing Sam': The Know Nothing Episode in Harrisburg." *Pennsylvania Magazine of History and Biography* 111, no. 3 (July 1, 1987): 305–40.

Egnal, Marc. "The Beards Were Right: Parties in the North, 1840–1860." *Civil War History* 47, no. 1 (March 2001): 30–56.

————. *Clash of Extremes: The Economic Origins of the Civil War*. New York: Hill and Wang, 2009.

Eiselen, Malcolm Rogers. *The Rise of Pennsylvania Protectionism*. Philadelphia: Porcupine Press, 1974.

Eisenhower, John S. D. *Agent of Destiny: The Life and Times of General Winfield Scott*. New York: Free Press, 1997.

Ellis, Franklin, and Samuel Evans. *History of Lancaster County, Pennsylvania: With Biographical Sketches of Many of Its Pioneers and Prominent Men*. Philadelphia: Everts & Peck, 1883.

Ellis, John B. *The Sights and Secrets of the National Capital a Work Descriptive of Washington City in All Its Various Phases*. New York: United States Pub., 1869.

Engle, Stephen Douglas. *All the President's Statesmen: Northern Governors and the American Civil War*. Milwaukee WI: Marquette University Press, 2006.

Ershkowitz, Herbert. "Consensus or Conflict? Political Behavior in the State Legislatures during the Jacksonian Era." *The Journal of American History* 58, no. 3 (1971): 591–621. http://www.jstor.org/stable /10.2307/1893726?ref=no-x-route:d160a5c6de3c9e1bb722363e 23cfa6e8. Accessed February 21, 2015.

Evans, Frank B. *Pennsylvania Politics, 1872–1877: A Study in Political Leadership.* Harrisburg: Pennsylvania Historical and Museum Commission, 1966.

Everett, Edward G. "The Baltimore Riots, April, 1861." *Pennsylvania History* 24, no. 4 (October 1, 1957): 331–42.

———. "Pennsylvania Raises an Army." *Western Pennsylvania Historical Magazine* 39 (Summer 1956): 83–108.

———. "Pennsylvania's Mobilization for War, 1860–1861." PhD diss., University of Pittsburgh, 1954.

Fahrney, R. R. "Horace Greeley and the New York Tribune in the Civil War." *New York History* 16, no. 4 (October 1, 1935): 415–35.

Fehrenbacher, Don E. "The Making of a Myth: Lincoln and the Vice-Presidential Nomination in 1864." *Civil War History* 41, no. 4 (December 1995): 273–90.

Ferry, Richard J. "Abraham Lincoln the Jacksonian Whig a Study in the Political Philosophy of Abraham Lincoln by an Examination of His Dealings with His Cabinet." PhD diss., SMU, 2007.

Finkelman, Paul. *Millard Fillmore.* New York: Times Books, 2011.

Flood, Charles Bracelen. *1864: Lincoln at the Gates of History.* New York: Simon & Schuster, 2009.

Foner, Eric. *Free Soil, Free Labor, Free Men: The Ideology of the Republican Party before the Civil War.* New York: Oxford University Press, 1970.

Ford, Worthington Chauncey, Charles Francis Adams, Charles Francis Adams, and Henry Adams. *A Cycle of Adams Letters.* Vol. 1. Boston and New York: Houghton Mifflin Company, 1920.

Forney, John W. *Anecdotes of Public Men.* New York: Harper & Brothers, 1873.

Freehling, William W. *The Road to Disunion.* Vol. 1. New York: Oxford University Press, 1990.

Fremont, John C. "Order of Martial Law throughout Missouri, August 30, 1861." Civil War Interactive Blue & Gray Daily. http://www.civilwarinteractive.com/DocsFremontMartialLaw.htm. Accessed March 11, 2015.

Furgurson, Ernest B. *Freedom Rising: Washington in the Civil War.* New York: Alfred A. Knopf, 2004.

G., Van Deusen Glyndon. *Thurlow Weed, Wizard of the Lobby.* Boston: Little, Brown and, 1947.

Gambone, A. M. *Major-General John Frederick Hartranft: Citizen Soldier and Pennsylvania Statesman.* Baltimore: Butternut and Blue, 1995.

Geary, Theophane. *A History of Third Parties in Pennsylvania, 1840–1860.* Washington DC: Catholic University of America, 1938.

George, Mary Karl. *Zachariah Chandler; a Political Biography.* East Lansing: Michigan State University Press, 1969.

Gerrity, Frank. "The Disruption of the Philadelphia Whigocracy: Joseph R. Chandler, Anti-Catholicism, and the Congressional Election of 1854."

Pennsylvania Magazine of History and Biography 111, no. 2 (April 1, 1987): 161–94.

———. "Joseph R. Chandler and the Politics of Religion, 1848–1860." *The Catholic Historical Review* 74, no. 2 (April 1, 1988): 226–47.

———. "The Masons, the Antimasons, and the Pennsylvania Legislature, 1834–1836." *Pennsylvania Magazine of History and Biography* 99, no. 2 (1975): 180–206. http://www.jstor.org/stable/10.2307/20090944?ref=no -x-route:ae48f42b90b48afc31c572a14fe3799a. Accessed February 21, 2015.

Gienapp, William E. "Nativism and the Creation of a Republican Majority in the North before the Civil War." *The Journal of American History* 72, no. 3 (December 1, 1985): 529–59.

———. "Nebraska, Nativism, and Rum: The Failure of Fusion in Pennsylvania, 1854." *Pennsylvania Magazine of History and Biography* 109, no. 4 (October 1, 1985): 425–71.

———. *The Origins of the Republican Party: 1852–1856.* New York: Oxford University Press, 1987.

Gienapp, William E., Stephen E. Maizlish, and John J. Kushma. *Essays on American Antebellum Politics, 1840–1860.* College Station: Published for the University of Texas at Arlington, by Texas A&M University Press, 1982.

Gilmore, James R. *Personal Recollections of Abraham Lincoln and the Civil War.* Boston: L. C. Page, 1898. Reprint, Mechanicsburg PA: Stackpole Books, 2007.

Glenn, William Wilkins. *Between North and South: A Maryland Journalist Views the Civil War: The Narrative of William Wilkins Glenn, 1861–1869.* Edited by Bayly Ellen Marks and Mark Norton Schatz. Rutherford NJ: Fairleigh Dickinson University Press, 1976.

Going, Charles Buxton. *David Wilmot, Free-Soiler: A Biography of the Great Advocate of the Wilmot Proviso.* Gloucester MA: P. Smith, 1966.

Goodwin, Doris Kearns. *Team of Rivals: The Political Genius of Abraham Lincoln.* New York: Simon & Schuster, 2005.

Goss, John Dean. *The History of Tariff Administration in the United States from Colonial Times to the McKinley Administration Bill.* N.p.: N.p.

Goss, Thomas J. *The War within the Union High Command: Politics and Generalship during the Civil War.* Lawrence: University Press of Kansas, 2003.

Grant, Ulysses S. *The Papers of Ulysses S. Grant.* Edited by John Y. Simon. Vols. 17–28. Carbondale: Southern Illinois University Press, 1991–2005.

———. *Personal Memoirs of U.S. Grant.* New York: C. L. Webster, 1886.

Greeley, Horace. *Proceedings of the First Three Republican National Conventions of 1856, 1860 and 1864: Including Proceedings of the Antecedent National Convention Held at Pittsburg, in February, 1856, as Reported by Horace Greeley.* Minneapolis MN: C. W. Johnson, 1893.

Green, Michael S. *Freedom, Union, and Power: Lincoln and His Party during the Civil War.* New York: Fordham University Press, 2004.

Grim, Webster. *Historical Sketch of the Doylestown Democrat, 1816–1916; with Biographical Sketches of the Editors; in Commemoration of the First Century of the Existence of the Doylestown Democrat.* Doylestown PA: Doylestown Publishing, 1916.

Grow, Matthew J. *"Liberty to the Downtrodden": Thomas L. Kane, Romantic Reformer.* New Haven: Yale University Press, 2009.

Gudelunas, William, Jr. "Nativism and the Demise of Schuylkill County Whiggery: Anti-Slavery or Anti-Catholicism." *Pennsylvania History* 45, no. 3 (July 1, 1978): 224–36.

Gurowski, Adam. *Diary, from March 4, 1861, to November 12, 1862.* Boston: Lee and Shepard, 1862.

Gutheim, Frederick Albert. *Worthy of the Nation: The History of Planning for the National Capital.* Washington: Smithsonian Institution Press, 1977.

Hackenburg, Randy W. *Pennsylvania in the War with Mexico.* Shippensburg PA: White Mane Pub., 1992.

Hailperin, Herman. "Pro-Jackson Sentiment in Pennsylvania, 1820–1828." *Pennsylvania Magazine of History and Biography* 50, no. 3 (1926): 193–240. http://www.jstor.org/stable/10.2307/20086610?ref=no-x-route:2c7c66 270ef51268a1c6c7e4e5891b7f. Accessed February 21, 2015.

Hamilton, Holman. *Zachary Taylor, Soldier in the White House.* Indianapolis: Bobbs-Merrill, 1951.

Hamlin, Charles Eugene. *The Life and times of Hannibal Hamlin.* Cambridge: Printed at the Riverside Press, 1899.

Hammond, Bray. *Banks and Politics in America, from the Revolution to the Civil War.* Princeton: Princeton University Press, 1957.

———. "Jackson, Biddle, and the Bank of the United States." *Journal of Economic History* 7, no. 1 (1947).

Harris, Alexander. *A Biographical History of Lancaster County . . . Being a History of Early Settlers and Eminent Men of the County; as Also Much Other Unpublished Historical Information, Chiefly of a Local Character.* Lancaster PA: E. Barr, 1872.

Harris, William C. *Lincoln and the Union Governors.* Carbondale: Southern Illinois University Press, 2013.

Harrison, Robert. "Blaine and the Camerons: A Study in the Limits of Machine Power." *Pennsylvania History* 49, no. 3 (July 1, 1982): 157–75.

———. "The Hornets' Nest at Harrisburg: A Study of the Pennsylvania Legislature in the Late 1870s." *Pennsylvania Magazine of History and Biography* 103, no. 3 (July 1, 1979): 334–55.

Harschlip, Rodney. "Simon Cameron and the War Contracts Committee." PhD diss., University of Wisconsin–Eau Claire, 1972.

Harvey, George. "Wayne MacVeath; a Passionate Patriot." *North American Review,* 1917, 337–44.

Hattaway, Herman, and Archer Jones. *How the North Won: A Military History of the Civil War.* Urbana: University of Illinois Press, 1983.

Hayes, Rutherford B. *Diary and Letters of Rutherford Birchard Hayes, Nineteenth President of the United States.* Edited by Charles Richard Williams. Vol. 3: *1865–1881.* Columbus: Ohio State Archaeological and Historical Society, 1922.

———. *Diary and Letters of Rutherford Birchard Hayes, Nineteenth President of the United States.* Edited by Charles Richard Williams. Vol. 4: *1881–1893.* Columbus: Ohio State Archaeological and Historical Society, 1922.

Hearn, Chester G. *Lincoln, the Cabinet, and the Generals.* Baton Rouge: Louisiana State University Press, 2010.

Heidler, David Stephen, and Jeanne T. Heidler. *Henry Clay: The Essential American.* New York: Random House, 2010.

Heiges, George L. *1860—The Year before the War.* Lancaster PA: Lancaster County Historical Society, 1961.

Heiss, John P. "Papers of John P. Heiss, of Nashville. With an Introduction and Notes by the Editor." *Tennessee Historical Magazine* 2, no. 1 (June 1916): 137–47, 208–30.

Hendrick, Burton Jesse. *Lincoln's War Cabinet.* Boston: Little, Brown, 1946.

Hensel, W. U. *The Attitude of James Buchanan: A Citizen of Lancaster County; towards the Institution of Slavery in the United States.* Lancaster PA: Press of the New Era Printing, 1911.

———. "Sidelights on an Early Political Campaign." *Historical Papers and Addresses of the Lancaster County Historical Society* 18, no. 4 (1914): 90–96.

Hesseltine, William Best. *Lincoln and the War Governors.* New York: A. A. Knopf, 1955.

———. *Ulysses S. Grant: Politician.* New York: F. Ungar, 1957.

Hewitt, Warren F. "The Know Nothing Party in Pennsylvania." *Pennsylvania History* 2, no. 2 (April 1, 1935): 69–85.

Hitchcock, Ethan Allen, and W. A. Croffut. *Fifty Years in Camp and Field, Diary of Major-General Ethan Allen Hitchcock, U.S.A.* New York: G. P. Putnam's Sons, 1909.

Hoar, George Frisbie. *Autobiography of Seventy Years.* Vols. 1 and 2. New York: C. Scribner's Sons, 1903.

Hofstadter, Richard. "The Tariff Issue on the Eve of the Civil War." *American Historical Review* 44, no. 1 (October 1, 1938): 50–55.

Holt, Michael F. *Forging a Majority: The Formation of the Republican Party in Pittsburgh, 1848–1860.* New Haven: Yale University Press, 1969.

———. *The Political Crisis of the 1850s.* New York: Wiley, 1978.

———. "The Politics of Impatience: The Origins of Know Nothingism." *The Journal of American History* 60, no. 2 (September 1, 1973): 309–31.

Holzer, Harold. *Lincoln President-Elect: Abraham Lincoln and the Great Secession Winter, 1860–1861*. New York: Simon & Schuster, 2008.

Hoogenboom, Ari Arthur. *The Presidency of Rutherford B. Hayes*. Lawrence: University Press of Kansas, 1988.

Horowitz, Murray M. "Benjamin F. Butler: Seventeenth President?" *Lincoln Herald* 77, no. 4 (December 1975): 191–203.

Howe, Daniel Walker. *What Hath God Wrought: The Transformation of America, 1815–1848*. New York: Oxford University Press, 2007.

Hudson, Frederic. *Journalism in the United States, from 1690 to 1872*. New York: Harper & Brothers, 1873.

Hunt, H. Draper. *Hannibal Hamlin of Maine: Lincoln's First Vice-President*. New York, 1968.

Huston, James L. "The Demise of the Pennsylvania American Party, 1854–1858." *Pennsylvania Magazine of History and Biography* 109, no. 4 (October 1, 1985): 473–97.

———. *The Panic of 1857 and the Coming of the Civil War*. Baton Rouge: Louisiana State University Press, 1987.

Hutchinson, C. H. *The Chronicles of Middletown, Containing a Compilation of Facts, Biographical Sketches, Reminiscences, Anecdotes, &c., Connected with the History of One of the Oldest Towns in Pennsylvania*. N.p.: Printed by the author, 1906.

Hyman, Harold Melvin. *The Radical Republicans and Reconstruction, 1861–1870*. Indianapolis: Bobbs-Merrill, 1967.

Jackson, Andrew. *Correspondence of Andrew Jackson*. Edited by John Spencer Bassett and David Maydole Matteson. 7 vols. Washington DC: Carnegie Institution of Washington, 1926–35.

Johnson, Andrew. *The Papers of Andrew Johnson*. Edited by LeRoy P. Graf, Ralph W. Haskins, and Paul H. Bergeron. 16 vols. Knoxville: University of Tennessee Press, 1967–2000.

Jones, James P. *John A. Logan: Stalwart Republican from Illinois*. Tallahassee: University Press of Florida, 1982.

Jordan, David M. *Roscoe Conkling of New York: Voice in the Senate*. Ithaca NY: Cornell University Press, 1971.

Jordan, Philip D. *The Capital of Crime*. Harrisburg PA: Civil War Times Illustrated, 1975.

Josephson, Matthew. *The Politicos: 1865–1896*. New York: Harcourt, Brace, 1958.

Journal of the Senate of the Commonwealth of Pennsylvania, Commenced at Harrisburg, on Tuesday the Seventh Day of January, in the Year of Our Lord One Thousand Eight Hundred and Fifty-One. Vol. 1. Harrisburg: Theo. Fenn, 1851.

Journal of the Senate of the Commonwealth of Pennsylvania of the Session Begun at Harrisburg, on the First Day of January, A.D., 1856. Harrisburg: A. Boyd Hamilton, 1856.

Journal of the Senate of the Commonwealth of Pennsylvania Which Commenced at Harrisburg, on Tuesday, the Fourth Day of January, in the Year of Our Lord One Thousand Eight Hundred and Forty-Two. Vol. 1. Harrisburg: Boas & Patterson, 1842.

Journal of the Thirty-Seventh House of Representatives of the Commonwealth of Pennsylvania Commenced at Harrisburg, Tuesday, the Fifth of December, in the Year of Our Lord One Thousand Eight Hundred and Twenty-Six. Vol. 1. Harrisburg: John S. Wiestling, 1826–27.

Kamm, Samuel Richey. "The Civil War Career of Thomas A. Scott." PhD diss., University of Pennsylvania, 1940.

Kelker, Luther Reily. *History of Dauphin County, Pennsylvania.* Vol. 3. New York: Lewis Publishing, 1907.

Kelley, Brooks M. "Fossildom, Old Fogeyism, and Red Tape." *Pennsylvania Magazine of History and Biography* 90, no. 1 (January 1, 1966): 93–114.

———. "A Machine Is Born: Simon Cameron and Pennsylvania, 1862–1873." PhD diss., University of Chicago, 1961.

———. "Simon Cameron and the Senatorial Nomination of 1867." *Pennsylvania Magazine of History and Biography* 87, no. 4 (October 1, 1963): 375–92.

Kenny, Kevin. "Nativism, Labor, and Slavery: The Political Odyssey of Benjamin Bannan, 1850–1860." *Pennsylvania Magazine of History and Biography* 118, no. 4 (October 1, 1994): 325–61.

Keyes, E. D. *Fifty Years' Observation of Men and Events, Civil and Military.* New York: Charles Scribner's Sons, 1884.

Kielbowicz, Richard B. "The Telegraph, Censorship, and Politics at the Outset of the Civil War." *Civil War History* 40, no. 2 (June 1994): 95–118.

King, Willard L. *Lincoln's Manager, David Davis.* Cambridge: Harvard University Press, 1960.

Klein, Maury. *Days of Defiance: Sumter, Secession, and the Coming of the Civil War.* New York: Knopf, 1997.

Klein, Philip Shriver. "The Inauguration of President James Buchanan." *Journal of the Lancaster County Historical Society* 61 (1957): 145–68.

———. "John Andrew Schulze-Dark Horse." *Historical Review of Berks County* 56, no. 4 (1942).

———. *Pennsylvania Politics, 1817–1832: A Game without Rules.* Philadelphia: Published under the Lamberton Fund, the Historical Society of Pennsylvania, 1940.

———. *President James Buchanan: A Biography.* University Park: Pennsylvania State University Press, 1962.

Korngold, Ralph. *Thaddeus Stevens: A Being Darkly Wise and Rudely Great.* New York: Harcourt, Brace, 1955.

Lamon, Ward Hill, and Dorothy Lamon. Teillard. *Recollections of Abraham Lincoln.* Lincoln: University of Nebraska Press, 1994.

Landis, Michael Todd. *Northern Men with Southern Loyalties: The Democratic Party and the Sectional Crisis.*

Lee, Elizabeth Blair. *Wartime Washington: The Civil War Letters of Elizabeth Blair Lee.* Edited by Virginia Jeans Laas. Urbana: University of Illinois Press, 1991.

Leech, Margaret. *Reveille in Washington, 1860–1865.* New York: Harper & Brothers, 1941.

Leib, Charles. *Nine Months in the Quartermaster's Department; Or, The Chances for Making a Million.* Cincinnati: Moore, Wilstach, Keys &, Printers, 1862.

"Letters of James K. Polk and Andrew J. Donelson, 1843–1848." *Tennessee Historical Magazine* 3, no. 1 (1917): 51–74.

Levin, Bernard. "Pennsylvania and the Civil War." *Pennsylvania History* 10, no. 1 (January 1, 1943): 1–10.

Libhart, Lemar Landon. "Simon Cameron's Political Exile as United States Minister to Russia." *Journal of the Lancaster County Historical Society* 72, no. 4 (Fall 1968): 189–228.

Lincoln, Abraham. *The Lincoln Papers.* Edited by David Chambers Mearns. Vol. 1. Garden City NY: Doubleday, 1948.

Lincoln, Abraham, and Charles M. Segal. *Conversations with Lincoln.* New York: Putnam, 1961.

Lincoln, Mary Todd. *Mary Todd Lincoln: Her Life and Letters.* Edited by Justin G. Turner and Linda Levitt Turner. New York: Knopf, 1972.

Lind, Michael. *Land of Promise: An Economic History of the United States.* New York: Broadside Books, 2012.

Loose, John Ward Willson. "Cholera in Lancaster and Columbia in 1854." *Journal of the Lancaster County Historical Society* 62 (1958).

———. *A Survey of 19th Century Iron Industry in Lancaster County.* Lancaster PA: Lancaster County Historical Society, 1954.

Lowe, William J. *Donegal Reformed Church at Milton Grove; Maytown Reformed Church at Maytown.* Vol. 22. Lancaster PA, 1918.

Luthin, Reinhard H. "Abraham Lincoln and the Tariff." *American Historical Review* 49, no. 4 (July 1, 1944): 609–29.

———. "The Democratic Split during Buchanan's Administration." *Pennsylvania History* 11, no. 1 (1944): 13–35. http://www.jstor.org/stable/10.2307/27766588?ref=no-x-route:8e08c983f00eade087608e17bf736543. Accessed February 21, 2015.

———. *The First Lincoln Campaign.* Cambridge MA: Harvard University Press, 1944.

———. "Pennsylvania and Lincoln's Rise to the Presidency." *Pennsylvania Magazine of History and Biography* 67, no. 1 (January 1, 1943): 61–82.

Macartney, Clarence Edward Noble. *Lincoln and His Cabinet.* New York: C. Scribner's Sons, 1931.

Mackay, Winnifred K. "Philadelphia during the Civil War, 1861–1865." *Pennsylvania Magazine of History and Biography* 70, no. 1 (January 1, 1946): 3–51.

Magness, Phillip W. "Morrill and the Missing Industries: Strategic Lobbying Behavior and the Tariff, 1858–1861." *Journal of the Early Republic* 29, no. 2 (July 1, 2009): 287–329.

Majority and Minority Reports of the Joint Committee of the Senate and House of Representatives Relative to an Investigation Into Any Corrupt Means Which May Have Been Employed by the Banks, of Their Agents, for the Purpose of Influencing the Actions of the Legislature, or Any Other Department of Government in Regard to Any Legislation for Their Benefit Accompanied with Testimony. Harrisburg: Henlock & Bratton, 1842.

Mangum, Willie Person. *Papers.* Vol. 4: *1844–1846.* Raleigh NC: State Department of Archives and History, 1950.

———. *Papers.* Vol. 5. Raleigh NC: State Dept. of Archives and History, 1950.

Marvel, William. *Mr. Lincoln Goes to War.* Boston: Houghton Mifflin, 2006.

McClellan, George Brinton, and Stephen W. Sears. *The Civil War Papers of George B. McClellan: Selected Correspondence, 1860–1865.* New York: Ticknor & Fields, 1989.

McClintock, Russell. *Lincoln and the Decision for War: The Northern Response to Secession.* Chapel Hill: University of North Carolina Press, 2008.

McClure, Alexander K. *Colonel Alexander K. McClure's Recollections of Half a Century.* Salem MA: Salem Press, 1902.

———. *Old Time Notes of Pennsylvania a Connected and Chronological Record of the Commercial, Industrial and Educational Advancement of Pennsylvania, and the Inner History of All Political Movements since the Adoption of the Constitution of 1838.* Philadelphia: J. C. Winston, 1905.

McCormick, Richard Patrick. *The Second American Party System: Party Formation in the Jacksonian Era.* Chapel Hill: University of North Carolina Press, 1966.

Mccrary, Royce C., Jr. "'The Long Agony Is Nearly Over': Samuel D. Ingham Reports on the Dissolution of Andrew Jackson's First Cabinet." *Pennsylvania Magazine of History and Biography* 100, no. 2 (April 1, 1976): 231–42.

McGinty, Brian. *The Body of John Merryman: Abraham Lincoln and the Suspension of Habeas Corpus.* Cambridge MA: Harvard University Press, 2011.

McNair, James Birtley. *Simon Cameron's Adventure in Iron, 1837–1846; New Biographical Material including an Account of the Formation and Dissolu-*

tion of a Partnership of Simon Cameron, S. F. Headley, Samuel Humes, and Thomas McNair for the Manufacture and Sale of Iron (principally to What Is Now the Pennsylvania Railroad) and Its Political Connotations. Los Angeles: Printed by author, 1949.

Meade, George Gordon. *The Life and Letters of George Gordon Meade: Major-General United States Army.* Vol. 1. New York: Charles Scribner's Sons, 1913.

Meneely, A. Howard. "Three Manuscripts of Gideon Welles." *American Historical Review* 31, no. 3 (April 1926): 484–94.

———. *The War Department, 1861: A Study in Mobilization and Administration.* New York: Columbia University Press, 1928.

Miers, Earl Schenck, and William E. Baringer. *Lincoln Day by Day: A Chronology, 1809–1865.* Dayton OH: Morningside, 1991.

Miller, Alphonse Bertram. *Thaddeus Stevens.* New York: Harper & Brothers, 1939.

Miller, David W. *Second Only to Grant: Quartermaster General Montgomery C. Meigs: A Biography.* Shippensburg PA: White Mane Books, 2000.

Mohr, James C. *Radical Republicans in the North: State Politics during Reconstruction.* Baltimore: Johns Hopkins University Press, 1976.

Montgomery, David. "Radical Republicanism in Pennsylvania, 1866–1873." *Pennsylvania Magazine of History and Biography* 85, no. 4 (October 1, 1961): 439–57.

Morrison, Chaplain W. *Democratic Politics and Sectionalism: The Wilmot Proviso Controversy.* Chapel Hill: University of North Carolina Press, 1967.

Mueller, Henry Richard. *The Whig Party in Pennsylvania.* Vol. 101. New York: Columbia University, 1922.

Murray, Robert B. "The Fremont-Adams Contracts." *Journal of the West* 5, no. 4 (October 1966): 518–19.

Myers, C. Maxwell. "The Influence of Western Pennsylvania in the Campaign of 1860." *The Western Pennsylvania Historical Magazine* 24 (1860): 229–50.

———. "The Rise of the Republican Party in Pennsylvania, 1854–1860." PhD diss., University of Pittsburgh, 1940.

Nash, Howard P., Jr. *Stormy Petrel: The Life and Times of General Benjamin F. Butler, 1818–1893.* Rutherford NJ: Fairleigh Dickinson University Press, 1969.

Neely, Mark E., Jr. "Civil War Issues in Pennsylvania: A Review Essay." *Pennsylvania Magazine of History and Biography* 135, no. 4 (October 1, 2011): 389–417.

———. *The Union Divided: Party Conflict in the Civil War North.* Cambridge MA: Harvard University Press, 2002.

Nevins, Allan. *The Emergence of Lincoln: Prologue to Civil War, 1859–1861.* New York: Scribner, 1950.

———. *The Emergence of Lincoln.* Vol. 1: *Douglas, Buchanan, and Party Chaos, 1857–1859.* New York: Scribner, 1950.

———. *Hamilton Fish: The Inner History of the Grant Administration*. New York: F. Ungar, 1957.

———. *Ordeal of the Union*. Vol. 1: *Fruits of Manifest Destiny, 1847–1852*. New York: Charles Scribner's Sons, 1975.

———. *Ordeal of the Union*. Vol. 2: *A House Dividing, 1852–1857*. New York: Charles Scribner's Sons, 1975.

———. *The War for the Union*. Vol. 1: *1861–1862: The Improved War*. New York: Scribner, 1959.

Newland, Samuel J. *The Pennsylvania Militia: Defending the Commonwealth and the Nation, 1669–1870*. Annville PA: Commonwealth of Pennsylvania, Dept. of Military and Veterans Affairs, 2002.

Nichols, Roy F. *The Democratic Machine: 1850–1854*. New York, 1923.

———. *The Disruption of American Democracy*. New York: Macmillan, 1948.

Nicklason, Fred. "The Civil War Contracts Committee." *Civil War History* 17, no. 3 (September 1971): 232–44.

———. "The Secession Winter and the Committee of Five." *Pennsylvania History* 38, no. 4 (October 1, 1971): 372–88.

Nicolay, John G. *An Oral History of Abraham Lincoln: John G. Nicolay's Interviews and Essays*. Edited by Michael Burlingame. Carbondale: Southern Illinois University Press, 1996.

Niven, John. *Gideon Welles: Lincoln's Secretary of the Navy*. Baton Rouge: Louisiana State University Press, 1994.

———. *Salmon P. Chase: A Biography*. New York: Oxford University Press, 1995.

Nolan, Dick. *Benjamin Franklin Butler: The Damnedest Yankee*. Novato CA: Presidio, 1991.

Oakes, James. "Reluctant to Emancipate? Another Look at the First Confiscation Act." *The Journal of the Civil War Era* 3, no. 4 (December 2013): 458–66.

Official Proceedings of the National Republican Conventions of 1868, 1872, 1876, and 1880. Minneapolis MN: C. W. Johnson, 1903.

Orr, Timothy J. "'We Are No Grumblers': Negotiating State and Federal Military Service in the Pennsylvania Reserve Division." *Pennsylvania Magazine of History and Biography* 135, no. 4 (2011): 447–80. http://www.jstor.org/stable/10.5215/pennmaghistbio.135.4.0447?ref=no-x-route:b6db56db63614730561acc0788593323. Accessed February 21, 2015.

Page, Elwin L. *Cameron for Lincoln's Cabinet*. Boston: Boston University Press, 1954.

Paludan, Phillip Shaw. *The Presidency of Abraham Lincoln*. Lawrence: University Press of Kansas, 1994.

Parrish, William E. "Fremont in Missouri." *Civil War Times Illustrated* 17 (April 1978): 4–45.

Parton, James. *Life of Andrew Jackson*. 3 vols. New York: Mason Brothers, 1860.

Paskoff, Paul F. *Industrial Evolution: Organization, Structure, and Growth of the Pennsylvania Iron Industry, 1750–1860*. Baltimore: Johns Hopkins University Press, 1983.

Patterson, Robert. *A Narrative of the Campaign in the Valley of the Shenandoah: In 1861*. Philadelphia, 1865.

Pendel, Thomas F. *Thirty-Six Years in the White House: Lincoln-Roosevelt*. Washington DC: Neale Publishing Company, 1902.

Perret, Geoffrey. *Lincoln's War: The Untold Story of America's Greatest President as Commander in Chief*. New York: Random House, 2004.

Peskin, Allan. *Winfield Scott and the Profession of Arms*. Kent OH: Kent State University Press, 2003.

Peterson, Merrill D. *The Great Triumvirate: Webster, Clay, and Calhoun*. New York: Oxford University Press, 1987.

Phillips, Kim T. "The Pennsylvania Origins of the Jackson Movement." *Political Science Quarterly* 91, no. 3 (1976): 489–508. http://www.jstor.org/stable/10.2307/2148938?ref=no-x-route:e9e2200ce225ea530f56e3c436628d04. Accessed February 21, 2015.

Pierson, William Whatley, Jr. "The Committee on the Conduct of the Civil War." *The American Historical Review* 23, no. 3 (April 1, 1918): 550–76.

Pincus, J. J. *Pressure Groups and Politics in Antebellum Tariffs*. New York: Columbia University Press, 1977.

Pindell, Richard. "'He Would Steal?' The Very Brief History Of The Very Brief Term Of Union Secretary Of War Simon Cameron." *Civil War Times Illustrated*, May/June 1990, 44–53.

Polk, James Knox. *Correspondence of James K. Polk*. Edited by Wayne Cutler. Vol. 8: *1844*. Knoxville: University of Tennessee Press, 1993.

———. *Correspondence of James K. Polk*. Edited by Wayne Cutler. Vol. 9: *January–June 1845*. Knoxville: University of Tennessee Press, 1996.

Polk, James K., and Milo Milton Quaife. *The Diary of James K. Polk during His Presidency, 1845–1849*. Vols. 1–4. Chicago: McClurg, 1910.

Potter, David M. *The Impending Crisis*. New York: Harper & Row, 1976.

———. *Lincoln and His Party in the Secession Crises*. New Haven CT: Yale University Press, 1962.

Prahl, A. J. "Bayard Taylor's Letters from Russia." *Huntington Library Quarterly* 9, no. 4 (August 1, 1946): 411–18.

Pratt, Harry E. "Simon Cameron's Fight for a Place in Lincoln's Cabinet." *Bulletin of the Abraham Lincoln Association* 49 (September 1937): 3–11.

Proceedings of The Convention, of the Integrity of the Union, Harrisburg. Harrisburg, 1837. http://library.duke.edu/digitalcollections/broadsides_bdspa012367/. Accessed March 10, 2015.

Proceedings of the National Democratic Convention: Held in the City of Baltimore, on the 5th of May, 1840. Embracing Resolutions, Expressive of the Sentiments of the Democratic Party of the Union: And an Address, in Support of the Principles and Measures of the Present National Administration. Baltimore: Printed at the Office of the Republican, 1840.

The Public Ledger Building, Philadelphia with an Account of the Proceedings Connected with Its Opening June 20, 1867. Philadelphia: George W. Childs, 1868.

Quarles, Benjamin. *The Negro in the Civil War.* Boston: Little, Brown, 1953.

Rafuse, Ethan Sepp. *McClellan's War: The Failure of Moderation in the Struggle for the Union.* Bloomington: Indiana University Press, 2005.

Randall, J. G. *Lincoln the President.* Vol. 1: *Springfield to Bull Run.* New York: Dodd, Mead, 1945.

———. *Lincoln the President.* Vol. 2: *Bull Run to Gettysburg.* New York: Dodd, Mead, 1945.

———. *Lincoln the President.* Vol. 3: *Midstream.* New York: Dodd, Mead, 1952.

Rawley, James A. *Edwin D. Morgan, 1811–1883: Merchant in Politics.* New York: Columbia University Press, 1955.

———. *The Politics of Union: Northern Politics during the Civil War.* Hinsdale IL: Dryden Press, 1974.

———. *Race and Politics: "Bleeding Kansas" and the Coming of the Civil War.* Philadelphia: Lippincott, 1969.

Rayback, Joseph G. *Free Soil; the Election of 1848.* Lexington: University Press of Kentucky, 1971.

Report of the Joint Committee on the Conduct of the War: In Three Parts. Washington DC: Government Printing Office, 1863.

Report of the Select Committee, Appointed to Investigate the Expenditures upon the Canals and Railroads of This State, Accompanied with the Minority Report and Testimony upon the Subject. Read in the House of Representatives, April 16, 1841. Harrisburg PA: J. S. Wallace, Printer, 1841.

Reports of the Joint Committee of the Legislature of Pennsylvania in Relation to Alleged Improper Influences in the Election of United States Senator. Harrisburg PA: A. Boyd Hamilton, 1855.

Reports of the Secretary of the Treasury of the United States. Vol. 5. Washington DC: John C. Rives, 1851.

Richards, Leonard L. *The Slave Power: The Free North and Southern Domination, 1780–1860.* Baton Rouge: Louisiana State University Press, 2000.

Richardson, Leon B. *William E. Chandler, Republican.* New York: Dodd, Mead, 1940.

Riddle, A. G. *The Life of Benjamin F. Wade.* Cleveland OH: W. W. Williams, 1886.

———. *Recollections of War Times; Reminiscences of Men and Events in Washington, 1860–1865.* New York: G. P. Putnam's Sons, 1895.

Rienow, Robert, and Leona Train Rienow. *Of Snuff, Sin, and the Senate.* Chicago: Follett Pub., 1965.

Risch, Erna. *Quartermaster Support of the Army: A History of the Corps, 1775–1939.* Washington DC: Center of Military History, U.S. Army, 1989.

Roadman, George. "Daniel Sturgeon, a Study in Obscurity." *Western Pennsylvania Historical Magazine* 37 (1954): 47–55.

Roberts, Jonathan. "Notes and Documents: Memoirs of a Senator from Pennsylvania: Jonathan Roberts, 1771–1854." *Pennsylvania Magazine of History and Biography* 61, no. 4 (October 1937): 446–74.

———. "Notes and Documents: Memoirs of a Senator from Pennsylvania: Jonathan Roberts, 1771–1854." *Pennsylvania Magazine of History and Biography* 62, no. 1 (January 1, 1938): 64–97.

———. "Notes and Documents: Memoirs of a Senator from Pennsylvania: Jonathan Roberts, 1771–1854." *Pennsylvania Magazine of History and Biography* 62, no. 2 (April 1938): 213–48.

———. "Notes and Documents: Memoirs of a Senator from Pennsylvania: Jonathan Roberts, 1771–1854." *Pennsylvania Magazine of History and Biography* 62, no. 3 (July 1938): 361–409.

———. "Notes and Documents: Memoirs of a Senator from Pennsylvania: Jonathan Roberts, 1771–1854." *Pennsylvania Magazine of History and Biography* 62, no. 4 (October 1938): 502–51.

Robinson, Elwyn Burns. "The 'Press': President Lincoln's Philadelphia Organ." *Pennsylvania Magazine of History and Biography* 65, no. 2 (April 1, 1941): 157–70.

Robinson, Michael. "William Henry Seward and the Onset of the Secession Crisis." *Civil War History* 59, no. 1 (March 2013): 32–66.

Romero, Matías. *A Mexican View of America in the 1860s: A Foreign Diplomat Describes the Civil War and Reconstruction.* Translated and edited by Thomas David Schoonover and Ebba Wesener Schoonover. Rutherford NJ: Fairleigh Dickinson University Press, 1991.

Roske, Ralph Joseph. *His Own Counsel: The Life and Times of Lyman Trumbull.* Reno: University of Nevada Press, 1979.

Rothman, David J. *Politics and Power: The United States Senate, 1869–1901.* Cambridge MA: Harvard University Press, 1966.

Russell, William H. "A. K. McClure and the People's Party in the Campaign of 1860." *Pennsylvania History* 28, no. 4 (October 1, 1961): 335–45.

———. "A Biography of Alexander K. McClure." PhD diss., University of Wisconsin, 1953.

Russell, William H., and Martin Crawford. *William Howard Russell's Civil War: Private Diary and Letters, 1861–1862.* Athens: University of Georgia Press, 1992.

Salter, William. *The Life of James W. Grimes Governor of Iowa, 1854–1858; a Senator of the United States, 1859–1869.* New York: D. Appleton, 1876.

Sandberg, Carl. *Abraham Lincoln: The War Years, 1861–1864.* New York: Dell Publishing, 1967.

Sandow, Robert M. "The Limits of Northern Patriotism: Early Civil War Mobilization in Pennsylvania." *Pennsylvania History* 70, no. 2 (April 1, 2003): 175–203.

Saul, Norman E. *Distant Friends: The United States and Russia, 1763–1867.* Lawrence: University Press of Kansas, 1991.

Savage, John. *Our Living Representative Men.* Philadelphia: Childs & Peterson, 1860.

Schuckers, J. W. *The Life and Public Services of Salmon Portland Chase, United States Senator and Governor of Ohio; Secretary of the Treasury and Chief-Justice of the United States.* New York: D. Appleton, 1874.

Schurz, Carl, Frederic Bancroft, and William Archibald Dunning. *The Reminiscences of Carl Schurz.* Vol. 2. Garden City: Doubleday, Page, 1908.

———. *The Reminiscences of Carl Schurz.* Vol. 3. Garden City: Doubleday, Page, 1908.

Sears, Stephen W. *George B. McClellan: The Young Napoleon.* New York: Ticknor & Fields, 1988.

Sellers, Charles Grier. *James K. Polk: Continentalist, 1843–1846.* Vol. 2. Princeton NJ: Princeton University Press, 1966.

Sewell, Richard H. *Ballots for Freedom: Antislavery Politics in the United States, 1837–1860.* New York: Oxford University Press, 1976.

Shankman, Arnold. "Francis W. Hughes and the 1862 Pennsylvania Election." *Pennsylvania Magazine of History and Biography* 95, no. 3 (1971): 383–93. http://www.jstor.org/stable/10.2307/20090572?ref=no-x-route :af057c9faf3ab6fc1d68c28d5bb8dcab. Accessed February 21, 2015.

Shannon, Fred A. *The Organization and Administration of the Union Army.* 2 vols. Bethesda MD: University Publications of America, 1994.

Sheep, James Thompson. *John W. Forney Stormy Petrel of American Journalism.* 1959.

Shelden, Rachel A. "Messmates' Union: Friendship, Politics, and Living Arrangements in the Capital City, 1845–1861." *Journal of the Civil War Era* 1, no. 4 (2011): 453–80. doi:10.1353/cwe.2011.0069.

———. *Washington Brotherhood: Politics, Social Life, and the Coming of the Civil War.* Chapel Hill: University of North Carolina Press, 2013.

Shelling, Richard I. "Philadelphia and the Agitation in 1825 for the Pennsylvania Canal." *Pennsylvania Magazine of History and Biography* 62, no. 2 (1938): 175–204. http://www.jstor.org/stable/10.2307/20087108?ref=no-x -route:8f50f1af1635cff4d3d83e51c23eef01. Accessed February 21, 2015.

Shenton, James P. *Robert John Walker, a Politician from Jackson to Lincoln.* New York: Columbia University Press, 1961.

Sherman, John. *John Sherman's Recollections of Forty Years in the House, Senate and Cabinet: An Autobiography.* Vol. 1. Chicago: Werner, 1895.

Sherman, William T. *Memoirs of General W.T. Sherman.* Vols. 1 and 2. New York: Literary Classics of the United States, 1990.

Sherman, William T., John Sherman, and Rachel Sherman Thorndike. *The Sherman Letters; Correspondence between General and Senator Sherman from 1837 to 1891.* New York: C. Scribner's Sons, 1894.

Shields, Johanna Nicol. *The Line of Duty: Maverick Congressmen and the Development of American Political Culture, 1836–1860.* Westport CT: Greenwood Press, 1985.

Simpson, Brooks D. "Review: Two More Roads to Sumter." *Reviews in American History* 17, no. 2 (1989): 225–31. http://www.jstor.org/stable/10.2307/2702923?ref=no-x-route:f68d80c725983fac18177078fe231c5b. Accessed February 21, 2015.

Sioussat, George L., ed. *Tennessee Historical Magazine.* Vol. 2. Nashville: Tennessee Historical Society, 1920.

———, ed. *Tennessee Historical Magazine.* Vol. 3. Nashville: Tennessee Historical Society, 1920.

Slaughter, Thomas P. *Bloody Dawn: The Christiana Riot and Racial Violence in the Antebellum North.* New York: Oxford University Press, 1991.

Smith, Adam I. P. *No Party Now: Politics in the Civil War North.* Oxford: Oxford, 2006.

Smith, Culver H. *The Press, Politics, and Patronage: The American Government's Use of Newspapers, 1789–1875.* Athens: University of Georgia Press, 1977.

Smith, David G. *On the Edge of Freedom: The Fugitive Slave Issue in South Central Pennsylvania, 1820–1870.* New York: Fordham University Press, 2013.

Smith, Elbert B. *Francis Preston Blair.* New York: Free Press, 1980.

———. *The Presidency of James Buchanan.* Lawrence: University Press of Kansas, 1975.

Smith, Wayne. "Pennsylvania and the American Civil War: Recent Trends and Interpretations." *Pennsylvania History* 51, no. 3 (July 1, 1984): 206–31.

Snyder, Charles McCool. *The Jacksonian Heritage: Pennsylvania Politics, 1833–1848.* Harrisburg: Pennsylvania Historical and Museum Commission, 1958.

Soldon, Norbert Carroll. "James Donald Cameron: Pennsylvania Politician." PhD diss., Pennsylvania State University, 1959.

Speiser, Matt. "The Ticket's Other Half: How and Why Andrew Johnson Received the 1864 Vice Presidential Nomination." *Tennessee Historical Quarterly* 65, no. 1 (April 1, 2006): 42–69.

Spout, Oliver S. "James Buchanan, "Big Wheel" of the Railroads." *Papers of Lancaster County Historical Society* 56 (1952): 22–34.

Sprague, Dean. *Freedom under Lincoln.* Boston: Houghton Mifflin, 1965.

Sprankling, Thomas. "'Pennsylvania's for Lincoln': Measuring the Keystone State's Impact on the Early Electoral Success of the Republican Party." *Foundations: An Undergraduate Journal in History* 3, no. 1 (2008): 5–16.

Stahr, Walter. *Seward: Lincoln's Indispensable Man.* New York: Simon & Schuster, 2012.

Stampp, Kenneth M. *America in 1857: A Nation on the Brink.* New York: Oxford University Press, 1990.

———. *And the War Came: The North and the Secession Crisis, 1860–61.* Chicago: University of Chicago Press, 1964.

Steele, Henry. "The Life and Public Service of Governor George Wolfe, 1777–1840." *Proceedings and Addresses of the Pennsylvania German Society* 39 (1930): 5–25.

Stenberg, Richard R. "Jackson, Buchanan, and the 'Corrupt Bargain' Calumny." *Pennsylvania Magazine of History and Biography* 58, no. 1 (1934): 61–85. http://www.jstor.org/stable/10.2307/20086857?ref=no-x-route:f299410cf86b26a9a2289699b5a7a0b9. Accessed February 21, 2015.

———. "The Motivation of the Wilmot Proviso." *The Mississippi Valley Historical Review* 18, no. 4 (1932): 535–48. http://www.jstor.org/stable/10.2307/1898562?ref=no-x-route:21a7376d0cf5853d90bdf6cd36db29b0. Accessed February 21, 2015.

Stevens, Thaddeus. *The Selected Papers of Thaddeus Stevens.* Edited by Beverly Wilson Palmer and Holly Byers Ochoa. Vol. 1: *January 1814–March 1865.* Pittsburgh: University of Pittsburgh Press, 1997.

———. *The Selected Papers of Thaddeus Stevens.* Edited by Beverly Wilson Palmer and Holly Byers Ochoa. Vol. 2: *April 1865–August 1868.* Pittsburgh: University of Pittsburgh Press, 1998.

Stewart, David O. *Impeached: The Trial of President Andrew Johnson and the Fight for Lincoln's Legacy.* New York: Simon & Schuster, 2009.

Stewart, John D. "The Deal for Philadelphia: Simon Cameron and the Genesis of a Political Machine, 1867–1872." *Lancaster County Historical Society* 77 (1972): 41–52.

———. "The Great Winnebago Chieftain: Simon Cameron's Rise to Power 1860–1867." *Pennsylvania History* 39, no. 1 (1972): 20–39. http://www.jstor.org/stable/10.2307/27771991?ref=no-x-route:b945aaa584cdf3660ea c18d231b5370b. Accessed February 21, 2015.

Stewart, William M., and George Rothwell Brown. *Reminiscences of Senator William M. Stewart, of Nevada.* New York: Neale Pub., 1908.

Street, Ida M. *The Simon Cameron Indian Commission of 1838.* N.p.: N.p., 1905.

Strong, George Templeton, and Allan Nevins. *Diary of the Civil War, 1860–1865.* New York: Macmillan, 1962.

Summers, Festus P. "The Baltimore and Ohio—First in War." *Civil War History* 7, no. 3 (September 1961): 239–54.

Summers, Mark W. "The Spoils of War." *North and South* 6, no. 2 (February 2003): 82–89.

Sumner, Charles. *The Selected Letters of Charles Sumner.* Edited by Beverly Wilson Palmer. Vol. 1: *1830–1859.* Boston: Northeastern University Press, 1990.

———. *The Selected Letters of Charles Sumner.* Edited by Beverly Wilson Palmer. Vol. 2: *1859–1874.* Boston: Northeastern University Press, 1990.

Tap, Bruce. *Over Lincoln's Shoulder: The Committee on the Conduct of the War.* Lawrence: University Press of Kansas, 1998.

Taussig, F. W. *The Tariff History of the United States.* New York: G. P. Putnam's Sons, 1931.

Taylor, Bayard, and John Richie Schultz. *The Unpublished Letters of Bayard Taylor in the Huntington Library.* San Marino CA, 1937.

Taylor, Bayard, Marie Hansen Taylor, and Horace Elisha Scudder. *Life and Letters of Bayard Taylor.* Vol. 1. Boston: Houghton, Mifflin, 1884.

Taylor, Brian. "A Politics of Service: Black Northerners' Debates over Enlistment in the American Civil War." *Civil War History* 58, no. 4 (December 2012): 451–80.

Taylor, John M. *William Henry Seward: Lincoln's Right Hand.* New York: HarperCollins, 1991.

Taylor, Zachary. *Letters of Zachary Taylor: From the Battle-Fields of the Mexican War.* Rochester NY: William K. Bixby, 1908.

Thomas, Benjamin Platt. *Abraham Lincoln: A Biography.* New York: Knopf, 1952.

Thomas, Benjamin Platt, and Harold Melvin Hyman. *Stanton: The Life and Times of Lincoln's Secretary of War.* New York: Knopf, 1962.

Thompson, William I. "The U.S. Sanitary Commission." *Civil War History* 2 (1956): 41–61.

Tinkcom, Harry Marlin. *John White Geary, Soldier-statesman, 1819–1873.* Philadelphia: University of Pennsylvania Press, 1940.

Tipton, Thomas Weston. *Forty Years of Nebraska at Home and in Congress.* Lincoln NE: State Journal, Printers, 1902.

Tomek, Beverly C. *Colonization and Its Discontents: Emancipation, Emigration, and Antislavery in Antebellum Pennsylvania.* New York: New York University Press, 2011.

Toomey, Daniel Carroll. *The War Came by Train: The Baltimore & Ohio Railroad during the Civil War.* Baltimore MD: Baltimore & Ohio Railroad Museum, 2013.

Trefousse, Hans L. "The Joint Committee on the Conduct of the War: A Reassessment." *Civil War History* 10, no. 1 (March 1964): 5–19.

———. *Thaddeus Stevens: Nineteenth-century Egalitarian.* Chapel Hill: University of North Carolina Press, 1997.

Trefousse, Hans Louis. *Benjamin Franklin Wade: Radical Republican from Ohio, Hans Louis Trefousse.* New York: Twayne Publishers, 1963.

Truman, Ben. "In the Convival Days of Old." *Overland Monthly and Out West Magazine* 55, no. 3 (March 1910): 317–22.

Tucker, Leslie R. *Major General Isaac Ridgeway Trimble: Biography of a Baltimore Confederate*. Jefferson NC: McFarland, 2005.

Turner, George Edgar. *Victory Rode the Rails: The Strategic Place of the Railroads in the Civil War*. Indianapolis: Bobbs-Merrill, 1953.

Tyler, Lyon Gardiner. *The Letters and times of the Tylers*. Vol. 2. New York: Da Capo Press, 1970.

United States. Congress. House. *Reports to the House of Representatives*. 25th Cong., 3d sess. H. Rept. 229. Washington DC, 1839.

United States. War Department. *The War of Rebellion: A Compilation of the Official Records of the Union and Confederate Armies*. Ser. 3, vol. 1. Washington DC: Government Printing Office, 1899.

Voss-Hubbard, Mark. *Beyond Party: Cultures of Antipartisanship in Northern Politics before the Civil War*. Baltimore: Johns Hopkins University Press, 2002.

Waggoner, Linda M. *"Neither White Men nor Indians": Affidavits from the Winnebago Mixed-Blood Claim Commissions, Prairie Du Chien, Wisconsin, 1838–1839*. Roseville MN: Park Genealogical Books, 2002.

Walton, Joseph S. "Nominating Conventions in Pennsylvania." *The American Historical Review* 2, no. 2 (1897): 262–78. http://www.jstor.org/stable/10.2307/1833866?ref=no-x-route:be7d2051e3234bddd9702ef322b0f501. Accessed February 21, 2015.

Ward, James Arthur. *J. Edgar Thomson: Master of the Pennsylvania*. Westport CT: Greenwood Press, 1980.

Ward, John William. *Andrew Jackson: Symbol for an Age*. New York: Oxford University Press, 1955.

Wasson, R. Gordon. *The Hall Carbine Affair; a Study in Contemporary Folklore*. New York: Pandick Press, 1948.

Weber, Thomas. *The Northern Railroads in the Civil War, 1861–1865*. New York: King's Crown Press, 1952.

Webster, Daniel. *The Papers of Daniel Webster*. Edited by Charles M. Wiltse and Harold D. Moser. Vol. 4: *1835–1839*. Hanover NH: Published for Dartmouth College by the University Press of New England, 1980.

———. *The Papers of Daniel Webster*. Vol. 6: *1844–1849*. Hanover NH: Published for Dartmouth College by the University Press of New England, 1984.

Weed, Thurlow, Harriet A. Weed, and Thurlow Weed Barnes. *Life of Thurlow Weed including His Autobiography and a Memoir*. 2 vols. Boston: Houghton Mifflin, 1884.

Weeden, William B. *War Government, Federal and State, in Massachusetts, New York, Pennsylvania, and Indiana, 1861–1865*. New York: Da Capo Press, 1972.

Weidman, John. *Rejoinder to the Defence Published by Simon Cameron, February 6th, 1855, to the Charges Made against Him as Commissioner to Carry into Effect the Treaty with the Half-breed Winnebago Indians. Also Public Document*

No. 229, of House of Representatives of U.S., 25th Congress, 3d Session: To the Members of the Senate and House of Representatives of Pennsylvania, and All Others Whom It May Concern. N.p., 1855.

Weigley, Russell Frank. *A Great Civil War: A Military and Political History, 1861–1865*. Bloomington: Indiana University Press, 2000.

———. *Quartermaster General of the Union Army: A Biography of M. C. Meigs*. New York: Columbia University Press, 1959.

Welch, Richard E. *George Frisbie Hoar and the Half-breed Republicans*. Cambridge: Harvard University Press, 1971.

Welles, Gideon. *Diary of Gideon Welles, Secretary of the Navy under Lincoln and Johnson*. Edited by John T. Morse. 3 vols. Boston: Houghton Mifflin, 1911.

West, Richard S. *Lincoln's Scapegoat General: A Life of Benjamin F. Butler, 1818–1893*. Boston: Houghton Mifflin, 1965.

White, Jonathan W. *Abraham Lincoln and Treason in the Civil War: The Trials of John Merryman*. Baton Rouge: Louisiana State University Press, 2011.

Widmer, Edward L. *Martin Van Buren*. New York: Times Books, 2005.

Wilentz, Sean. *The Rise of American Democracy: Jefferson to Lincoln*. New York: W. W. Norton, 2005.

Williams, Kenneth P., and Clark Ray. *Lincoln Finds a General: A Military Study of the Civil War*. Vol. 1. New York: Macmillan, 1949.

Williams, T. Harry. *Lincoln and the Radicals*. Madison: University of Wisconsin Press, 1941.

Wilson, Henry. "Edwin M. Stanton." *Atlantic Monthly* 25 (1870): 238.

Wilson, Mark. *The Business of Civil War: Military Mobilization and the State, 1861–1865*. Baltimore MD: Johns Hopkins University Press, 2006.

Wilson, Rufus Rockwell. *Intimate Memories of Lincoln*. Elmira NY: Primavera Press, 1945.

Winkle, Kenneth J. *Lincoln's Citadel: The Civil War in Washington DC*. New York: W. W. Norton, 2013.

Winston, James E. "Pennsylvania and the Independence of Texas." *The Southwestern Historical Quarterly* 17, no. 3 (1914): 262–82. http://www.jstor.org /stable/10.2307/30234601?ref=no-x-route:613a3fda709fa42c407a6221 f42c600e. Accessed February 21, 2015.

Withers, Robert Enoch. *Autobiography of an Octogenarian*. Roanoke VA: Stone Print. & Mfg. Press, 1907.

Woodford, Frank B. *Lewis Cass: The Last Jeffersonian*. New Brunswick: Rutgers University Press, 1950.

Woodward, C. Vann, ed. *Mary Chesnut's Civil War*. New Haven CT: Yale University Press, 1983.

Zornow, William Frank. *Lincoln (and) the Party Divided*. Westport CT: Greenwood Press, 1972.

INDEX

abolition of slavery: abolitionism and, 3, 28, 69, 77, 80–82, 113, 116, 123, 126, 129–30, 132, 134, 136, 143, 184, 188–91, 195, 197–99, 201–2, 215, 219, 222, 228, 231, 258; abolitionists and, 3, 77, 81–82, 113, 116, 123, 126, 130, 132, 143, 184, 189–91, 195, 198–99, 202, 215, 222, 228, 231; Abraham Lincoln and, 143, 190–91, 195, 198–99, 202, 215; Simon Cameron and, 3, 28, 81–82, 116, 126, 184, 189, 198–99, 202, 215, 222

Adams, John, 7

Adams, John Q.: 1824 presidential election and, 16–17; 1828 presidential election and, 18–19; cabinet of, 18; "corrupt bargain" and, 16–17; presidential administration of, 17–20; Simon Cameron and, 17–19

Alexander II (Czar of Russia), 219–21. *See also* Russia

Anderson, Robert, 159

Army, U.S.: American War of Independence and, 5; Brua Cameron and, 79; Civil War and, 210–14, 292; enlistment of African Americans into, 3, 203, 205, 292; Simon Cameron's attitude toward, 79, 165–66; volunteers in, 78–79, 163, 170–72, 176, 180, 185–86, 197, 199, 203, 223, 229, 236

Arthur, Chester A., 283–84

Baltimore & Ohio (B&O) railroad, 94–95, 161–64. *See also* Garrett, John W.

Baltimore MD: 1832 Democratic National Convention in, 25; 1844 Democratic National Convention in, 42; 1848 Democratic National Convention in, 88; riot in, 161–62, 193

Bank of Middletown, 22–23, 31, 50, 56, 93, 129, 187, 287

Bates, Edward, 141, 150, 194, 196, 201, 206–8, 210, 215

Beauregard, Pierre G. T., 159, 184

Belknap, William W., 268

Benton, Thomas H., 50, 53

Bigelow, John, 207, 211

Bigler, William, 99, 102, 111, 118, 121

bimetallism, 265. *See also* monometallism

Bingham, John A., 247

Blaine, James G., 268–69

Blair, Francis P., 46–51, 61, 114. See also *Globe* (newspaper)

Blair, Montgomery, 195–96, 200, 202, 204, 208, 213. See also *Globe* (newspaper)

Borie, Adolph E., 250

Breckenridge, John C., 143, 148

Brewster, Benjamin H., 215, 242, 284

Bristow, Benjamin H., 277, 280

Brodhead, Daniel M., 31, 34–38, 40. *See also* Winnebagos (Native Americans)
Brodhead, Richard, 97, 115, 119, 123
Brooks, Preston, 122. *See also* Sumner, Charles
Bryant, William C., 189
Buchanan, James: 1856 presidential election and, 112–15; and "Buccaneers," 20, 130; and Kansas-Nebraska Act, 103, 106–7, 112; and Lecompton constitution, 119–20; Pennsylvania's Democratic Party and, 19, 42, 52–56, 62, 85–86, 88, 97–100; presidential administration of, 119, 121, 127, 129–33; as secretary of state, 48, 61–62, 64–65, 67, 79, 83–85; Simon Cameron and, 19–20, 26, 28, 54–55, 88–91, 97–102
Buckalew, Charles R., 109, 225–26
Bucks County PA, 9–10, 47
Bull Run, Battle of, 183–86, 190, 286

Cadwalader, George, 192, 227–28
Calhoun, John C., 16, 23–24, 47, 49, 59, 76–77, 80, 119, 206
California, 78, 113, 115
Cameron, Catherine (daughter), 26
Cameron, Catherine (sister), 285
Cameron, James (brother), 13–14, 19, 26–27, 42, 79, 87, 185, 190, 286–87
Cameron, J. Donald, 14, 27, 95, 97, 105, 163, 220–21, 243, 249, 251, 257–58, 261–63, 265, 267–72, 275, 278, 282–84, 286–87, 290
Cameron, John (brother), 13, 26, 94–95
Cameron, Maggie, 14, 218, 288–89
Cameron, Margaret (wife), 264, 289
Cameron, Rachel, 14, 27, 128, 220, 264
Cameron, Simon: 1864 presidential election and, 231–37; as adjutant general, 13–14; as ambassador to Great Britain, 272; as ambassador to Russia, 218–19, 222; apprenticeship of, 6–7, 9, 19, 104; and Bank of Mid-

dletown, 22–23, 31, 50, 56, 93, 129, 187, 287; and Battle of Gettysburg, 229–30; birthday of, 6, 28, 283, 285, 288; and bribery allegations, 35, 110, 117, 120, 149, 226; and canals, 13, 18, 20–22; and Catholicism, 105–6; censure of, by House of Representatives, 216–17, 267; and champagne, 14, 256, 277, 284; and civil service reform, 258, 270, 291; and Committee on Foreign Relations, 253–56, 268; and contraband, 198, 200; and corruption allegations, 1, 3–4, 31, 35, 38–39, 54, 99, 102, 108–9, 117–18, 149, 151, 155, 165, 168–69, 175–76, 182, 191, 213, 237, 243, 259–60, 291; death of, 283, 287–88, 290; departure of, from Lincoln's cabinet, 205, 207–8, 210–11, 215, 223; and Donegal (estate), 129, 222, 281, 283–84, 286, 289; and Emancipation Proclamation, 223; and enlistment of African Americans, 3, 203, 205, 292; and Fort Monroe, 197–98, 233–34; and Fort Sumter, 157–59, 178–79; and Fugitive Slave Law, 107; funeral of, 289–90; generosity of, 2, 7, 27, 96, 126, 128, 145, 239, 245, 286–87; and *Globe*, 48–51, 114; grandchildren of, 276, 283, 285–87, 289; as "Great Winnebago Chief," 29–57, 108, 168; and Habeas Corpus Act, 192; and Hall Carbine Affair, 174; Harrisburg home of, 217, 239, 271, 283, 289; and iron business, 22, 72; and John Merryman, 192, 227–28; Know-Nothings and, 2, 104–16; and Maryland state legislature, 193–94; and nativism, 10, 53, 106; opinion of, of Abraham Lincoln, 145; and patronage, 7–8, 11, 13, 17–18, 20, 28–30, 52, 62, 65, 97, 101–4, 133, 155, 168–69, 212, 215, 217, 224, 237–39, 241, 246, 250, 254, 257–60, 262, 266–67, 271, 292; and *Pennsylvania Reporter and*

Democratic Herald, 14, 22; and Pierce Butler, 192–93, 215–16; and Presbyterianism, 54, 253, 286; and procurement, 173–74, 180–82, 188, 213, 291; and railroads, 22, 93–95, 126, 139, 153, 161–64, 171, 224, 226–27, 245, 257–58, 261, 264–65, 285; resignations of, 221–23, 271; as secretary of war, 95–96, 155, 157–93, 195–200, 202–14, 216–17, 232, 236, 238, 247, 264, 268, 291; and sectionalism, 2, 75–76, 81, 121, 124, 245–46; as senator, 19–20, 30, 52–53, 86, 89–91, 93, 95–99, 103–4, 107–9, 111, 113, 115, 132–33, 137, 144, 146, 149, 153, 157, 169–70, 183, 209, 212, 215, 217–18, 220, 224–28, 235, 238–39, 271, 279, 282, 284; as senator in 1845–49, 54–55, 59–60, 64–69, 71–76, 81–82, 86; as senator in 1857–61, 117–28; as senator in 1867–77, 245–46, 251–58, 263–64, 266, 271; and slavery, 3, 107, 126, 134, 136, 143; and spoils system, 1, 25–26, 30, 169, 260, 271, 291; and suffrage for African Americans, 243, 251; and tariffs, 15, 41, 46, 53, 57, 68–75, 121, 126–29, 134, 144, 243; visit of, to France, 218; and Wilmot Proviso, 81–82, 98, 107; and Winnebago scandal, 28–57, 108, 118, 149, 168–69, 191

Cameron, Simon (younger), 14, 128–29, 278, 283, 288–90

Cameron, Virginia, 14, 27, 242, 277, 288–89. *See also* MacVeagh, Wayne

Cameron, William (brother), 26, 94, 220, 285

Cameron, William Brua, 27, 79, 97

Campbell, James, 102

Carnegie, Andrew, 166, 286

Casey, Joseph, 149, 153

Cass, Lewis, 44, 86, 88–90, 99–100, 114

Centennial International Exposition, 272

Chandler, Zachariah, 123, 258

Chase, Salmon: 1856 presidential election and, 113; 1860 presidential election and, 137, 141–42; as "Attorney General for Fugitive Slaves," 113; death of, 264; and enlistment of African Americans, 200, 203; and patronage, 217–18, 224; as secretary of the Treasury, 152, 155, 168–69, 206; and Simon Cameron's departure from Lincoln's cabinet, 207–9, 211–13, 223; and the War Department, 166, 169, 179–80, 190–91, 209; and William Seward, 211, 221

Chicago IL, 31, 133–35, 138–39, 141–43, 149–50, 248–49, 282

Clay, Cassius M., 209, 219–20, 222–23

Clay, Henry, 15–20, 46, 49, 209, 219–20, 222–23

Cleveland, Grover, 282

Clymer, Hiester, 242

Cochrane, John, 200–202

Colfax, Schuyler, 262

Congress, U.S., 40, 110, 117–19, 130, 187–89, 192, 215, 268

Conkling, Roscoe, 258, 273

Constitution, U.S., 16, 251, 252

Cooke, Jay, 187, 249, 265

Coryell, Lewis, 30, 50

Covode, John, 130, 228, 230

Cowan, Edgar, 153, 241–43

Crawford, William, 15–16

Crippen, Lee F., 44, 88, 111

Crittenden, John J., 120–21

Cummings, Alexander, 154, 173, 216, 238

Curtin, Andrew G.: 1863 gubernatorial election and, 228–31; 1866 Senate campaign and, 241–50; 1868 presidential election and, 248–50; as ambassador to Russia, 250, 259; efforts of, to prevent Simon Cameron from joining Lincoln's cabinet, 151, 154; as governor of Pennsylvania, 145–48, 162, 171, 174, 215, 225–26;

Curtin, Andrew G. (*cont.*)
Liberal Republicans and, 250–52;
Ulysses S. Grant and, 250–52; War
Department and, 167, 176–77, 185.
See also McClure, Alexander

Dallas, George M., 9, 24, 53–56, 59–
63, 72–73, 75, 86, 88, 91
Dana, Charles, 236
Datcher, Francis, 205–6
Dauphin County PA, 13, 15, 17, 19, 27,
79, 85, 95–96, 112, 229
Davis, David, 140–41, 143–44, 147,
149–50, 152
Davis, Jefferson, 44, 81, 87–88, 98,
124–25, 238, 252
Dawes, Henry, 168, 206, 212
Dayton, William L., 114, 142, 218
Delahay, Mark, 139
Democratic Party: 1832 Democratic
National Convention and, 25; 1844
Democratic National Convention
and, 42; 1848 Democratic National
Convention and, 88; 1860 presiden-
tial election and, 131–32, 138, 142–
43; factionalism of, 41, 51–53, 56,
61–63, 85–86, 97, 102–3; Jacksonians
and, 23; James K. Polk and, 44–46,
61, 66, 90; and Liberal Republicans,
261–62; Pennsylvania and, 29, 41, 51,
53–57, 75, 85, 91, 100, 103, 115, 119,
143, 224–26, 229, 237; two-thirds
rule and, 43
Dennison, William, Jr., 164, 177
Dix, John A., 174, 194
Donelson, Andrew J., 48–51. See also
Washington Union (newspaper)
Douglas, Stephen A., 100, 103, 114,
120, 131–32, 137, 142, 148
Doylestown PA, 9, 11–12
Dred Scott v. Sanford, 113, 125, 131–32,
252

Eaton, John, 25
Emancipation Proclamation, 201–2,
223, 236

Errett, Russell, 122, 133, 230, 236, 249,
258, 261
Europe, 127, 190, 218, 256, 285, 287

Family Party. *See* Dallas, George M.;
Ingham, Samuel D.
Federalist Party, 7, 19
Fessenden, William P., 235
Fillmore, Millard, 115
Findlay, William, 12
Fish, Hamilton, 250–51, 256, 267
Florida, 65, 76, 178, 270, 276, 282, 285
Forney, John W.: 1857 Senate election
and, 116–17; 1860 presidential elec-
tion and, 133; 1867 Senate election
and, 243; and Andrew G. Curtin,
228; death of, 285; and Pennsylvania
gubernatorial elections, 240, 261–
62; and *The Pennsylvanian*, 62, 99;
and Simon Cameron's desire to enlist
African Americans, 202; and Ulysses
S. Grant, 256
Fort Pickens, 159, 178, 180
Fort Sumter, 157–59, 178–79
Frazer, Reah, 96, 137
Free Soilers, 90, 112
Fremont, John C.: 1856 presidential
election and, 113–15; and the Civil
War, 174, 191, 194–97, 200, 202, 208;
and Pennsylvania, 114; removal of,
from command, 194–97, 200, 202,
208

Garfield, James A., 281, 283
Garrett, John W., 95, 162, 164
Garrison, William L., 81
Geary, John W., 240–42, 260–61
Germany, 96, 105, 136, 218, 221, 256,
290
Gettysburg, Battle of, 229–30
Gettysburg PA, 228–30
Globe (newspaper), 46–51, 61, 114. *See
also* Blair, Francis P.
Grahl, Peter, 6
Grant, Ulysses S.: and *Alabama* claims,
255; and annexation of Santo

Domingo, 253; cabinet of, 250, 258, 266–71, 278, 283–84; and corruption allegations, 259–60; and Inflation Bill of 1874, 265; and Liberal Republicans, 259, 261–63; and Oregon, 255; presidential administration of, 250, 253, 255–56, 258–59, 267–68; relationship of, with Charles Sumner, 253–55, 264; and Senate Committee on Foreign Relations, 253–56, 268

Great Britain: and Oregon Territory, 60, 83–84; Russia and, 218–19; Simon Cameron as potential ambassador to, 272, 275; U.S. commerce with, 23, 76

Greeley, Horace, 259, 263

Grow, Galusha, 183, 242–43

Hall Carbine Affair, 174

Halleck, Henry W., 169

Hamlin, Hannibal, 143, 146, 232, 234–35

Harrisburg PA, 186–87

Harrison, William H., 41, 76

Hartranft, John F., 261–62, 271

Hay, John, 144, 175, 189

Hayes, Rutherford: 1876 presidential election and, 246, 269–70; 1880 presidential election and, 282; cabinet of, 270, 284; and civil service reform, 258, 270–71, 291; opinion of, of Charles Sumner, 254; opinion of, of Simon Cameron, 258, 283; presidential administration of, 273; and Simon Cameron as potential ambassador to Great Britain, 272–73, 275

Heiss, John P., 47–50. See also Globe (newspaper)

Hitchcock, Ethan A., 31, 33–38, 169. See also Winnebagos (Native Americans)

Holt, Michael, 106, 112, 120

Horn, Henry, 62–65, 67

Illinois, 16, 100, 103, 112, 115, 120, 131, 138–39, 142, 177, 183, 191, 204, 210

Indiana, 27, 115, 120, 137, 181, 216, 258

Ingham, Samuel D., 9, 11, 16, 24, 26

Iowa, 103, 112, 138, 177

Jackson, Andrew: 1824 presidential election and, 15–17; 1828 presidential election and, 18–19, 26; 1832 presidential election and, 42, 231; cabinet of, 24; Globe and, 46–51; and Jacksonians, 15–20, 23, 25, 28, 40–41, 44–46, 65, 80, 87, 291; James Buchanan and, 19–20, 24, 29; James K. Polk and, 44–47; Mexico and, 76; opinion of, of Simon Cameron, 24, 51; Pennsylvania and, 23–25, 41, 61; presidential administration of, 23–26, 30, 41; Simon Cameron and, 15, 18–19, 25, 28–29, 41, 51, 231; as a "symbol for an age," 1;

Jefferson, Thomas, 8, 15, 87, 237

Johnson, Andrew: cabinet of, 247; and Edwin Stanton, 247–48; impeachment of, 247–48; presidential administration of, 240; Reconstruction policies of, 240–42, 246–47; as vice president, 234–36

Johnston, William F., 114

Kane, John K., 45–46, 63, 71–72, 85. See also tariffs

Kane, Thomas L., 251, 259

Kansas-Nebraska Act, 103, 106–7, 112

Kelley, Brooks M., 41, 164, 168

Kemble, William H., 257, 260

Kentucky, 16, 120, 171, 175, 194, 201, 205, 219, 222, 276

Kirkpatrick, John M., 106–7

Know-Nothings, 2, 104–16. See also nativists

Krause, David, 14, 17, 19

Lancaster County PA, 5, 96, 105, 222, 289

Lancaster PA, 13, 22, 55, 83, 87

Leib, Charles, 134, 138, 143, 213
Liberal Republicans, 259, 261–63
Lincoln, Abraham: and administration policy toward escaped slaves, 194–99; and allegations of Simon Cameron's corruption, 175–76; cabinet of, 3, 140–41, 145, 167, 169–71, 173, 176–78, 180, 182, 189–91, 195–97, 201–4, 206–10, 212, 214–15, 223, 230, 233, 236, 247, 262, 264, 290; death of, 234, 239; defense of Simon Cameron by, 216–17; and Fort Sumter, 157–59, 178–79; funeral of, 239; and habeas corpus, 192; John C. Fremont and, 194–97; management style of, 177; opinion of, of Simon Cameron, 182; patronage and, 170; presidential administration of, 152, 155, 157, 166, 170, 174, 176, 180, 183–84, 187–94, 197–200, 202, 204, 206–7, 211, 217, 221, 227–28, 231–32, 236, 238; and Simon Cameron's annual report, 203–6; Simon Cameron's appointment to cabinet of, 148–49, 151–55; Simon Cameron's departure from cabinet of, 208–10; and tariffs, 134, 144
Lockwood, Belva, 279
Louisiana, 21, 165, 254, 270, 285
Louisville KY, 276
Lyon, Nathaniel, 191

Mackey, Robert W., 260, 263
MacVeagh, Wayne, 236, 242, 250, 256, 258, 272, 283, 286, 289. *See also* Cameron, Virginia
Maine, 100, 176, 181, 268
Mangum, Willie P., 81
Maryland, 193–94
Massachusetts, 60, 122, 161, 186, 200, 248, 253, 255, 258, 263
Maytown PA, 5, 290
McClellan, George B., 168–69, 180, 185, 198, 204, 206, 236–37
McClure, Alexander: 1860 gubernatorial election and, 147; 1863 Senate

election and, 224–26; 1864 presidential election and, 232, 234–35; 1868 presidential election and, 249; Andrew G. Curtin and, 109, 146, 228, 238, 241, 244–45; and Liberal Republicans, 259; opposition of, to Simon Cameron entering Lincoln's cabinet, 151; as Pennsylvania legislator, 128, 135; and Simon Cameron's departure from Lincoln's cabinet, 209
McDowell, Irvin, 169, 184–85. *See also* Bull Run, Battle of
Meade, George, 211
Meigs, Montgomery, 175, 178–82, 195–97, 206, 208, 214
Meneely, A. Howard, 1, 213
Meredith, William A., 215–16, 226
Merryman, John, 192, 227–28
Mexican-American War, 77–78, 81, 83, 86, 100, 113, 219, 264
Mexico, 76–78, 80–81, 84, 207, 264, 285
Michigan, 29, 44, 100, 123, 258
Mississippi, 21, 30, 43–44, 252
Missouri, 16, 53, 84, 101, 107, 122, 171, 186, 191, 194, 235, 254, 259
monometallism, 265. *See also* bimetallism
Morgan, Edwin, 119, 146, 174
Morton, Oliver P., 181–82, 258
Mowry, Charles, 12–13, 21
Muhlenberg, Henry A., 51–52, 55, 72, 85–86
Murray, James, 30–34, 36–40. *See also* Winnebagos (Native Americans)

nativists, 53–54, 90, 102, 105–7, 112
Nebraska, 103. *See also* Kansas-Nebraska Act
Nevins, Allan, 61, 117, 165, 214
Nicolay, John, 189, 196, 211, 232, 234, 237
Norristown PA, 87, 132
nullification, doctrine of, 23, 27. *See also* secession

Ohio, 11, 16–18, 94, 112–13, 123, 137, 142, 160–61, 164, 172, 177, 185, 195, 249, 254, 268–69, 278, 283
Oklahoma, 78
Oliver, Mary S., 264, 275–81
Oregon, 44, 60, 83–84, 255

Pennsylvania, 7, 13, 24, 29, 52, 56, 82, 90–91, 94–95, 99, 104–6, 108–11, 117–18, 124, 128, 134, 176, 224–25, 231–33, 242, 248–49, 259–63, 266, 271, 282, 288
Pennsylvania Railroad (PRR), 94–95, 162–63, 170. See also Scott, Thomas A.
Pfoutz, Martha, 5
Philadelphia PA, 9–10, 20–22, 31, 34, 36, 40, 45, 50, 62–63, 75, 78, 88, 94–95, 102, 112, 134–35, 143, 146–47, 154, 163, 172–73, 192, 215, 225, 229, 241, 249–50, 257, 259, 262–63, 270, 272, 282, 288
Pierce, Franklin, 100–103, 114
Pittsburgh PA, 17, 21, 112, 122, 154, 211, 290
Poinsett, Joel R., 30, 36–38. See also Winnebagos (Native Americans)
Polk, James K.: cabinet of, 48, 53, 56, 60–61; and Mexican-American War, 77–78, 81, 83, 86, 100, 113, 219, 264; and Oregon, 44, 60, 83–84; presidential administration of, 44, 46–53, 55, 57, 60–64, 66–67, 70–71, 73, 75; and tariffs, 41, 44–46, 53, 57, 60, 68–75, 90; as "Young Hickory," 44, 47, 71
Pollock, James, 110, 150
Porter, David, 41–42, 102
Prairie du Chien WI, 30, 32, 35, 149. See also Winnebagos (Native Americans)
Purviance, Samuel, 148, 238

Quay, Matthew, 243, 257, 263, 269

Reconstruction, 246, 268–70, 291
Republican Party: 1856 presidential election and, 114–15; 1860 presiden-

tial election and, 132, 138; 1864 presidential election and, 232, 236; 1868 presidential election and, 248; 1872 presidential election and, 255, 262; birth of, 112; factionalism of, 146–48, 171, 232, 241–43, 248–50, 257–61, 266; and Liberal Republicans, 259, 261–63; Pennsylvania and, 113, 135, 171, 215, 231, 242, 244–45, 249–50, 257–60, 263, 268; slavery and, 82, 112, 115, 119, 140, 143, 222
Revels, Hiram, 252
Riddle, Albert G., 278–79, 281. See also Oliver, Mary S.
Ritchie, Thomas, 44–45, 49–50. See also Washington Union (newspaper)
Romero, Matias, 207–8, 212. See also Mexico
Russia: Andrew Curtin and, 250, 259; James Buchanan and, 20, 114; Simon Cameron and, 208–9, 212, 217–23, 289. See also Alexander II (Czar of Russia)

Sanderson, John P., 149, 153, 169, 238
Scott, Dred, 113, 125, 131–32, 252
Scott, Thomas A., 94, 139, 163, 166, 170–71, 199, 209, 224, 229, 264, 285. See also Pennsylvania Railroad (PRR)
Scott, Winfield, 101, 152–53, 158, 163, 166, 185, 227. See also Pennsylvania Railroad (PRR)
secession, 119, 129, 160–61, 167, 171, 188, 192–94, 198, 220, 235, 238, 240, 252
Second Bank of the United States, 11
Seigfried, Simon, 9–10
Senate, U.S.: in 1845–49, 54–55, 59–60, 64–69, 71–76, 81–82, 86; in 1857–61, 117–28; in 1867–77, 245–46, 251–58, 263–64, 266, 271; atmosphere of, 59, 119, 123–24; and Committee on Foreign Relations, 253–56, 268; courtesy in, 253; James K. Polk and, 60–62; Simon Cameron

Senate, U.S. (*cont.*)
and, 19–20, 30, 83–84, 89–91, 93, 95–99, 103–4, 107–9, 111, 113, 129, 132–33, 137, 144, 146, 149, 153, 157, 169–70, 183, 209, 212, 215, 217–18, 220, 224–28, 235, 238–39, 279, 282, 284; violence and, 59, 122
Seward, Augustus H., 170
Seward, William H.: as presidential candidate, 113, 135–37, 139–42; resignation of, from cabinet, 223; as secretary of state, 148, 150, 152–54, 160, 168–69, 177–82, 185, 191, 196, 209, 211, 219, 221, 223, 227–28; Simon Cameron and, 135–37, 177–80
Sherman, John, 185
Sherman, William T., 247, 276
Shulze, John A., 12–14, 21, 237
Shunk, Francis R., 52–53, 55, 63, 72, 85–86
Sickles, Daniel, 234
slavery: and contraband, 198, 200; and emancipation, 194, 199, 252; expansion of, 80, 84–85, 104, 107, 112; freedom from, 43, 116, 197, 240–41; and fugitive slaves, 101, 107, 113, 197–99, 203; as "peculiar institution," 21, 103, 121
Smith, Caleb, 141, 201–2
Snyder, Charles M., 52, 71
South Carolina, 8, 16, 23, 119, 122, 157, 159, 192, 198, 238, 270, 286
spoils system, 1, 25–26, 30, 61, 130, 148, 169, 259–60, 271, 291
Stanton, Edwin: and Andrew Johnson, 247–48; and Simon Cameron, 202–3, 211–13, 224, 229, 238
Stevens, Thaddeus, 116, 145, 153–54, 174, 189, 204, 216, 232, 235–36, 240, 242–43, 247, 277
Sturgeon, Daniel, 52, 59, 71–73, 97
Sumner, Charles, 122, 200, 205, 212, 253–55, 264
Supreme Court, U.S. See *Dred Scott v. Sanford*

Swett, Leonard, 141, 149–50, 152
Taggart, David, 95–96
Taney, Roger B., 192. See also *Dred Scott v. Sanford*
tariffs: and Abraham Lincoln, 134, 144; and James K. Polk, 41, 44–46, 53, 57, 60, 68–75, 90; and Pennsylvania, 15, 24, 41, 45–46, 53, 70–75, 90, 121, 143–44, 243. *See also* Walker Tariff
Taylor, Bayard, 218, 220, 222–23, 230
Taylor, Zachary, 78, 86–88, 90, 115
Tennessee, 15, 47–48, 189, 234
Texas, 43–44, 60, 76–78, 83, 101, 165
Tilden, Samuel J., 246, 269
Tower, Charlemagne, 263
Trumbull, Lyman, 138, 145, 152, 158, 183, 189, 191, 212
Tyler, John, 50, 76–77
Van Buren, Martin, 8, 23, 25, 28–30, 41–46, 57, 62, 76, 80, 83–84, 86, 90
Van Wyck, Charles H., 188–90
Virginia, 14, 16, 27, 101, 160–61, 184, 197–98, 242, 276–77, 281, 288–89
Wade, Benjamin F., 123, 183, 195, 216, 232, 238, 248–49
Walker, Robert J., 44–45, 50, 68–69, 72–75, 126
Walker Tariff, 68–69, 72–75, 126
War Department: bureaus of, 166, 174; and Simon Cameron as secretary of war, 95–96, 155, 157–93, 195–200, 202–14, 216–17, 232, 236, 238, 247, 264, 268, 291
Washington Union (newspaper), 50, 60, 73, 86. See also *Globe* (newspaper)
Webster, Daniel, 60, 73
Weed, Thurlow, 3, 136, 140–41, 174, 208, 228
Weidman, John, 89–90, 108. *See also* Winnebagos (Native Americans)
Weigley, Russell, 214
Welles, Gideon: and impeachment of Andrew Johnson, 247–48; opinion

of, of Simon Cameron, 2, 258; as secretary of the navy, 158, 178–80, 191, 203, 216

West Point (U.S. Military Academy), 25, 79

Whig Party, 41–42, 53–57, 60, 65–67, 70, 74–75, 77, 80–81, 85–88, 90, 95, 99, 101, 103–6, 111–12, 115, 128, 130

Wilkins, William, 9, 20

Wilmot, David, 66, 80–84, 88, 98, 101, 107, 113–14, 116, 121, 136–37, 149, 218, 224–26

Wilmot Proviso, 80–84, 98, 107, 113–14

Winnebagos (Native Americans), 28–57, 108, 118, 149, 168–69, 191

Wolf, George, 20

Woodward, George W., 52–55, 63–67, 76, 97, 99, 111, 228, 230